Settler Common Sense

Settler Common Sense

QUEERNESS AND EVERYDAY COLONIALISM
in the
AMERICAN RENAISSANCE

Mark Rifkin

University of Minnesota Press
MINNEAPOLIS • LONDON

Portions of chapter 1 were previously published as
"Settler Common Sense," *Settler Colonial Studies* 3, no. 4 (2013): 322–40.
Portions of chapters 1 and 3 were previously published as "Settler States
of Feeling: National Belonging and Erasure of Native American Presence,"
in *Blackwell Companion to American Literary Studies,* ed. Robert Levine
and Caroline Levander (New York: Wiley–Blackwell, 2011), 342–55.

Published by the University of Minnesota Press
111 Third Avenue South, Suite 290
Minneapolis, MN 55401–2520
http://www.upress.umn.edu

Library of Congress Cataloging-in-Publication Data

Rifkin, Mark, author.
Settler Common Sense : Queerness and Everyday Colonialism
in the American Renaissance / Mark Rifkin.
Includes bibliographical references and index.
ISBN 978-0-8166-9057-2 (hc : acid-free paper)
ISBN 978-0-8166-9060-2 (pb : acid-free paper)
1. Indians in literature. 2. Queer theory.
3. Homosexuality in literature. I. Title.
PN56.3.I6R54 2014
809´.933520397—dc23
2013038694

Printed in the United States of America on acid-free paper

The University of Minnesota is an equal-opportunity educator and employer.

20 19 18 17 16 15 14   10 9 8 7 6 5 4 3 2 1

For Rich

Contents

Acknowledgments

This book began as a request. Bob Levine and Caroline Levander asked
me to contribute something to the Blackwell *Companion to American Literary Studies.* I wasn't sure what I wanted to write, but since previously I'd
been focusing primarily on struggles around Native self-representation, I
decided that I would think about questions of settler subjectivity. As an
experiment I began to consider Henry David Thoreau's *Walden* and William Apess's "Eulogy on King Philip" for what they might say about the
relation between citizenship, settler colonialism, and everyday nonnative
experience. The short essay that came of that intellectual exercise served as
the initial kernel for this book, and for that reason I am deeply grateful to
Bob and Caroline for the invitation and for all of the feedback they offered
on that piece.

This project marks a welcome return to the nineteenth century, bringing me back to the period about which I wrote my dissertation. In this
vein, I owe thanks to those who provided my initial training in nineteenth-
century American literary studies at the University of Pennsylvania, especially Eric Cheyfitz, Nancy Bentley, Colin Dayan, and Chris Looby. I also
am deeply grateful to those who read and offered comments on the manu-
script, whether whole or in part, including Beth Piatote, Lisa Brooks, Nancy
Bentley, Colin Dayan, Pete Coviello, Dana Nelson, Kyla Tompkins, and the
anonymous reader from the press. Thank you so much for your time, support, and incisive readings; they have strengthened the project immensely.
Parts of this project were presented at the University of Minnesota, the University of North Carolina at Charlotte, Pomona College, the Huntington
Library, and the Native American and Indigenous Studies Association, and
I am grateful to all of the organizers of the various conferences, symposia,
speakers' series, and panels for inviting me and to all of the participants for

their help in shaping what appears here. I also have benefited incalculably from my ongoing conversations with a range of fellow scholars over the years. In addition to those already mentioned, I would like to include Joanne Barker, Kevin Bruyneel, Jodi Byrd, Jessica Cattelino, David Chang, Jennifer Denetdale, Jean Dennison, Qwo-Li Driskill, Tol Foster, Mishuana Goeman, Alyosha Goldstein, Lisa Kahaleole Hall, Shona Jackson, Daniel Heath Justice, Scott Morgensen, Jeani O'Brien, Bethany Schneider, Audra Simpson, Andy Smith, Lisa Tatonetti, Patrick Wolfe, and Craig Womack.

The University of North Carolina at Greensboro has offered a wonderful place to be for the past five years. In particular, I would to thank Risa Applegarth, Becca Black, Danielle Bouchard, Liz Bucar, Sarah Cervenak, Tony Cuda, Michelle Dowd, Asa Eger, Jen Feather, Tara Green, Mary Ellis Gibson, Ellen Haskel, Jennifer Keith, Karen Kilcup, Derek Krueger, Christian Moraru, Noelle Morrisette, Kelly Ritter, Gene Rogers, Scott Romine, Hepsie Roskelly, María Sánchez, Ali Moore, Amy Vines, Anne Wallace, and Karen Weyler for their friendship and support. I owe much to my dissertation students—Rose Brister, Jason Cooke, Zach Laminack, Gene Melton, Matt Mullins, Andrew Pisano, David Rogers, and Belinda Walzer—who have kept me on my toes, introduced me to new ways of thinking, and reminded me consistently of why I chose this profession. I also would like to thank the students in my course "Representing Indians: Writings by and about Native Americans in the Nineteenth-Century U.S." for their intellectual energy and acuity. This project also was aided immensely by a one-year research leave from UNCG as well as a Regular Faculty Research Grant.

Working with University of Minnesota Press continues to be a wonderful experience, due largely to my wonderful editor Jason Weidemann and his assistant Danielle Kasprzak.

For keeping me going when I'm ready to stop, and for reminding me how wonderful things can be when I look up from my computer and step out of my office, I owe a great debt to Sheila and Alex Avelin, Zivia Avelin, Jon Dichter, Kevin and Justin Dichter, Mike Hardin, Marc Smith and Lisa Dilorio Smith, Tiffany Eatman Allen and Will Allen, Alicia and Bobby Murray, Debbie and Andy Johnson, Tammy Sears, Craig Bruns, Keith Brand, Kent Latimer, JJ McArdle, and Jon Van Gieson. For Erika Lin, you already know (and there isn't enough space). My parents, Neal and Sharon

Rifkin, and sister, Gail Dichter, remind me of where I've been and help orient me to where I'm going, and knowing that there will always be a place for me in their hearts and homes means more than I can say.

The most stunningly miraculous thing happened just after I started work on this project. I met Rich Murray. Everything has been different, and better, since. This book is dedicated to him.

Note on the Cover

Upon first view, the cover may raise some questions, particularly the use of a headdress for a book concerned with peoples from the Northeast. Such regalia was not, to my knowledge, part of the cultural repertoire of Native nations in New England and New York. I admit that when I first viewed the cover, I was not sure what it had to do with the book. I wondered whether the use of such an image from a different region would continue the process by which peoples in the Northeast, from the eighteenth century onward, have been judged not truly "Indian" enough to be recognized as Native. Moreover, since the nineteenth century, such questions of authenticity often have turned on a supposed failure of Haudenosaunee, Wabanaki, and Algonquian peoples to embody an idea of indigeneity drawn from Plains peoples. Prior to my seeing the cover, people at the press had already had lengthy conversations about this question and then raised the issue with me.

Then I got it: the feather taken from the headdress becomes the quill. Those juxtaposed images encapsulate my central argument, that settler ways of being and modes of representation are affected by processes of colonial relation without always being explicit about that influence. Settler occupation shapes the materiality of daily life without necessarily highlighting directly the ways everyday nonnative experiences remain dependent on past and present practices of institutionalized expropriation. Instead, the results of such continuing colonial dynamics appear as the ready-to-hand means of settler expression and self-elaboration. Conversely, the pairing of the quill and the headdress suggests the ways that Native peoples in the Northeast needed to perform a particular kind of Indianness in order be legible as such, to be able to represent themselves as Indians in ways nonnatives could understand.

For these reasons, I think the cover quite evocatively captures the spirit of the book, and I am deeply grateful to the designer.

Introduction

A few years ago, I bought a house, my first venture into owning real estate. At first, I was a bit disoriented in it, adjusting to the new—and larger—dimensions of my living space.[1] Having moved many times over the prior ten years, I was familiar with the perceptual and physical realignment that occurs when in a new home-place. However, I soon realized that my dysphoria was of a different kind than previously; my sensations seemed to be less about where things were in relation to my body than the ways the entire house and the lot on which it is located felt like an *extension* of my body. The fact that this place was my possession translated into an expansion of self—somewhere between the realms of the tactile and the imaginary—to encompass the area covered by the official property lines. I began to think that such an impression was not all that weird, given the ways personal identity under liberal modes of political economy often is conceptualized and lived as self-ownership. Extending my sense of selfhood to the land I legally owned seemed like a corollary of that ingrained way of understanding personhood. In the wake of this set of sensations, I began to consider more so than I had before the ways the macrological dynamics and institutionalized frameworks of settlement—the exertion of control by nonnatives over Native peoples and lands—give rise to certain modes of feeling.[2] I started to think about how institutionalized relations of settlement, such as law and policy, help generate forms of affect through which they become imbued with a sensation of everyday certainty. In this sense, quotidian affective formations among nonnatives can be understood as normalizing settler presence, privilege, and power, taking up the terms and technologies of settler governance as something like a phenomenological surround that serves as the animating context for nonnatives' engagement with the social environment.

My experience productively can be understood as an instantiation of what more broadly may be characterized as *settler common sense*. By this phrase, I mean to suggest the ways the legal and political structures that enable non-native access to Indigenous territories come to be lived as given, as simply the unmarked, generic conditions of possibility for occupancy, association, history, and personhood. Addressing whiteness in Australia, Fiona Nicoll argues that "rather than analysing and evaluating Indigenous sovereignty claims . . . , we have a political and intellectual responsibility to analyse and evaluate the innumerable ways in which white sovereignty circumscribes and mitigates the exercise of Indigenous sovereignty" (19). My felt sense of possession of my property, such that my senses seem to extend over it as if it were contained within my individual body schema, can be conceptualized as coming at the expense of Indigenous claims to that same space, the former emerging through the phenomenological translation of the settler-state's jurisdiction and property law as the material from which my experience of selfhood and inhabitance arises. The fact that there is not, or I do not perceive there to be, an active political struggle over the place I inhabit does not mean it and my apprehension of it somehow exist outside or beyond ongoing histories of settler–Indigenous negotiation, antagonism, and conflict.

How would taking such a perspective as the lens alter how we read nineteenth-century writing in the United States? How do texts from the period register and recirculate everyday modes of settlement, drawing on them as an unacknowledged basis in developing social imaginings, geographies, and ethics not apparently related to "Indians" or processes of conquest? What might reading such texts in this way tell us about how settler sovereignty functions as a form of quotidian perception and possibility? In *The Common Pot*, Lisa Brooks asks, "What happens to our view of American history when Native narratives are not just *included* but *privileged?*": "What happens when we put Native space at the center of America rather than merely striving for inclusion of minority viewpoints or viewing Native Americans as a *part* of or on the *periphery* of America? What does the historical landscape look like when viewed through the networks of waterways and kinship in the northeast[?]" (xxxv). Building on the insights of Brooks and others with respect to the centrality of Indigenous presence and sovereignties to U.S. history, politics, and culture, and the profound alteration attending to the former brings to the latter, I want to examine how Native networks are excised from "the historical landscape," how Indigenous peoples and geographies become unseen as part of ordinary, nonconscious non-native praxis and writing. To that end, this study engages with a select group of authors—Nathaniel Hawthorne, Henry David Thoreau, and Herman Melville—chosen for their canonicity, for the ways they continue to occupy an overdetermined place within nineteenth-century American literary studies. I argue that regularized aspects of settler colonial administrative procedures, statutes, and legal debates shape the trajectory of the critiques of contemporary political economy offered by their texts and the ways they imagine opposition to the state. *Settler Common Sense* demonstrates how the construction and maintenance of the settler-state implicitly frames the ways these writers address place, personhood, and political belonging. It indicates how texts that are written and set far from "the frontier" and that do not feature Indians can be theorized and historicized as relying in critical ways on the institutionalized dynamics through which Indigenous presence and polities are translated, managed, and/or elided, demonstrating how everyday instantiations of settlement provide the materials out of which non-native ethics, ideals, and orientations emerge.

Hawthorne, Thoreau, and Melville all write in and about New York and New England, areas from which Native peoples either were thought to be "extinct" or were considered as somewhat pathetic "remnants" who would disappear soon, and none of the three main texts I address—*The House of the Seven Gables* (1851), *Walden* (1854), and *Pierre* (1852)—can be said to be about Indians. Native people(s) do appear in them, but as peripheral figures. These writers and writings, then, seem particularly bad choices for a project that centers indigeneity and the critique of settler colonialism. However, that set of critical problems is precisely what makes these texts and authors attractive. How do entrenched and normalized settler experiences of inhabitance, individual identity, and collective belonging appear when not directly connected to depictions of Indians, and what work do they do? How does one conceptualize and locate such dynamics, and how might they provide a broader set of interpretive questions and problems for other texts and for the analysis of everyday sensations of settlement—of quotidian settler structures of feeling?

These authors cast their work as engaged in a critique of contemporary political economy, particularly of the role of the state in enforcing unjust relations of property. Rather than dismissing such claims as merely putative (they think they are contesting the state but are not really), I take them seriously, arguing that the texts I address develop what might be understood as specifically *queer* critiques of the state. All of them displace bourgeois homemaking in ways that open room for thinking other possibilities for inhabitance and association, developing notions of personhood and placemaking askew with respect to an emergent heteronormative imaginary. These texts bracket increasingly dominant conceptions of household and family formation and feature identities, practices, and spaces deemed perverse, opening room for envisioning modes of occupancy and self-identification not dependent on state authorization. Hawthorne, Melville, and Thoreau critique lineage-based understandings of property holding, casting such genealogically inflected notions of landholding less as indicating insulation from the state (as in liberal ideologies of familial homemaking, privacy, and intimacy) than as means of implementing and naturalizing state-sanctioned projects of speculation, consumption, and exploitation. They signal the possibility for alternative modes of life based less on existing legal regimes by highlighting statuses, desires, and practices that would appear sexually deviant from the perspective of bourgeois norms, including bachelorhood, spinsterhood, onanism, homoeroticism, and incest.

Instead of suggesting that these texts and writers do not truly offer an oppositional perspective, I argue that their forms of opposition depend on taking for granted the conceptions of place, politics, and personhood normalized in the settler-state's engagement with Indigenous peoples. The legalities of settlement form the commonsensical background in and through which these texts envision possibilities for dissent and engage in a critique of contemporary political economy. All of these texts imagine a kind of place to which one might flee from geographies of property endorsed by the state and in which one might discover more ethical principles for living than those embedded in existing law and policy. The normative frameworks they develop depend on presuming the coherence of U.S. jurisdiction, envisioning an extrapolitical relation to space (particularly through figures of "nature"), and recirculating modular notions of self-possessed personhood, all of which emerge out of Anglo-American legal ideologies and which defer the possibility of reckoning with Indigenous sovereignty or ongoing processes of settler occupation. While differently configured (nonnuclear

Lockean homesteading, masturbatory exploration in an unowned wilderness, immersion in the atomizing mysteries of the cityscape), these visions all require that the space of retreat/regeneration not be understood as a site of political contestation, as located within another polity or as a place in which a struggle is occurring among competing sovereignties. They conjure the image of a place *within* the nation but yet somehow not *of* it. However, the very spaces the texts cast as outside of, or as resistant to, political and legal norms become available for settler inhabitance as a function of effaced settler–Indigenous conflict and negotiation, itself displaced into an archaic past when acknowledged at all.

After an initial chapter that lays out the project's theoretical and methodological commitments, each of the chapters situates the central text under discussion within the struggles of particular Native peoples, analyzing the text's settler mappings and ethics in relation to specific Indigenous histories and geopolitical formations. The chapters further illustrate how the nongenealogical and individualist models of personhood these texts privilege emerge out of changes in the legal subjectivity of white men that themselves arise out of the increasing occupation of Native territory, moving from the text least concerned with Native dispossession to the text for which it seems most haunting.

In the late eighteenth and early nineteenth centuries, small-scale landholders in the District of Maine waged a virtual war of insurgency against efforts by largely absentee owners to survey their lands and demand payment for them, marshaling Lockean arguments in defense of their claims. Nathaniel Hawthorne's *The House of the Seven Gables* (1851) alludes to this decades-long battle in and over the Maine backcountry, which provides the paradigm for the text's ethical claims in favor of individual labor on the land. Hawthorne's critique of the aristocratic Pyncheon family and their overreliance on government largesse positions "toil" in the "wilderness" as a counterpoint to the corrupt machinations of the state. The text's image of extrapolitical labor in nature—including the numerous references to the virtue of life in the "country"—provides a conceptual space from which to critique the government-backed generational transmission of unearned inherited wealth. Moreover, forms of midcentury deviance—including bachelorhood, spinsterhood, onanist monomania, and socialist communalism— all can be rehabilitated through movement to the unencumbered elsewhere of rural landholding. These proliferating queernesses illustrate the ethical capaciousness of the text's inclination toward a Lockean romance of labor. However, envisioning an extrapolitical right to property through labor entails suspending the politics of settler–Indigenous conflict over the character and limits of nonnative jurisdiction, positing a "nature" that precedes institutions of governance and validates them but that presupposes Euro-modes of political economy and effaces Native polities as such. The "Indian deed" at the center of the text—the Pyncheon claim to lands in Maine—provides the trace of such continuing struggle, which I explore through attention to the history and politics of Penobscot sovereignty and relations with other Wabanaki peoples. In the text's imagination, the Pyncheons are like a "tribe," taking the latter as too queer to be redeemed—as an undemocratic form of genealogically based landedness. Doing so positions indigeneity as a reservoir for signifiers of aberrance instead of as a potential challenge to the legitimacy of U.S. law and jurisdiction. However, by associating deviations from normative home and family with possibilities for alternate modes of spatiality and inhabitance, the text opens the potential for a queer engagement with the "deed" that could foreground the ongoing processes through which settler sovereignty is normalized.

For Thoreau "Nature" serves as a realm of innocence and integrity in stark contrast to the corruption, artificiality, and excesses of industrialization, commercial agriculture, and bourgeois homemaking. "Nature" allows for the imagination of modes of being that defy the debt-inducing and enervating forms of labor, homemaking, and patriotic submission that *Walden* suggests characterize routine life in Concord and the nation more broadly. This scene of withdrawal from the conventional attachments of home and work registers as a kind of excessive stimulation within prominent discourses of health, particularly those decrying the evils of masturbation. *Walden* upends anti-onanist warnings by making reverie and associated forms of apparently unproductive sensation and wasteful activity into the prism through which to recast normative personhood, articulating a queer conception of personhood. However, this vision takes shape through the effacement of Native geopolitics in New England. "Nature" can be understood as marking the trace of prior Native sovereignty, taking up the exceptionality already attributed to Native polities and lands in Massachusetts law. Thoreau articulates an ethics that draws on Native people(s) as an example of how to occupy an ajurisdictional space of exception while disowning any need to attend to the varied forms of abjection produced for Indigenous peoples in New England by their abandonment to such a legal limbo—a dynamic addressed in William Apess's *Indian Nullification* (1835) and petitions from Native peoples to the state government. However, when interpreted in light of this history, aspects of *Walden* can be reread as envisioning a critical (masturbatory) relation to place and legally privileged modes of personhood that also might expose the settler self to its limits. In this way, the text opens the potential for something like a queer solidarity with Indigenous self-determination that can acknowledge the politics of Native endurance rather than sublimating it as an Indianness available for settler self-fashioning in (an illusory and empty) nature.

In the 1840s, tensions between tenants and landlords in upstate New York exploded into what became known as the "Anti-Rent Wars," in which small landholders insisted on their right to the fields they had worked as against legally backed claims by proprietors. Much like the struggle in Maine a few decades earlier, farmers marshaled arguments in favor of the legitimacy of their occupancy based on their sustained toil in the soil. Initially set on a manorial estate just like those in question in New York, *Pierre* offers a critique of this aristocratic mode of landedness. While drawing on the political energies and charges unleashed by tenants, the text evades the question of land reform, implying that an ethics of rural territoriality cannot escape the orbit of the kinds of force necessary to sustain private property holding and the enchaining genealogical entailments of inheritance it engenders. Unlike Hawthorne and Thoreau, Melville does not posit a rural space of retreat and rejuvenation, and the text less provides a positive ground for envisioning more just social relations than defers the possibility of instantiating a new norm, casting urban space as a democratic site in which elite forms of familial alliance and property corrode and disintegrate. In its anonymity, density, and opacity, the city facilitates the profusion of "mysteries" (including perverse forms of association and desire borne from the country). Through its investment in such "ambiguities," the text stages an antirevolutionary ethics more interested in the queer undoing and dissolving of existing arrangements than the construction of an alternative sociality, a project of negation for which the city provides the perfect locale. This emphasis on a metropolitan rupture in elite inheritance, though, leaves the status of the land in the country in question while also casting urban space as a kind of ethical elsewhere from the problems that haunt the former. In this way, Melville treats the city-space as itself a given rather than as having depended for its growth on access to transportation and commercial networks that required ongoing forms of rural displacement, including of the Oneidas and the Senecas. Yet, the figure of the Indian in *Pierre* links the sovereignty of Native peoples and the movement for land reform by tenants in the state (who referred to themselves as "the Indians") in ways that, if read against the grain, suggest less the need to supersede the anachronistic and aristocratic politics of rural landedness than the unavoidable enmeshment of the metropolis (and its queer excesses) in the political economy of settler land tenure.

1

ORDINARY LIFE AND THE
ETHICS OF OCCUPATION

In "Eulogy on King Philip" (1836), Pequot minister and activist William Apess explores how forms of citizen-feeling emerge in the context of institutionalized structures and imperatives that are themselves predicated on the disavowal of Native sovereignty. The project of settlement appears as crucial in the construction and persistence of U.S. modes of governance: "a foundation was laid in the first Legislature to enslave our people by taking from them all rights, which has been strictly adhered to ever since. Look at the disgraceful laws, disfranchising us as citizens. Look at the treaties made by Congress, all broken. Look at the deep-rooted plans laid, when a territory becomes a state, that after so many years the laws shall be extended over the Indians that live within their boundaries" (134). The dynamics of U.S. state formation axiomatically constrain and displace Native peoples, *extending* "laws" over them and their lands that deny their "rights" as autonomous polities. This political infrastructure provides the context in which settler sentiments take shape. Apess offers an imaginary conversation between the president of the United States and Native peoples that lays out the implicit terms of Indian relations and national belonging: "We want your land for our use to speculate upon"; "it aids us in paying off our national debt"; "our fathers carried on this scheme of getting your lands for our use"; "this has been the way our fathers first brought us up, and it is hard to depart from it" (135). The continual reproduction of national membership as such depends on the extension of a geopolitical claim to Indigenous "lands," and the topos of familial inheritance here connects quotidian feelings of citizenship to propertyholding, indicating that the experience of national belonging is shaped by ongoing processes of settlement through which the national "we" (literally) is given form.

Through the figure of inheritance, Apess suggests that the legacy of displacing Natives and effacing their survival remains ongoing, connected as it is to the sensation of intimate filiation to the nation. Enumerating the violent acts and retrospective justifications by English settlers in New England throughout the seventeenth century, Apess exhorts, "Let the children of the Pilgrims blush while the son of the forest drops a tear and groans under the fate of his murdered and departed fathers" (114). The shame borne by these "children" lies in their relation to those Indigenous peoples whose decimation and dispossession cleared the space for their occupancy and, by implication, that of all subjects of the state. Moreover, Apess's repeated invocation of the trope of parenthood emphasizes that the broader dynamics of expropriation and erasure he addresses are realized as quotidian forms of private landholding passed through legally recognized family lines. He observes, "[I]t does appear that the Indians had rights, and those rights were near and dear to them, as your stores and farms and firesides are to the whites, and their wives and children also" (116). The everydayness of settler domestic life occurs in places whose availability for such inhabitance depends on the suspension of Native "rights." The practice of citizenship both reveals and engenders an orientation toward settlement regardless of one's apparent sympathies: "Although in words they deny it, yet in the works they approve of the iniquities of their fathers" (115). As opposed to something like a conscious repudiation of indigeneity, subjects in the contemporary moment live their citizenship as a structure of feeling and set of routine orientations in ways that arise from and propel the extension of claims to Native lands and dismissal of Native polities.

Turning to Nathaniel Hawthorne, Henry David Thoreau, and Herman Melville, I take Apess's insights on the ordinariness of settlement as a guiding frame for rethinking approaches to the field of nineteenth-century American literary studies. My aim in reading these authors is not to investigate how they represent Native peoples, but instead to track how nonnative texts are affected by histories, legalities, and policies of Indigenous dispossession and settler jurisdiction in ways that do not appear to have anything to do with Indians. If we understand the United States as a settler-state, one founded on top of polities that precede its existence, which then are pro-claimed to be "domestic" and thus made subject to the authority of the settler government, that massive and continuing project of interpellation, invasion, and domination must have effects that extend beyond the explicit depiction of Native peoples.[1] To the extent that critical engagement with writing produced in and about the United States functions as a significant means of envisioning, narrating, and revaluing the national past, present, and future, it serves as an important scholarly site for engaging with the meaning and consequences of the centrality of settlement to the ongoing existence of the U.S. nation-state. Moreover, the kinds of textual interpretation devel-oped and deployed within literary studies address modes of social imagi-nation, engagement, and maneuver that are not constrained by the specific functional demands of governance but that also are not exactly the stuff of everyday life. In other words, close reading provides a means of concep-tualizing and analyzing the ways that ideas, feelings, and commentary are coalesced as conscious projects in extant public discourses while at the same time tracing the unacknowledged conditions of possibility for such partici-pation, contestation, and mediation. Textual production points back toward modes of ordinary perception that serve as background and for which there is no document, and analysis of such texts indicates how quotidian modes of sensation and sense-making provide the impetus and frame from which the texts themselves emerge.

Each of the three central texts I discuss cultivates and features what might be understood as queer potentials in its development of a democratic ethics it treats as antagonistic to the existing regime. In this way, *Settler Common Sense* traces a heretofore unexamined strain of what might be termed queer antistatism within mid-nineteenth-century writings.[2] However, while open-ing room for envisioning queer possibilities for occupancy and selfhood (deviations from nuclear domesticity), these writings treat processes of set-tlement as a given in developing their ethical visions. *House of the Seven Gables* makes settlement in Maine ethically paradigmatic without attending to the persistent landedness of Wabanaki peoples; *Walden* invests in Indian-ized inhabitance in nature without recognizing the existence and struggles of Native peoples in Massachusetts (including the highly visible "revolt" of the Mashpees); and *Pierre* presents the vast, and brutal, anonymity of New York City as a counterpoint to the entrenched hereditary hierarchy of estates upstate without considering how the city's massive growth in the period depended on the transport and commercial network made possible by contemporaneous efforts to displace the Six Nations. Thus, I seek to provide something of a genealogy for the ways (queer) opposition to the state can reiterate everyday modes of settler sensation and occupation as its condition of possibility, how in Apess's terms "in the works they approve of the iniquities of their fathers."

Yet, in illustrating the pervasiveness and momentum of settlement in shaping ordinary experience, indicating how it animates articulations and formulations that are not "about" conquest or Native people(s), I also work to suggest the possibility for reorientation offered in these texts, for a sensuous realignment of perception in which settler personhood and placemaking might come into critical focus. Pursuing this line of analysis involves rethinking prominent tendencies in Indigenous and settler colonial studies (to focus on the everyday experience of nonnatives), in nineteenth-century American literary studies (to engage Native peoples and their dispossession in ways neither centered on representations of Indians nor overdetermined by critical paradigms developed with respect to slavery), and in queer studies (to foreground questions of place-based political collectivity and the ways counterhegemonic queer imaginings can normalize settlement), as well as addressing the dynamics of canon formation and the role of "diversity" in choosing our objects of analysis. That process of methodological and theoretical reformulation, setting the conceptual stage for the rest of the study, is the work of this chapter.

Looking for Indians and Structure

The figure of the vanishing Indian still remains prominent within U.S. popular and scholarly discourses, both explicitly and implicitly. Within this narrative, Native peoples may have had prior claims to the land, but they, perhaps tragically, were removed from the area, or died out, or ceased to be "really" Indian, or simply disappeared at some point between the appearance of the "last" one and the current moment, whenever that may be.[3] As against this tendency, scholars in nineteenth-century American literary studies have sought to indicate the significance and pervasiveness of Indigenous presence within U.S. writing, politics, and culture. In doing so, the focus can lie on locating figurations of Indianness, either to document the survival of

Native peoples and their ongoing importance to nonnative social life or to index the ways that representations of Indigenous absence illustrate forms of settler self-definition. These approaches, however, can direct attention to the modes through which "Indians" appear in U.S. textual production rather than addressing how settler modes of governance and inhabitance become normalized and what role they play in giving shape to articulations, ideals, and imaginings that do not directly refer to Native people(s). Conversely, analyses of settler colonialism have developed ways of addressing the systemic quality of settler seizures, displacements, and identifications, arguing that the claiming of a naturalized right to Indigenous place lies at the heart of nonnative modes of governance, association, and identity. Such articulations of the pervasive and enduring quality of settler colonialism, though, can shorthand its workings, producing accounts in which it appears as a fully integrated whole operating in smooth, consistent, and intentional ways across the sociospatial terrain it encompasses. Doing so, particularly in considering the exchange between the domains of formal policy and of everyday life, may displace how settlement's histories, brutalities, effacements, and interests become quotidian and commonsensical.

In seeking to consider the everyday phenomenology of settlement and the ways it affects forms of textual production in the nineteenth century, *Settler Common Sense* builds on the extensive body of work concerned with the representation of Native people(s) in the period.[4] While addressing the significance of Indians to nonnative writing and modes of self-representation, this scholarship has tended to focus more on the varied ways Native subjects appear as a kind of representational content rather than on the (material and discursive) processes by which nonnative presence, jurisdiction, and occupancy come to appear as given and how those normalizations give rise to particular visions of social life, modes of ethics, and conceptions of placemaking that participate in processes of settlement without specifically referring to Native people(s). In *Removals*, Lucy Maddox insists on the relative ubiquity of engagement with "Indian–white relationships" in nineteenth-century writing and culture, suggesting that such representations are organized around the choice between "civilization" and "extinction" (6–9). As against this emphasis on dichotomy, Joshua David Bellin argues in *The Demon of the Continent* that scholars need to attend to "processes of 'mutual acculturation'" (2), suggesting that too often analysis of depictions of Native people(s) think in terms "of white and red sides that clash at some Turnerian frontier" (4). Instead, Bellin emphasizes the space/scene of "encounter," drawing attention to how interaction with Native peoples affects nonnative social life and cultural production. In *The Insistence of the Indian*, Susan Scheckel observes that after 1812, "Indians mattered during this period not primarily as a physical or political threat to the American nation but as a threat to Americans' sense of themselves as a moral nation—a threat, in short, to American national character and legitimacy" (6–7). She suggests that Native peoples came to function less as a source of "political" conflict than as a "symbolic" means of representing the United States to itself (11). Also addressing the role of Indians as a residual marker of past violence, Renée Bergland in *The National Uncanny* explores how figures of Indian ghosts index the "interior logic of the modern nation" in which "the very texts that inscribe United States nationalism require the presence of ghostly Natives" (4), such that spectral Natives serve as a sign of the national past, register the violence of conquest, and function as a disavowal of the (ongoing) colonial dynamics of U.S. nationalism. Exploring the affective life of settlement, Laura Mielke's *Moving Encounters* seeks to address how nineteenth-century representations of Native people(s) by nonnatives "proposed the possibility of mutual sympathy between American Indians and Euro-Americans, of community instead of division" (2), seeking to restore a prior relation of "Indian–white intimacy" understood as lost through the violence of warfare and removal (4).

This body of work largely has bound analysis of U.S. imperial absorption of Native peoples and lands in nineteenth-century writing to the body of the Native. In focusing primarily on the ways nonnative texts manifest Indian figures, the contours of those depictions, and the kinds of feelings and relations borne by them, scholars treat the force of settler colonialism and of its shaping of nonnative discourses, ethics, materialities, and affects as residing in tropes of Indianness. In *The Erotic Life of Racism*, Sharon Holland addresses the ways race is localized as a phenomenon that attaches to black persons. Describing what she characterizes as "the catch-22 of race," she observes, "[I]t renders theorizing about 'it' impossible because it stabilizes identity for those who *impose* it and for those who work to *expose* it" (6). In response, she asks, "[H]ow can we mark and make this history without attaching it to some bodies rather than others?" (57). Similarly, to the extent that the discussion of settler colonialism and indigeneity with respect to nonnative texts turns on the locating and interpretation of "Indian" moments, this practice of reading "stabilizes" settlement as a dynamic that inheres in Native bodies, rather than understanding it as a phenomenon that shapes nonnative subjectivities, intimacies, articulations, and sensations separate from whether or not something recognizably Indian comes into view. How does one trace the presence and influence of settlement without looking for Indianness, or at least without ordering analysis around such textual traces? How can such work consider the ways everyday forms of perception are pervaded by the settler-state's exertion of jurisdiction and erasure/management of Indigenous self-determination? In this vein, *Settler Common Sense* reads representations of Indians less as indicative of a particular attitude, discourse, or ideological framing than as symptomatic of an unstated set of nonnative inclinations, orientations, modes of perception, forms of networking, and durable lived assemblages shaped by processes of settlement and experienced as the stability of the given. The content of "Indian" images matters less than the ways they serve as textual traces of quotidian ways that the dynamics of settler occupation operate as the phenomenological background, against which Indigenous survival registers as anomaly and is hived off from routine nonnative experience as an aberrant (and anachronistic) eruption.[5] As Apess suggests, the force of colonialism inheres for nonnatives in "the way our fathers first brought us up" and their relation to their "farms and firesides." Rather than going in search of moments of discernible Indianness, then, critics can map the contours of unmarked, normalized settler geographies of the everyday as they give form to explicit and implicit textual imaginings and effects.

If nineteenth-century American literary studies tends to focus on the ways Indians enter the narrative frame and the kinds of meanings and associations they bear, recent attempts to theorize settler colonialism have sought to shift attention from its effects on Indigenous subjects to its implications for nonnative political attachments, forms of inhabitance, and modes of being, illuminating and tracking the pervasive operation of settlement as a system. In *Settler Colonialism and the Transformation of Anthropology*, Patrick Wolfe argues, "Settler colonies were (are) premised on the elimination of native societies. The split tensing reflects a determinate feature of settler colonization. The colonizers come to stay—invasion is a structure not an event" (2).[6] He suggests that a "logic of elimination" drives settler gover-nance and sociality, describing "the settler-colonial will" as "a historical force that ultimately derives from the primal drive to expansion that is generally glossed as capitalism" (167), and in "Settler Colonialism and the Elimination of the Native," he observes that "elimination is an organizing principle of settler-colonial society rather than a one-off (and superceded) occurrence" (388). Rather than being superseded after an initial moment/ period of conquest, colonization persists since "the logic of elimination marks a return whereby the native repressed continues to structure settler-colonial society" (390). In Aileen Moreton-Robinson's work, whiteness functions as the central way of understanding the domination and displacement of Indigenous peoples by nonnatives.[7] In "Writing Off Indigenous Sover-eignty," she argues, "As a regime of power, patriarchal white sovereignty operates ideologically, materially and discursively to reproduce and main-tain its investment in the nation as a white possession" (88), and in "Writ-ing Off Treaties," she suggests, "At an ontological level the structure of subjective possession occurs through the imposition of one's will-to-be on the thing which is perceived to lack will, thus it is open to being possessed," such that "possession . . . forms part of the ontological structure of white subjectivity" (83–84). For Jodi Byrd, the deployment of Indianness as a mobile figure works as the principal mode of U.S. settler colonialism. She observes that "colonization and racialization . . . have often been conflated," in ways that "tend to be sited along the axis of inclusion/exclusion" and that "misdirect and cloud attention from the underlying structures of set-tler colonialism" (xxiii, xvii). She argues that settlement works through the translation of indigeneity as Indianness, casting place-based political collec-tivities as (racialized) populations subject to U.S. jurisdiction and manage-ment: "the Indian is left nowhere and everywhere within the ontological premises through which U.S. empire orients, imagines, and critiques itself"; "ideas of Indians and Indianness have served as the ontological ground through which U.S. settler colonialism enacts itself" (xix).

These accounts are differently configured, but in all of them, the contours of settlement appear analytically as clear and coherent from the start, as a virtual totality. What, though, might be lost in an analytical investment in tracing settlement as a structure or ontology—a somewhat self-generating, uniform whole? The ongoing processes by which settler dominance actively is reconstituted as an embodied set of actions, occupations, deferrals, and potentials can slide from view, deferring discussion of how the regularities of settler colonialism are materialized in and through quotidian nonnative sensations, dispositions, and lived trajectories. Holland notes of discussions of antiblack racism that "when we return to [racist] practice, we can only see something produced by the machinations of large systems like the university or the state. We often only have eyes for the spectacularity of racist practice, not its everyday machinations" (27), later observing, "[W]e might come to think differently about the historical—we might find a grounding for racist practice that acknowledges both systemic practices *and* quotidian effects that far exceed our patterned understanding of how history has happened to us" (52). When and how do projects of elimination, replacement, and possession become geographies of everyday nonnative occupancy that do not understand themselves as predicated on colonial occupation or on a history of settler–Indigenous relation (even though they are), and what are the contours and effects of such experiences of inhabitance and belonging? Quotidian forms of sensation—processes of routine *happening*—fade from view in the move away from the "everyday" and toward the "systemic." In *Reassembling the Social,* Bruno Latour argues against kinds of analysis in which "the social" functions as an explanatory tool that exceeds and precedes the particular sets and sites of relations under discussion: "every activity—law, science, technology, religion, organization, politics, management, etc.—could be related to and explained by the same social aggregates *behind* all of them" (8).[8] Doing so short-circuits the investigation by a priori positing an integrated set of connections that is then treated as a sufficient cause for the "activity" in question, which itself functions in the analysis as merely a bearer of that self-same "social aggregate"—not doing anything on its own.

The dynamics by which legislative and administrative agendas come to function as an animating part of daily life, the differences such realization and localization make in the terms and trajectories of those explicit projects, and the possibilities for forms of disjuncture between the state apparatus and everyday experience are bracketed by the positing of a clear, direct, and inevitable relation characterized as "ontological." Raymond Williams observes, "A lived hegemony is always a process. It is not, except analytically, a system or a structure. . . . In practice, that is, hegemony can never be singular," instead needing "continually to be renewed, recreated, defended, and modified" (112), and he describes the tendency to speak and think in terms of *systems* as a "procedural mode" that emphasizes "formed wholes rather than forming and formative processes" (128). Following this line of thought, accounts of settlement as always-already a "formed whole" leave aside the ways the institutions of the settler-state become "actively involved" in the daily life of nonnatives, serving as "formative" but in ways that cannot be understood as always taking the same shape and thus known beforehand. Moreover, this *processual* approach leans away from the tendency to look to a limited set of federal laws, cases, and policy determinations as the means of defining the legal terms (the structure) of settlement, particularly given the unevenness of the application of federal norms generally, the development of divergent patterns in states and territories, and the fact that states in the Northeast sought to present themselves as not bound by the terms of federal Indian affairs.[9] The notion of settler common sense seeks to address how the varied legalities, administrative structures, and concrete effects of settler governance get "renewed" and "recreated" in ordinary phenomena by nonnative, nonstate actors, in ways that do not necessarily affirm settlement as an explicit, conscious set of imperatives/initiatives or coordinate with each other as a self-identical program. As a project of reading, then, it looks for the textual traces of quotidian ways of (re)producing the givenness of settler jurisdiction, placemaking, and personhood, attending to the means by which writings that feature neither Indians nor the expropriation of Native lands register the impression of everyday modes of colonial occupation.

Settler Sensoria

In the absence of a processual (as opposed to "procedural") methodology, settlement can appear as a de facto monolith, forestalling discussion of the divergence and attendant (uneven) relations among its manifestations, the mediums and modes of its nonofficial proliferation/realization, and the character and contours of its abiding influence in situations (and representations) in which Native people(s) do not lie at the center. Fiona Nicoll suggests the importance of nonnatives "mov[ing] towards a less coercive stance of reconciliation *with* [ceasing to center nonnatives as the givers of recognition] when we fall ... into an embodied recognition that we already exist within Indigenous sovereignty" (29). Flipping over that call, the kind of analysis I am suggesting begins by investigating the embodied conditions

of possibility for the historical and persistent deferral of Native s
the ways settler sovereignty continually is activated, circulated, ar
ized within and through the "lived hegemony" of everyday experience.-- How
do nonnatives actively participate in the ongoing remaking of settlement as
a shifting assemblage of ordinary actions, occupancies, ethics, aspirations,
dispositions, and sensations?[11] Settler jurisdiction inhabits the everyday
experience of nonnatives as affect, less determining effects and relationships
than inducing inclinations and coalescing/catalyzing possibilities that serve
as the animating context from which texts such as Hawthorne's, Thoreau's,
and Melville's emerge.[12]

Queer and feminist work in Native studies has addressed the role of
Native emotion and eroticism in daily life, seeking to bridge the divide
between intimacy and sovereignty and exploring how representations of the
ostensibly personal register histories of political struggle and legacies of
attempted genocide. In "Dildos, Hummingbirds, and Driving Her Crazy,"
Deborah Miranda investigates nonnative blindness to, and unwillingness to
circulate, depictions of Native eroticism, particularly that of and by women.
She suggests, "Stereotypes about Native women . . . may take up all the available space in the American public's head, leaving no room for writers who
are not either squaw sluts, Pocahontas, or Indian princesses" (138). More
than crowding out fuller, richer accounts of Indigenous experience, this
profusion of skewed images defers and disavows the persistent violence of
settlement: "[W]e cannot be allowed to *see* indigenous women in all their
erotic glory without also *seeing* and acknowledging all that has been done
to make those women—their bodies and cultures—extinct" (145). To represent Native women's bodily and emotional sensation in a substantive way
entails conveying the continuing impress of their displacement, exploitation, and erasure as Indigenous people. Moreover, Native accounts of affective life provide insight into the ways the exertion of authority by the state
operates as an ongoing process. Discussing the effects of sexual violence
in Indian boarding schools and the narration of those experiences within
public discourse, Dian Million argues that "emotional knowledges" function
as "community knowledges" (54), indicating not merely an idiosyncratic
account but an implicit analysis of and response to the structures—governmental, economic, cultural—through which Native people(s) are regulated
and self-determination is managed or denied. She further observes that such

expressions "d[o] not always 'translate' into any direct, political statement" (64), indicating how quotidian sensations often do not operate in a register that would be understood as "political" and do not usually produce articulated propositions that would function as political claims.[13]

Taking a cue from this body of scholarship, which traces the ways macrological dynamics of conquest inhabit and move within everyday experience, I seek to address how settlement operates as a structure of feeling, how the ordinary "emotional knowledges" of nonnatives work to circulate, instantiate, and normalize settler sovereignty.[14] Tracing a dialectical relation between policy and the everyday, Moreton-Robinson notes in "Writing Off Indigenous Sovereignty" that the "possessive investment in patriarchal white sovereignty is enhanced through private property ownership. This security produces affect that is encapsulated in a sense of home and place, mobilising an affirmation of a white national identity" (95). Here she raises the issue of how the legal discourses that sustain the settler-state's sovereignty become part of ordinary nonnative routine and feeling. In drawing on Moreton-Robinson's work, Chris Andersen has suggested the importance of attending to the "density" of Indigenous being, "com[ing] to terms with a more serious and infinitely less schematic *livedness* which defies easy (academic) description" (92), and doing so also entails attending to the forms of "colonial critique" enabled by Indigenous knowledges about the terms and dynamics of settlement. In this way, attending to the "*livedness*" and "density" of settler experience works as a way of exploring the operation of settler colonialism without falling into what Andrea Smith has described as "ethnographic entrapment" (43), the effort to account for Native particularity as a means to argue for increased recognition.[15]

Aspects of law and policy orient, shape the trajectory of, and provide momentum for quotidian modes of sensation and contextualization. In *Phenomenology of Perception*, Maurice Merleau-Ponty suggests, "[S]ince sensation is a reconstitution, it pre-supposes in me sediments left behind by some previous constitution" (249), adding, "The *person who* perceives is not spread out before himself as a consciousness must be; he has historical density, he takes up a perceptual tradition" (277).[16] The "previous constitution" of the space one occupies as part of the U.S. nation-state provides nonconscious "historical density" to nonnatives' engagement with the landscape, *reconstituting* settlement as part of assessing the material "field of possibility" for present action (509): "I do not so much perceive objects as reckon with an environment" (483). Attending to the ways settler law operates as an historically dense field of everyday possibility enables consideration of what precedes nonnative subjects in their individual inhabitance, how state policies engender inclinations and tendencies. In *Queer Phenomenology,* Sara Ahmed suggests, "Familiarity is shaped by the 'feel' of space or by how spaces 'impress' upon bodies. . . . The familiar is an effect of inhabitance; we are not simply in the familiar, but rather the familiar is shaped by actions that reach out toward objects that are already within reach" (7), and she adds, "The work of inhabitance involves orientation devices; ways of extending bodies into spaces that create new folds, or new contours of what we could call livable or inhabitable space" (11). If the familiarity of inhabitance depends less on the inherent character of the place one inhabits than the iterability and duration of occupancy itself, the sensation of belonging—of properly extending into the place one occupies—arises out of an "impress" that also *orients,* directing attention to some things and not others while providing a working map of extant relations and potentials in the space of inhabitance as well as an animating impetus in traversing it. Governmental acts and agencies can be understood as providing such orientation through mechanisms like property law, zoning ordinances, rules of inheritance, regulation of commerce, police presence, and the construction and maintenance of infrastructure. While themselves arising out of processes of contestation, negotiation, and compromise, such state-enacted geographies in their (albeit mutable) implementation help provide shape and structure to the quotidian networks that individuals engage, and the sense of relative stability such geographies generate facilitates the normalization and becoming-given of the ways they contour place, association, and belonging as well as the particular kinds of actions, connections, and dispositions they incite and incentivize.[17]

Reciprocally, everyday practice realizes and projects those geographies, materializing them by drawing on them as a guide in processing and responding to affective and sensory input and thus (re)constituting them as given in ordinary modes of meaning-making, feeling, and movement.[18] Ahmed notes, "we do not have to consciously exclude those things that are not 'on line.' The direction we take excludes things for us, before we even get there" (*Queer* 15). The legalities in and through which placemaking occurs and personhood is defined bear a propulsive force, not simply installing something like a social cartography or diagram but endowing it with a dynamic character that incites kinds of engagement, practice, and subjectivity, what Merleau-Ponty characterizes as the "momentum of existence" (159). Inasmuch as law and policy help define and delimit the horizon of the possible, providing a nonconscious frame that informs and guides the phenomenological experience of selfhood, situatedness, and connection to others, they bear a "momentum" that contributes to their material (re)actualization. In Apess's terms quoted earlier, "a foundation was laid in the first Legislature to enslave our people by taking from them all rights, which has been strictly adhered to ever since," and that set of institutional discourses and practices orient a generationally iterative, and naturalized, process of occupation—"our fathers carried on this scheme of getting your lands for our use."

The legal and political mappings that influence everyday life in the United States remain predicated on the assertion of an underlying and incontestable national sovereignty that itself animates the work of law and policy-making in putatively domestic space. The routine actualization of state-licensed mappings depends on reactivating the jurisdiction-setting procedures that establish settler presence and governance as given, as a necessary context through which commonplace sense-making occurs. Merleau-Ponty observes, "[I]t is essential to the alleged fixed points underlying motion that they should not be posited in present knowledge and that they should always be 'already there.' They do not present themselves directly to perception, they circumvent it and encompass it by a preconscious process, the results of which strike us as ready made" (326), and in this way they provide "anchorage" in nonconsciously composing varied affective impressions into a sense of locatedness and possible movement, of the potential for engagement with the world (326–27). The apparent absence of struggle among incommensurate claims to sovereignty over one's space of occupancy, and an attendant impression of one's dwelling in that place as itself having no inherent political dimension or as not conditioned on state action, provides nonnatives with a "ready made" background against which to register opportunities for agency and for interaction with their surroundings.

More than simply clearing away or containing Native presence and claims, such sovereignty-making policies, ideologies, and practices affect the composition of the ensuing/encompassing legal regime. As Ahmed suggests,

"Histories shape 'what' surfaces: they are behind the arrival of 'the what' that surfaces" (44). Conceptions of sovereignty, territoriality, and personal identity inherited from shared Anglo-American legal and philosophical traditions, operative within the relatively integrated political economy of the transatlantic British colonial system, and recontextualized in the struggle for independence gain new implications and momentum in its wake (a transmission and reconfiguration addressed in particular in chapter 2).[19] Everyday experiences of dwelling, personal autonomy, relation to others, and (non)relation to the state remain *anchored* in settler sovereignty, in the sense of being dependent on forms of state jurisdiction and policy that themselves subsume and displace Indigenous presence and territoriality. Merleau-Ponty observes that "former experience is present to" current perception "in the form of a horizon which it can reopen" (26), and state-endorsed geographies, shaped in their initial construction by extant political discourses and pressures, function as such experience due to the ways they are materialized as given in the contours of everyday occupancy, providing both the background and implicit horizon for present thought, feeling, and action.

Thus, the intellectual and political technologies for justifying the assertion of jurisdiction over Native peoples and expropriation of their lands do not simply disappear when Indians are (declared to be) no longer there. Rather, they remain vital in the ongoing performance of quotidian modes of inhabitance and selfhood. When discussing the absence of an "underlying hidden structure," Latour observes, "this is not to say that there doesn't [*sic*] exist *structuring templates* circulating through channels most easily materialized by techniques—paper techniques and, more generally, intellectual technologies being as important as gears, levers, and chemical bonds" (196), and he describes the effects of such "techniques" on the experience of subjectivity as "plug-ins" (207). Everyday enactments of place, personhood, and belonging rely on the reiteration of settler sovereignty and the redeployment of its accompanying legal and normative templates. In that process, relevant plug-ins might include narrations of national history as progress or as expansion into politically empty space, stories of inevitable Native disappearance, articulations of the extralegal character of individual agency, the categorization of noncommercial or public land as authentic/pure "nature," characterizations of domestic issues as necessarily distinct from foreign/international ones, equations of political existence and peoplehood with the nation-state form, and calls to increase intimacy with one's place of inhabitance. These framings reaffirm, normalize, and propel settlement as the "ready made" against which new information, sensation, experience affectively is managed.

The orientations and momentum emerging out of everyday life—including the templates circulating through and actualized in it—give rise to texts (and other forms of cultural production) for which U.S. legal and political mappings serve as the unacknowledged frame. Such texts certainly do not merely reproduce experience, instead engaging in imaginative explorations and reflexive meditations that allow for a reconsideration and refashioning of the everyday (as well as breaks from its contours and normalizations). However, any act of representation foregrounds some things and not others, highlighting particular persons, objects, events, ideas, and relations for consideration while treating others as given. As Bruce Smith suggests in defining his notion of "historical phenomenology," it engages with the "presence effects" of everyday sensation on textual production, "ask[ing] the reader to take words, not as symbols, signs with only an arbitrary relation to the thing toward which they point, but as indexes, signs with a natural or metonymic connection with somatic experience" (326). Characterizing settlement as operating as a form of embodied "common sense" suggests that the normalized legalities and geographies of settler policy—its displacement, containment, and erasure of Indigenous landedness and implementation and routinization of modes of nonnative dwelling—function largely as backdrop, as the unacknowledged condition of possibility for textual representations in which other issues occupy the foreground. Such texts then themselves circulate as possible templates, potentially influencing ordinary experience by providing part of the "perceptual tradition" through which sense data is processed.

Such "templates" are efficacious not because of an ideological hold they have over consciousness, which can be broken through falsification or deconstruction. They are not logical propositions or beliefs that can be disposed of by being shown to be incorrect. Rather, "plug-ins" are integrated into everyday life via the material "techniques" and networks through which they circulate, and those templates and techniques function as part of quotidian, nonconscious processes of orientation, (re)producing a phenomenological sense of givenness and projecting it as the horizon of future possibility.[20] In this sense, nonnatives need not function directly as agents of the state or as

conscious purveyors of state aims in order to rematerialize state-effects by
drawing on extant geographies, discourses, and normative frames as anchors
in processes of affective sense-making and "reckon[ing] with [their] environment." Moreover, these actualizations and enactments of "familiarity"
may not be identical or congruent with each other. Multiple histories of
state action that inhabit, orient, and stimulate the present "impress" in ways
that might produce different (even incommensurate) forms of engagement.
Comfort in the Lockean privatized autonomy of one's home(stead) (chapter 2), an inclination toward "nature" as a space of escape from the extant
regime of property ownership (chapter 3), and immersion in the obscure
anonymities of urban dwelling (chapter 4) do not resemble one another and
arise out of disparate affective—and perhaps ethical—commitments. Yet,
all of them iterate, to varied effects, the geopolitical self-evidence and security of the state whose unquestioned endurance anchors and animates them.
The point, then, is not what nonnatives consciously think or believe about
Native people(s), and the critical task is not to disprove, refute, or replace
such conscious commitments. I am not making claims about Hawthorne's,
Thoreau's, or Melville's attitudes toward Indians or their conscious principles with respect to Indian policy. Instead, what is at issue is how the juridical dimensions and dynamics of settlement impress upon and are lived
and reconstituted as the material animating ordinary nonnative experience:
how settlement is actualized, stabilized, and extended through modes of
settler sensation and how such sensation serves as the context from which
textual representation emerges. In addition, though, texts provide an archive
of available templates, how those templates are mobilized in projects of representation, and the material conditions of possibility (the modes of everyday sense-making) through which the texts' terms become intelligible. When
engaged from a perspective that disorients the givenness of settler phenomenologies—that does not take for granted the familiarity of, in Apess's terms,
"the way our fathers first brought us up"—those same texts (such as those
on which I focus) can be read in ways that track the process of template making and circulation, drawing on them as a resource in thinking back toward
everyday forms of normalization so as to open increased possibilities for
imagining otherwise.[21]

Given the continued presence of Native peoples, including in areas from
which they putatively have "vanished," though, the question remains as to

how the endurance of indigeneity and nonnatives' encounters with Natives intersect with the kinds of settler orientation and momentum I have been addressing.[22] In describing how sensation gets resolved into a coherent perceptual field, Merleau-Ponty observes, "Our perception in its entirety is animated by a logic which assigns to each object its determinate features in virtue of those of the rest, and which 'cancel out' as unreal all stray data; it is entirely sustained by the certainty of the world," providing a sense of "the primordial constancy of the world as the horizon of all our experiences" (365), and he later notes, "My thought, my self-evident truth is not one fact among others, but a value-fact which envelops and conditions every possible one," such that the various phenomena apprehended "must figure in my universe without completely disrupting it" (463). To the extent that the legal geography of the settler-state engenders ordinary modes of personhood, placemaking, and belonging, it provides, in Merleau-Ponty's terms quoted earlier, "fixed points" through which one "reckons with the possible," and from that perspective, Indigenous landedness, sovereignty, and collectivity appear as "stray data" that function as "unreal," challenging the apparent "constancy of the world" in nonnative experience. In this way, discourses and accounts of Native disappearance may function as the conscious translation of disturbances to the perceptual "self-evident truth" of U.S. jurisdiction and attendant geographies of everyday life.

Furthermore, following this line of thought, tropes of Indianness may be understood as a kind of plug-in that allows Native presence to enter settler phenomenologies without "completely disrupting" them. The entry of discourses and figurations of Indianness can be interpreted as a form of crisis management that enables nonnatives to accommodate and engage with Indigenous presence so as to contain the threat it poses to quotidian modes of affective anchorage, in which the settler-state and its legal and political mappings are lived as given and projected as the basis for engaging with one's "environment." In other words, the deployment of various modes of *Indianization* through which Native peoplehood and sovereignty are converted into forms of anomaly—conceptually and perceptually segregated from the space of routine experience as a kind of categorical, geographic, political, and/or temporal aberration—can be understood as an expression of an ongoing process of making "unreal" Native sovereignties in the ordinary enactment and stabilization of U.S. sovereignty as the basis for nonnative sensation.[23] This approach can be distinguished from the interpretation of such figuration as part of an explicit project of dispossession that articulates directly with existing institutional aims (although such exceptionalization also operates as a vital mechanism of state practice).[24] Moreover, the coding of Native people(s) as Indians allows for the articulation of propositional statements about them—including expressions of ambivalence, support, sympathy, and guilt—in ways that may still make constant the regularity of the legalities, jurisdiction, and mappings of the (settler-)state. However, in seeking to manage potential disruptions to settler certainty, the process of Indianization also may signal possibilities for reorientation, moments when settler phenomenologies might shift into something new. In this way, the "Indian" emerges both as a figure of dismissal and foreclosure and of potential transformation. That trope implicitly marks the unacknowledged presence of a quotidian settler phenomenology while also holding out the potential for opening into an engagement with enduring Native presence, landedness, and self-determination, as well as with the routinized and ongoing violences through which the self-evidence of settler inhabitance is secured.[25]

(CRITICAL) LEGACIES OF ENSLAVEMENT

Over the past twenty years, scholars have given greater prominence to slavery and its legacies and the intertwined processes of (re)producing blackness and whiteness as ubiquitous features of U.S. history, politics, and culture, understanding these dynamics as pervading all aspects of national life. In *Playing in the Dark* (1992), Toni Morrison asks the landmark question of how the presence of black people and the practices and legacies of enslavement might be registered in texts that do not foreground either, providing "the very manner by which American literature distinguishes itself as a coherent entity" (6). She demonstrates how texts illustrate "the impact of racism on those who perpetuate it" (11), "even, and especially, when American texts are not 'about' Africanist presences or characters or narrative or idiom" (46).[26] This conceptual and methodological turn helps propel the emergence of immensely rich and important developments within nineteenth-century Americanist scholarship, enabling a centering of slavery and its legacies, blackness as a mode of racialization and anti-black racism, and African American experience within the field as a whole by indicating their relevance across the entire spectrum of U.S. political economy, cultural production, and social life. While *Settler Common Sense* owes an immeasurable debt to this set of conceptual and methodological innovations, these salutary developments also have had the effect of reaffirming what has been characterized as the "black/white binary."[27] Even more than taking the specifics of one vector of racialization and the modes of oppression that sustain it (and that it sustains) and potentially generalizing them to all forms of racialization in ways that may ill-fit other histories, the black/white binary tends to foreground citizenship, rights, and belonging to the nation, miscasting Indigenous self-representations and political aims in ways that make them illegible.[28]

From a perspective organized around bondage, emancipation, labor, political participation, and formal versus substantive freedom, Native articulations of peoplehood, sovereignty, and collective landedness can appear confusing at best and at worst are taken as indicative of an investment in a form of reactionary ethnic nationalism. As Byrd argues in *The Transit of Empire*, "The generally accepted theorizations of racialization in the United States have, in the pursuit of equal rights and enfranchisements, tended to be sited along the axis of inclusion/exclusion. . . . When the remediation of the colonization of American Indians is framed through discourses of racialization that can be redressed by further inclusion into the nation-state, there is a significant failure to grapple with the fact that such discourses further reinscribe the original colonial injury" (xxiii). More than simply leaving out Indigenous political aims, the substitution of racialization for colonization "masks the territoriality of conquest by assigning colonization to the racialized body . . . [;] land rights disappear into U.S. territoriality as indigenous identity becomes a racial identity and citizens of colonized indigenous nations become internal ethnic minorities within the colonizing nation-state" (xxiv), a process "of making racial what is international" (125).[29] Such "conflation," confusion, obfuscation results in a tendency in American studies to treat Native presence and violence against Native peoples as a kind of originary sin of white supremacy that can be quickly noted on the way to a discussion of other apparently more significant and enduring modes of racial domination. Byrd observes that American studies often "sees it as enough to challenge the wilderness as anything but vacant" while then "relegat[ing] American Indians to the site of the already-doneness that begins to linger as unwelcome guests to the future" (20). She suggests that a critical and historical lens developed to examine modes of racialization—a form of study itself overdetermined by the black/white binary—not only cannot grasp the contours and stakes of indigeneity but translates it in ways that redouble colonial incorporation.[30]

Scholarship within nineteenth-century American literary studies that has sought to consider both settlement and slavery often displaces the former on the way to the latter in ways that leave aside the question of the self-determination of Indigenous peoples, as well as the process by which the occupation of Native lands comes to be lived and represented as the "ready made" of everyday nonnative possibility. In *Captivity and Sentiment,* Michelle Burnham suggests that the popularity of narratives of captivity from the seventeenth through the nineteenth centuries (including slave narratives) can be understood in terms of the ways they worked to manage the "resistant and unrecuperable surplus of cultural difference always left over by the process of cultural exchange" (9): "The experience of captivity across cultural boundaries transports them [captives, the texts produced by and about them, and the readers of such narratives] to interstitial zones of contact, where dominant values, standards, and modes of representation fail, alter, or are brought to crisis" (170). Characterizing "boundaries" as *cultural* makes "space" and "zone" almost entirely metaphorical, delinked from actual places, land claims, and modes of occupancy, abstracting from the particular kinds of sociopolitical mappings at play in different instances in order to place them in the same analytic frame. "Culture" comes to mark the difference of nonwhiteness per se rather than indexing the normalization of specific formations of residence, land tenure, and political belonging. Ezra Tawil's *The Making of Racial Sentiment* similarly enfolds American Indians into a critical narrative that defers questions of Native sovereignty, reading representations of settler–Indigenous conflict as a coded way of addressing slavery. He explores "the attribution of certain qualities of character and emotion to race," which he characterizes as "racial sentiment" (11): "In the most general terms, it stands to reason that the Indian and the slave could operate at times as analogous figures in Anglo-American political discourse. Both could be represented as members of alien populations that vexed the smooth operation of Anglo-American power on the continent" (59). He later indicates that "the thematics of Indian dispossession was one aspect of a contemporary discussion about property conflict in which the politics of slavery, no less than Indian land ownership, was at stake" (86), naming Native "dispossession" as a struggle around "property" in ways that allow the contested geopolitics of sovereignty to be cast as similar in kind ("analogous") to "the slavery debate." In *Fugitive Empire*, Andy Doolen observes that the book's title "invokes the heretofore hidden imperialism . . . that shaped our culture and institutions in America's formative years" while then indicating that he seeks to attend "to the histories of slaves and the institutions of slavery" (xiii). For Doolen, U.S. *imperialism* refers to a "logic of racial domination" that shapes "the American rhetoric of equality" (xvi), as opposed to indicating a territorial project of expansion/incorporation in which governmental and jurisdictional authority is exerted over nonmember polities who do not seek such belonging, and from this perspective, Native political projects (such as that of Mashpees in the 1830s, which I discuss in chapter 3) appear as the pursuit of "cultural autonomy" within the broader achievement of "civil rights" (162–68).

If an existing analytics of race produces distortion, what is the alternative? Or, approached from a slightly different angle, in addressing the implicit operation and reproduction of settler legalities in quotidian geographies of lived nonnative experience, what happens to the notion of *whiteness*? Work within Indigenous studies coming out of Anglophone settler-states other than the United States has foregrounded the role of whiteness as a principal mode through which settlement is realized and naturalized.[31] In "Whiteness, Epistemology, and Indigenous Representation," Moreton-Robinson distinguishes "between a racialised subject position and the power and knowledge effects of racialised discourse," positioning whiteness not simply as a particular embodied social location but as a means of naming the structure through which Indigenous territory comes to be understood as possessable by nonnatives and by which that logic of expropriation/ownership by the settler nation comes to be experienced as given (84). However, in the context of the United States, in which the de facto racial divide is not white/Native but white/black, can whiteness provide the principal means of naming the operation of everyday formations and sensations of settlement? Moreton-Robinson suggests as much in "Writing off Treaties," which addresses how whiteness studies in the United States takes the black/white binary as given in ways that efface settler colonialism and Indigenous dislocation: "The

USA as a white nation state cannot exist without land and clearly defined borders, it is the legally defined and asserted territorial sovereignty that provides the context for national identifications of whiteness. In this way I argue Native American dispossession indelibly marks configurations of white national identity" (85). If racializing attributions of Indianness work as a way of displacing indigeneity, does that dynamic make settlement equivalent to whiteness or identification with it? Moreton-Robinson observes that "the sovereignty claims" of Indigenous peoples "are different from other minority rights at the center of the struggle for racial equality," because "their sovereignty is not epistemologically and ontologically grounded in the citizenship of the white liberal subject of modernity" (87). Describing Native "dispossession" as *marking* "white national identity," though, need not be the same as characterizing whiteness as the primary vehicle through which Indigenous "sovereignty claims" are disowned.

In other words, whiteness in the United States conventionally has signified in terms of a racial hierarchy through which populations' access to citizenship rights and social wealth are managed, but given that all positions in that hierarchy are predicated on the continued existence of the settler-state, settlement may be conceptualized less as a function of whiteness than whiteness may be understood as expressing a particular privileged position within the allocation of Native lands and resources among nonnatives. As Scott Morgensen suggests, "Racialization under white supremacy will grant non-Natives distinct, often mutually exclusive, abilities to represent or enact settler colonial power. But all non-Natives still will differ in their experiences of settler colonialism from the experiences of Native peoples" (21).[32] Put a little differently, if whiteness names the mechanisms by which settler land tenure and jurisdiction are legitimized, it may not be the same whiteness as that of the black/white binary, even if both are lived in the same body, such that people of color may enact and aspire to whiteness-as-settlement while still contesting whiteness-as-allocation-of-entitlements-within-citizenship.[33] Moreover, settlement may itself not depend on a routing through whiteness. In *Creole Indigeneity*, Shona Jackson addresses the dynamics of belonging in Guyana, analyzing how black subjects make themselves "native" in the process of emancipation and producing a postcolonial national identity. Jackson suggests that engaging with the history of the Caribbean "requires the difficult assessing of Creoles as themselves settlers," adding that "we must begin to address the ways in which, in the Caribbean and even within settler states like the United States. . . , those brought in as forced labor (racialized capital) now contribute to the disenfranchisement of Indigenous Peoples" (3). Specifically, casting labor as nationalizing and nativizing allows formerly enslaved people to be narrated as having an intimate connection to the place of the state, a belonging made possible by the ongoing settlement of Native lands. Jackson argues, "[L]abor by formerly enslaved and indentured people is precisely what they are able to make into and reify as the new *prior* time of their belonging[,] . . . with which they supplant the prior time of Indigenous peoples" (69). Doing so reaffirms the legitimacy and inevitability of the nation-state's existence, which itself depends on the translation and efface-ment of Native governments and geographies. Yet, in Guyana and elsewhere in the Caribbean, articulations of national identity come from majority non-white populations, largely of African descent. For these reasons, it may ana-lytically be more productive to refer to the process of settlement in other terms than as "whiteness," especially in the U.S. context in which the latter de facto is understood as referring to a struggle *within* the nation-state rather than as one over the nation-state's domestication of Indigenous peoples and territories.[34]

The operation of the United States as a settler-state cannot be under-stood in isolation from the naturalization of racial identities and racialized access to resources, particularly inasmuch as the privileging of whiteness shapes nonnatives' experience of possession and personhood. However, for the reasons sketched above, I do not foreground race as the primary modality through which to conceptualize processes of settlement and the dynamics of settler phenomenology, even as I address the (racial) coding of Native people(s) as Indians as part of how nonnatives edit out indigeneity and settler occupation from their sensation of the ordinary.[35] I seek to address the ways that the legalities of the settler-state shape everyday expe-riences of givenness for all nonnatives, such that antiracist projects (along with other articulations of opposition, as in the texts I address) can recycle those lived grids of intelligibility as a basis for their alternative imaginings. In addition, bracketing the methodological centrality of race, while still engaging with dynamics of racialization, works as a way of forestalling the gravitational pull of citizenship and analogy with African Americans as the means for approaching settler colonialism, while also potentially opening up my analyses to a comparative frame that addresses settler-states in which whites are not predominant.

Queer Geographies and Temporalities

To be *queer* means to be askew with respect to dominant, institutionalized modes of household and/or family formation.[36] That disjunction further suggests possibilities for occupying everyday life in ways other than those ordered around the imaginary and political economy of nuclear home-making. In this vein, work in queer studies has sought to trace how non-heteronormative subjectivities, identifications, practices, and processes of world-making enable the potential for orientations that decenter official mappings and narratives of historical continuity and succession. As J. Jack Halberstam suggests in *In a Queer Time and Place,* "Queer uses of time and space develop, at least in part, in opposition to the institutions of family, heterosexuality, and reproduction" (1), further observing that "the time of inheritance" "connects the family to the historical past of the nation, and glances ahead to connect the family to the future of both familial and national stability" (5). Yet, while accessing possibilities for being in the world and critical vantage-points other than those naturalized as properly familial, queer critique does not necessarily engage with the ways that settler sovereignty can provide the field of possibility and horizon for such counterhegemonic articulations, political aspirations, and ethics. As Janet R. Jakobsen suggests in "Queer Is? Queer Does?," "What we would resist—the norm, the normal, or heteronormativity—is a site of frequently over-looked complexities" (513), adding that "the call to resist the regime of the normal can be (misleadingly) appropriated as if resistance to normaliza-tion undid the question of normativity rather than moved us into another normativity" (520): "[T]he network of power relations that forms a given normativity implies that agency can be constituted not just from differ-ent iterations of the norm and the ambivalence within the subject but also from various norms played off against each other within the network" (526). To the extent that the jurisdictional coherence of the settler-state continues to shape the "network" within which queer analyses, spatialities, and temporalities are envisioned and lived, the contestation of one set of norms (the heterosexual imaginary of familial order)[37] may be predicated on the unreflexive mobilization of other norms (ordinary modes of settler

personhood and placemaking). Conversely, though, queer studies' attention to errant, residual, opaque, and perversely misdirected kinds of sensation, desire, and association within even the most apparently normative
of sites offers the possibility for reading processes of Indianization against
the grain, emphasizing their potential to reorient nonnatives' perceptions of
their environment.[38]

In naming the maneuvers, imaginings, and ethical formulations at play in
the texts I address as *queer,* I aim to indicate their self-conscious divergence
from (although not necessarily direct resistance to) only recently consoli-
dated norms of bourgeois homemaking as well as the ways they may be situated genealogically in relation to contemporary formations.[39] Rather than
taking part in the project of imagining the *before* to the epochal shift brought
on by sexology and its institutionalization of homo/hetero as contradis-
tinguished categories of personhood,[40] my argument participates in the
ongoing effort to open queer analysis in all periods to varied, intersecting
vectors of normalization and deviance, especially as connected to processes
of racialization.[41] To this end, it addresses how Hawthorne, Thoreau, and
Melville explore relations among eroticism, intimacy, property, and family
in ways that envision alternative modes of placemaking and selfhood to
forms of state-endorsed, genealogically ordered, privatizing ownership and
inheritance. However, in doing so, these texts rely on the givenness of U.S.
jurisdiction and accompanying legal formulations of inhabitance and personhood, elevating one set of settler potentialities over another cast as
inherently less democratic. Put another way, each text generates its critique
by deploying (queerly inclined) aspects of settler occupation against other
aspects of settler occupation, presenting the former as outside or antagonistic to the will of the state as embodied/embedded in the latter. Such engagement in the extant social field *is* counterhegemonic while also recirculating
settlement as a constant through which the challenges, deviations, qualifications, and/or contestations offered by the texts gain meaning.

This knotted relation between continuity and change can be understood
in terms of the relative absence of attention to questions of jurisdiction and
landedness within accounts of the history of sexuality. In theorizing the
emergence of "sexuality" in the nineteenth century and its distinction from
the prior "deployment of alliance," Michel Foucault suggests that the latter
"is firmly tied to the economy due to the role it can play in the transmission

and circulation of wealth," and it, therefore, depends on a "privileged link with the law" that enables "a homeostasis of the social body." In contrast, "sexuality" has more "mobile, polymorphous, and contingent techniques of power," "proliferating, innovating, annexing, creating, and penetrating bodies in an increasingly detailed way." The move from the one to the other constitutes a shift from "a system of . . . kinship ties" that transmits "names and possessions" to one focused on "the sensations of the body" that "engenders a continual extension of areas and forms of control" (106–7). Juridical articulation and force along with the territoriality of property characterize alliance, whereas sexuality partakes of forms of affection, attraction, pleasure, and other "sensations" as means of defining personhood and populations. Yet, how do we situate patterns of placemaking, occupancy, and governance within the movement from the former to the latter? Institutional mappings of inhabitance and the question of territoriality more broadly seem to fall out once we shift to "sexuality." Foucault further suggests that "the deployment of sexuality" takes part in the broader emergence of biopolitics, "the right of the social body to ensure, maintain, or develop its life" (136), and in this process, as a means of validating public policy, "the juridical existence of sovereignty" gives way to "the biological existence of a population" (137), in which the operation of power works by "effect[ing] distributions around the norm" (144). The role of national boundaries in defining the geographic contours of "the social body" as such—the *geopolitical*—fades from view, leaving unremarked upon the ongoing dynamics through which state jurisdiction is constituted, normalized, and experienced as self-evident. Instead, attention turns to the constitution and categorization of populations and the operation of "sexuality" within that process, seemingly separate from the (outmoded) performance of, contestation over, and alternative enactments of sovereignty.

This tendency to overlook territoriality and legal geography can be viewed as both conceptual and historical, as an inclination within contemporary scholarship but also as indicative of how the emergence of "sexuality" as a set of "techniques of power" drew on, and helped solidify, the coherence of the state as such by apparently suspending/displacing the question of sovereignty. Foucault observes, "The family is the interchange of sexuality and alliance: it conveys the law and the juridical dimension in the deployment of sexuality; and it conveys the economy of pleasure and the intensity of sensations in the regime of alliance" (108). The emergence and institutionalization of the ideal of nuclear family homemaking entails its linkage to privileged modes of feeling such that deviations from it, alternative modes of inhabitance and landedness, appear as expressions of aberrant feelings and tendencies. Rather than disappearing, the geopolitics of sovereignty, both vis-à-vis other states and as the state's right to control its "domestic" territory, are rearticulated as biopolitical norms, casting social formations that do not fit the legal geography of the state as expressions of bodily inclinations that belong to particular populations or types of persons. From this perspective, generationally discrete and reproductively organized forms of landholding come to be understood as fostering proper forms of personhood and nationhood (a point developed further in chapter 2). While particular ways of arranging and occupying place emerge as normative and legally privileged ideals, they are validated in terms of the *development of (national) life*—procreation, well-being, health, comfort, inculcation of moral capability—rather than as enactments of sovereignty. That shift, though, leads contemporary and later commentators to underaddress the crucial spatial and jurisdictional dynamics at play in discourses of sexuality.

Conversely, when nineteenth-century texts mobilize forms of feeling against legalized structures of property holding, that opposition envisions queer possibilities that rely on dissociation from the juridical apparatus. The state and its modes of mapping (the exercise of sovereignty, the geopolitical bounding of the nation-state, the implementation of jurisdictional grids and principles) appear as either an unremarked-upon background or as the site of critique—as that which must be evaded, displaced, replaced, and/or transcended due to the ways they indicate a nonmodern and tyrannical effort by the government to manage the terms of ownership and inhabitance. In other words, the kinds of representations, discourses, political maneuverings that I am collating as *queer* inhabit an implicit distinction between "alliance" and "sexuality," in which the former signifies as outmoded, monarchical, and undemocratic as against modes of feeling, association, and inhabitance that themselves are envisioned as autonomous from law and policy. While Hawthorne, Thoreau, and Melville offer varied formations of queerness, each deferring nuclear normality in different ways, they all locate spaces in which such relations can unfold in ways that are cast as free from state mappings, as not meaningfully transected and shaped by state sovereignty.

Each disowns the politics of placemaking as an inappropriate government imposition while imagining nonjuridical spaces of exception (a concept addressed in particular in chapter 3) in which to live out the queer potentials they imagine. However, the existence of the settler-state, its mechanisms of geopolitical (re)production and legitimation, and the realization of settler legalities in/as the landscape of everyday life serve as the unexamined material out of which these queerings take shape. One of *Settler Common Sense*'s aims, then, is to suggest how the anarchronizing of sovereignty—with its supposedly regressive and repressive linkage of political rule to forms of territoriality—within queer critique can lead not only to underexamining such critique's own privileged mappings and spaces, but to an implicit evasion of how those critical geographies may derive from ongoing processes of settlement.

The conceptual problem sketched above lies in the ways that landedness (including the legalities of placemaking and jurisdiction) comes to be understood as temporally disjointed from questions of "sexuality," as something of a holdover from an earlier era that needs to displaced in favor of more fluid geographies.[42] Recent work on temporality within queer studies offers the possibility of directing critical attention toward the role of processes of anachronism-making in everyday experiences of settlement, including the ways it informs queer projects.[43] In *Time Binds,* Elizabeth Freeman explores the possibility of a queer relation to time that explores "what has been forgotten, abandoned, discredited, or otherwise effaced" (xvi), accessing the potential of "temporal drag"—"[the] pull of the past on the present" (62). Such affects and identifications work to counter forms of "chrononormativity," how "manipulations of time convert historically specific regimes of asymmetrical power into seemingly ordinary bodily tempos and routines" (3). Seen from this angle, stagings of historical succession and proper chronology work as means of casting dominant regimes as the natural expression of bodily rhythms and/or as the necessary unfolding of progress, and in this way, the passage of time itself comes to appear as if it confirmed particular social logics and projects. As Valerie Rohy suggests in her study of discourses of racial and sexual atavism in the nineteenth century, this insistence on the forward movement of history "mimes the heteronormative demand for proper sexual sequencing" (130), enacting what she characterizes as "straight time" (xiv). Similarly, Dana Luciano has argued that discourses of grieving in the nineteenth century served as a way of organizing the relation between the present and the past by subjecting it to a teleology of nuclear family futurity, but as she suggests, such formations also produced queer aberrations: "[T]he asynchronic traces that haunt narrative dispositions of the grieving body in nineteenth-century American literature . . . [facilitate] forms of connection in and across time that fall outside or athwart the confines of both recognized history and familial generationality" (18). Those forms of feeling "rearrange the dominant chrono-biopolitical dispositions of the historical moments in which they were produced," engendering "a self-conscious distance from the 'official' materials of history" (21).

Attending to that which seems out of time, then, can generate queer possibilities for disjointing "regimes of asymmetrical power" experienced and legitimized in temporal, particularly reproductive, terms. Although work on queer temporality usually places emphasis on recuperating elements of social life cast as old-fashioned, passé, stunted, primitive, or obsolete, the investigation of affects that circulate around the supposedly residual or anachronistic also can address forms of institutionalized authority whose operation partially depends on being cast as outdated, as no longer truly efficacious. From within this frame, queer analysis might take up sovereignty and territoriality by investigating the normative work performed when they are presented as an antidemocratic *drag* on the present (such as in other queer arguments). How does the management of landedness and jurisdiction through law and policy come to be lived as "seemingly ordinary bodily tempos and routines," especially when political struggle over territory and the pursuit of sovereignty are treated like anachronisms? Put another way, how does the normalization and routinization of state geographies work as a *chronogeopolitical* project, including within many forms of queer challenge to "official" history?

How are discourses and experiences of temporality part of the quotidian dynamics of settlement,[44] and how might everyday nonnative sensation be opened to the presentness of indigeneity and ongoing settler colonialism? Earlier, I suggested that the figure of the *Indian* operates as a way of dislodging Native peoples (and their continuing dispossession) from the phenomenal nonnative present, containing the disruptive effects of evidence of Indigenous self-determination and the violence of settler occupation by

presenting them as a form of aberrance. As Tavia Nyong'o suggests, "A critical approach to race should encompass both the history of racial ideas and
the forms of historicity and temporality embedded in those ideas and practices" (10). The process of racializing Indigenous peoples as Indians often
operates through a temporal dislocation in which Native peoples are perceived as properly inhabiting the past, such that their appearance in the
present can be experienced as mere oddity with settler expansionism functioning as the evident horizon through which the present moves toward the
future. In *Firsting and Lasting,* Jean O'Brien observes of ways of thinking
about Native peoples in New England in the nineteenth century, "Indians
could only be ancients, and refusal to behave as such rendered Indians in-
authentic in their minds. Indians, then, can never be modern. These ideas
provided fertile ground for the idea of extinction" (xxii): "[T]he implicit
argument posed is that Indians reside in an ahistorical temporality in which
they can only be the victims of change, not active subjects in the making of
change" (105). Prominent and repeated narrations to this effect function as
a plug-in, or structuring template,[45] that enables the ordinary perception of
Indians as out of time, as a surprising *remnant* necessarily awry with respect
to nonnative modernity. However, more than dislocating Native peoples in
time, such sensations of their belatedness implicitly cast the political negotiation of place that their presence marks as itself a bygone process, presenting
the extension/cohesion of settler jurisdiction as accomplished rather than
an open-ended and continuously fraught project. Not only do Native peoples
appear as holdovers from the past, rather than active agents and claimants in
the contemporary sociopolitical landscape, but the processes through which
the United States secures its sovereignty over "domestic" space seem already
to have been completed, such that one's engagement with the environment
in the present has little to do with the means by which the nation-state
appropriates Native territory for/as itself. The impression of anachronism
that surrounds *Indianness,* then, helps orient and provide momentum for the
feeling of givenness that marks nonnatives' relation to place.

Reciprocally, though, instances of such Indianization also offer the possibility for a different felt connection to that which has been declared past.
When approached from a queer perspective, these moments open up the
potential not only for engaging with Native presentness but for disjointing
the settler field of possibility produced through the routine normalization of

state sovereignty. In *Time Binds*, Freeman observes that, "distinct from the desire for a fully present past, a restoration of bygone times," what she terms *erotohistoriography* "does not write the lost object into the present so much as encounter it already in the present, by treating the present as hybrid" (95). With respect to nineteenth-century discourses of Indianness, eroto-historiography might speak to the ways the representation and experience of Indigenous sociospatialities and sovereignties as a residue from the past might, instead, come to be perceived as an *anachronized* relation with the present. In other words, a shifted relation to discourses and phenome-nologies of *presentness* could enable nonnatives to see the *making past* of Indians as itself a contemporary structure of feeling—part of, in Raymond Williams's terms noted earlier, the "forming and formative processes" of ongoing settler colonialism. Whether attending to the meaning of a recov-ered "Indian deed" to territory in Maine (chapter 2), the presence of camp-ing Penobscots and Indian basket-sellers in Concord (chapter 3), or the significance of Native land claims in upstate New York (chapter 4), the texts I address all open the potential for disjointing the self-evidence of quotidian geographies of settler inhabitance. They offer moments where nonnatives come into intimate proximity with Native persons, legacies, and landedness only to swerve away from the implications of this sensuous contact, dis-placing the possibility of engaging with the ways settler violence animates ordinary life in favor of envisioning forms of nonnative escape from the his-tory of state imposition—Lockean labor in the countryside, sovereign self-elaboration in "Nature," disappearance into the anonymous density of urban space. The texts contain, in Merleau-Ponty's terms, the "stray data" of Native peoplehood and colonial conquest by presenting them as temporal anom-alies. Yet, each text also has queer tendencies that, if further pursued, could lead to a different field of possibility, a reorientation in which not only the normalization of "straight time" but the everyday (re)making of state sover-eignty can come into focus.

CANONICAL MOMENTUM AT THE LIMITS OF DIVERSITY

I've been addressing the ways settlement becomes part of quotidian non-native perception, how that process influences experiences and modes of (textual) representation that are not "about" Indians, the limits of a race-based analysis (implicitly organized around the history and legacies of enslavement) for tracking these dynamics, and the complicity of queer imaginings and critique in settler colonial geographies, as well as the possibilities offered by queer analytics. However, the question remains, why focus on Nathaniel Hawthorne, Henry David Thoreau, and Herman Melville? Why illustrate those dynamics by attending to already quite well interpreted texts by these canonical writers? As I've suggested, my interest in analyzing these particular authors and texts comes from the fact that they are so canonical. I do not seek to make any claim to their representativity, in terms of the processes of settlement that concern me or with respect to writing in midcentury New England (never mind writing anywhere else, or for the antebellum period or nineteenth century as a whole). Rather, the fact that Hawthorne, Thoreau, and Melville lie at the heart of American literary study—dating at least back to F. O. Matthiessen's field-making *American Renaissance* (1941)—is what makes them a desirable subject for my study.[46] I aim to draw on the existing institutional momentum coalesced around and through their canonicity in order to argue for the need to address the presence of indigeneity and ongoing projects of settlement in ways that are not disciplinarily and methodologically territorialized onto the Indian (as represented figure or as author) as the sign of diversity.

Potentially indicating a social justice project within knowledge-production and institutions of higher learning, "diversity," along with "multiculturalism," also can name a containment of that very impulse, binding it to the body of the *different* as a substantialized content that surrogates for an analysis of persistent structural inequity and the violences of state-enabled modes of exploitation and expropriation.[47] The aim of incorporating diversity into literary studies often takes the form of (calls for) increasing the representation of writers of color within disciplinary research and curricula.[48] Doing so seeks to challenge habituated processes through which certain (kinds of) authors come to serve as representative of *the literary*, implicitly understood as producing texts worthy of serious study with the systemic result that writings by women and people of color come to be seen as marginal, specialized, niche—positioned as less deserving of substantive engagement because they have not received such engagement previously. In *Making Multiculturalism,* her sociological study of approaches to multiculturalism in a range of English departments, Bethany Bryson observes of choices made about objects of scholarly study and teaching, "[W]hen a gender or race boundary becomes aligned with a more legitimate boundary (such as a disciplinary boundary or a status distinction), 'innocent' boundary work *can* function as discrimination" (190), and as Sara Ahmed suggests in *On Being Included,* which examines the operation of diversity policies in universities in Great Britain, "A habit is *a continuation of willing what no longer needs to be willed,*" adding that "no individual has to block an action that is not continuous with what has already been willed" (129). The habit of looking to particular texts as the proper objects of interpretive and pedagogical attention—like those by Hawthorne, Thoreau, and Melville—creates an institutional momentum such that those texts continue to function as the privileged bearers of disciplinary value. The maintenance of the boundary of an area of study based on such repeated intellectual investments can function in discriminatory ways absent any will to discriminate, such that the marginality of a vast range of writers persists despite the absence of any explicit effort to "block" study of them.[49]

In this way, canonicity can be conceptualized less as a matter of conscious commitment to a particular set of ideologies/values than as participation in a dense matrix of existing linkages to sites of routine disciplinary (re)production. As with the forms of settler sensation discussed earlier, the privileging of certain authors may have arisen out of intentional projects at one point, but once they have become part of the material, everyday life of the discipline, they serve as, in Merleau-Ponty's terms, a means of *anchoring* oneself by drawing on an existing "perceptual tradition" in orienting oneself toward a "horizon" of interpretive possibility. In *Reassembling the Social,* Latour argues, "Macro no longer describes a *wider* or a *larger* site . . . but another equally local, equally micro place, which is *connected* to many others through some medium transporting specific types of traces. No place can be said to be bigger than any other place, but some can be said to benefit from far safer connections with many *more* places than others" (175–76). Texts that are canonical can be thought of as mediators (modes of transportation across sites) that connect sites to each other, providing "macro" or *generalist* effects due to their service as bearers of value/meaning/relation that help sustain the durability of the knowledge-production/teaching/publication network that is nineteenth-century American literary studies. Even as interpretations of these texts change, they aid in generating cohesion for the network itself, helping to engender disciplinary continuity, contours, and boundaries. While new books can become canonized (extensively networked) over time, doing so entails repeatedly bucking existing institutional flows mediated by already canonical texts.

Native texts, then, can function within the phenomenal life of the field as an alien presence, not unlike the process of everyday excision-by-Indianization discussed earlier (in which Native peoples and accounts of ordinary settler inhabitance as colonial occupation appear as something other than part of quotidian nonnative sensation). As such, engagement with indigeneity and settlement via such texts can be experienced as something other than "literary"—as beyond the (implicit) boundaries, procedures, networks that constitute the field as such in everyday ways. While arguing for a conscious project of altering the choice of what texts we study and discuss functions as a way of trying to intervene in the institutional orientations produced toward certain writers (largely white men), that effort can be blunted by the ways the aim of diversifying objects of study gets bound to the new objects as bearers of "diversity." As Ahmed indicates, "If diversity becomes something that is added to organizations, like color, then it confirms the whiteness of what is already in place" (*On Being*, 33), and she later notes, diversity "seems to be used as a way of accruing value, as what adds value to something" such that "diversity in being attributed creates a certain kind of body" that adds value to the institution by its presence (58). From this perspective, texts by writers of color come to be seen as bringing to the monograph or the classroom a quantum of "diversity," including a new perspective in ways that do not necessarily shift existing interpretive habits, forms of boundary construction, and modes of linkage within the disciplinary/field network. Such additions are not necessarily understood as implicating or affecting the "generalist" concerns of those who study and teach the authors toward which the field already is oriented. Additionally, in *The Reorder of Things*, Roderick Ferguson argues that the representation of minority voices and perspectives within academic and pedagogical projects can function as a means of "archiving modes of difference" (171), noting that over the past fifty years "the university arose as a prominent site of minority reconciliation" in which "it was responsible not only for incorporating racial, gender, and ethnic minorities but also for giving the world a language for how to engage and tolerate the respective differences of those minorities" (189).[50] For this reason, although increased attention to Indigenous

36 ORDINARY LIFE AND THE ETHICS OF OCCUPATION

intellectuals and their textual productions is desirable and to be lauded, it does not inherently eventuate in an engagement with settler colonialism broadly stated, instead potentially leading to a fetishizing celebration of the *inclusion of Indianness* (as value-added vehicle of "reconciliation" and "tolerance") into a now expanded discipline.

While my previous work has focused primarily on forms of Native self-representation, my choice here to address three of the most familiar and central writers in nineteenth-century American literary studies emanates from a desire to draw on the number and scope of networks in which those writers are enmeshed and the ease with which they move across scholarly sites in order to insinuate attention to indigeneity and settler colonialism within the quotidian life of the field. My turn to these writers, then, is less about the special content of their texts than their role in ongoing processes of field-construction, a tactical means of inserting and disseminating consideration of everyday forms of settlement in ways that are not about the adding-on of Indians.[51] One could argue, though, that the turn away from Native voices to white men whose representations already are privileged redoubles that privilege, giving it the sheen of a commitment to engage the violence of settler colonialism while proceeding in a way that reaffirms the extant network and its marginalizing tendencies and recenters settler framings and experiences. Methodologically, I seek to ameliorate that dynamic by focusing on particular Native histories, territorialities, political struggles, and forms of self-representation in each chapter (the Penobscots and the Wabanaki Confederacy, the Mashpees and other peoples in southern Massachusetts, the Senecas and Oneidas), offering them as a necessary context/counterpoint for understanding the particular configuration of settler common sense at play in the central text under discussion. As Ahmed observes, however, within diversity work often "antiracism becomes a matter of generating a positive white identity that makes the white subject feel good. The declaration of such an identity sustains the narcissism of whiteness" (*On Being*, 170). While I am suggesting less the delineated addition of "Native" topics than the reconceptualization of the field around the heretofore largely unacknowledged ways settler geographies become normalized, it could contribute to such "narcissism" by enabling something like a form of collective self-flagellation for an oppressive past that can be transcended in the experience of redemptive expiation of national sins, thereby allowing nonnatives (particularly whites) to "feel good."[52] The kind of analysis in which I'm engaged, then, potentially slides into a form of settler solipsism that implicitly reinvests in the canon as a site of remediation.

My aim in inhabiting the canon and its modes of disciplinary circulation through my choice of writers, though, is not to endorse its sufficiency (we need just read these same authors/texts differently) or to denounce its inherent limitations (they're all settler colonial, so why can't we just abandon them already?). Rather, I seek to point to the endurance of nonconscious modes of settler habitation, habituation, and recalcitrance that displace engagement with ongoing Indigenous presence and peoplehood, and in doing so, I hope to facilitate in the field something like the reorientation I've described with respect to the texts themselves, in which a potential emerges of disturbing the "fixed points" of extant legal geographies that help stabilize the phenomenal field of settler possibility. In Fiona Nicoll's terms quoted earlier, nonnatives need to "move towards a less coercive stance of reconciliation *with*" Native peoples through "an embodied recognition that we already exist within Indigenous sovereignty," and I have offered "settler common sense" as a means of theorizing the ordinary felt sense of *nonrelation* and the work it performs in making given settler colonial occupation. However, tracing such dynamics with respect to these authors and texts works as a way of trying to open the field of nineteenth-century American literary studies more than previously to unacknowledged possibilities for engaging with Indigenous self-determination, to take the latter as an ethical horizon toward which the field might turn by exploring the forms of boundary work (conceptual, institutional, and national) that implicitly have blocked such movement. Attending to nonnative representations alone certainly cannot fully index Native presence, histories, self-articulations, and political aims, but on the other hand, the foregrounding of Native textualities can be territorialized as marginal to the field through the coding of Indianness as "diversity." Thus, both are valuable, the one helping to produce the conditions of possibility whereby the other appears as central to knowledge-production, rather than as an inclusionary addendum.

In this sense, the conceptual and methodological project of queering returns as an animating impulse in my project. Rather than revealing minoritized presence or a position of exteriority from which to offer an unimplicated perspective, to queer something suggests revealing previously unacknowledged tendencies or inclinations that open a text, figure, or relation to alternative possibilities. While highlighting *queer* elements or dynamics enables one to trace processes of normalization through which deviance is constructed as such (as well as effaced, contained, and regulated), the impulse of such an effort also moves toward embracing the ways other potentials already may dwell immanently within even the most apparently dominant objects, institutions, frameworks. Similarly, even as *Settler Common Sense* questions the capacity of queerness (as both identity and political project) to name something other than the operation of settler colonialism, suggesting the enmeshment of antiheteronormative aims in ordinary forms of nonnative occupation, I draw on the openness to risk in strategies of queering as a way of thinking the stakes of my readings. Eve Kosofsky Sedgwick suggests that queer reading can defer the "paranoid temporality" of a sense of structural totality in favor of a sense of "contingency" and "possibility" that "the future may be different from the present" (146–47). Drawing on canonical texts as a way of pointing back toward networks of the ordinary and of disciplinary practice works as a way of envisioning how both might be opened to the unexpected, how they could be made strange with respect to themselves in ways that are not knowable beforehand as the unvarying unfolding of a logic, structure, or ontology.

By tracking routine processes of nonengagement through which settler geographies, modes of inhabitance, and forms of selfhood are lived as the "ready made" basis for action in the world, I hope to suggest the ways indigeneity dwells within nonnative experience as its effaced/negated condition of possibility, reciprocally suggesting how a perceptual shift might alter nonnatives' sense of the quotidian landscape of their lives. Doing so less manifests an affirmable subject of Indigenous difference, with whom nonnatives can identify, than brings into focus how the everyday realization of (settler-)state legalities and jurisdiction influences affect, textual production, and scholarly investigation in ways that thwart the potential for acknowledging the persistence and significance of Native sovereignties. The aim, then, is to shift the momentum of nonnative feeling, imagination, and knowledge away from a field of possibility bounded by and oriented around settlement, instead taking Indigenous survival and self-determination as the ethical horizon toward which we all may move.

2

ROMANCING THE
STATE OF NATURE

Speculation, Regeneration, and the
Maine Frontier in *House of the Seven Gables*

In the late eighteenth and early nineteenth centuries, small-scale landholders in the southern part of the District of Maine waged a virtual war of
insurgency against efforts by largely absentee owners to survey their lands
and demand payment for them. Those who had moved into the area in
order to start farms in the last decades of the eighteenth century largely had
fled increasingly overcrowded conditions in eastern Massachusetts, in which
prices were escalating quickly due to the growing paucity of available land,
and they hoped to settle enough territory to provide for themselves and their
families.[1] At stake in the antagonism between farmers and proprietors was the
proper character and basis of land tenure, the legacy of the war for independence, and the kind of political economy that would be taken as normative in
the new republic.[2] Writers favoring the farmers observe that instead of gaining control over the land through labor, actually improving it through cultivation and building permanent structures like houses, elites seek to extend
their reach and profit through "stratagem and artifice."[3] Rather than endorsing concrete relation to the land in the form of agricultural work as the only
legitimate means of defining ownership, the state has sided with predatory
speculative schemes built on the circulation of paper—"deeds"—that gain
authority by receiving the official imprimatur of the government. This Lockean logic privileges labor as the basis for property, a sacrosanct relation that
precedes and exceeds the specific arrangements of any given political order.

In *The House of the Seven Gables* (1851), Nathaniel Hawthorne alludes
to this decades-long battle in and over the Maine backcountry, a struggle of

which he would have been well aware.[4] He observes of the lands in Waldo
County, Maine, claimed by the Pyncheon family based on a seventeenth-
century deed that "in the course of time, the territory was partly re-granted
to more favored individuals, and partly cleared and occupied by actual settlers," adding that "[t]hese last, if they ever heard of the Pyncheon title,
would have laughed at the idea of a man's asserting a right—on the strength
of mouldy parchments, signed with the faded autographs of governors and
legislators, long dead and forgotten—to the lands which they or their fathers
had wrested from the wild hand of Nature, by their own sturdy toil" (15).
Hawthorne's juxtaposition of the Pyncheons' long lost "deed"—the "mouldy"
state-endorsed paper claim—with the work of "actual settlers" whose "sturdy
toil" carved farms out of the wilderness replicates almost term for term the
arguments made by Maine settlers and their supporters a half century earlier. The search for that deed animates much of the plot, and its discovery
and the proclamation of its supposed worthlessness propels the novel to its
close. In its vision of farmers who "wrested [lands] from the wild," the opening chapter suggests that the text's account of ownership and economy will
be oriented by the struggles of the Maine settlers and the Lockean principles
at play in their arguments.[5] The novel's implicit invocations of this perspective help circulate a narrative of labor in the country as a counter to the
hoarding of ill-gotten gain by elites (cast as themselves residually European)
and as a path to individual and collective regeneration.

The novel's orientation toward a state-of-nature ethics shapes its participation in midcentury political discourses, specifically the extant critique
of speculation. Between the time of the struggle in Maine and the writing of
House of the Seven Gables, two financial panics had occurred, in 1819 and
1837, followed by years of crushing depression and mass unemployment
and dislocation. They revealed precisely how vast chains of credit and debt
were and the degree to which virtually the entire populace was enmeshed in
extended volatile financial and commercial networks predicated on paper,
promises, and public policy that facilitated transregional and transnational
linkages.[6] However, amid the ever-growing proliferation of capitalist entanglements, the Democratic Party, to which Hawthorne belonged and from
which he benefited as a government employee during the late 1830s and late
1840s,[7] legitimized itself by recycling the image of the agrarian laborer as a
figure of republican virtue, trading on the promotion of itself as representing

the interests of working people who desired the supposed self-sufficiency of family farm ownership.[8] Moreover, this image fueled a vision of Democratic ideals and initiatives as not really *of* the state, as emanating from a prepolitical sphere of yeoman inhabitance whose principles should animate governance but were not themselves generated by the workings of the institutions of government. Drawing on the history and rhetoric of the Maine settlers to provide a normative counterweight to existing forms of property law, the novel positions itself within a lineage that resonates with extant party rhetoric, including its positioning of itself as outside of—and as normatively superior and prior to—actually existing political structures. In this way, *House* suggests, in Brook Thomas's terms, that "the ideal of the law contains within it a standard of equity that allows us to measure the failure of individual laws to correspond to that standard" (17).[9] Thus, Hawthorne speaks to contemporary political discourses but in ways that less confirm the legitimacy of government action than suggest how extant law and policy has failed to live up to the philosophical principles and material possibilities that supposedly drove the American Revolution, mounting a critique of the state that does not so much seek to dismantle it as to install a regime (particularly of property) more consonant with an implicitly Lockean standard.

In being framed as a "romance," however, the text expresses some skepticism toward the possibility of realizing the ideals at play in the history of land conflict in Maine (and recirculated as Democratic sensibility).[10] Hawthorne's representation of the tensions around land tenure at the heart of the story (the enmity between the Pyncheons and the Maules, the original possessors of the plot on which the House of the Seven Gables sits) defers discussion of the specific dynamics of contemporary public land policy, bearing the normative force gathered around the employment of Lockean principles in earlier struggles while remaining somewhat agnostic as to their ability to be implemented in the present.[11] Hawthorne's invocation of the legacy of Maine settlement provides an ethical frame and trajectory for his romance of labor, but *House* proliferates queernesses in ways that intimate both the capaciousness of the text's vision and its misgivings about whether Lockean ideals can provide a workable frame for public policy. The image of extrapolitical labor in nature provides a conceptual space from which to critique the speculative excesses of the market and their generational translation into unearned inherited wealth, and the neo-Jeffersonian vision of (re)claiming the "wild" through "sturdy toil" appears in the text to hold out the potential for redeeming kinds of persons who from the perspective of conjugally centered homemaking would appear aberrant.[12] Forms of mid-century deviance—including bacherlorhood, spinsterhood, onanist monomania, and communalism—all can be rehabilitated through movement to the unencumbered elsewhere of rural landholding. However, the very profusion of such figures in the text also suggests some wariness about the possibilities for saving the nation through a journey to "the country."

In staging this (queer) drama about land, commerce, and the meaning of property, though, the text defers the question of how such territory is acquired from Native peoples and what happens to them in the wake of that supposed transfer. The project of developing a theory of the right to land-holding that can challenge state authority runs headlong into the problem of validating nonnative access to Native space. Creating an extrapolitical right to property through labor entails negating the politics of settler–Indigenous conflict over the character and limits of nonnative jurisdiction. Positing a "nature" that precedes institutions of governance and validates them, an empty wilderness in which settlers can "toil," presupposes Euro-modes of political economy and effaces Native polities as such. While in no sense *about* Indians, *The House of the Seven Gables* bears the trace of this imperial legacy in the figure of the "Indian deed" at its center. At issue, though, is less the mere fact of the absence of Native people(s) than the ways the text's narration of speculation, family, history, and personhood depends for its intelligibility on the givenness of settler presence and jurisdiction. The deed to lands in Maine stands as a figure of deceptive claims invented by elites and speculators to block popular access to forms of work-based yeoman subjectivity. In this way, the narrative creates the impression of an unmediated and regenerative relation to supposedly unoccupied land. Such "nature"-alization of settler logics of possession serves as the condition of possibility for the novel's ethical imaginary, suspending questions raised by the imposition of U.S. legal geography onto existing Native political mappings. Hawthorne presents conflict over land tenure as a function of competing modes of house-hold formation on a landscape itself treated as geopolitically given and uncon-tested, but which remains haunted by "Indian deeds" and ongoing Indigenous territoriality, particularly of the Penobscots. The shadows of Indian landed-ness in the novel point toward the ways its Lockean inclinations, as well as the queer excesses it calls forth and seeks to manage, emerge out of an ongoing process of normalizing settler ideologies, while also indicating how the lingering anxieties engendered by settlement perforate the ethical appeal to a nationally regenerative state of nature.

LOCKEANISMS PAST AND PRESENT

The novel's running juxtaposition of labor on/in nature with elite accumulation of property, itself sanctioned by the state, provides the ethical center for the tale of a century-and-a-half-long struggle between two families. The patriarch of the one—Colonel Pyncheon—engineered a grant of title to land claimed and worked by Matthew Maule, who ends up accused, convicted, and executed for witchcraft in the Salem trials of 1692,[13] and the Maules periodically return to chastise and punish the Pyncheons for this theft. The House of the Seven Gables built on this plot is passed down undivided through wills to male heirs (although often not sons, but more distant relatives),[14] but the deed to vast territory in Maine purchased by the colonel goes missing upon his death, which occurs the very day of the completion of his mansion—itself built by the son, Thomas Maule, of the land's former occupant. The reader eventually discovers that Thomas hid the deed in a portrait of the colonel hung in the House's study, which remained there until the present of the novel.[15] This fact is revealed by Holgrave, the daguerrotypist renting a room in the mansion who only indicates his status as a Maule at the end and whose marriage to Phoebe—the Pyncheon cousin from the country—holds out the ambivalent possibility for regeneration at the novel's conclusion. The question of land in Maine, with its potential to satisfy Pyncheon pretensions to aristocracy, appears repeatedly, and the vastness of those claims is contrasted with the much smaller scale of their possessions in Salem. Yet more than providing a distant figure of ephemeral riches, the mention of Maine indexes a long-running struggle over the terms and dynamics of legitimate property claims in the United States, offering a Lockean prism through which to approach midcentury public debates over landholding.[16]

Hawthorne portrays the House as exemplifying broader principles with respect to property. It offers a concrete manifestation of the problem of inheritance as an unearned encumbrance through which progenitors unintentionally stifle the imagination, ingenuity, and ethical sense of future generations. The preface offers "a moral" that animates the story of the Pyncheons:

"the folly of tumbling down an avalanche of ill-gotten gold, or real estate on the heads of an unfortunate posterity, thereby to maim and crush them, until the accumulated mass shall be scattered abroad in its original atoms" (3–4). Rather than offering security, wealth in money and land "crush" one's posterity, temporarily holding off an inevitable process of *atomization* that appears as a kind of natural entropy. The narrator notes, "From father to son, [the Pyncheons] clung to the ancestral home, with singular tenacity of home-attachment," yet they remain "troubled with doubts as to their moral right to hold it," and the narrator wonders "whether each inheritor of the property—conscious of wrong, and failing to rectify it—did not commit anew the great guilt of the ancestor, and incur all its original responsibilities" (16). Clifford Pyncheon, the recently released and wrongly jailed brother of the House's current resident Hepzibah, observes late in the novel once he and she have temporarily left the House, "What we call real estate—the solid ground to build a house on—is the broad foundation on which nearly all the guilt of this world rests," suggesting that the very act of such building with the intention of leaving it to one's "remotest great grandchildren" constitutes a violation of natural law (185)—a "guilt" in which all of one's descendants will share. The problem lies less in the idea of building a household than the aim of creating an edifice, an "estate," that circumvents the need for anyone after you actually to build anything. Holgrave offers the most ringing denunciation of the enervation that results from this inertial and oppressive preservation of the monumentalized past. He asserts, "A Dead Man sits on all our judgement-seats, and living judges do but search out and repeat his decisions," beginning a litany of *deadening* influences that culminates in his declaiming, "I ought to have said, too, that we live in Dead Men's houses; as, for instance, in this of the seven gables!" (130–31).[17] Less a source of comfort than a kind of tomb, the House saps life from the living by replacing present independent judgment with repetition, movement with stasis, innocent creation with complicity in sedimented wrongs. Holgrave adds, "[I]f each generation were allowed and expected to build its own houses, that single change, comparatively unimportant in itself, would imply almost every reform which society is now suffering for" (131). As against a sense of genealogical continuity, those in "each generation" should do their own work in constructing a place—literally homes—for themselves, signaling not so much the fall of a family dynasty as the rise of an iterable ethos of self-sufficiency.

That proliferating process of self-making, however, does not occur just anywhere. Rather, the text consistently locates it in areas coded as nature. Readers are told that "with his own toil," Matthew Maule "had hewn [his "acre or two of earth"] out of the primeval forest," the land gaining value through this improvement and the growth of the town of Salem around it such that "after thirty or forty years" of work it had "become exceedingly desirable" to Colonel Pyncheon (6). The settlers in Maine, who presumably occupy the territory granted to Pyncheon in the vanishing deed, are described in almost identical terms. Their "lands" were "wrested from the wild hand of nature" through "their own sturdy toil" (15). These moments point toward the value of building a house and improving land for oneself. The labor expended in that process serves as the basis for its value, enacting a kind of independence that provides one with a palpable feeling of autonomy and a capacity for creation separate from the deadening institutions inherited by others. Cast as a space apart from the "accumulated mass" of "property," "nature" offers regenerative possibilities by forcing one to renew oneself through work. Holgrave extends his Maule ancestor's propensity for "toil" in the soil in his care for the House's garden. His first meeting with Phoebe occurs there, and he notes, "I dig, and hoe, and weed, in this black old earth, for the sake of refreshing myself with what little nature and simplicity may be left in it, after men have so long sown and repeated here" (66). Despite its having been worked for generations and its enclosure within the confines of the ever-expanding city, this plot of "earth" carries the potential for "refreshing" those who choose to labor honestly on it. The text also links Holgrave's penchant for "turn[ing] up the earth" to his time in the "country": "[H]e had already been, first, a country-schoolmaster; next, a salesman in a country-store; and . . . the political-editor of a country-newspaper. He has subsequently traveled New England and the middle states as a peddler" (125). Yet, "[h]omeless, as he had been—continually changing his whereabouts, and therefore responsible neither to public opinion nor to individuals— . . . he had never violated the inmost man, but had carried his conscience along with him" (126). This "conscience" forged in rural space provides ethical orientation for him when he enters the city, as indicated by his interest in the garden.

Additionally, the novel directly connects the transformation Phoebe enacts in the lives of Hepzibah and Clifford to her status as "a little country-girl,"

born to a cast-out Pyncheon cousin "who had married a young woman of
no family or property" (20). As "a native of a rural part of New England"
(52), she brings with her a set of skills in "practical affairs" that endows
work inside and outside the home "with an atmosphere of loveliness and
joy," learned "in a state of society" quite different from that inhabited by
Hepzibah—one "where ladies do not exist" (55). In fact, Hepzibah insists
that Phoebe's capacity to enliven quotidian tasks and relations is not a Pyncheon trait: "She takes everything from her mother!" (59), who herself was
a poor country girl lacking in "property."[18] Through Phoebe, the novel offers
a privileged model of rural womanhood in which everyday labor becomes
the source of joy and care for others, a fit pairing with Holgrave's "refreshing" work in the garden. The garden reminds Phoebe of her home: "It being
her first day of complete estrangement from rural objects, Phoebe found
an unexpected charm in this little nook of grass, and foliage. . . . The eye of
Heaven seemed to look down into it, pleasantly, and with a peculiar smile;
as if glad to perceive that Nature, elsewhere overwhelmed, and driven out
of the dusty town, had here been able to retain a breathing-place" (64). The
fact that they meet there—in this "breathing-place" of rurality in the city—
signals at the outset that their relationship, and eventual marital union, bears
within it the potential to displace the *wrongful, estranging* legacy of Pyncheon
landedness with an alternative whose rejuvenating power comes from its
connection to "toil" in "the wild."[19]

The Maine settlers invoked at the beginning of the text provide the privileged model of such regenerative labor in the wilderness. The novel draws on
their late-eighteenth- and early-nineteenth-century struggle over land tenure
and ownership in the very area—Waldo County—covered by the Pyncheons'
lost "Indian deed." As Bruno Latour suggests in *Reassembling the Social*,
"framing things into some context is what actors constantly do" (186), and
more than merely setting the scene the act of framing shapes the trajectory
of the narrative by providing it with a particular direction and momentum,
as discussed in chapter 1, mobilizing prior meanings and associations while
also mediating them. The territory in Maine toward which the text turns had
been known as the Waldo Patent, a million-acre parcel that gained its name
from its former proprietor Brigadier General Samuel Waldo, and from 1771
to 1793, portions of the patent were purchased by General Henry Knox.[20]
The Waldo Patent along with two other proprietary grants (the Plymouth

and Pejepscot) covered the area from the Androscogin River to the Penobscot River. Dating back to seventeenth-century agreements with Native
peoples and royal grants, they had been subject to much confusion, due to
abandonment during long periods of warfare, competing grants by the king
prior to independence, and overlapping and ill-defined boundaries among
the patents. In the decades just before and in the wake of the Revolution,
numerous settlers, largely from eastern Massachusetts, migrated inland in
this region to establish family farms for themselves and their children. As the
proprietors were able to consolidate their legal claims in the area, receiving
confirming grants from the Massachusetts legislature, they began prose-
cuting settlers for trespass unless the latter were willing to purchase the land
at rates considered by the settlers to be exorbitant, especially since ultimate
title to the land still remained questionable given ongoing court battles over
the complex and muddled history and geography of grants in the region. In
response to efforts to sue settlers or survey their lands, they began to engage
in forms of low-level guerilla warfare with the proprietors and their agents—
an intermittent insurgency that lasted until roughly when Maine was separated from Massachusetts as its own state in 1820.[21]

Several writers did offer favorable commentary on settler resistance, and
in legitimizing the actions of small landholders, they articulate a Lockean
framework that helps provide ethical orientation for Hawthorne's *House*.
Settlers argue that their right to the land comes from the fact of actual inhabitance and improvement, rather than paper title. In *A Concise Review of
the Spirit which Seemed to Govern in the Time of the Late American War*
(1798), James Shurtleff offers "an apology for the settlers upon wild lands in
the District of Maine" in which he "calls for their being immediately quieted
in their possessions" (3), insisting that the land was "wild" prior to residence
by those who seek to farm it for themselves.[22] In defining what should constitute property, Shurtleff pegs ownership to a physical relation with the
land and actual use, observing that "titles to wild land ought only to be derived by taking possession and occupancy" (17). Furthermore, "when large
tracts of wilderness lands are held by individuals or companies," that fact
"prevent[s] the lands being appropriated to the use for which they were
originally designed" (11), and the only means by which "to detach any part
of the common mass and give it the stamp of exclusive right" is for a person to "annex his labor to it" (19). This line of thought seems drawn most

directly from James Sullivan's *The History of the District of Maine*, published three years earlier.[23] In it, Sullivan repudiates speculation, insisting that the notion "of obtaining vacant lands to sell again, is clearly wrong . . . because the very form of the purchase, is evidence that the soil is not then wanted for subsistence" (140).[24] The hoarding of lands by the wealthy denies access to those who, in Hawthorne's terms, are willing to exert "sturdy toil" to carve a home out of "Nature." As Sullivan argues, though, the "subsistence" gained by such work is not just of any sort: "This improvement must, in the nature and constitution of the world, be progressive," meaning that territory will "become subject to the hand of agriculture" (130). This image seems of a kind with that Hawthorne offers of "Nature" as providing a "breathing-place" from the stultifying effects of living in "town" (64). Texts that describe the conflict over territory in Maine, then, offer a theory of the value of agricultural labor that appears as at least one of the inspirations for the critique of estate-building in *House*, especially given the role in the narrative of an inherited deed to lands in Waldo County.

These texts about the Maine struggle further construct a Lockean account of the relation between property and political legitimacy in which principles of proper landedness precede and exceed governmental oversight, and Hawthorne takes up this connection as a way of posing an ethical challenge to the validity of state determinations of ownership. In his history, Sullivan invokes "Mr. Lock[e]" as "having considered property" as "hav[ing] originated from man's annexing his labor to some part of the great mass of matter": "[W]hile the portion thus rendered apt for use, holds the form . . . to which the exertion of the agent has brought it, the property will remain in the man, who has thus acquired it" (131). Here he essentially reiterates Locke's contention in the *Second Treatise* that, for a given man, "[t]he labour of his body, and the work of his hands . . . are properly his" (111), such that "[a]s much land as a man tills, plants, improves, cultivates, and can use the product of, so much is his property. He by his labour does, as it were, enclose it from the common" (113).[25] Defining the basis for ownership, Locke develops a normative vision in which the absence of such improvement, of "husbandry" on "enclosed and cultivated land," amounts to territory "lying waste in common" (116).[26] As against extant notions of a divinely ordained monarchical right to control the distribution of territory or a need for collective consensus of some sort prior to the allocation of land to individuals, Locke emphasizes the validity of individual appropriation for "tillage" of what otherwise lies "wild" and uncultivated.[27] One possible implication of this logic, pursued by the writers in Maine and recirculated in Hawthorne's text, is that a space counts as "wild" or "nature" not because it is unclaimed by any governmental entity but because it is not being put to use, is being left in a *state of nature*. Those whose labor can transform it from waste to productivity have a right to it that transcends administrative declarations of title and attempts to seize it from those who actually have worked it. Locke observes that "the municipal laws of countries . . . are only so far right, as they are founded on the law of nature" (105), and "the community perpetually retains a supreme power of saving themselves from the attempts and designs of any body, even of their legislators," to thwart their natural rights (166). Since political society according to Locke is formed "for the preservation of property" (137), state acts that violate these principles of occupancy constitute just cause for rejecting governmental authority.

Those writing about the claims of settlers in Maine extend this Lockean intimation, suggesting that their right to landholding does not emanate from the state and that to seek to extort exorbitant prices from them on penalty of forced removal violates the principles for which they fought the Revolution. As Sullivan asserts, if a man "can find a spot not thus appropriated, he has clearly a right to seize upon it as his own. The difference of nation or country, is no objection, because the earth belongs to the sons of man indiscriminately, until there is an exclusive appropriation" (133). In addition, the assertion by a government of control over such territory "appropriated" by agricultural labor amounts to nothing but "a legal fiction" due to the fact that a man happens to be the subject of a given sovereign: the "title originated by taking the land at first as the gift of God to man" (136–37). Thus, the "fiction" of jurisdiction cannot supplant the legitimacy endowed by actual possession and labor. James Shurtleff further develops this idea, arguing that "in acting against the settlers you act against the peace, prosperity, and dignity of the commonwealth," committing a "treason" against freedom (36),[28] and he earlier observes that "principles of equality . . . ought to be legal principles" and statutes "against the spirit of the law" do not count as law (17), adding "for law subverted is not law" (38). The actual users of the land have the right to challenge tyrannical modes of governance that threaten their extragovernmental relation to the part of nature they have made property through occupancy and work. Moreover, given that "these settlers have joined in the adventure of contending for their just rights" from Great Britain, they "ought to be sharers in the happy effects of the revolution" (16). For what was the Revolution fought if not for liberty from oppressive and arbitrary government? In *The Deformity of a Hideous Monster* (1797), Samuel Ely amplifies this sense that confirming the proprietors' claims betrays the goals of independence.[29] He observes, "if one that conquered and defended the land against the King, presumes to take a lot of land, he may not hold it, say the rulers (we want to make gentlemen)" (9), and this preference for "gentlemen" over the small landholder gives power to the "proprietors who will plague him like the despots of Europe," a "restriction of liberty" substantively worse than when "the British King held the claim" (10). Toil on the land endows rights that precede and exceed the jurisdictional powers of the state, and that very principle, these texts suggest, served as the animating force for independence, citing the Revolution in ways that pit natural law against the corrupt promotion of the interests of the wealthy through the state apparatus and that cast the proprietors' claims as an antinational residue of European aristocracy.

In appealing to the example of the Maine settlers, *House* puts this set of associations in motion, giving an ethical trajectory to its indictment of the Pyncheons. Possessing officially recognized status in his position as a "colonel," the Pyncheon patriarch has his landholdings ratified by the government (6, 14), suggesting an alignment of his interests with that of the Massachusetts General Court against that of the Maules and actual settlers on the eastern frontier. The spirit of the colonial legislative endorsement of the elder Pyncheon's land seizures and speculations persists in the public acclaim of Jaffrey Pyncheon, the most recent inheritor of the House.[30] Jaffrey has served as a judge, earning him the title for life, and "having a natural tendency towards office," he also has served "in both branches of the state legislature" and for "two terms in Congress" (19), as well as being in the process of seeking his party's nomination for governor (191–93). The novel suggests that this office-seeking indicates less public-spiritedness than the judge's self-interested participation in elite manipulation of the political system. Those who seek to nominate him "are practiced politicians, everyman of them skilled to adjust those preliminary measures, which steal from the people, without its knowledge, the power of choosing its own rulers"

(193).[31] Furthermore, the judge dissimulates his own desires and character by playing the role of benevolent democrat: "As is customary with the rich, when they aim at the honors of a republic, he apologized, as it were, to the people for his wealth, prosperity, and elevated situation" (94). In addition to his hollow pretense of republican sympathies in pursuit of state power, Jaffrey remains driven by the pursuit of the deed to the territory in Maine, terrorizing Clifford—and framing him for the death of their uncle—as part of an effort to extract information he believes Clifford has about that long-lost landed wealth (214, 223). Not only does his attempt to consolidate and extend elite privilege through the mechanisms of governance resemble that of the seventeenth-century family patriarch,[32] but Jaffrey pursues the very same illegitimate land claims as his ancestor. The novel highlights the parallel by repeatedly indicating the striking physical resemblance between them, and the genera-tional transmission of Pyncheon property marks a parallel continuity of cor-ruption in which the state colludes with the already privileged to increase their power and wealth at the expense of the working populace.

However, as with the arguments around Maine settlement, the novel couches its suspicion of government institutions, and their embrace of the interests of *gentlemen*, within a nationalist imaginary, signaling the un-Americanness of Pyncheon sentiments through the family's running identi-fication with things European. The colonel appears attracted to the Maine lands because they "were more extensive than many a dukedom, or even a reigning prince's territory, on European soil," an expanse that "would be the source of incalculable wealth to the Pyncheon blood" (15). The lost pro-prietary deed serves as a dense site at which the transmission of wealth, landedness, and a monarchical concern with inherited title intersect—an anti-republican symbol of Tory leanings. That intimation becomes more explicit in later Pyncheon generations. In a tale told by Holgrave to Phoebe, the colonel's grandson, Gervayse Pyncheon, returns from his sojourn in England, having married "a lady of fortune" (135), with dreams of returning there once "the eastern claim" enables him to purchase "an earldom" "from the British monarch" (142). Earlier, the narrator reveals, "During the revolu-tion, the Pyncheon of that epoch, adopting the royal side, became a refugee, but repented, and made his re-appearance, just at the point of time to preserve the House of the Seven Gables from confiscation" (18),[33] and Hepzibah fantasizes about being rescued from her penury (despite her residency in the House) by "the head of the English branch of the family," now a "member of parliament," and whisked off to England to dwell there in "Pyncheon Hall" (48). To be in favor of unearned claims to land and office based on elite status, reinforced by the undemocratic workings of government policy, means endorsing British modes of hierarchy as against the true principles of the Revolution, itself grounded in the natural law ideals of virtue through "sturdy toil."[34] "Nature" and nation converge in the Lockean negation of a politics of inheritable paper titles, understood as fundamentally antagonistic to the rights and welfare of "the people."

In this way, the text enacts a longstanding Democratic Party politics of critiquing speculation and circulating a neo-Jeffersonian conception of yeoman labor as a sign of national virtue, but it simultaneously thematizes the problem of realizing such ideals in the present moment.[35] Stretching from the time of Jefferson to that of Jackson and beyond, interdependent tropes of yeoman virtue, banking/mercantile collusion with political officials, and the danger of anti-revolutionary identification with Great Britain were staples of political discourse in the United States, employed against Federalists and Whigs for decades by the time of the text's composition.[36] Yet, in representing *House* as a "romance," Hawthorne calls on the ostensibly extrapolitical principles of Lockean philosophy (at play in the Maine controversy) while wondering about the degree to which they can influence or supplant existing laws. In the preface, Hawthorne explicitly distinguishes between the "novel" and the "romance," suggests that the former "is presumed to aim at a very minute fidelity, not merely to the possible, but to the probable and ordinary course of man's experience." On the other hand, while it "must rigidly subject itself to laws," "romance" "has fairly a right to present that truth ["of the human heart"] under circumstances to a great extent, of the writer's own choosing or creation" (3). Its "laws," then, are those of the "possible," or the desirable, rather than being bound to the "probable" circumstances generated by existing legal and administrative structures. The term *laws*, though, suggests less a realm utterly alien to that of public policy than one that occupies similar territory and attends to related concerns but from a perspective that can be normative ("truth") rather than descriptive, introducing "laws" and forms of *rights* that should guide thought and action while acknowledging that they may not currently do so. Hawthorne adds that the "Romantic" quality of this particular story "lies in the attempt to connect a by-gone time with the very Present that is flitting away from us" (3). In this sense, the text presents its ethical imagination as a project of conjuring a residual formation as a model for the present.[37]

Hawthorne casts the narrative as the resuscitation of ideas from "a by-gone time" (such as small property-holding in Maine before the triumph of proprietors in the decade before statehood) that offer an alternative set of "laws" to those currently operative. Thus, he positions the text as speaking from outside the extant terms of political debate but in an ideological register not totally foreign to such debate either. In doing so, he suggests the potential for revaluing such subordinated or forgotten principles in ways that might alter the present, in Latour's terms constructing a new formation by *mediating* ideas from the past so as to have them carry a different set of meanings or implications in the present.[38]

The preface further intimates that the notions it seeks romantically to put into play in public discourse specifically bear on questions of land tenure: "He trusts not to be considered as unpardonably offending by laying out a street that infringes upon nobody's private rights, and appropriating a lot of land which had no visible owner" (4). This framing of "the possible" has a distinctly Lockean cast to it, "appropriating" unused territory otherwise lying waste in order to make it productive through one's improving labor. The vision of romance as an effort to find "a lot of land" for one's own rather directly invokes the issue of the public lands, since the question of who could stake a claim on the frontier and under what circumstances had been a running policy conundrum for decades.[39] The settlement of the public lands historically had played a key role in public discourses critiquing speculation more broadly—the expansion of markets, banking, credit, and paper money—and had precipitated the financial panics of 1819 and 1837, engendering the fiercest outcries against speculation.[40] The image of a settler seeking to "appropriat[e] a lot of land that has no visible owner" situates Hawthorne's romance as a recollection of the devastating effects of speculation (largely forgotten by younger Democrats in the late 1840s and early 1850s)[41] and as a call to remember other possibilities for conceptualizing property, such as the Lockean logics employed by Maine settlers. Thus, as Walter Benn Michaels suggests in "Romance and Real Estate," "The romance . . . is the text of clear and unobstructed title" (157), but rather than seeking to "render property secure" by "attempt[ing] to imagine an escape from capitalism" (168), the text's appeal to romance draws on the example of Maine in offering a Democratically inflected (Lockean) account of the value of homesteading, suggesting a normative ground for the national economy—as opposed to that currently licensed by law and government policy—while still holding on to a certain skepticism about the realizable efficacy of this vision.[42]

The text presents the Maine deed as a figure for the co-implication of speculation in the public lands with other mysteries of the market, highlighting the danger of sacrificing the materiality of labor in "nature" to "a world given over to the radical immateriality of the paper economy" particularly as managed by the state.[43] While Hepzibah fantasizes about "the great claim to the heritage of Waldo County" (49), "her shadowy claims to princely territory" (59), Jaffrey threatens Clifford with commitment to an asylum unless he can reveal the whereabouts of the rest of his uncle's estate, of which Jaffrey is convinced he has received "not one third" and of which Clifford claimed to have knowledge in their youth (93, 165–67).[44] While earlier in the text Jaffrey insists to Hepzibah that this missing portion of the estate has been hidden in "distant and foreign investments" that are "familiar enough to capitalists" (165–66),[45] readers later learn that the only knowledge Clifford possessed was the location of the Maine deed in the hidden chamber in the portrait of Judge Pyncheon hanging in the House's study (although at the time Clifford did not understand what he accidentally had discovered) (222). Thus, the phantom investments known to "capitalists" become merged with the "shadowy" claims to a princely territory in Maine. In addition, the text's representation of Jaffrey emphasizes the fictional quality of both his reputation and authority. The narrator observes, "The Judge, beyond all question, was a man of eminent respectability. The church acknowledged it; the state acknowledged it," but "buried so deeply under a sculptured and ornamented pile of ostentatious deeds . . . there may have lurked some evil and unsightly thing." The text adds that men like Jaffrey "possess vast ability in grasping, and arranging, and appropriating to themselves, the big, heavy, solid unrealities, such as gold, landed estates, offices of trust and emolument, and public honors" through which each "individual of this class builds up, as it were, a tall and stately edifice" (162). The judge's "respectability" is a kind of shell generated through its acknowledgment by entities of public trust, which themselves function as *edifices* built out of "unrealities." His construction of himself through a "pile" of "deeds" recalls the "deed" to the Maine territory, suggesting his identity and his power come from a kind of speculative investment given force by extant institutions (like the state, which ratifies Pyncheon land claims).[46] As Brook Thomas suggests, "If the legal documents essential to the maintenance of America's rule by law do not embody the authority they claim, the entire structure of government may rest on a false foundation" (54).

Yet, rather than presenting itself as a window onto the (rural) real, the text insists on its own status as a kind of *unreality*—a romance that speaks more to the "possible" than the actual. While such a designation can be read as playing on prominent public accounts of the paper economy of the market as lacking substance, as a kind of fevered dream, it differs markedly from the self-presentation of writings more directly responsive to financial crisis. In *Reforming the World*, María Carla Sánchez traces the claims to authenticity that characterized fiction in the wake of the Panic of 1837. She suggests that for such writers, "the real reform must be in our characters, and fundamental to that is learning to properly read, to distinguish between 'romance' and 'life'" (73).[47] Doing so required a sort of textuality that hewed closely to the truth, rather than the ostentatious and inflated fictions that characterized the workings of the market system itself and that produced national economic catastrophes. However, while indicating the unreality of the economy of reputation, prestige, and investment in which men like Judge Pyncheon move and thrive (and, by extension, the other Pyncheon inheritors stretching back to the colonel as founding patriarch), Hawthorne refuses to cast his tale as providing a firm ground on which to (re)build the nation.

Instead, in highlighting the text's status as something of a counterspeculation,[48] Hawthorne calls forth a sense of natural-law-based nationalism that exists apart from, and potentially against, the state while raising questions as to the possibility of locating or realizing that normative ideal. The preface insists, "When romances do really teach anything, or produce any effective operation, it is usually through a far more subtle process than the ostensible one" (4). In this way, the text offers its "moral" of the evils of "real estate" and inheritance while demurring from the notion that a work of fiction could produce direct effects in the world. In "The Other Hawthorne," Robert Milder argues, "What Hawthorne sought in and through fiction were exemplifications of universal moral law, which his experience of actual persons in concrete situations rarely, if ever, produced" (568), later adding that "the problem Hawthornean romances sought ontologically to resolve" was "that of establishing a post-theological ground for moral and spiritual belief" (591). *House* itself foregrounds that problem as irresolvable, and one of the principal ways the text does so is through the figure of *law*, particularly as it circulates around Holgrave. As noted earlier, Hawthorne aligns the Pyncheons with the state, in ways that accord with the representation of proprietors' claims by Maine settlers, and as the fiercest critic of the "lifeless institutions" that enable the accumulation and transmission of property (128), Holgrave provides the counterpoint to Jaffrey, his "country" affiliations and work in the garden implying Lockean conceptions of labor. At one point, Hepzibah lumps him with the "community-men" with whom he associates "who acknowledged no law," but in response to Phoebe's concern that he "is a lawless person," Hepzibah muses, "I suppose he has a law of his own" (62–63). His condemnation of speculative wealth, including the *unreality* of "landed estates," and "refreshing" of himself through direct engagement with the "earth" suggests a kind of "law" that challenges the anti-democratic (and anti-Democratic) workings of the web of institutions that make Jaffrey possible and sustain him. Although, once Holgrave has pledged himself to Phoebe, his perspective seems to change fairly dramatically: "The happy man inevitably confines himself within ancient limits. I have a presentiment, that, hereafter, it will be my lot to set out trees, to make fences—perhaps, even, in due time, to build a house for another generation—in a word, to conform myself to laws, and the peaceful practice of society" (216). In envisioning the house as "for another generation," he seems to embrace the notion of "plant[ing] a family" he earlier decried quite vociferously (131–32). He appears to substitute the kind of "laws" that undergird and extend Pyncheon-like property for the version of Lockean natural law he had endorsed. However, this image also suggests something of the kind of self-sufficiency represented by Matthew Maule in *hewing* a home out of the surroundings—the actual physical construction of a house and working of the land around it.

While one could read this change as jettisoning Holgrave's earlier radicalism in the adoption of bourgeois norms, or casting his prior views as a kind of juvenile acting-out he has outgrown,[49] it can be taken as indicative of the text's own ambivalence about the possibility of sustaining an alternative set of principles within the context of existing "practice[s] of society." The Maule-like activity of building one's own house and Holgrave's, and the others', move to "the country" at the end recalls the romantic sensibilities articulated in the preface, distantly alluding as well to the "actual settlers" in Maine. Simultaneously, the resistance to the genealogical impingement of inheritance on the present seems to have waned, recognizing the difficulty of finding a space not already encompassed within the "laws" of "lifeless institutions."

Framing the text as a "romance," then, serves as a way of both offering and qualifying opposition to the speculative dynamics of U.S. political economy. Through this conceit, Hawthorne suggests another way of conceptualizing property and personhood is *possible* (one organized around "by-gone" values of labor and small-scale commodity production and circulation). Yet the text simultaneously indicates the difficulties of connecting such broadly democratic (and Democratic) ideals to "the very Present that is flitting away" (3)—of mobilizing a *country* philosophy to the increasingly urban and commercial dynamics of mid-nineteenth-century life in the United States.[50] Although demurring from the possibilities of realizing the Lockean ethics toward which it tends, the text pivots around the sense of individual work in nature separate from the oversight and interference of governance, using this ideal as the basis for its portrayal of Pyncheon degeneration and the regenerative potential carried by Holgrave, Phoebe, and their union.

NEEDING THE DEED, OR
WHAT COMES PRIOR TO OCCUPANCY?

If the text remains doubtful about the practicality of instituting natural law, it retains that vision as the normative horizon toward which it moves. Following Sara Ahmed's formulation, as discussed in the chapter 1, *House* illustrates the notion that "[t]he direction we take excludes things for us, before we even get there."[51] Hawthorne's adoption of a Lockean perspective emerging out of the earlier struggles in Maine points the text in a direction and gives it a trajectory that leaves aside consideration of the dynamics of Indigenous landedness and settler expropriations, even as Hawthorne appears to disown governmental recognition as the basis of legitimate landedness. As against the ultimate authority of state laws, the text offers the wilderness as a counterpoint, as that which provides a moral ground not

predicated on governmental logics and as an imaginative space from which to
critique speculative investments and the policies that make them possible. In
We Have Never Been Modern, Latour argues that the post-Renaissance "constitution" in which "nature" and "culture" are held to be distinct from each other
allows for the proliferation of *hybrids*.[52] He observes, "In spite of its transcendence, Nature remains mobilizable, humanizable, socializable," and self-
described "moderns" "transfer thousands of objects from Nature into the
social body while procuring for this body the solidity of natural things" (37).
Within *House*, figures of "natural" presence like the garden and the country
function as hybrids, generating the impression of a set of principles distinct
from—and potentially antagonistic to—the legal apparatus even as natural
law emerges within and remains dependent on the jurisdictional imaginary
of the state. The normative leverage the text gains through images of labor
depends on making settler legal geography both invisible and immutable. In
recycling aspects of the struggles on the Maine frontier, the text runs into
two related conceptual impasses: how can one claim as a subject of the state,
occupying land within the jurisdiction of that state, to be exempt from such
jurisdiction without fundamentally challenging the existence of the state?
Additionally, how can one acknowledge Native presence without engaging
with the question of how settlement on Indigenous lands requires intervention and negotiation by the state? In both the Maine texts and Hawthorne's
narrative, these two problematics swirl around the figure of the "Indian deed."

Endowing forms of legally mediated settler occupancy with natural associations, a sense that they precede and transcend the terms of state governance, gives them an ethical momentum that orients them away from the
questions raised by historical and contemporary sites of settler–Indigenous
confrontation and negotiation. The narrator in *House* states that the territory in Waldo County covered by the Pyncheon deed was "in course of
time ... partly re-granted to more favored individuals, and partly cleared and
occupied by actual settlers," but the text's immediate insistence that they
have "wrested [the land] from the wild hand of Nature" effaces the actual
conflicts over their right to title (15), in terms of both Native claims and
extant property law. This formulation suspends discussion of the dependence of such Lockean legitimacy on the extension of state jurisdiction over
the territory in question, instead locating "wild"-ness as a site within the
state yet beyond its authority. In *A Concise Review* Shurtleff decries "one

individual . . . hold[ing] thousands of acres of wild lands by virtue of con-
veyances from those [the legislature] who had no right to convey" (22), and
he later observes, "But as the wilderness comprehended within the limits of
the commonwealth ought to be the property of the commonwealth, it ought
to be the privilege of the poor, who incline to cultivate it, to have lands sufficient to farm at a cheap rate, and not to lay at the mercy of the avaricious"
(27). Here, "the wilderness" suggests less a space outside the sphere of law
than an unused portion of the territory of "the commonwealth" itself, which
should be distributed and utilized in ways that better benefit the interests
of "the people." In fact, the jurisdictional conceit of the land belonging to
the commonwealth is central to the ethical force of settlers' claims as less
privileged members of that polity. As Samuel Ely asks in *The Deformity of a
Hideous Monster*, if "a poor man . . . puts his life in his hand and turns out into
the wilderness with his family" (5–6), by what authority can the legislature regulate his possession of it? Ely extends this critique, insisting, "While
other parts of the union enjoy the great blessings of liberty and a very happy
constitution, we are tied up and bowed down under oppression, our just
rights are threatened to be taken from us . . . ; we are loth to fight for liberty
again, we do not delight in war; but if it must be we will try it once more" (13).
The legitimacy of armed struggle, then, appears to lie in a *right* to develop
wild lands held by settlers *as citizens*, to resist forms of "oppression" that distinguish the Maine district from the rest of the "union." In this way, the conflict in Maine highlights how invocations of nature/wilderness function as
a maneuver in negotiating the jurisdictional field of the state rather than a
position simply external to state logics, projects, and forms of recognition.

This torsion in the geopolitics of land tenure is both marked and suspended by the citation of *Indianness*. Settlers who engaged in violence
against officials and the proprietors' agents were known as "white Indians,"[53]
and such tactics might have been brought to Hawthorne's attention by the
Anti-Rent struggle in upstate New York in which protestors in 1841 started
calling themselves "the Indians" and by 1845 numbered around ten thousand.[54] The use of such disguise when assaulting or threatening surveyors
and land agents was so prominent in backcountry Maine that in 1808 the
Massachusetts legislature enacted a statute making "it a high crime for any
person to disguise himself in the likeness of an Indian."[55] In *The Deformity of
a Hideous Monster*, Samuel Ely describes one such scene:

Mr. Ballard, running the east line of the land which the Court released to the
Plymouth proprietors, was found in the night camping by a fire by a number
of Indians, as was reported, who broke his compass and got away with his role
and papers. Whether these Indians came from Fort-Halifax or from Penobscot I have never heard; probably they had heard the tumult that was among
the people, that many companies of men were seeking to dispossess the settlers, and fearing lest their land at Penobscot would in such a way be taken
from them; to prevent it, it is like they broke Ballard's compass; and if Indians
should break every compass they should find in the woods, how would the
people hinder it? (17)

The implied threat at the end of this description suggests that the citation of
"Indians" from an unknown location serves as a way of figuring "tumult . . .
among the people." This practice of disguise hides the specific identity of
the assailants, making them harder to prosecute although certainly well
known to those familiar with the area. Additionally, playing Indian in this
fashion would have been familiar in the late eighteenth and early nineteenth
century as a mode of potentially revolutionary resistance to existing laws
that questioned not just the legitimacy of a given policy but the claim to
jurisdiction itself, while also indicating a patriotic commitment to the emergent nation.[56] In donning this disguise, nonnatives simultaneously evoke
the notion of the wilderness and of the independence of the nation while
displacing onto a noncitizen population the jurisdictional conundrum of
asserting land rights under the state while flouting state laws.

Such an invocation of Indians, though, is not tantamount to an acknowledgment of Native peoples' sovereignty or collective rights to land. In fact,
the association of them with the wilderness depends on the belief that they
do not, in Lockean terms, constitute *political societies*. Even as Ely references
Native "land at Penobscot" and the "fear" it will "be taken from them," he
also repudiates the possibility of understanding Indigenous presence and
land tenure as anything resembling sovereignty. Arguing that the fact of
Indian presence cannot serve as de facto evidence of legitimate geopolitical
claims, he asserts that "we may observe that all the Indian deeds are a number of years since the King's claim, and it is well known that the subjects of
the British King were in as strong possession of New-England at the time of
these deeds being given as the natives and more so, we were waxing stronger

and stronger, and they were waxing weaker and weaker" (30). In addition to rehearsing a version of the vanishing Indian narrative, itself already well established by the late eighteenth century,[57] Ely's argument primarily turns on the absence of proper Native landholding from which a collective claim to the territory could arise: "[T]he natives had never taken any legal possession to those lands which they have deeded away; . . . they had no legal possessions no otherways than the moose or wolves; they had no certain dwelling place" (4). The figure of "natives" may signify externality with respect to the laws of the state, particularly in terms of property in contested areas in Maine, but it does not point to an alternative legal-political regime.

In order for appeals to "Nature" to provide a pre- or extrapolitical basis for landholding, one needs rhetorically to manage and efface the ways the "Indian deed" signifies not only the existence of a prior political regime over the territory in question but, consequently, the fact that all current claims to that land are rooted in the legal structures of the sovereign that acquired it from the Indigenous polity to which it previously had belonged. From within the terms of Lockean argumentation, Indian deeds cannot have any real significance because Native peoples' relation to the land did/does not constitute a claim to property. As Shurtleff insists, "And does not this logic forbid the use of Indian deeds in proving titles? for, according to this, a man must occupy lands in order to gain an exclusive right in them" (20). This line of thought draws on the argument in Sullivan's *History*: "There has been, no doubt, a practice for distinct tribes to divide the wilderness for the purpose of hunting; and that they have generally held such divisions sacred, there may be good evidence of; but those divisions were never intended as the lines marked for tillage or other improvements" (134). Indian deeds do not signify prior Native sovereignty, since there was no permanent connection to place as indicated by use—implicitly defined as "tillage." "Tribes" exist as coherent entities, differentiated from one another and recognized as distinct by Natives and nonnatives alike, but that placemaking and collectivity remains prepolitical. If Natives have no "property" claim, then the elites who supposedly purchased it can have no legitimate authority over the land, which remained a "wilderness" waiting to be developed by those willing to improve it through the labor of husbandry.

Such claims about rightful access to Native lands formed a significant part of the arguments that led to and helped legitimize the fight for independence, thus historically linking Lockean land claims to assertions of national sovereignty.[58] Authorities in England claimed the colonies as a *conquered* space over which they, therefore, could assert uncircumscribed jurisdiction, and colonists presented themselves as having conquered/settled a wild land, which gave them the right to form a distinct political society on it, one allied with England and under the Crown's overriding authority but not within the regular legislative and representational sphere of Parliament. As part of this conflict over which government could claim the right to regulate settlement on Native lands, figures of the "natural" did not so much mark kinds of privileges and immunities that preceded or exceeded any government at all (although sometimes the usage had this kind of rhetorical cast) as indicate the rights thought to attend one's status as an Englishman anywhere within the sphere of the king's authority and, thus, not alterable by Parliament. Prior to the Revolution and in the lead-up to it, the "natural" had the quality of being both within and without the law, which appears in the Maine texts. *Nature* functions as a discursive and ethical switch point for indexing kinds of claims made within the sphere of the sovereign's territorial reach but irreducible to the terms of existing policy. In light of this history (protecting their rights as Englishmen denied to the colonists by the actions of Parliament and the king), the trope of "Nature" would continue to have nationalist connotations in the wake of the Revolution, signaling the process of according proper rights to national subjects to access "wild" lands within the sphere of the state's sovereignty, and in this sense, it operates as, in Latour's terms, a "structuring template" in the ongoing (re)construction of networks of property.[59] Additionally, English authorities had cited treaties and other agreements with Native peoples as a limit on colonial projects of development and as a sign that Native peoples also formed collectivities under the protection of the Crown, so the rejection and invalidation of such documents became part of the legal argument for colonial, and then national, autonomy. Thus, the refusal to acknowledge "Indian deeds," and the use of Lockean arguments to do so, appears to cite the existence of a pre-political wilderness while continuing in a trajectory shaped by an extended jurisdictional debate within English law which then becomes a part of the revolutionary legacy, a set of claims given momentum by their role in justifying the validity and coherence of U.S. national sovereignty.

Hawthorne's *House* draws on this discursive matrix—the juxtaposition of labor in the wilderness with the Indian deed—in ways that implicitly reproduce the elision of Native geopolitics. As noted earlier, the text contrasts the "strength of mouldy parchments" with the action of "actual settlers" "wrest[ing land] from the wild hand of Nature" through "sturdy toil" (15). When the deed reappears at the end of the novel, retrieved from deep inside Colonel Pyncheon's portrait by Holgrave, he proclaims that the long sought "treasure" "has long been worthless." However, we also are told by the narrator that the "ancient deed" is "signed with the hieroglyphics of several Indian sagamores" and that it "convey[ed] to Colonel Pyncheon and his heirs, forever, a vast extent of territory at the eastward." Assessing the meaning of Matthew Maule's theft of the deed when he built the House, Holgrave concludes that "they bartered their eastern-territory for Maule's garden-ground" (223).[60] This metaphoric *bartering* among whites depends on the meaninglessness of the literal signatures of "Indian sagamores." Describing them as "hieroglyphics" emphasizes their nonsensicality, their lack of significance within and to property holding *within* the United States. The presence of apparent consent by Native leaders to the transfer of land to nonnatives (although, later I will return to the question of what such documents might signify) must be taken as having no value, as an empty gesture that can have no effect on the "rights" of claimants to the territory or on its political status.

In recognizing the existence of Native peoples, in the form of the signature of "sagamores," the Indian deed does not so much counter the deletion of Indians from the past (and present) of Salem and Massachusetts more broadly as render Native presence politically meaningless—dissociating Indians from indigeneity. As Ahmed suggests in *Queer Phenomenology*, "It is important that we think not only about *what* is repeated, but also about how the repetition of actions takes us in certain directions: we are also orienting ourselves toward some objects more than others, including not only physical objects . . . but also objects of thought, feeling, and judgment, as well as objects in the sense of aims, aspirations, and objectives" (56). Being ethically oriented through the Lockean terms of the struggles in Maine, and similar battles over property in the early republic, turns the text away from considering the self-determination of Native peoples as such. Addressing Matthew Maule's claims to the land on which the House eventually is built, the text observes, "The House of the Seven Gables . . . was not the first habitation

erected by civilized man, on precisely the same spot of ground. Pyncheon-
street formerly bore the humbler appellation of Maule's Lane, from the
name of the original occupant of the soil" (6). To say that Maule is the "original occupant" is not the same as saying no one lived there prior, instead
claiming that his is the first "habitation erected by civilized man." Native
peoples cannot properly be *occupants* on land, nor have *habitations*, since
their presence cannot constitute a *property* claim. Thus, the Indian deed
testifies not to, in Timothy Powell's terms, a "multicultural unconscious"
that implicitly recognizes Indians' co-existence within the space of the
nation,[61] but to the impossibility of their prior and continuing presence constituting a geopolitical claim that could compete with the rights of settlers to
develop/improve land currently lying "waste."

In both *House* and texts about settlement in Maine, the improved wilderness appears as both inside the state and outside the bounds of property law
per se, and in this way, the figure of "Nature" operates as a jurisdictional hinge
concept, or hybrid in Latour's terms, endowing particular arrangements
of land tenure, activity, and subjectivity with a quality of transcendence—
they precede and exist beyond the terms of extant "laws." However, doing so
does not raise the possibility that this ensemble could belong to another
political order than that of the state.[62] Thus, the effort to mobilize the priorness of labor as a normative discourse against acts by juridical institutions
(such as the Massachusetts legislature in its awarding of Maule's land to
the Pyncheons or its endorsement of the empty legalities of elites over labor
by "actual settlers") runs into the difficulty of justifying the sovereignty of
the political entity to which such complaints are articulated and on which
such complaints depend for their intelligibility.[63] Taking Indigenous sovereignty seriously as political possibility would displace claims like those of
Matthew Maule to be the "original occupant of the soil" whose "toil" had
"hewn [the land] out of the primeval forest" (6), instead highlighting the
ways such occupancy requires that, in Shurtleff's terms, the "wilderness
[be] comprehended within the limits of the commonwealth" (27). Topoi of
nature in Hawthorne's text, then, gesture toward a perception/experience
of inhabitance—of labor in the wilderness as the basis for making normative claims—that not only does not disturb the sovereignty of the state
but requires the presumption of such sovereignty as its enframing context
and horizon of rhetorical/moral address. In this way, the novel's apparently

antistatist Lockean tendencies construct an ethics that itself takes for granted the existence of the settler-state as its condition of possibility.[64]

The treatment of existing sociopolitical formations as if they merely expressed natural tendencies is a hallmark of Lockean definitions of property. As noted earlier, he argues in his *Second Treatise* that "every man has property in his own person" and that the "labour of his body, and the work of his hands, we may say, are properly his" (111–12), but the only kind of labor that counts is European modes of agriculture, such that "the wild woods and uncultivated waste of America" are understood as "left to nature" due to the absence of "improvement, tillage, or husbandry" (116). As James Tully argues in *An Approach to Political Philosophy*, "Locke's concepts of political society and property" are generated "in contrast to Amerindian forms of nationhood and property in such a way that they obscure and downgrade the distinctive features of Amerindian polity and property" (138–39).[65] The existing parameters of English political economy appear as a universal norm that exists prior to political society, as the supposedly pre-political frame through which to evaluate the validity of human land tenure per se. In Uday Mehta's terms, there is an "anthropological common denominator" that Locke inserts as the basis for what he presents as first principles (52): "Locke presumes on a complex constellation of social structures and social conventions to delimit, stabilize, and legitimize, without explicitly restricting, the universal referent of his foundational commitments" (57). In assessing the non-use of Native territory, he argues that "the benefit mankind receives from the one [cultivated land] in a year is worth 5*l.* and from the other [Native land held 'in common'] possibly not worth a penny, if all the profit an Indian received from it were to be valued and sold here" (118). "Value" here emerges out of the possibility of growing crops for circulation in a (transatlantic) market, and the *use* and *improvement* is measured in pounds, indicating the importance of currency as the frame through which to understand legitimate land tenure.[66] That already developed system of commerce is cast as pre-political, as coming to exist through mutual agreement "out of the bounds of society, and without [the] compact" through which a political society is founded (121), since such society is created in order to guarantee preexisting property rights (133–41). Locke presents the entire system of land distribution, land use, commerce, and currency that emerged in uneven and contested ways in Britain and British trade over the prior two hundred years as *preceding* juridical and jurisdictional structures and as not dependent for its normative appeal or ethical operation on them.[67] As Mehta suggests, "by imagining nature as a physically and emotionally vacant space, with no binding potential, he makes it all but conceptually impossible to articulate the origins and the continued existence of distinct political societies or nations" (129), adding "Locke's account cannot give significance to nor account for the fact that political societies have territorial boundaries" (130). From within a Lockean frame, therefore, the portrayal of Native placemaking as *waste*, as the absence of improving labor, arises from the implicit installation of Anglo-American political economy as itself a first principle, as logically and ethically a priori. Native peoples appear not as polities with their own distinct territorialities but as negative examples within a vision of political order that appears to be derived from the prior state of nature while being projected backward from the actual dynamics of contemporary jurisdictional logics. Locke's account foundationalizes a certain vision of sociospatiality as generically human and, therefore, universally applicable—treating it, as in Williams's terms quoted earlier, "the pressures and limits of simple experience and common sense."[68]

Such Lockean inclinations provide the "perceptual tradition" through which Hawthorne's *House* envisions a contemporary "field of possibility."[69] The text champions the claims of "actual settlers" in Maine as against the "mouldy parchments" of Indian deeds (and of Matthew Maule as the "original occupant" versus the acts of the legislature awarding the land to Colonel Pyncheon), and in doing so, it implicitly relies on the jurisdictional geography of Anglo-American institutions of governance as the commonsensical frame through which to articulate claims to space. Labor in the wilderness only gains oppositional meaning once one has taken the geopolitics of settler inhabitance as the unreflexive organizing frame/template.

Asserting the obviousness of the natural right to "toil" in "the wild," however, requires effacing recent, competing, and continuing Native claims to sovereignty over that same territory. With respect to Waldo County, the area covered by the Pyncheons' Indian deed, Penobscot history indicates longstanding struggles over land continuing throughout the period covered by the novel and the time of Hawthorne's writing of it.[70] In his *History of the District of Maine*, Sullivan observes, "The Penobscott tribe who now exist there are considered as the ancient possessors of a quantity of land there.

The government has in consideration of that, assigned them a larger tract of about the contents of twelve miles wide, and thirty miles long" (134–35), suggesting simultaneously that the Penobscot people continue to live on their traditional lands (toward the headwaters of the Penobscot River in the vicinity of what came to be known as "Indian Island") and that such occupancy comes as a gift from the state of Massachusetts ("assigned them"). The representation of lands in Waldo County as a *wilderness*, then, requires bracketing the political significance of persistent Penobscot presence and self-governance in their homeland, as well as the approximately eight decades of intermittent warfare between Native peoples in the region (including the Penobscots) and the English from the late seventeenth century through the mid-eighteenth century that rendered sustained nonnative settlement virtually impossible.[71]

That extended deferral of the possibility of English authority in the region provides much of the unstated context for the questions raised about the legitimacy of the deeds. Secured primarily in the mid-seventeenth century, these agreements to allow forms of Anglo occupancy functionally were suspended until about a century later due to ongoing military conflict, which at points entailed Native claims to land just north of Portsmouth and raiding as far south as Salem.[72] As Samuel Ely asks in *The Deformity of a Hideous Monster*, "if these deeds are good, why have they not been established before now?" (5), adding, "if a man produces a deed from a native for ten thousand acres, dated a hundred and forty years ago, executed ten years ago, let it stand, it may make him a gentleman" (6). The century and a half that Ely mobilizes as a sign of falsity, of the perfidy of claiming ownership over undeveloped land in violation of Lockean natural law,[73] marks less the absence of all occupancy than the exertion of Indigenous sovereignty—sustained struggle generated by Anglo-American aggression and movement into territory understood by Native peoples as rightfully belonging to them.

In *House*, the "hieroglyphics of several Indian sagamores" on the "Indian deed" appear as nothing more than ciphers, stand-ins for the machinations of speculators and officials whose interests bear little relation to those of "the people." However, if one takes seriously such signatures, what do they signify? If one refuses to treat the time between the deed and the period in which the territory was properly *improved*—such that the deed became "worthless"—as politically empty, what happened to the peoples whom those sagamores represented? The territory that eventually came to be known as the Waldo Patent was not originally acquired through purchase of Native land, instead being awarded in March 1630 by the Plymouth Company to John Beauchamp and Thomas Leverett "expressly for the purpose of an exclusive trade with the natives" and "contain[ing] no powers of civil government" (and known for the next ninety years or so as the "Muscongus Patent").[74] However, land below the head tides on the St. Georges River, which became part of the Waldo claim, was secured through agreements in the mid-1690s with Madockawando, the leader of the Penobscots.[75] In nearby territories to the west where nonnative inhabitance was secured through mid-seventeenth-century agreements with Native leaders, part of the condition was that Native people be allowed to remain in their villages and to access the hunting and fishing grounds they previously had utilized.[76] Whatever territoriality such documents granted, it could not have constituted something like sale, in the sense of complete transfer of exclusive rights to the land as property.

In the early to mid-eighteenth century, English colonists began to move back into areas west of the Kennebec River that had been settlements prior to almost forty years of virtually nonstop fighting from King Philip's War through Queen Anne's War. After the Treaty of Utrecht (1713) extended British authority over all of Acadia, which France had asserted stretched as far west as the Kennebec,[77] English settlers began moving into territory to the east of the river, creating increased conflict with the Penobscots and neighboring peoples. From the 1710s through the 1730s, they repeatedly protested such incursions, challenging English narratives of prior Native consent and repudiating the rights claimed by nonnatives to their lands. Such disturbances and dislocations were facilitated by government efforts to assert the supremacy of English political mappings. Claiming sovereignty over the region, English authorities repeatedly sought to secure Native confirmation of their subordination as subjects of the Crown. Beginning in 1693, treaties of peace with the Penobscots and their allies included a clause in which they agreed to place themselves under British authority in return for recognition of their lands, as well as fishing and hunting rights, "as formerly." However, statements and actions by Native leaders throughout the first half of the eighteenth century, as well as continued warfare—Governor Dummer's War (1721–26) and King George's War (1744–48)—suggests that they had a very different understanding of the agreements than that of the colonial government.[78] In the wake of the treaty of 1727, the Penobscot leader Loron summarized his understanding of the treaty in a letter to English officials: "Much less, I repeat, did I, become his subject, or give him my land, or acknowledge his King as my King. This I never did, and he never proposed it to me. . . . Yes, I recognize [the King of England as] King of all his lands; but I rejoined, do not hence infer that I acknowledge thy King as my King, and King of my lands. Here lies my distinction—my Indian distinction."[79] The repeated need of the English to call on Native leaders to declare their submission to English authority suggests not only the tenuousness of such claims but that officials could not narrate the territory east of the Kennebec as simply a "wilderness" awaiting settlement.

Moreover, the need for Penobscot participation in the American Revolution led the Provincial Congress to agree during the Watertown Conference in June 1775 to recognize Penobscot lands six miles up on both sides from the head of the tide of the river, indicating their perceived importance to the war effort.[80] In the wake of the Revolution, the Massachusetts government attempted to secure cessions of Penobscot land in 1784 and 1786, claiming that they rightfully had claims to the Penobscots' territory as a "conquered" people,[81] but in response Penobscot leaders during the treaty conference of 1784 reminded the commissioners of "the agreement which was made in the first of the War" which promised "that we would not suffer any persons to come on our lands": "The Almighty placed us upon the land and it was ours. The General [who oversaw the 1775 agreement] said that no person should interfere, and take away any of our lands, but that we should have them. Now why should we not hold the lands, as the Almighty gave them to us?"; "Concerning our selling the lands, we never sold any to our knowledge and never will while we live."[82] Throughout the late seventeenth and eighteenth centuries, nonnative governments continually grappled with the problem of needing to assert sovereignty over Penobscot space as against insistent evidence of Native opposition and self-determination.

In Abenaki, closely related to the language spoken by the Penobscots, the root word for writing and mapping is the same (*awigha-*),[83] suggesting that the signing of treaty documents might have been conceptualized as similar to the act of mapmaking. Following this logic, treaties likely would have been situated within extant Native geographies, a connection that provides a different perspective on the map that appears in Hawthorne's *House*. The map of prospective Pyncheon lands in Maine that perennially hangs in the House's study, right next to the colonel's portrait, stands as the ultimate figure for the lack of any substantive connection to the land. When first describing the study, the narrator notes that one of its "ornamental articles of furniture" is "a map of the Pyncheon territory at the eastward, not engraved, but the handiwork of some skillful old draftsman, and grotesquely illuminated with pictures of Indians and wild beasts, among which was seen a lion; the natural history of the region being as little known as its geography, which was put down most fantastically awry" (26). The lack of any direct experience working the land vitiates the claim to ownership over it.[84] However, this reference to "wild beasts" on the map as part of the proof of the illusory claims of the deed might appear somewhat ironic in light of the fact that, at times, Penobscot leaders used animal images as their signature on petitions, treaties, and other official documents—a kind of "hieroglyphic" indicating kinship belonging as well as the nature of the individual's representativity as a signatory.[85]

Envisioning an empty space into which nonnatives could enter, as the novel says of Matthew Maule, as "original occupant[s] of the soil"—such that they can "wrest" farms from "the wild hand of nature"—presumes the jurisdictional contiguity and coherence posited by the English starting in 1693. Doing so disavows the Indigenous sense of place in which their signatures would have signified, including broader Native geopolitical networks whose existence challenged the geography of sovereignty on which English (and then U.S.) authorities insisted. The Penobscots had extensive connections with other peoples, participating in what scholars have described as two overlapping sets of alliances—both of which at different times have been termed "the Wabanaki Confederacy." One of them, which likely emerged prior to the other, involves connections among the peoples of what is now eastern Maine, Nova Scotia, and New Brunswick—namely, the Penobscots, Passamaquoddies, Maliseets, and Micmacs.[86] While there was running conflict between Micmacs and peoples to the west through the 1610s,[87] growing connections with French missions, participation in English and French trade routes, extreme population decline due to European epidemics, shared enmity and organization against the Mohawks, and resistance to English encroachment brought them into increasing relation to one another.[88] In *History*

of the Indian Wars in New England (1677), William Hubbard observes that
at the beginning of King Philip's War in 1675 Madockawando's people "for-
sook their Fort [on the Kennebec River] presently and went Eastward and
abroad to [the St.] Johns River and to the Sea Side to get all the Indians they
could together to come up Penobscot River,"[89] suggesting the existence of
a sociopolitical network by the late seventeenth century, with those on the
Penobscot taking a notable position of leadership.

The Penobscots would become even more central as both speakers for
an ensemble of peoples ranging from the Androscoggin to the St. John
Rivers in peace negotiations and treaty conferences in the eighteenth century and as elder figures in the emergent alliance with the Seven Nations of
Canada and the Iroquois Confederacy that emerged in the mid-eighteenth
century.[90] After the Great Peace in Montreal in 1701, which resolved existing conflicts over the fur trade stretching back several decades between
Iroquois and Algonquian peoples, missionized Native peoples living in territory claimed by New France joined together in an alliance that became
known as the Seven Nations of Canada. Possibly at the same time, Wabanaki
peoples may have been incorporated into the Iroquois Covenant Chain, and
by the mid-eighteenth century, a union had emerged between the Wabanaki
peoples of Maine and the Seven Nations. The council fire lay in Kahnawake, Mohawk territory located opposite Montreal on the St. Lawrence
River, and meetings were held every three years. Decisions on the terms
of peace and of land cessions in Maine may have involved consultations with
this broader confederacy, and the Penobscots and Passamoquoddies maintained their place within it until the late nineteenth century.[91] Additionally,
during the eighteenth century and throughout most of the nineteenth century, leaders for the Wabanaki peoples of Maine and the Maritimes took
part in choosing one another's sagamores and in the condolence ceremon-
ies through which those leaders were raised to positions of authority.[92]
Once one begins to inquire about the political geographies in which the
"Indian sagamores" of the Penobscot area would have participated, Waldo
County and its environs appear as embedded in the extended matrix of
Wabanaki territoriality. Axiomatically proclaiming the "deed" to be "worthless," then, does not simply recognize the passage of time but requires that
one disavow the Native mappings that accompany such signatures and per-
sist in their wake.

Furthermore, discounting the "Indian deed" as merely "mouldy parchment" leaves one with no way of explaining precisely how land claimed by the "sagamores" becomes available for Euramerican development. With respect to Waldo County and areas to the north along the Penobscot River, that process of acquisition via treaties and agreements continues up through the mid-nineteenth century. In 1796 an agreement was reached to sell the land for thirty miles above the head of tide—about 230,400 acres or ten townships—while retaining the land and islands above that point.[93] In their report prior to the treaty meeting, the commissioners sent to negotiate with the Penobscots indicate their concern that "the said tribe will soon become a public charge," suggesting that "in their opinion it would be expedient for the Commonwealth that a treaty should be held with the said Indians to induce them upon fair and honourable considerations to relinquish all claim to the aforesaid land and to put themselves completely under the care and protection of the government."[94] As against this vision of them as helpless dependents awaiting government "care and protection," Penobscot leaders responded to the initial offer of the commissioners by noting, "We are willing to let you have our land. We don't wish to sell it right out. If we sell it out right, we don't know the value of it. The great God who put us on the land, did not give us the privilege of knowing what the value of it is," and later in the treaty conference, they observe, "Brothers—we take this opportunity to let you know that we think you have not offered us quite enough for the land. You may think the tribe to be very small, but there are a great many of them absent," adding, "now we have great many children growing up, and we may want to improve some of this land. Brothers—we reserve that land for our children to hunt upon for the present."[95] Beyond reaffirming that the territory belongs to them as a matter of right not emanating from English or American governance ("great God who put us on the land"), the Penobscots engage in significant bargaining, refusing commissioners' narratives of the land's "value" and calculating this cession in terms of securing the futurity of the Penobscot people ("we have great many children growing up") while asserting the legitimacy of extant practices as modes of inhabitance ("to hunt upon for the present"). In addition, the assigning of an agent to them the next year comes not as a matter of settler management, but as a result of a visit by Penobscot representatives to Boston to speak with the governor in which they complain of nonnative intrusion and logging and "request the protection of Government and that some Agent of respectable character in their neighborhood may be appointed to assist them in obtaining redress if such injuries should be repeated."[96]

By 1818, as a result of losing access to fishing and hunting resources due to settler presence and development further down river, the Penobscots desired to sell some of their land, negotiating for the transfer of all but four townships of their non-island territory.[97] They justify this action in notably non-Lockean terms. In a petition to the legislature, Penobscot leaders observe that "in 1796 they relinquished their title to two townships of the same in consideration of an annual payment which they receive from this Commonwealth," and they indicate that "they still own a large tract of valuable and fertile land which owning to their mode of living and limited knowledge of agriculture does not produce them any income or profit. They therefore propose to sell two more townships to the Commonwealth": "And in order to render the remaining part of their land more profitable, they humbly request permission to let or lease any parts of the same to individuals for the purpose of agriculture for any period not exceeding one hundred years and to receive the rent annually under the direction of an agent who may be appointed for that purpose."[98] While the petition indicates that their "limited knowledge of agriculture" results in a lack of "income," the absence of that kind of *improvement* does not vitiate their claim to the land, and in fact, the Penobscots seek to lease parts of their territory to those who do engage in "agriculture" in order to increase its marketable output, presenting such use as irrelevant with respect to the question of possession—the prospective lessees not gaining a more legitimate claim to the land via the activity of farming.

Under increasing pressure from fishing, logging, and timber mill interests, as well as settlers desiring access to Penobscot land, the state of Maine ratified an agreement in 1833 in which the Penobscots supposedly agreed to cede the four remaining townships (retaining their islands), in the wake of which numerous delegations and petitions insisted on the document's fraudulence on the grounds that those who signed either were not endowed with representative authority to do so and/or were misinformed as to its nature.[99] In a letter to the Penobscot agent in 1851, Governor Hubbard of Maine unilaterally declared that the Penobscots were subject to state criminal laws while also insisting that they should no longer use monies from the

state (which actually were drawn from the Penobscots' own funds from
land sales and annuities held by the state) to support "useless festivities,"
including meetings related to the Wabanaki Confederacy—in relations with
other peoples in Maine and the Seven Nations of Canada.[100] While the state
sought to exert direct jurisdiction over the Penobscots, in ways that would
cast them as geopolitically isolated and beholden for their continued existence on state largesse, formal political relations with Kahnawake and other
Wabanaki peoples persisted for at least another decade after state warnings
to stop. Moreover, the ongoing negotiations for territory with the Penobscots
for over fifty years after independence belies claims made by Massachusetts,
and then Maine, that Penobscot territory simply was part of the "commonwealth" of the state to do with as the legislature pleased. This history foregrounds the fact of competing mappings in which the territory claimed by
the United States as Maine (first as a district of Massachusetts and then its
own state) cannot be understood as jurisdictionally neutral—as separable
from negotiations over sovereignty and the geopolitics of collective placemaking. In order for "actual settlers" in Maine to serve as paradigmatic, the
text needs to bracket ongoing Penobscot and Wabanaki history and territoriality as the emptiness between the ostensibly deceptive *Indian deeds* of the
seventeenth century and the occupancy of small landholding farmers in the
late eighteenth and early nineteenth centuries,[101] further effacing continuing
negotiations with Native peoples in Maine after this period.

   The text's deployment of a Lockean ethics gains momentum by taking as
given the contours of state jurisdiction, even as Hawthorne critiques the
operation of law and policy, but the retreat to the "country" becomes less
extrapolitically pastoral if one needs to contend with the issue of Native
claims and the jurisdictional questions they raise. The dismissal of the
"Indian deed" as a vehicle for transferring control over land remains com-
plexly enmeshed in the difficulty of negotiating settler jurisdiction given
that the treaty system continued to serve as the only legal means for the
United States to gain authority over Native territories.[102] The assertion that
tribes in New England were mere "remnants" on the way to extinction,
and/or that they were so mixed with other populations as to cease to be
truly Indian,[103] provided justification for not negotiating federal treaties
with them, despite the requirement in the various Indian Trade and Intercourse Acts that the cession of Native lands must occur "under the authority

of the United States" rather than individual states like Massachusetts or Maine.[104] Thus, the forceful assertion in *House* of the "worthless"-ness of the "Indian deed" implicitly registers both the exemption of New England from the treaty system and the anxieties that persist around continuing Indigenous territoriality.[105]

The invocation of Lockean wilderness holds constant not only much of the conception of landholding already present within Anglo-American law (albeit with an emphasis on work rather than formal title) but also the jurisdictional boundaries of the state. The trope of "the wild," and associated figures like the garden and the country, serves as a hybrid or intermediary in Latour's sense, offering "the solidity of natural things" to aspects of "the social body" (37). Although the characterization of the text as a "romance" suggests a certain ambivalence about the efficacy of this normative ideal, it remains central to the text's critique of aristocratic and speculative wealth. While Hawthorne certainly is not writing as a representative of any political party, he is recycling prominent forms of Democratic Party discourse, and more importantly, his ethical inclinations cast the juridical stability of the United States as given. However, if one foregrounds the Indian deed and the map, an alternative history of Waldo County and its environs comes into view, one in which Native alliances and modes of placemaking do not merely precede sustained Euramerican presence (as a kind of evolutionary forerunner to proper cultivation and development) but take precedence as prior Indigenous political geographies. Such mappings necessarily are overwritten by a settler experience of place in which "toil" in "Nature" transcends questions of jurisdiction and sovereignty.

Familial Feeling and Its (Tribal) Limits

Toward the end of the text, in the wake of Jaffrey's death, Hawthorne envisions all the prior generations of Pyncheons stretching back to the colonel "jostling and elbowing each other" in trying to grasp the portrait in which the deed to the Maine territory is hidden, and the narrator characterizes them as "the whole tribe" (197). Given that they are seeking a document signed by "Indian sagamores" that supposedly endows them with property rights to an estate the size of a dukedom, what is the aim or effect of referring to the Pyncheons as a *tribe*? As noted earlier, the novel is not in any sense about Native people(s), and the text renders prior and ongoing Indigenous inhabitance politically meaningless as part of its Lockean orientation. The association with Indianness, in particular with Native collectivity, appears as a means of denigrating the Pyncheon family, or at least ironizing their desire for familial title to such vast territory. As against the chaining of the present to the past via inheritance, which circumvents the need for "each generation . . . to build its own houses" (131), the depiction of proper land-holding in the text emphasizes labor by individuals on their own discrete parcels, each toiling in the interests of his own family. In this way, possessive individualism serves as a prominent, mediating feature of the text's repre-sentation of legitimate placemaking—the self-owning person whose work-ing of the land extends his possession over himself to that which he has improved.[106] This model of generic personhood entails a direct relation to nature, envisioned as independent from state policies and interests in ways that allow the text to suspend the question of how that formation is articu-lated to and through existing modes of (settler) governance. The text sus-pends bourgeois homemaking per se, opening up room for forms of "queer sociability" in the present,[107] but that potential reaches its limits in kinds of generational territoriality that appear as improperly *tribal*, positioning Indianness as a reservoir for signifiers of aberrance.

At times Hawthorne seems to endorse the affective life of conjugal cou-plehood as the basis for the critique of Pyncheon aristocracy,[108] but despite such intimations, the text does not ultimately privilege the nuclear family unit. The text works to expose the naturalization of family history and prop-erty, indicating the ways such conventions come to appear as if they were as given as the landscape itself. Describing the force of inheritance, the narra-tor observes, "[T]hey inevitably sow the acorns of a more enduring growth, which may darkly overshadow their posterity" (6), and in characterizing Jaffrey's uncle's decision to leave the House to him, the text insists that "the strong prejudice of propinquity . . . impels the testator to send down his estate in the line marked out by custom, so immemorial that it looks like nature" (19). These moments speak to the generational force of genealogy, and Hawthorne offers a similar depiction of the House itself. The Pyncheon-elm next to the House "gave beauty to the old edifice, and seemed to make it a part of nature" (22); the narrator later proclaims, "So little faith is due to external appearances," offering as evidence that "the lines and tufts of green moss, here and there [around the House], seemed pledges of familiarity and sisterhood with Nature; as if this human dwelling-place, being of such old date, had established its prescriptive title among primeval oaks" (201). The sensation of the natural that attaches to entrenched modes of familial possession and transmission of wealth (particularly in land) derives from the effects of legal "title," falsely attributing to such ownership an inevitability that safeguards against any attempt to dismantle or redirect the accumulated property including by the owners themselves.[109] Holgrave's denunciation of the idea of "plant[ing] a family" distills this suspicion of elite forms of inheritance, rejecting an aristocratic preservation of lines of lineage (as if they somehow grew from the soil) in favor of a democratizing disintegration of kinship so as to make it more modular: "once in every half-century, at longest, a family should be merged into the great, obscure mass of humanity, and forget all about its ancestors" (132). In making a transgenerational claim to place that makes its existence seem obvious, lineage takes root as if in the ground itself, wrongly presenting itself *as* nature rather than making inhabitance contingent on labor *in* nature.

This insistence on the need to shrink "family" into a more generationally discrete household unit seems to fit with increasingly established norms of middle-class domesticity, in which children were expected to move away from their parents in order to form conjugally centered households of their own.[110] The privatizing political economy of bourgeois homemaking, though, often is justified through, in Dana Luciano's terms, a "reprosexual" narrative of the nuclear family as the unit of procreation and thus the basis around which to build social life. While challenging Pyncheon inheritance and landedness, Hawthorne ironizes the citation of reproductivity to validate the self-evident naturalness of conjugal homemaking. When first introducing Jaffrey, the text observes, "There were few of the Pyncheons left. . . . In respect to natural increase, the breed had not thriven; it appeared rather to be dying out" (19), and the narrator bemoans that Jaffrey's resemblance to his ancestor the colonel "implied that the weaknesses and defects, the bad passions, the mean tendencies, and the moral diseases which lead to crime, are handed down from one generation to another, by a far surer process of transmission than human law has been able to establish" (86). The Pyncheons as a "breed" have not done well, possibly having something to do with the "mean tendencies" and "moral diseases" passed down generationally.[111] The moments attributing failings and difficulties to Pyncheon reproductivity are the only characterizations *House* offers of the implications of procreation. One could read this indictment of semi-aristocratic modes of lineage as implicitly endorsing bourgeois homemaking as more healthful and productive due to its smaller generational reach and greater modularity, but as Robert Levine notes, readers never hear anything of Holgrave and Phoebe's children (145), suggesting a quite muted sense of the reproductive potential/validity of middle-class domesticity. Thus, Hawthorne does not provide an account of the nuclear family model as more natural due to its supposed status as the unit of procreation.[112]

Even as the text links Holgrave and Phoebe's courtship to regenerative figures of rurality and closes with their declaration of their intent to wed, positioning the marital union of Maule and Pyncheon descendants as the resolution of the conflict at the story's center, it defers the creation of a couple-centered household. Robert Levine asks, "Why is it that Hawthorne leaves us not with two characters—a loving couple—choosing to live together happily ever after, but with five characters, three of whom are elderly, two of whom are brother and sister, and one simply the friendly town vagrant? . . . [This configuration] raises questions about what sort of 'family' has emerged in this supposedly conventional resolution" (144–45). That somewhat queer assemblage pushes beyond the limits of bourgeois homemaking, but they are not creating a community based on new principles of property, like many utopian projects in the mid-nineteenth century. Instead, they form a single household, heading as they all are to inhabit Jaffrey's country house which the remaining Pyncheons—Phoebe, Hepzibah, and Clifford—seem to have inherited equally (220). Holgrave suggests that he eventually plans "to set out trees, to make fences—perhaps, even, in due time, to build a house for another generation" (216), but at the text's close, they are all set to cohabit in the "country" (with Uncle Venner residing in a cottage in the garden) (224). This domestic arrangement conforms neither to the singularity of male heirship that had defined Pyncheon inheritance until this point nor to the middle-class norm of the affectively saturated conjugal-parental unit. However, it in some ways resembles the more loose sense of family, as members of a single household, at play prior to the early nineteenth century, although at that time the sense of all other residents as dependents of the head of the household would have been far stronger. Within that frame, inhabitants also were understood as potential workers, rather than being connected through marriage and childrearing understood as bonds of emotional support and care.[113] If the retreat to the country is not a return to an earlier political economy, it does shift emphasis from feelings to place as a way of envisioning the household, focusing less on their (procreatively defined) relations with one another than the where and how of land tenure. Put another way, the text places focus less on the *naturalness* of the relations among members of the household than on the relation between household formation (and property holding) and *nature* as place—the regenerative and antispeculative effects of working in the wilderness, the garden, and the country.

Such a shift in the figuration of homemaking does open room for deviations from middle-class domesticity,[114] and those forms of queerness can be recuperated, even if cast as in need of relative subordination to a more (if not entirely) couple-centered version of homemaking. As with Hawthorne's characterization of the text as a "romance," the emergence of queer forms of subjectivity in the text indicates both its articulation of a vision of home and land at odds with existing bourgeois conventions and its anxiety about the possibility of realizing that vision.[115] Hepzibah, Clifford, and Holgrave all are associated with forms of sexual and gender nonnormativity that also are correlated with ways of conceptualizing place that the text casts as tyrannical or chaotic. Hepzibah's singleness marks her as potentially perverse, while linking her to a desire for patriarchal inheritance. In light of the growing influence of the "cult of true womanhood" in the nineteenth century, her choice not to marry could be understood as indicative of unhealthful and disruptive tendencies.[116] However, as Nina Baym argues, Hepzibah is positioned as the protagonist of Hawthorne's narrative, clashing with Jaffrey, sympathizing with Holgrave, and offering a counterpoint to "Clifford's lunatic liberation" (613). In this way, she appears as a predominating perspective from within the Pyncheon line from which to dissent from its greed and dislocating violence. The text casts her celibacy, though, less as powerful than a bit pathetic. The narrator asks, "Can it have been an early lover of Miss Hepzibah? No; she never had a lover—poor thing, how could she?—nor ever knew, by her own experience, what love technically means" (25). More than indicating a sad lack, the absence of such "experience" means that she remains "poor" in another sense—unsupported by the income of a husband. While that fact might be read as giving her a kind of feminist autonomy, especially in light of the political campaigns for women's rights in and outside of marriage in the period,[117] the text portrays it as marking an ongoing identifi-cation with the legacy of Pyncheon landedness. As contrasted with Phoebe's rural simplicity, the narrator characterizes Hepzibah as "our forlorn old maid, in her rustling and rusty silks, with her deeply cherished and ridicu-lous consciousness of long descent, her shadowy claims to princely terri-tory" (59). While later apparently renouncing such desires ("Alas, Cousin Jaffrey, this hard and grasping spirit has run in our blood, these two hun-dred years!" [168]), they shape her character throughout the narrative, and she seems quite happy to occupy a position of elite noblesse oblige at the novel's end, having inherited the speculative gains of Jaffrey and her uncle (if not property in the eastern lands) and endowing her former customer Ned Higgins with a heaping helping of silver as her last act in the text (224–25). In light of existing coverture laws, which only gradually were altered over a half century starting in the 1830s,[118] married women did not retain control over their property unless put in trust by their fathers. From this perspective, Hepzibah's singleness also signifies as a refusal to surrender her status as a Pyncheon, in particular as a potential individual inheritor of the Pyncheon estate. Thus, even as Hepzibah (along with the other charac-ters) seems to renounce the aristocratic dream of a dukedom in Maine, accepting the *worthlessness* of the "Indian deed," her status as an "old maid" suggests a residual alignment with the unearned "princely" accumulations of state-endorsed lineage.

As against the potential for a generational entailment of the future by the past, via the bonds of inheritance, Clifford points toward the dangers of a complete rupture with familial landholding. He certainly seems to be the queerest, no matter how defined, of any of the characters in the text. Characterized as a "Sybarite" (or sensualist) with an overinvestment in the pleasures of physical experience, he also expresses feminine tendencies: "burst[ing] into a woman's passion of tears" (82); possessing "too fine and delicate" a constitution (100); having an "affection and sympathy for flow-ers" which is "almost exclusively a woman's trait" (105). These descriptions portray his heightened attention to aesthetics, his delight in the senses, and his emotional sensitivity as somewhat aberrant.[119] Such traits could also mark one as a chronic masturbator, expressing a broader enervation and lack of pro-ductivity due to the wasting of one's nerves caused by self-abuse, and while the narrator never explicitly says as much, Clifford's general anxiousness, bouts of manic excitement, lack of romantic attachment, and semicoherence (and possible madness) fit the profile laid out in extant medical discourses and warnings to young men.[120] More than appearing nonnormative with respect to the ideal of marital couplehood, his deviant character seems to affect his ways of apprehending time and space. The narrator observes of him: "With a mysterious and terrible Past, which had annihilated his memory, and a blank Future before him, he had only this visionary and impalpable Now, which, if you look closely at it, is nothing" (107). This imprisonment in the "Now" seems like a reductio ad absurdum version of Holgrave's critique of inheritance as an enchaining relation to the past and his insistence on the need for each generation to start building anew. Fixation on the sense impressions of the present moment leaves Clifford wasted by an overanimation that can be linked neither to the past nor future. This impression of existing in a kind of limbo is amplified in Clifford and Hepzibah's retreat from the House in the wake of Jaffrey's death. As they speed away from Salem by train, Clifford asserts, "My impression is, that our wonderfully increased, and still increasing, facilities of locomotion are destined to bring us round again to the nomadic state" (183), but the older man with whom he is conversing retorts, "I should scarcely call it an improved state of things . . . to live everywhere and nowhere!" (184). The breaking of ties to the past and future in Clifford's sensation of "Now," his feminizing immersion in the immediate pleasure of the senses, correlates with an alienation from any claim to place, a new *nomadism* made possible by the railroad in which the connection between location, duration, and community is broken. Given that the text previously codes Clifford as perverse, his vision of space appears as an extension of his aberrance, threatening to disjoint the normative vision of *toil* on the land toward which the text inclines.[121]

While Holgrave in many ways bears the text's "moral," his relationship with Phoebe and transformation at the end moves him away not only from what may appear as an extreme perspective on family property and inheritance but the sorts of sexual excesses often associated with the rejection of conventional logics of ownership.[122] Hepzibah characterizes him as one of the "community-men and come-outers" with whom he associates (62). Later, in speaking with Phoebe, he observes that working together in the garden will make them "fellow-laborers, somewhat on the community system" (68), and in discussing his past with her, he notes that "he had spent some months in

a community of Fourierists" (126). The references to "community" allude to
the various kinds of socialist collectives that emerged in the mid-nineteenth
century United States, and those organized around the philosophy of Charles
Fourier were the most popular, particularly during the 1840s. Born in France
in the late eighteenth century, Fourier advocated the creation of communities, called phalanxes, in which labor would be divided equitably and shift
based on individuals' desires, and in which each person through seeking
to satisfy individual passions and appetites would contribute to both the life
of the collective and his or her own personal fulfillment.[123] Fourier's comments on the stultifying circumscription and privatization of desire within
conjugal homemaking led many of his critics in the United States to connect
Fourierism to the kinds of "free love" advocated within other extant socialisms. While neither seeking to challenge the preeminence of monogamous
marital union nor renouncing private property (the Fourierian model for
the phalanx was as a joint-stock company with each individual or family purchasing shares), as Andrew Loman notes, Fourierism in the United States
"became increasingly intertwined with discourses on free love, spiritualism,
and anarchism" (6), and thus, "Fourierist communities raise the specter of a
world of ambiguated property and marriage" (91). Holgrave's desire to tear
down "lifeless institutions" (128), his connection to Mesmerism with its
intimations of sexual access and excess (126, 151–52), his frequent changes
in profession (125–26), and his attraction to the garden all imply the presence of countercultural identifications.[124] Moreover, in distending the nuclear
family unit, the somewhat odd collection of people in the judge's country
house at the end can make it begin to appear a bit like a phanlanstery—the
single building in which all members of the phalanx were supposed to live (an
arrangement that if it did not undo conventional marriage certainly diverged
from the ideal of the single-family home). Although not presenting Holgrave as deviating from the dominant sociosexual ideal as much as Hepzibah
and Clifford, the text indicates and intimates his connection with somewhat
amorphously defined socialisms in ways that hint at the potential for license.
The very ellipticality of his radical commitments (he does not declare himself a Fourierist or an Owenite, for example) taps into ambient popular anxieties about the perversity lurking within all modes of communitarianism.[125]

The novel's proliferation of queernesses suggests possibilities for lifeways
beyond that of heteroconjugal homemaking, but all of these other options

offer matrices of family, place, and selfhood cast as immoral, chaotic, and/or pathological. *House* displaces reproductive couplehood as the central means of defining legitimate homemaking, instead orienting it toward the labor of household (re)construction—primarily in non-urban spaces. However, the image of the single-family home persists as a kind of phantom norm: stripped of explicit reference to emotional bonds and reprosexual aims but present as a kind of conceptual and affective surround, offering a common-sense frame for what constitutes proper personhood.[126] The semi-Lockean household at the end of the novel, then, restrains the characters' sociospatial deviance, bending it toward a kind of dwelling that matches the simultaneous settledness and modularity of the bourgeois household.

The ability of this modified middle-class household to incorporate queer deviations, though, reaches its limit in the figure of the "tribe." Given the prior portrayal of the Pyncheon family and their claims as exploitative, deceptive, tyrannical, and anti-republican, *tribe* cannot be understood as a term of approbation. In being characterized as a *tribe*, the Pyncheons appear insufficiently distinct from the "sagamores" who signed the "Indian deed" for which the family searches. Within incipient forms of ethnology, starting at least in the early nineteenth century, a central and repeated claim was that tribal peoples lacked a sufficient sense of private ownership over plots of land, a lapse in terms of individuation that also correlated with an ill-defined sense of family. Albert Gallatin, one of the chief promoters and the first president of the American Ethnological Society (founded in 1842), said in an 1805 letter to Thomas Jefferson that Indians have a "want of the social institutions which establish and secure *property* and *marriage*," a lack which is "the greatest obstacle to [their] civilization."[127] These two—property and marriage—signify in terms of each other, indicating an inevitable relation between proper modes of familial order/distinction and landholding. Without marriage, property threatens to become communally indistinguishable, large numbers of people making shared, quasi-familial claims to vaguely defined territory. Native peoples were understood as agglomerating together and confusing kinship relations in ways that showed either an undeveloped or degenerated sociality.

Lewis Henry Morgan's *League of the Ho-de-no-sau-nee, or Iroquois* (1851) offers an instructive example of this perspective, published as it is in the same year as *House*. It casts Haudenosaunee matrilineal clans as systemically

misrecognizing the natural categories of mother, father, aunt, and so forth—
the guiding terms of genealogy being taken from Roman law and Blackstone's
Commentaries with Haudenosaunee understandings (such as referring to
one's "mother" and "mother's sister" by the same term) appearing as an
underdifferentiated aberration from the apparently self-evident dynamics
of (Roman/Anglo conceptions of) family.[128] Morgan's later work pivots
around a distinction between "descriptive" and "classificatory" kinship relations, in which, as Thomas Trautmann observes, "the Roman side will remain
the standard and the Iroquois, the problem variant to be explained" (54).
Thus, when Morgan concludes that the Iroquois League "was established
on the principles . . . of the Family Relationships" (60), that "each tribe" is
"in the nature of a family" and combined together in the league to form "one
political family" (78–79), "tribe" appears as a barbaric distension of "family"—a developmental failure to appreciate the necessary centrality of the
procreative unit and its rightful separation from the field of *politics*. Furthermore, in describing the existence of a limited number of sachems whose
positions are passed through complex forms of familial inheritance, Morgan
characterizes the Haudenosaunee, and this kind of social formation, as an
"oligarchy," suspended between the more primitive "monarchical" stage of
governance and the more advanced "democratical" one (127–46). Although
he seeks to distinguish oligarchy as "rule by a few" from aristocracy (rule
by a wealthy elite), the term still carries many of the same implications, indicating a consolidation of authority (transmitted genealogically) that suggests the potential for an undemocratic concentration of resources.[129] While
using different terminology, this line of thought seems reminiscent of Locke's
speculations about the historical origins of commonwealths. He notes,
"[W]here a family was numerous enough to subsist by itself, and continued entire together, without mixing with others, as it often happens, where
there is much land and few people, the government commonly began in the
father" (145), pointing to the "people of America" as an example of such a
dynamic and casting this mode of collectivity as antecedent to the formation of a true "political society."[130] The depiction of Native sociality as a network of relatives suggests a nonpolitical basis for landholding such that the
spatiality of Native occupancy appears to extend far beyond the needs of a
properly defined household-family unit. In this way, they seem oligarchic
like the proprietors in Maine, seeking to hoard large amounts of land for a

small group whose definition through an expansive matrix of blood-relations undemocratically limits possible participation in the land's resources and wealth while also swelling beyond the implicit norm of the insulated, self-reproducing household.

With respect to the Pyncheons, their description as a "tribe" suggests the presence of a distended, and thus somewhat perverse, notion of "family" that engenders claims to a vastly disproportionate share of available lands and abnormal modes of genealogical and territorial continuity. Unlike the sorts of individual aberrance associated with Hepzibah, Clifford, and Holgrave that can be incorporated into the household in the country, the Pyncheons collectively represent a queering of place that runs counter to the text's ethical orientation toward modular forms of homemaking and occupancy. In *The Empire of Love*, Elizabeth Povinelli argues that dominant liberal ideologies of autonomous selfhood—"the autological subject"—depend on their juxtaposition to the "genealogical society," "discourses, practices, and fantasies about social constraints placed on the autological subject by various kinds of inheritances" (4). If family illiberally restrains the possibility for personal freedom, couplehood, or "the intimate event," provides a minimum condition for reproduction, intimacy, and love; however, "if the magical features of the intimate event are to be animated socially and psychically, then others must be trapped in liberal intimacy's nightmare—the genealogically determined collective" (181–82). In this way, we might read the *tribalness* of the Pyncheons as marking a kind of undifferentiated genealogical mass, one that specifically speaks to the ways identity as a Pyncheon and its various inheritances travels not through the *lineality* of procreation but along *collateral* pathways (crooked lines of transmission such as in the wake of the deaths of Alice Pyncheon, Jaffrey and Hepzibah's bachelor uncle, and Jaffrey himself).[131] However, as I have been suggesting, the genealogical not only signals the unfreedom of being enfolded within a generational collective but the reciprocal unfreedom for those who cannot claim parts of the territory over which genealogical right and belonging illegitimately is extended. At the moment they are categorized as a "tribe," the assembled ghosts of the Pyncheon dead all are reaching for the Indian deed hidden within the portrait of the family patriarch, an image that further fuses the problem of diffuse familial genealogy to that of wrongfully expansive territoriality. The document that marks the desire for territory the size of a "dukedom" lies inside the symbol of the Pyncheon legacy as a family. This figure of the deed in the portrait suggests that, for Hawthorne, the "nightmare" of "the genealogically determined collective" lies in the fact that the core organizing principle of such a familial entity is the accumulation of unused lands such that others—"actual settlers"—cannot gain access.

The "Indian deed" at the heart of Pyncheon identity signals a perverse degeneration into Indianness: an insupportable claim to vast territory by a small collection of relatives coupled with an enduring embeddedness in a particular locale that enchains the present to a (primitive) past. In presenting the Pyncheons as engaged in "tribal" thieving rather than proper grieving in the moment of Jaffrey's death, *House* casts the history of Indigenous–settler confrontation and negotiation as an inclination toward outmoded tendencies. The text codes Pyncheon desires through, in Dana Luciano's formulation discussed in chapter 1, a chronobiopolitics that converts the *chronogeopolitics* of sovereignty (the memory of diplomatic encounters with Native polities and associated recognition of the persistence of unceded territory and claims) into a set of specifically *Indian* relations to time, land, and family.[132] As an unmanageable distension of homemaking that enables monstrously excessive pretentions to place, the tribal is perverse, presenting longstanding landedness as a form of deviance through association with wrong kinds of family. The Pyncheons, therefore, appear to have an immoral relation to place, because indiscrete and enduring rather than contained in a single household and renewed in a new place each generation. Their association with the tribal suggests a kind of collectivity whose nonlaboring relation to place renders its inhabitance, and existence, primitive and/or immoral. Luciano observes that nonnative depictions transpose the supposed "*anteriority*" of Native presence into a means of signifying the "*interiority*" of nonnative subjectivity (71). However, to render the Indian as a marker of perverse nonnative forms of interiority, or inclination/orientation, not only displaces Native people from the normative vision of time (individual and collective) but also undoes their spatiality, instantiating settler occupancy, including Lockean improvement, as the milieu for understanding and experiencing healthful personhood.

Translating the Pyncheons' elite landedness as tribal identity genealogizes Native peoples as (failed) families rather than recognizing them as polities, and from this perspective, their modes of territoriality appear excessive and unethical—at odds with a republican ethos of individual/household toil in the wilderness—rather than as exertions of sovereignty. Yet, if interpreted against the grain, Hawthorne's text suggests that personal dispositions, including those deemed perverse, are expressive of spatiotemporal orientations, ways of envisioning placemaking and its historicity. *House* suggests that certain kinds of divergence from bourgeois homemaking (especially when lived as individual tendencies) can be incorporated, in the terms of the text's preface, into a Lockean vision of "possible" modes of inhabitance at odds with the increasingly normalized—"probable"—ideal of the nuclear family. Moreover, such deviations partake in an acceptable kind of anachronism, hailing from a "by-gone time." Hawthorne's critique of extant forms of speculation and property law, as well as imagination of a place apart from state-endorsed geographies, then, engages in a kind of "temporal drag," as discussed in chapter 1. This implicit challenge by the text to the forward movement of progress opens onto ways of perceiving the landscape that are disjointed from state mappings, which facilitate an aristocratic accumulation of property. However, the text defers the potential for alternative political cartographies by treating U.S. jurisdiction as a constant in envisioning the existence of a state (or perhaps states) of nature within its boundaries.

When shifted away from its Lockean frame, including the impression of a governmentally unmediated relation to place, though, the novel raises the question of what a queer ethics predicated on engaging with the "Indian deed" might entail. As Valerie Rohy suggests, "anachronism, however abjectly attributed to racial and sexual others, is structurally implicated in white patrilineage. Notions of linear time depend on atavism: the fantasy of a straight time assailed by racial or sexual atavism actually produces the lineage temporality that it takes as primary" (xv). Contesting the "white patrilineage" of the Pyncheons potentially undoes the nonnative impression that Native peoples belong to a properly superseded past (for which the *tribal* functions as the unwelcome residue) by challenging not only the linear continuity of inheritance but the geopolitical presumptions upon which it rests and that it helps render self-evident. The destabilizing possibilities represented by Hepzibah, Clifford, and Holgrave direct attention toward the fragility of the normative order of toil in the country toward which the text moves (for which "actual settlers" in Maine serve as the model). Yet, the insistence that the "Indian deed" cannot signify anything meaningful in the present generates a sense of certainty, a boundary beyond which the disruption of sociospatial order cannot go. The critique of "straight time" runs headlong into the spatiality of settlement: the deed operates as the point at which queer potential becomes something else. In Merleau-Ponty's terms, it functions as "stray data," indexing that which must be made "unreal" in order to sustain the feeling of "the primordial constancy of the world as the horizon of all our experiences" (365). Proximity to the deed indicates the Pyncheons' regressive inclinations, but beyond their apparently delusional "tribal" desire to claim their "princely territory," no other current relation to the place of Maine appears at the text's end. In other words, the deed only can signal an aberrant relation to the past, not one to the present.

However, as discussed earlier, the Penobscots continue to exist as a landed polity, and as part of the Wabanaki Confederacy, into the time of *House*'s publication, far beyond the period in which they supposedly were displaced or replaced by "actual settlers" engaged in properly Lockean labor. While this *data* cannot enter the text's perceptual frame, it is what lies behind the "horizon" of settler regeneration in the country with which the text closes. A queer relation to the deed would require a reintegration of "the tribal" into the present as other than a marker of atavistic regression. Such engagement with the temporality of Indianness does not so much take up and revivify a remnant from the past as grapple with the ways that a phenomenal dislocation in time (experiencing something/someone as of the past) works as a form of spatial disavowal, specifically in this case as a foreclosure of Native sovereignty. Reckoning with the ongoing legacy of struggle in which documents like the deed are inscribed engages the possibility of them bearing other geographies, associations, and affects than those (re)constructed in and through settler law. Doing so locates nonnative trajectories of desire within a landscape thick with ongoing Indigenous stories while also suggesting how the phenomenological experience of "distance from the 'official' materials" of governance may itself constitute a mode of settler sensation.[133]

In troubling the legitimacy of elite claims and inheritance, *House of the Seven Gables* brings to the foreground the work of the state in securing them, but its counterhegemonic momentum in challenging speculative investment comes from its recirculation of narratives drawn from prior intra-settler conflicts over property. Indigenous peoples can only seem to occupy space improperly once one has erased their *political* claims to that space. In *An Approach to Political Philosophy*, James Tully observes of Locke's discussion of Native peoples, "[H]e describes their national forms of government in such a way that they are not full 'political societies' and thus native Americans can be dealt with as if they are in a late stage of the state of nature" (151). Taking up Lockean notions of labor that emerge out of earlier controversies in Maine, Hawthorne's *House* bears within it this depoliticization of Native presence. Even as the text challenges state-endorsed policies with respect to ownership, its celebration of "actual settlers" and demonization of the "Indian deed" is oriented around the jurisdictional contours of U.S. governance. "Nature" appears in the text as an ostensibly extrapolitical space to which one can have recourse in developing notions of valid occupancy, drawing on such ideas as part of a normative critique of U.S. law and policy. That very act of normative grounding, though, involves taking as given—as *settled*—the geopolitical status of the ground in question, the land for/from which one wants to envision a republican ethics of inhabitance. The jurisdictional schemas whose continuing performance secures settler access to the area themselves appear and are experienced as if emanating from the land itself, rather than as mediating the perception and inhabitance of the territory in question.

Once one displaces the question of geopolitical legitimacy, the modular forms of ownership and residency already contained within state-endorsed regimes of property can be treated as norms arising out of regenerative contact with the *wilderness*. Furthermore, ethical claims about proper modes of landedness remain inscribed within a national imaginary, in which government actions are critiqued from the perspective of their failure to sustain the interests of the nation's people. The Penobscots, along with other Wabanaki groups, do not count as part of that people or as an alien polity. The signatures of the sagamores on the Pyncheon deed indicate their significance in the Euroamerican acquisition of territory, but the deed's putative *worthlessness* empties their signatures of any political meaning while still providing neither a frame through which to understand the character of Wabanaki presence nor an indication of when and how they ceased to have such collective claims to occupancy. Moreover, that very process of simultaneously recognizing and effacing the political implications of Native peoples' presence in the construction of a supposedly pre-political Lockean ethics of inhabitance follows the trajectory of pre-Revolutionary and Revolutionary arguments over title in the backcountry—the call for a change in the political order so as to allow for an apolitical claiming of Native land through labor in the state of nature. Similarly, the wilderness—and the garden and country as figures for its residual presence—appears in Hawthorne's text to be both outside the sphere of legal order (providing a place from which to contest the letter of the law) and inside the boundaries of the nation (displacing the problem of state jurisdiction and sovereignty). This scheme casts the Indian as the antinormative figure for genealogical and territorial excess, as the perversion of the self-evident ethics of proper homemaking, even as the implicit association with things Native is what endows the land with the sense of being wild in the first place, such as in Maine settlers' self-presentation as "white Indians."

In presenting the narrative as a "romance," Hawthorne insists on the presence of older principles at odds with current "laws" while remaining ambivalent about the possibility of actualizing the garden/country/wilderness ethos in the present, and the text's proliferation of queer figures helps index that skepticism. *House* suggests that the Lockean logic of building a household in the country may be capacious enough to accommodate and ameliorate various tendencies with respect to generationality, temporality, and landedness, but the *tribal* signals that which by definition cannot be absorbed within that normative imaginary. As Luciano notes, "The progressive substitution of Indian melancholia, the ultimately fatal embrace of the past, by white melancholy, the reflective look backward that enabled one to continue moving forward, thus bespoke, to whites, their own more sophisticated comprehension of the 'true' nature of time's passage" (82). In this vein, the effort "to connect a by-gone time with the very Present that is flitting away from us" gains meaning through its distinction from a tribal kind of "melancholia." However, if the "Indian deed" is no longer read as testifying to the presence of elite estate building and/or as a "worthless" marker of a politically empty claim to occupancy, it could suggest a (queer?) rupture in the geography of the present. From this perspective, dislodging one's everyday sense of place and personhood from its anchoring in an implicitly Lockean matrix of labor, possession, and state jurisdiction raises the potential for the apparently anachronistic presence of signs of Indianness to open out into a more multivalent experience of the contemporary landscape, itself marked by persistent (if not always legally recognized) Indigenous political cartographies and the effects of superimposed and routinized settler mappings.

3

LOVING ONESELF LIKE A NATION

Sovereign Selfhood and the Autoerotics of Wilderness in *Walden*

In a journal entry on September 1, 1842, Nathaniel Hawthorne observes of Henry David Thoreau that he is "inclined to lead a sort of Indian life among civilized men," noting in particular "the absence of any systematic effort for a livelihood."[1] He suggests an "Indian life" entails being outside of the capitalist economy, existing in some space other than that of "civilized men." Native peoples in New England in this period, however, very much were enmeshed in the political economy of indenture, debt, itinerant seasonal labor, diaspora in search of wage work, and ongoing land loss due to nonnative agricultural and logging interests.[2] In *Indian Nullification*, written as part of advocating for greater Mashpee self-governance and control over their state-recognized territory, William Apess asserts, "The laws were calculated to drive the tribes from their possessions and annihilate them as a people; and I presume they would work the same effect upon any other people; for human nature is the same under kinds of all colors. Degradation is degradation, all the world over" (212). The systemic "degradation" of Native peoples through "laws" and state-sanctioned policies creates ongoing and intensifying forms of imbrication in the settler economy, a steady and coercive incorporation whose aim appears to be to "annihilate them as a people" by making life unliveable in their homelands. Yet, Hawthorne's offhand reference to the unlikelihood of an *Indian* livelihood suggests occupancy in a kind of elsewhere in which one might no longer be bound by the norms and imperatives that seem to govern the lives of others. From this perspective, to "lead a sort of Indian life" means simultaneously to be within the sociospatiality of mid-nineteenth-century New England and exterior to it, inhabiting a kind of limbo that puts in abeyance the seemingly inevitable requirements of life in a *civilized* country.

While the comment is Hawthorne's, Thoreau repeatedly characterizes himself in similar terms throughout *Walden*.[3] For Thoreau "Nature" serves as an (imaginary) realm of innocence and integrity in stark contrast to the corruption, artificiality, and excesses of industrialization, commercial agriculture, and bourgeois homemaking, and in order to enter that space of sublime transcendence, one must occupy a kind of subjectivity consistent with it, for which *Indian* is the name. As Jodi Byrd argues, "The transit of empire . . . depends upon the language, grammar, and ontological category of Indianness to enact itself" (xxxv), earlier noting, "To be in transit is to be made to move" (xv). The notion of the Indian functions as a transit into a supposed realm apart from marriage, commerce, and the crush of population. Unlike in *The House of the Seven Gables* where Indians mark a wrong form of landholding and generationality, Indianness in *Walden* helps concretize the existence of a simplified mode of being in/as nature at odds with expanding and intensifying capitalist networks. However, that space must be voided of Native presence in order for it to offer the possibility of a nonnative ethics of purifying regeneration—living *like* an Indian, not *among* them.[4]

The notion of a kind of place separated from circuits of production and consumption provides an avenue for Thoreau to rethink dominant understandings of personhood that tie health to participation in extant economies. In the discourse of the health reform movement of the mid-nineteenth century, "nature" refers to tendencies within the body that contribute toward the smooth working of the polity. Sylvester Graham, one of the movement's most important figures, argues in his exceedingly popular *A Lecture to Young Men on Chastity* "that moral and civil laws, so far as they are right and proper, are only the verbal forms of laws which are constitutionally established in our nature," "however destitute society might be, of all moral and civil restraints, in regard to sexual commerce" (29). For Graham, obedience to the "laws" of "our nature" enacts a biopolitics in which the promotion of personal health necessarily contributes to the promotion of national welfare. In *Walden*, however, "Nature" suggests less an inbuilt set of propensities that guide behavior in ways that make one a better-functioning citizen than a space beyond the demands of the *constitution* of the state. For Thoreau,

"[i]ndividuals, like nations, must have suitable broad and natural boundaries, even a considerable neutral ground, between them" (95).[5] This vision
of personhood takes shape as a reversal of Graham's assumptions, and those
of other crusaders against masturbation, in that it amplifies the self in ways
that would seem dangerously insular and narcissistic from an anti-onanist
perspective.[6] Although retaining an emphasis on self-discipline and a wariness of bodily pleasure for its own sake, Thoreau's account of individual
identity freed from the quotidian imperatives of market-oriented means
of work and ways of sustaining a household emphasizes time for imagination, non(re)productive modes of bodily expenditure, and the restorative
possibilities of being alone. From this perspective, *Walden* articulates a queer
conception of personhood,[7] and in this sense, the text can be said to offer
"an alternative hegemony" by "practical[ly] connect[ing] ... forms of struggle ... not easily recognizable as and indeed not primarily 'political' and
'economic.'"[8] Writing in a similar context to Hawthorne in the wake of the
Panic of 1837 and the decade-long depression that followed brought on
largely by the bursting of the bubble in public land purchases, *Walden* sub-
stitutes speculation in the self for that in property, investing in imaginative
excess as opposed to that of the debt accrued in seeking to possess additional territory.

Existence in the purifying space of nature situates that experience of individuality outside the routine requirements and invasions cast as endemic
to *civilization*. In providing a masturbatory theory-in-the-flesh for trying out
other ways of making a life at odds with those of contemporary discourses
of health, *Walden* offers a vision of individuality that depends on its immersion in a location apart, constructing a form of selfhood that has attributes
of sovereignty that make it immune to nationalism and the jurisdictional
claims of the state. In this way, personhood in the text becomes *Indian-like*
in its occupancy of this pristine, extrapolitical locale. As argued in the previous chapter, Hawthorne's *House* orients itself through a Lockean conception
of toil in the wilderness as the basis for legitimate property claims, as against
government judgments favorable to large landholders, but in doing so, the
text brackets the history of how the land is cleared of "Indian sagamores" in
order to be developed by "actual settlers." While Thoreau forswears possession itself, his oppositional queer conception of personhood also takes shape
around the voiding of Native geopolitics in New England, casting nature as

immune from political contestation and the eruption of competing sover-eignties.[9] Furthermore, that sense of a place within the state yet distinct from its legal geography arises out of and gains momentum from the ongo-ing legal representation of Native presence and territoriality as an anomaly. The coding of Indigenous polities and landedness as a legal and political aberration helps give shape to the notion of "Nature" as a place apart, such that the state operates as the condition of possibility for the construction of a given location as wild/wilderness. Additionally, *Walden's* normative account of personhood—including its oppositional queer dimensions—gains its form and trajectory from the kinds of legal subjectivity for white men that had become increasingly prominent in the United States over the previous half century. The text's ideal of individual autonomy emerges through the expansion of the franchise, the increased possibility for single-family land-holding, and changing logics of contract all driven by the making available of (Native) land on the "frontier." The conditions of *degradation* endured by Indigenous peoples in New England, chronicled in part by *Indian Nullifica-tion*, then, serve as the precondition and corollary for Thoreau's ethics (both autoerotic and ecological), which take shape around modes of narrating place made possible by the subjection of Native peoples to the very condi-tions of destitution the text seems to repudiate.[10]

However, what might happen if Thoreau's vision of masturbatory person-hood were not bound to a conception of sovereign selfhood? What if the psychic and discursive energies decried as self-pollution on which Thoreau draws were rechanneled into a critique of the property and jurisdictional logics at play in settler subjectivity? *Walden* envisions a kind of withdrawal from existing modes of naturalization that also might expose the (settler) self to its limits and the potential for imaginative engagement beyond the terms of the law. Following this line of thought, might Thoreau's negation of the biopolitics of *civilization* come to work in solidarity with the Mashpees' and other peoples' negation of the right of the state to superintend them and their lands? In the final section, I will explore how *Walden* might be reread as offering the possibility for forms of queer solidarity with Indigenous self-determination, acknowledging the politics of Native endurance rather than sublimating it as an Indianness available for settler self-fashioning in (an illu-sory and empty) "Nature" and, thereby, allowing for a more capacious en-gagement with the politics of place.

Reverie against Debt

Walden rejects bourgeois wage-work, agricultural production, and home-making, presenting them as predicated on forms of extensive and perennial indebtedness. Such dependence does not simply impinge on the self but actually produces a kind of speculative personhood in which enmeshment in capitalist networks proves actively enervating, sapping physical resources and thereby wasting the bodies and minds of those so imbricated. In re-sponse, the text articulates a vision of masturbatory personhood, in which what otherwise might be understood as aimless daydreaming and the absence of productive labor facilitates states of sensation that generate more life energy and open the potential for imagining less utilitarian and debili-tating ways of being in the world than those of the villagers and neighbors he derides. Thus, the text's portrayal of embodied personhood inverts the terms of antimasturbation discourses of the period, which largely present bodily expenditure beyond the requirements of one's livelihood and repro-duction to be a drain on the nervous system. From this perspective, nature marks less an innate set of bodily tendencies and norms than a space of rela-tive solitude in which occupancy without ownership allows one to avoid the dissipating forms of subjectification entailed by quotidian bourgeois prac-tices and aspirations.[11]

Thoreau presents the pursuit of property holding as compromising a man's autonomy, portraying attempts at self-sufficiency through ownership into a being for others that leeches away his vitality. In the late eighteenth and early nineteenth centuries, the possession of property served as a sign of one's independence and, therefore, one's suitability to participate in the polity, but in the wake of both the increase in the number of landholders due to the expansion of white settlements and the democratization of political partici-pation through the widespread elimination of property restrictions on vot-ing and public service, more white men were able to envision themselves as full subjects and to aspire to homeownership even as the possibilities for fully owning one's home and for agricultural or artisanal work not depen-dent on wages declined.[12] Thoreau plays on the tensions among the persistent connotations of landholding as republican self-sovereignty, the economic difficulties of actually achieving that goal, and the potential for envision-ing a kind of (political) selfhood not legitimized through the possession of an estate.[13] Toward the beginning of "Economy," he observes, "I see young men, my townsmen, whose misfortune it is to have inherited farms, houses, barns, cattle, and farming tools; for these are more easily acquired than got rid of" (2). He suggests that this intergenerational transmission of landed wealth, increasingly rare in Concord and southern New England generally,[14] functions as an encumbrance of which one would want to "rid" oneself. In order to explain this paradox, he asks a series of questions: "Who made them serfs of the soil? Why should they eat their sixty acres, when man is condemned only to eat his peck of dirt? Why should they begin digging their graves as soon as they are born?" (2). What might appear as an index of self-determination, a capacity to set the terms of one's own life without needing to rely on others, actually functions as a mode of *serfdom* in which fealty to "the soil" alters the very structure of one's body in ways that incapacitate it. Working the land you own means digging your own grave, turning your body into the soil by *eating* it until it eats you. The labor expended in caring for the farm threatens bodily integrity and personhood, making the work of sustaining one's property into an act of self-destruction that starves you of nourishment.

While serving as the conventional symbol of personal and political autonomy, the family farm, Thoreau suggests, remains embedded in a web of commercial relations that vitiates its ability to engender or signify true self-sufficiency. He remarks,

> When I consider my neighbors, the farmers of Concord, who are at least as well off as the other classes, I find that for the most part they have been toiling twenty, thirty, or forty years, that they may become the real owners of their farms, which commonly they have inherited with encumbrances, or else bought with hired money, ... but commonly they have not paid for them yet. It is true, the encumbrances sometimes outweigh the value of the farm, so that the farm itself becomes one great encumbrance. (22)

Inheritance and purchase merge into each other, since neither escapes the orbit of the "encumbrance" of debt. He adds, "On applying to the assessors, I am surprised to learn that they cannot at once name a dozen in the town who own their farms free and clear. If you would know the history of these homesteads, inquire at the bank where they are mortgaged" (22). Whether due to the need to borrow money in order to purchase it or inheriting the debts incurred in trying to sustain the farm's operation, the mortgage mediates between the territory and its putative owners. Describing these properties as "homesteads" ironically highlights the gap between nominal/indebted and *real* ownership, drawing on the rhetoric surrounding the decades-long campaign to get the U.S. government to make public lands available for free to those willing to inhabit and work them (as opposed to gaining lands through purchase at auction or through preemption followed by purchase)— a movement already well-established by the early 1850s.[15] As discussed in chapter 2, this movement pitched itself against the excesses of speculation in which one buyer would amass large tracts and either wait to sell them until they had appreciated in value or sell them to small landholders at exorbitant rates that could only be accommodated through extensive borrowing. One stands as a "serf" less to the soil itself than to "the bank," which maintains the relation to the land once reserved for the lord of the manor, and the notion of a consolidation of the self through homeownership is revealed as a virtually impossible fantasy that actually incites a disintegration of that self—a process of becoming "dirt." The very desire for the apparent self-sufficiency of homeownership creates an enslaving dependence on creditors and access to the market in which you become "the slave-driver of yourself," forcing your "fancy and imagination" toward an ideal that yokes selfhood to the extant economy of homemaking and agricultural production (4).[16]

Thoreau's neighbors mortgage bodily capacity for the illusion of security and independence, enacting an enfeebling kind of personhood.[17] Such speculative subjectivity trades physical well-being in the present for a phantasmatic future state: "Making yourselves sick, that you may lay up something against a sick day" (4). He suggests that in calculating value, including that of a home or farm, one needs a formula attentive to the true "cost of a thing" which "is the amount of what I will call life which is required to be exchanged for it, immediately or in the long run" (21). Not only is the possession of property not a privileged means of coalescing and insulating one's self, it directly compromises selfhood by bleeding one of the very substances of "life," siphoning and exhausting through the parasitical extraction of labor necessary to sustain the household or farm as an enterprise.[18]

If *Walden* refuses the republican vision of achieving self-sovereignty through the linked statuses of homeownership and landholding, it also repudiates the notion of domesticity as a preservative enclosure. While the

creation and sustaining of a stand-alone household became more dependent on wage work and consumption of mass-produced goods in the early
to mid-nineteenth century, it increasingly was represented as a refuge from
the aggression, competition, and contingency of the market—a contained
place for the protection and cultivation of individual (bourgeois) identity.[19]
As against this vision of the home as a space of retreat, Thoreau targets feminized homemaking as one of the chief means of depleting "life," a significant
drag on the possibilities for achieving a more truly autonomous and healthful (male) personhood.[20] In sketching the problems posed by current means
of getting a living, he proclaims, "At last, we know not what it is to live in the
open air, and our lives are domestic in more senses than we think. From the
hearth to the field is a great distance" (19). This contrast seems to turn on
the distinction between interior and exterior, the healthful results of spending less time indoors and more time working "in the open air," but the idea
of having a "domestic" life pivots away from a question of literal enclosure
to concern over the goods with which one fills that space and the relations
created by their manufacture and purchase. He describes the "modern drawing room" as having "divans, and ottomans, and sunshades, and a hundred
other oriental things, which we are taking west with us, invented for the
ladies of the harem and the effeminate natives of the Celestial Empire" (25).
Indicting not just the invasion of foreign objects but the importation of
commercial desires that are themselves *effeminizing*, the passage insinuates
that conventional home life dissipates men's capabilities, losing Yankee vigor
in exchange for "oriental" luxuriance and thereby alienating a man's subjectivity from itself in laboring to maintain such a household. While domestic
advice manuals called for greater restraint in terms of what one buys and
uses, *Walden* suggests that the enervating effects of consumption extend far
beyond what could be considered exotic commodities to items that would
be taken as commonsensical daily fare. Describing the quotidian diet of
John Field and his family, an Irish laborer living nearby,[21] Thoreau observes,
"as he began with tea, and coffee, and butter, and milk, and beef, he had to
work hard to pay for them, and when he had worked hard he had to eat hard
again to repair the waste to his system" (138). In order to purchase these
everyday items, Field must "waste . . . his system," becoming trapped in the
same kind of vicious cycle as the farmers trying to save for the future and purchase their land. The ubiquity of these items marks the destructive effects of

domesticity ("hard" labor) on the working (male) body even in the most
seemingly ordinary efforts at providing physical sustenance.

   Moreover, the text presents the labor of sustaining the household, primarily done by women, less as making possible the lives and well-being of its
members than as an index of the degree to which selfhood has become
immersed in sensual excess. As part of his promotion of vegetarianism in
"Higher Laws," Thoreau notes, "there is something essentially unclean about
this diet and all flesh, and I began to see where housework commences,"
emphasizing the "filth" generated by the preparation of animals for eating
(143). The somewhat strict focus on the routine messiness created by a non-
vegetarian diet, though, subtly shifts to a different set of concerns, focused
less on the problem of cleanliness than moral "cost": "It is neither the quality nor the quantity, but the devotion to sensual savors. . . . If the hunter
has taste for mud-turtles, muskrats, and other such savage tid-bits, the fine
lady indulges a taste for jelly made of a calf's foot, or for sardines from over
the sea, and they are even. . . . The wonder is how they, how you and I,
can live this slimy beastly life, eating and drinking" (146). The bodily expenditure of "housework" slides into the more general indulgence of "sensual savors," exemplified by "the fine lady" whose appetites resemble the
excessive, "oriental" decoration of the "modern drawing room." The text
repeatedly associates such yearnings with an implicit enmeshment in extended commercial networks, a "cost" to men in terms of their labor and
the drain on their "life" it entails, and a dangerous proximity/resemblance
to women.[22] Thoreau insists, "All sensuality is one, though it takes many
forms; all purity is one. It is the same whether a man eat, or drink, or cohabit,
or sleep sensually," while characterizing "chastity" as the ultimate aim—calling it "the flowering of man" (147). Although the latter term could indicate
"exclusion of excess, modesty, restraint" (in the words of the OED), it could
not shake its connotation of celibacy, and Thoreau clearly plays on this
connection by yoking eating and drinking to cohabiting and impure sleep-
ing, suggesting that the difficulties of "housework" stand as a symptom of
the broader *sensualizing* effect of relations with women while also implicitly
casting the "taste" of the "fine lady" as expressive of sexual excess. Conjugal
homemaking appears as itself a drain on the male body, instigating and per-
petuating modes of impurity that waste the self. Thus, when Thoreau declares that "[e]very man is the builder of a temple called his body" (148),

that "body" in its sacral self-relation exists outside of the gross sensuality of the bourgeois home.[23]

A contemporary review of *Walden* in the *New York Churchman* notes that Thoreau's economy "would not be adequate to the support of a family in respectability" and that "[t]o many of his moral speculations we could take exceptions. He carries the opposition to society too far. A self-pleasing man should have a more liberal indulgence for the necessities of others," and the review later decries Thoreau's need to publish "his philosophic ejaculations" rather than simply "carving his elegies on the bark of trees," adding that "[l]ife and reality seem oozing out of his feeble grasp."[24] From this perspective, *Walden*'s refusal of bourgeois homemaking takes Thoreau beyond the bounds of "respectability," indicating a "self-pleasing" bent that makes his commentary less (re)productive than a form of masturbatory eruption better kept to himself in solitude, and the image of a "feeble" grasping from which the vitality of life *oozes* further intimates that Thoreau's writing bespeaks the weak, broken, seeping physique—as well as the polluted morals and imagination—of the perennial onanist. While not common, this response suggests how Thoreau's challenge to the political economy of homeownership, landholding, and middle-class domesticity—and specifically his portrayal of them as a *wasting* drain on somatic resources—runs against the grain of existing discourses of health, in which the employment of vital energy beyond a man's family and livelihood threatens to incapacitate him entirely. This fear of bodily expenditure reaches its apotheosis in the proliferation of tracts warning of the catastrophic implications of masturbation. *Walden*'s vision of liberated personal well-being can be understood as working through and against the account of self-regulation such texts provide, reorienting the critique of masturbation to offer a counterhegemonic vision of selfhood freed from dependence on the dialectical relation between the bourgeois home and the market.

Offering a model adopted in various forms by other health experts for decades afterward, Sylvester Graham's *A Lecture to Young Men on Chastity* locates the destructive effects of masturbation in the shock it causes to the nervous system.[25] While noting that "self-pollution" is "by far the worst form of venereal indulgence" (87), Graham dissents from prior claims about its fundamental difference from other kinds of sexual experience,[26] instead arguing that orgasm in all its forms provided the most intense version of a

more diffuse physiological dynamic: "All extraordinary and undue excite-
ments, . . . whether caused by mental, moral or physical stimuli, increase the
excitability and unhealthy activity of the nerves of organic life; and tend to
bring on, and establish in them, a state of diseased irritability and sensitivity" (44). Whether through genital gratification, the overconsumption
of rich foods (including meat), or the use of alcohol, the overstimulation of
the body led to sickness by unduly exciting the nerves, thereby producing a
range of co-amplifying forms of inflammation. However, due to "convulsive
paroxysms attending venereal indulgence," "sexual desire" does more damage to the system than other kinds of stimulation, unleashing something like
the "tremendous violence of a tornado" (47–49). Graham offers a theory of
homeostatic balance in which disease can be defined as an overcommitment
of somatic resources to sensations that exceed the provision of basic needs,
with sexual indulgence proving most costly due to its intensity.

   This conception of human physiology can be understood as taking the
problem and ubiquity of debt as a basis for thinking the inherent dynamics
of sustainable personhood. As discussed in chapter 2, the early to mid-
nineteenth century was a time of extreme economic instability. Graham and
those of his generation had lived through the Panic of 1819,[27] and such concerns would have been even more prominent for those who lived through
the depression caused by the Panic of 1837, including those Grahamite health
reformers who gained prominence in the 1840s and early 1850s. Graham
characterizes "the present depraved state of man's instinctive propensities"
as a "lawless commerce" (66), and the text's introduction insists that "the
prosperity of the state, and the welfare of the people, may suffer decay" if
readers fail to acknowledge "practical interests" such as the prevalence of
nerve-destroying stimulation (28). These moments suggest that the promotion of bodily well-being will increase the wealth of the nation while reciprocally implying that foregoing sensual (particularly sexual) indulgence
partakes of the logic of proper financial management.[28] In this way, Graham
and his followers aim to distinguish between a properly self-sufficient bodily
economy and one that depends on a regular and unsustainable taxing of the
reserves of the nervous system. As Thomas Laqueur suggests, "the imaginative foundations of credit posed the same moral and psychological question
as masturbation" (278): "The diseases of the masturbator were very much
like those of the commonwealth addicted to the new fictions of paper"

(292). In *Amativeness,* Orson Fowler makes this relation even more explicit by warning those who engage in "promiscuous, and matrimonial, and solitary indulgence" of an "excess of expenditure over supply" created by their behavior that will "render them *bankrupts of life*" (20, 23), adding that male orgasm "overtax[es]" the supply of semen" and "withdraws energy from all other parts to re-supply the draft" (25).[29] Such figurations presume the possibility of a functional circulation of energy that does not eventuate in the degradation of the nerves through *overdrafting,* envisioning a kind of bodily economy not predicated on speculation that, therefore, provides a model for how to engage in commerce.

Graham further links the proper functioning of the body to that of the country—the natural to the national—by indicating that both must follow the shared "laws" of their "constitution." He insists, "The constitutional nature of man is established upon principles which, when strictly obeyed, will always secure his highest good and happiness; and every disease, and every suffering which human nature bears, results from the violation of the constitutional laws of our nature" (34). While "constitution" could refer to bodily order, linking it to "laws" cannot but call to mind for readers the U.S. Constitution.[30] Pursuing unhealthful forms of stimulation threatens the body politic as well: "In every condition of the human race, the physical, as well as the moral state of the people, is of the highest consideration; but more especially in a country like ours, where the aggregate of individual character and individual will, constitutes the foundation and efficiency of all our civil and political institutions" (28). Failing to attend to the proper functioning of the bodies of the citizens, their compliance with the "constitutional" order of "nature," leaves "our civil and political institutions" open to the derangements caused by overstimulation and physical excess due to the role of "the people" in processes of governance in "a country like ours." The individual's decision to embody healthful personhood by living within his physical means—attending to "the legitimate and undisturbed economy of your original constitution" (35)—sympathizes with and contributes directly and inevitably to the welfare and happiness of the people, enacting what Orson Fowler terms "self-government" (60).[31]

In envisioning the operation of a lawful and sustainable natural economy, Graham positions conjugal couplehood as a conceptual hinge, aligning the somatic with the social by harmonizing the proper mobilization of bodily resources with the management of the household as part of sustaining the nation. Early on, the text insists that "efforts to encourage illicit and promiscuous commerce between the sexes," an allusion to advocates of what would come to be known as "free love" such as Robert Dale Owens, endeavor "to show that marriage is not a divine institution" (20), and Graham condemns such arguments as "spreading corruption in their course" (22). In contrast, he assures readers that "the Bible doctrine of marriage and sexual continence and purity, is founded on the physiological principles established in the constitutional nature of man" (24). Essentially, marriage poses little danger, because it's just that unsexy.[32] Husbands and wives "become accustomed to each other's body, and their parts no longer excite an impure imagination" (73), and due to such loss of excitement—that is, the general nerve-preserving boringness attributed to matrimony—marriage "is an institution founded in the constitutional nature of things" that is "inseparably connected with the highest welfare of man, as an individual and as a race!" (75). Moreover, in casting Owenite and other socialist critiques of marriage as a danger to bodily well-being, Graham also displaces their analysis of the waste that attends the single-family household and privatization generally, implicitly presenting ascendant modes of bourgeois homemaking as the best way of ensuring physiologically proper forms of natural/national restraint.[33]

Although in some ways just one among many potential forms of (sexual) excitation that strains bodily resources, masturbation does pose particular problems to the happy conjunction of bodily, domestic, and national economies. According to Graham, what makes it "wholly unnatural" is its reliance on "mental action, and the power of the imagination on the genital organs" (88), allowing it to be "a secret and solitary vice, which requires the consent of no second person" (96). Onanism disjoints one from constitutionally regulated and nonstimulating engagement with others through an "unnatural" unleashing of "solitary" fantasy, making possible a potentially endless process of erotic speculation that, in Fowler's terms quoted earlier, can bankrupt the body by overdrafting its resources—putting it into something like nervous debt.[34] Graham insists that the masturbator "has no relish for the ordinary amusements and pleasures of life—no enjoyment of society" (127), and he earlier argues that "those LASCIVIOUS DAY-DREAMS, and amorous reveries, in which young people too generally—and especially the

idle, and the voluptuous, and the sedentary, and the nervous—are exceedingly apt to indulge, are often the sources of general debility, effeminacy, dis-
ordered functions, and even premature death, without the actual exercise of
the genital organs!" (58–59). Drawing away from others and engaging in
forms of "reverie" leads, almost inevitably, to "general debility." It wastes
the body by subjecting it to nerve-destroying, imagination-induced stimulation that fatally deviates from the *constitutional* imperatives subtending participation in the bourgeois household and the wage economy.[35] In fact, the
lure of onanism can appear strongest at precisely that period in life in which
young men are finishing their education and just beginning to enter the
economy but do not yet have (marital) homes of their own—the period of
bachelorhood.[36]

   In their concern over debt, as well as portrayal of the aims of life as for
"higher" purposes than physical stimulation and appetite, Graham's *Lecture
to Young Men* and other writings inspired by it seem in accordance with
Thoreau, leading some to describe him as something of a Grahamite,[37] but
for Thoreau *nature* does not appear as an immanent set of physical principles that tie people to one another in a "constitutional" order, instead functioning as a space into which to withdraw from the destructive bodily effects
of a social life organized around a political economy of speculation and debt.
Walden makes the very characteristics associated with onanism as sources
of bodily incapacitation and nervous derangement into the basis for envisioning a kind of personhood not drained and enchained through a commitment to property holding and conjugal domesticity, thereby articulating a
queer ethics.[38] The withdrawal of the bachelor into a solitary space of reverie indicates the power of imagination to engender more livable modes
of being.[39] In "Solitude" he observes, "I find it wholesome to be alone the
greater part of the time. To be in company, even with the best, is soon weari-
some and dissipating. I love to be alone. I never found the companion that
was so companionable as solitude" (91), and the "Conclusion" charges readers, "Do not trouble yourself much to get new things," "Do not seek so anxiously to be developed, to subject yourself to many influences to be played
on; it is all dissipation" (219). While *dissipation* potentially indicates a wasting of the self through indulgence in pleasure, often used in precisely this
way in antimasturbation discourse, Thoreau refigures it as something more
like the anxious dissolving of discrete personhood, an effect of participating

in the everyday sociality of the village. As opposed to leading one toward a diseased and degenerating retreat into fantasy, being alone offers a "wholesome" insulation from companions who take one away from the proper care of the self and its well-being.

The text takes up such masturbatory subjectivity in ways that approach the relation between personal identity and social processes as a specifically spatial problem. Solitude opens up distance between oneself and others, thereby creating the potential for envisioning a different kind of life than that made possible by enmeshment in the pressing demands of property, commerce, and marital domesticity. What is required is a space into which a person might go in order to recover a sense of himself. After assuring readers that he "never felt lonesome, or in the least oppressed by a sense of solitude," he notes that "a few weeks after I came to the woods,"

> for an hour, I doubted if the near neighborhood of man was not essential to a serene and healthy life. . . . But I was at the same time conscious of a slight insanity in my mood, and seemed to foresee my recovery. In the midst of a gentle rain while these thoughts prevailed, I was suddenly sensible of such sweet and beneficent society in Nature, . . . an infinite and unaccountable friendliness all at once like an atmosphere sustaining me, as made the fancied advantages of human neighborhood insignificant, and I have never thought of them since. (89)

Rather than "solitude" giving rise to "*amorous reveries*" that drive one to exhaustion and madness, as in Graham's account, the desire for company appears as a sign of "insanity."[40] In its separation from "human neighborhood," "Nature" provides a means of *recovering* from the derangement the village produces, forming an "atmosphere" conducive to the non(re)productive action of imaginative speculation. In "The Ponds" Thoreau speaks of his time at Walden "when [he] was younger," "having paddled my boat to the middle, and lying on my back across the seats, in a summer forenoon, dreaming awake, until I was aroused by the boat touching the sand . . . ; days when idleness was the most attractive and productive industry. . . . I was rich, if not in money, in sunny hours and summer days, and spent them lavishly" (129). He earlier observes in "Sounds" that he "sat in my sunny doorway from sunshine till noon, rapt in a revery, amidst the pines and hickories and sumachs, in undisturbed solitude and stillness," periods that "were far better than any work of the hands would have been": "They were not sub-tracted from my life, but so much over and above my usual allowance" (75). Offering scenes of masturbatory excess (including the sly pun on "aroused" and reference to the "work of the hands"), Thoreau distinguishes this period of "revery" or "dreaming awake" from what would be considered by others to be "productive industry." This reveling in one's own fantasy life does not so much take one away from the real as generate a kind of bodily and psychological wealth through solitude that is irreducible to the calculation and circulation of value in the market ("not in money," "above my usual allowance").[41] An onanistic ethos provides a kind of self-possessive occu-pancy promised through homeownership but actually deferred by it. In *Inti-macy in America* Peter Coviello argues that whiteness in this period works less as a stable identity than as a shifting process of identification that provides a means of experiencing a "binding intimacy" with fellow citizens through an "*affective* language" (6–10), later adding that "*whiteness realizes and concret-izes the fiction of an inalienable property in the self*" in the antebellum period (48). Thoreau envisions a way of performing whiteness that dislodges it from the matrix of bourgeois homemaking, in which whiteness accrues as a form of procreative inheritance,[42] and from this perspective, Thoreau's emphasis on a kind of autoerotic withdrawal/self-possession can be under-stood as a particular way of conceptualizing and experiencing the affective dynamics of whiteness that is oriented around solitary relations to place.[43]

Dwelling in "Nature" entails extending the onanistic capaciousness of the daydream to Thoreau's relation with the land more broadly—cultivating a "rich" imaginative life rather than a household or marketable crop.[44] "Where I Lived, and What I Lived For" chronicles Thoreau's process of choosing a space to inhabit, one in which he spent a good deal of time visiting others' farms: "My imagination carried me so far that I even had the refusal of several farms,—the refusal was all I wanted,—but I never got my fingers burned by actual possession" (55). He observes of this kind of survey, "I have frequently seen a poet withdraw, having enjoyed the most valuable part of a farm" and "fairly impounded it, milked it, skimmed it, and got all the cream" (56). As opposed to "actual possession," "imagination" entails a kind of connection with the land in which the *value* lies in a non(re)productive expenditure that yields pleasure as "cream," with all of the latter's ejaculatory insinuations.[45] A similar dynamic animates his discussion of his relation to seed. Thoreau assures readers that while surveying potential farms, "[I] had had my seeds ready" for "when at last I shall plant" (56–57), correlating dropping his seed(s) with a kind of enduring connection to place at odds with his imaginative *creaming*. In describing the bean field he planted while at Walden, he observes, "I was much slower, and became much more intimate with my beans than usual" (105), adding that he "was determined to know beans" in ways that provided "a rare amusement, which continued too long, might have become a dissipation" (109). These moments somewhat flirtatiously hint at a nonproductive connection to place in which his seed is spilled in an amusing, "intimate" pleasure that could lead to "dissipation."[46] He declares, "I desire to speak impartially on this point, and as one not interested in the success or failure of the present economical and social arrangements. I was more independent than any farmer in Concord, for I was not anchored to a house or farm, but could follow the bent of my genius, which is a very crooked one, every moment" (38). Thoreau insists that his "crooked"-ness (intimating his possession of perverse inclinations) signals his *independence*, the absence of "a house or farm" bespeaking a kind of personal orientation that dislodges him from the political economy in which he otherwise would be "anchored." The text's play on masturbatory idleness and dreaming signals a way of inhabiting place that severs one from the supposed "laws" of bourgeois political economy while also calling forth the idea of literal distance—a clearly demarcated space of solitude that Thoreau designates as "Nature."

SETTLERS GONE WILD

The invocation of "Nature" appears to bracket the question of jurisdiction, opening into a different conceptual and phenomenological register that displaces the problem of locating oneself in relation to the boundaries of the state. However, the very feeling that one has moved beyond geopolitics depends on the presence of an encompassing sovereignty that licenses one's access to that space. Who is the subject that can understand himself as beyond the sphere of legal authority? Native peoples must already cease to exert sovereignty (or at least cease to be understood as exerting sovereignty) in order for a place to be narrated or occupied as "Nature." However, Native peoples and presence return in the text, with *Indians* coming to serve as a sign of something beyond state-endorsed modes of personhood—as figures of the wilderness as an extrapolitical elsewhere. As such, they function as vehicles, as transitive objects, for a nonnative imagination/ethics of escape from the state.

Thoreau consistently presents his residence at Walden as divorcing him from the state. Early in the text, he notes, "I began to occupy my house on the 4th of July" (30), and while he does not elaborate on this fact, it clearly signals a connection between the act of living in his cabin and the American Revolution.[47] However, more than presenting his practice of economy as a more truly national way of living, a means of completing the work of the Revolution (as in the narrative of Lockean toil in the country offered by settlers in Maine and taken up in Hawthorne's *House*, discussed in the previous chapter), the image of breaking away from the jurisdictional sphere of an unjust government parallels the text's (masturbatory) refusal of Grahamite arguments about the necessary relation between bodily and national "laws."[48] Of the cabin he eventually builds near the pond, Thoreau observes, "from my door . . . I did not feel crowded or confined in the least. There was pasture enough for my imagination," adding, "We are wont to imagine rare and delectable places in some remote and more celestial corner of the system. . . . I discovered that my house actually had its site in such a withdrawn, but forever new and unprofaned, part of the universe" which was "at an equal remoteness from the life which I had left behind" (59). In indexing that he has "withdrawn" from "the life . . . left behind" in ways that give "pasture" for the imagination, "Nature" both indicates a physical context that occasions reverie and serves as a sign that the thoughts one is having can be understood as not "anchored" to "present economical and social arrangements." His presence in a place apart insulates him from the operation of the state, suggesting activity in solitude that puts him beyond the national/natural matrix suggested by Grahamite visions of bodily order. The state only can gain access to him when he returns to "the village": "One afternoon, near the end of the first summer, when I went to the village . . , I was seized and put into jail, because . . . I did not pay a tax to, or recognize the authority of, the state which buys and sells men, women, and children, like cattle at the door of its senate-house. I had gone down to the woods for other purposes. But, wherever a man goes, men will pursue and paw him with their dirty institutions" (115). The "institutions" of a government that sanctions enslavement may seek to "pursue" him, but they do not actually enter the "woods," presenting the latter as a space separate from the workings of the state in which one can achieve a perspective not encumbered by it—a place of independence.[49]

Instead of being under U.S. rule, Thoreau envisions the acquisition of a kind of autonomous jurisdiction over himself. In speaking of conversations with guests who visited his cabin, he observes in "Visitors," "Individuals, like nations, must have suitable broad and natural boundaries, even a considerable neutral ground, between them" (95). This comment speaks to the significance of giving people room for their individuality, as against the earlier description of "the nation" and "its so called internal improvements" as "cluttered with furniture and tripped up by its own traps" (62).[50] Yet more than suggesting the need for something like personal space, the use of the idiom of nationhood, especially in light of the text's initial declaration of independence, suggests a kind of political distinction.[51] This selfhood appears to precede and/or exceed the state that exerts jurisdiction over it but is modeled on, and thus only becomes intelligible through, the discursive and institutional matrix of state sovereignty—its exclusive authority over those people and lands within its boundaries.[52] Thus, being *like a nation* entails embodying a selfhood that has the properties of sovereignty—enacting what might be termed *sovereign selfhood*. The text envisions a sphere in which the powers of the state are suspended or held in abeyance, producing the possibilities for absenting oneself from the political economy that transects the rest of the nation (such as the forms of exchange that engender "internal improvements"). Rather than offering a Lockean vision of establishing property through toil, a kind of claim that provides the legitimate basis for state-making and governance, the text casts embodiment as self-contained insularity beyond the life of the state, suggesting that relations with others should be shaped around the recognition of such nation-like separation and autonomy. Moreover, while the wholeness of individuality one finds in nature suspends the intrusive influence of governmental logics and the dynamics of the market, it does not institute its own political economy, allowing a person to achieve a kind of independence that does not constitute an example of *imperium in imperio*—a state within a state.

"Nature" names a specific kind of space capable of providing the basis for an alternative ethics and experience of personhood, and Thoreau characterizes that space primarily through negation.[53] "Where I Lived, and What I Lived For" proclaims, "Every morning was a cheerful invitation to make my life of equal simplicity, and I may say innocence with Nature herself" (60), and in "The Ponds," Thoreau notes that Walden "needs no fence. Nations come and go without defiling it" (127). In these moments, the text emphasizes the absence of the encumbrances and dissipations of the village, the market, and the conjugal household. "Innocence" and "simplicity" are not descriptions of the qualities of that space but of a negative relation to "present economical and social arrangements," the projection backward or outside from a "defil[ed]" state. Similarly, "The Bean-Field" positions nature as a conceptual foil to farming and bourgeois landholding: "By avarice and selfishness, and a groveling habit, from which none of us is free, of regarding the soil as property, or the means of acquiring property chiefly, the landscape is deformed, husbandry is degraded with us, and the farmer leads the meanest of lives. He knows Nature as a robber" (111). "Nature" signifies a kind of inhabitance and relation to place other than that dependent on regimes of "property" and participation in the political economy of the market. It indicates that from which the "us" have fallen, into a "deformed" and "degraded" mode of being. This sense of a prior/exterior wholeness, though, depends on a narration of the negative relation to the village and the market—of *distance, remoteness, withdrawal.* The imaginative act of separation, retreating from the "institutions" of the state and the "serf[dom]" of commerce, creates the sense of a place in which one can gain autonomy from such relations, envisioning relocation to the "woods" as enabling an experience at the outer limits of sociality in which one encounters and imbibes the qualities of that location.[54]

However, to what does "nature" refer? Or more precisely, what does it mean to collate and give a unity to a disparate collection of phenomena, organic and nonorganic beings, and topographic and geologic formations as a singular "Nature"? In *Green Writing: Romanticism and Ecology,* James C. McKusick argues that by taking up "a non-human perspective, Thoreau affirms that nature possesses intrinsic value, distinct from any utilitarian value that it may have for human beings. This non-human perspective marks Thoreau as America's first Deep Ecologist" (147). Similarly, Lawrence Buell in *The Environmental Imagination* describes environmental understanding, including Thoreau's, as a "mode of vision" that "opens itself up as well as it can to the perception of the environment as an actual independent party entitled to consideration for its own sake" (77), indicating the importance of "find[ing] a way of conceiving the literal level" as against the "fallacy of derealization"—inculcating a "respect for environmental facticity" that recognizes "the implacable *thereness* of the external world" (90, 111).[55] In "Spring," Thoreau observes:

> Our village life would stagnate if it were not for the unexplored forests and meadows which surround it. We need the tonic of wildness . . . At the same time that we are earnest to explore and learn all things, we require that all things be mysterious and unexplorable, that land and sea be infinitely wild, unsurveyed and unfathomed by us because unfathomable. We can never have enough of Nature . . . We need to witness our own limits transgressed, and some life pasturing freely where we never wander. (211–12)

The "wildness" that makes possible a revitalization of life in the "village," that undoes convention and breaks one free from what is "surveyed" and "fathomed," requires contact with "Nature," itself conceptualized as the "unexplored" place of *mystery* that exceeds human community.[56] Thus, to be "wild" (to "transgress" one's "own limits") is to partake in the wilderness, defined by the phenomenological experience of outsideness.[57] To occupy nature is to be apart from the state and to have the freedom of oneself in ways that are *like a nation*, suggesting a kind of selfhood that derives from something other than the exercise of or participation in political sovereignty. In this way, "Nature" functions as a placeholder, catachrestically gesturing toward an experience of asocial fullness by substantializing absence as an identity—a determinate kind of space. How is that space realized as such? How is it cohered as an extrapolitical location that one phenomenologically could experience as "the environment"?[58]

The announcement of Thoreau's separation from the state invokes nature as a kind of place to which legal order does not apply, and in this way, it functions as a space of exception. For Giorgio Agamben, the exception marks the process by which the sovereign ruler decides "what is included in the juridical order and what is excluded from it" (19), and "[i]n this sense, the exception is the originary form of law" (26). He adds, "The relation of exception is a relation of ban. He who has been banned is not, in fact, simply set outside the law and made indifferent to it but rather *abandoned* by it, that is, exposed and threatened on the threshold. . . . It is literally not possible to say whether the one who has been banned is outside or inside the juridical order" (28–29). To place someone or a group in the state of exception is to exercise sovereignty in ways that deny a person or persons the protections of the law without placing them beyond state jurisdiction, instead *abandoning* them to violence on the "threshold"—neither included as a full political subject nor excluded as the subject of another political entity.[59] In *Walden*, "Nature" appears as a space within the boundaries of the state in which the state's authority is suspended, but that opening of a place neither incorporated into the matrix of state power nor exterior to the territory over which the state claims jurisdiction comes not as an act of state sovereignty, instead appearing as the alegal sphere for the self's exercise of its own nonpolitical form of sovereignty. The assertion of the exceptional quality of nature, though, can be understood as animated by existing modes of juridical exception—exertions of sovereignty by the state—that have been transposed into a different discursive register. In *Politics of Nature*, Latour suggests that "'nature' is made . . . precisely to eviscerate politics" (19–20), creating a sense of wholeness and unity apparently free from political negotiation, contention, and conflict through which to avoid, displace, or trump such necessary dialogue and debate.[60] Following this line of thought, the concept of nature might be understood as oriented by, and gaining momentum from, prior political acts and processes that come to be experienced as if immanent within the landscape itself.

Walden's envisioning of a place outside the circuits of U.S. law while inside the boundaries of the nation-state is shaped and propelled by the prior juridical exceptionalization of indigeneity. Repeatedly described as occupying a "special," "peculiar," or "unique" place in U.S. law, Native peoples continually have been cast as an anomaly, thereby suspending the question of their existence as distinct polities with sovereignties that precede and exceed that of the United States. As Stephen Rockwell notes, "federal officials *created* the 'uninhabited wilderness' we romanticize by removing Indians from the land" (217).[61] In this vein, we can trace Thoreau's conception of "Nature" as unfolding from the prior legal narration of Native lands as both a space apart and as lacking distinct political status. Native peoples in New England did not have treaties with the federal government as did peoples elsewhere, and Indian affairs were considered to be state matters. By the 1840s and 1850s Massachusetts had eight reservations whose boundaries had been determined and regulated under colonial and then state law,[62] and the maintenance, usage, and sale of such tribal lands were administered largely by state-appointed overseers or commissioners. Written in response to a legislative mandate, the *Report of the Commissioners Relating to the Condition of the Indians in Massachusetts* was submitted in 1848 and published in 1849. Often called the Bird report, after its lead author, it repeatedly describes the legal and political situation of Native peoples and their lands in the state as "imperfectly defined," "anomalous," and "peculiar."[63] These terms refer not only to the ambiguity of the relevant statutes as to certain key points, but also to the general fact of having populations and places governed by a set of policies not applicable to the rest of the population and property in the state. The report describes these peoples as "among the 'stricken few' who remain of the once undisputed sovereigns of the Western World. The blood of Samoset and Massasoit runs in their veins" (5), and in decrying the fact that Indians do not hold citizenship in the state or the nation, the report observes, "The Indian alone, the descendant of monarchs, is a vassal in the land of his fathers" (49). Indians bear a relation to place unlike that of all other inhabitants, which renders them exceptional. As observed in the 1861 report on Indian affairs in the state, authored by John Milton Earle, "Here are . . . communities within the State, but not of it, subject to its laws, but having no part in their enactment; within the limits of local municipalities, yet not subject to their jurisdiction; and holding real estate in their own right, yet not suffered to dispose of it, except to each other" (121). These reports circle around a conceptual impasse: Native peoples once were completely "sovereign," but now they are not; they live "within" the state but are not subject to most of its laws; they cannot live as subjects of the state/nation and not be citizens, but they do not desire citizenship.

Native territoriality must be aberrant to the state/nation, since to engage with the persistence of Indigenous sovereignty would undo existing settler jurisdictional mappings. Moreover, Native peoples refuse the overture of inclusion, negating this gesture of imposed identity.[64] Tribes in Massachusetts also are cast as exceptional with respect to Indians elsewhere. The 1848 report declares of the Mashpees, "They are not a domestic nation, as the Cherokees are declared to be, by the supreme court of the United States.

They have no rights secured by treaty" (50).[65] The Mashpees, and by extension other peoples in the state, exist as territorial entities of some sort, but they are not *nations* and do not possess specifically political "rights." The Mashpee, Chappequiddic, Christiantown, and Gay Head tribes, among others, all have land; yet according to the 1848 report, that land has no determinate legal or political status, existing merely as an exception to the constitutional principles of the state. If, as Agamben suggests, sovereignty comes into being through the exception, through the power to impose the state of exception, the sovereignty of the state of Massachusetts here depends on the production of Native peoples and their lands as exceptional, as a kind of alegal limbo within its jurisdiction.[66] Thoreau's citation of nature-as-exception (re)constructs this sense of a jurisdictional void while presenting that space as available for the cultivation of forms of extrapolitical personhood, thereby performing settler sovereignty as a condition of possibility for an apparent exit from the state by nonnatives.

The figure of the Indian marks the presence of already existing spaces of exception within the legal geography of the settler-state that provide the basis for conceptualizing "Nature" as a place neither quite within nor outside U.S. sovereignty. Robert Sayre suggests that "what has not been sufficiently recognized by Thoreau's critics and biographers is that for any American to go live in the woods immediately calls to mind living like an Indian" (60), and Mark David Spence observes, "Antebellum Americans did not conceive of wilderness and Indians as separate; indeed, the felicity with which we can speak of one *and* the other, wilderness *and* Indians, would not have been so readily conceivable" in the period (10).[67] For Thoreau, the figure of the "savage"/"Indian" stands for the kind of stripped-down, self-sufficient personhood made possible by withdrawal into the wilderness.[68] In "Economy" Thoreau repeatedly references Native peoples as models of how to live in simpler and heartier ways. As Joshua David Bellin suggests in *Demon of the Continent*, these moments engage in a form of "Noble Savagism" in which Native peoples are less cast as "displaced by the economy" than "deprived of an economic existence altogether," and within this frame, "savage nobility" functions as "freedom from the market" (58). Bellin adds that for Thoreau to consider the ways Native peoples "may live by institutions . . . of their own" would have been "to lose a space from which to launch his critique" (67). Additionally, many of the pressures on Native land bases in southern

New England in the early to mid-nineteenth century came from logging interests, so the forests and Indianness would have been even more tightly braided in the minds of many Massachusetts residents, with them possibly narrating a defense of Native homelands from settler exploitation as an effort to preserve an embattled "Nature."[69]

In *Walden*, Indians personify the potential for having a perspective that can exceed that engendered by the debt-inducing encumbrances of commerce and bourgeois homemaking. Thoreau observes in "Visitors" that "all honest pilgrims, who came out to the woods for freedom's sake, and really left the village behind, I was ready to greet with,—'Welcome, Englishmen! welcome, Englishmen!' for I had had communication with that race" (104). Here he envisions himself as Samoset, an Abenaki leader from Pemaquid whose people had been trading with the English for more than a decade who greeted the Pilgrims in English soon after their landing at Plymouth.[70] This instance of playing Indian, though, correlates with his presentation of himself as a representative from/of the "woods." Notably, while Samoset came to the English settlement, Thoreau greets visitors only once they have "left the village behind," and thus, an act of diplomacy becomes a gesture of incorporation into the space of the wilderness, taken as a place outside or beyond politics. Having already abandoned "the village," Thoreau has become one who can "greet" others who might join him, his Indianization indicating his occupancy of a location beyond the *enslaving* dynamics of the state and the market.[71] Further, the space that he inhabits testifies to prior Native presence in ways that the text suggests seem to confirm, rather than challenge, its naturalness. In "The Bean-Field," he notes, "it appeared by the arrow-heads, which I turned up in hoeing, that an extinct nation had anciently dwelt here and planted corn and beans ere white men came to clear the land" (105). He adds, "As I drew a still fresher soil about the rows with my hoe, I disturbed the ashes of unchronicled nations who in primeval years lived under these heavens," observing that their "small implements of war and hunting . . . lay mingled with other natural stones," and in the same paragraph, after describing the movement of a night-hawk around him while hoeing, he exclaims, "such kindredship is in Nature" (106–7). The fact of the previous existence of Native "nations" in the place of Walden does not mark an intrusion of politics into "Nature," instead suggesting a continuity "with other natural" phenomena, such that an ability to relate to and inhabit the space of (former) Indianness provides the measure of one's closeness to ("kindredship" with) "Nature." Previous Indian inhabitance appears to authenticate the place as wilderness, and the ability to live like an Indian in that space marks it as still wild, as beyond contemporary "economical and social arrangements." While one could critique the ways the text makes Native peoples continuous with the wilderness, what seems more pressing here is the emergence of the topos of "wilderness" or "Nature" as the means of designating Indigenous inhabitance and placemaking. Jodi Byrd argues that through the recoding of Native peoples as *Indians*, "American Indian national assertions of sovereignty, self-determination, and land rights disappear into U.S. territoriality as indigenous identity becomes a racial identity" (xxiv). However, the process of Indianization also can be understood as marking the translation of Indigenous geopolitics as the space of "Nature," a *derealization* of Native sovereignty through its *realization* as the *wilderness*. Unlike a Lockean denial of Native claims to "Nature" because of a lack of property or proper labor, as addressed in the previous chapter, Indigenous territoriality here *makes* a space "Nature."

Thoreau continually figures himself as in some sense becoming one with his surroundings ("I go and come with a strange liberty in Nature, a part of herself" [87]), but that supposedly *Indian-like* merger into the natural landscape can be understood less as an evasion of legalized modes of personhood, an escape from state sovereignty into the "woods," than as exercising the potential for settler personhood made possible through the exceptionalization of Native peoples and lands (albeit here mobilized as part of a critique of aspects of contemporary political economy). In *Natural Life: Thoreau's Worldly Transcendentalism*, David M. Robinson describes Thoreau as "seeking a more passive surrender to the natural world, one based less on an intellectual mastery of it than on a sensuous merging with it" (19), attempting to achieve a "will-less but participatory engagement with the natural environment" (23).[72] However, the feeling of becoming one with a place, including the space of "Nature," may be understood less as a loss of discrete or sovereign embodiment than a symptom of the ease with which one fits within normative (political) geographies. In *Queer Phenomenology*, Ahmed notes, "To be comfortable is to be so at ease with one's environment that it is hard to distinguish where one's body ends and the world begins. One fits, and in the act of fitting, the surfaces of bodies disappear from view," but that sense of comfort and fit arises due to the fact that places are organized around some bodies more than others: "White bodies are comfortable *as they inhabit spaces that extend their shape*" (134). Feeling merged into nature, then, may indicate the fact that one's experience of personhood and embodiment takes shape around legally endowed categories, like whiteness, that allow one to occupy particular places as an extension of one's selfhood. Thoreau's "savage" sensation of having his "limits transgressed" or of finding "a strange liberty in Nature" can be seen as taking shape in and through state-sanctioned modes of personhood.[73]

The feeling of autonomous (settler) selfhood that appears in *Walden* arises out of policy changes in the first half of the nineteenth century as a result of incorporating Native lands into the nation and legally opening access to them for nonnative inhabitance. In "Thoreau, Manhood, and Race," Dana Nelson suggests that Thoreau casts himself as "representative" by "imagining he somehow stands *for* all those men with whom he might otherwise long to have such tender relationships," "fail[ing] to provide the emotional exchange he accuses capitalist citizenship of denying to men" (88–89). That "representativity" also indexes Thoreau's recirculation of a generic model of personhood that emerges in this period. Beginning in the 1820s there was a radical expansion of the franchise to include all white men, eliminating prior property qualifications and thereby offering legal confirmation of the sense of oneself as a self-governing, self-possessed subject.[74] That trend in the East may be thought of as part of an effort to retain people there, given the possibility of both more land and greater political privilege in territory further west. By 1850 approximately 1.5 million people had moved to the West from the East, and over the half century from 1810 to 1860, the population of the Old Northwest rose by a factor of twenty-eight, increasing from 4 to 25 percent of the total population of the United States.[75] In the 1810s, seven states entered the union with extremely democratic provisions in their constitutions for participation by white men, which along with increasingly liberal terms for the purchase of public lands would have proven quite attractive to those in the Northeast (particularly southern New England) who continued to endure an escalating land crisis that made transfer of a workable amount of agricultural property to one's children virtually impossible. Moreover, the growing extension of chains of trade and credit led to changes in contract law, whereby the voluntary assent of contractors served as the index of the legal legitimacy and judicial enforceability of the contract rather than its measurement against a notion of communally acceptable standards. Thus, rather than treating individual transactions as subsets of collective practice, transactors appear as singular, self-determining entities whose own will defines the terms of legally binding action. Political discourse and public policy confirmed the sense of the possibility for the exercise of unencumbered selfhood in the figuration and regulation of access to the public lands. Over the first half of the nineteenth century, the cost of purchasing territory from the federal government and the scope of what one had to buy decreased greatly, and starting in 1803 Congress began sporadically passing statutes to extend a preemptive right to those who already had settled illegally on the public domain, a concession that began to balloon in the 1830s. Such measures consistently were articulated as for the benefit of "actual settlers," meaning male-headed single families who planned to reside on and farm the land as opposed to speculators. In this way, the law helped consolidate a privileged white yeoman subjectivity as the de facto model of citizenship, with politicians from all parties circulating this image as a means of legitimizing a range of policy formulations in ways that suggested that ideal's existing normative force while also further consolidating and institutionalizing it.[76]

This kind of selfhood, then, derives less from an engagement with the "implacable *thereness*" of the landscape than through the particular kinds of inhabitance made possible through Indian policy and the Indian wars, generating modes of settler occupation that come to be legally coded and lived as the phenomenological contours of whiteness (mediated by a shifting patriarchal regime of labor and property holding). By 1850 the federal government held approximately 1.2 billion acres in public land, not including what already had been granted,[77] and *all of that land* was gained through purchase from or the removal of Native peoples.[78] The material and policy conditions that made possible the survival of yeoman subjectivity depended on the cession or coercive claiming of Native territory, and inasmuch as political and property-holding possibilities in the West helped spur the opening of suffrage in the East, the emergence of institutionally sanctioned kinds of autonomous (white, male) personhood was made possible by the potential for settlement opened by the exceptionalization of Native peoples. Political and administrative discourses characterized them as other than fully sovereign polities such that the *anomalous* status of their lands allowed for the incorporation of Indigenous territories into U.S. jurisdiction as private property—space that could *extend the shape* of emergent modes of legal self-hood. Moreover, military service functioned as a significant means of defining citizen subjectivity, serving as one of the principal ways of arguing for enfran-chisement (veterans should be able to vote) and reasons for extending it (promise of the vote if you will serve), while also operating as a central tech-nology of settlement. In addition to granting veterans of the Revolutionary War and the War of 1812 land bounties in "military districts" that could serve as buffer zones between existing settlements and Indigenous peoples farther west, the federal government used the promise of access to public lands as a tool in recruitment for the Mexican-American War in 1847, as part of an effort to shift the burden away from the military to civilians at the end of the Second Seminole War in 1842, and in 1850 to reward all those who had served in any military conflict (including against Indians) since 1790.[79] In other words, service in the military and militia over the period involved engaging in con-flict with Native peoples as well as gaining increased access to Native lands.[80]

Thus, while Thoreau decries property holding and the demands of citi-zenship, the vision he articulates of the construction of an autonomous household in the wilderness depends on interdependent dynamics of legal subject formation as they emerged over the prior several decades.[81] By the time he took up residence at Walden in the mid-1840s, this privileged norm for thinking (white male) selfhood already was circulating as a form of com-mon sense that helped shape and give momentum to his critique of debt, speculation, and bourgeois homemaking (serving as the frame through which to register his masturbatory appropriation/deviation), as well as providing a phenomenological matrix through which to experience his own act of occu-pancy in the woods. In this way, his dwelling in the "wild" enacts a mode of personhood that arises in multivectored ways out of the displacement of Native peoples and the settlement of Native lands, a dynamic that builds on the legal and economic tendencies already at play in southern New England in the wake of more than two hundred years of settler occupation. The notion of developing an *Indian-like* mode of sovereign selfhood through encounter with "Nature," then, turns the effects of the exercise of U.S. sover-eignty over Native peoples, the production of a state of exception through which to enable settler access to Indigenous lands, into the condition of possibility for Thoreau's vision of oppositional subjectivity.

In "Higher Laws," that dependence manifests itself rather directly, but in a way that transposes the politics of settlement into the experience of autonomous personhood in the "wild." The chapter begins with the famous anecdote of Thoreau having "a strange thrill of savage delight" in his desire "to seize and devour" a woodchuck due to the "wildness which he represented," and this appreciation of "wildness" arises out of practices from when he was a child. He observes, "I have owed to this employment [fishing] and to hunting, when quite young, my closest acquaintance with Nature," adding, "Fishermen, hunters, woodchoppers, and others, spending their lives in the fields and woods" are "in a peculiar sense a part of Nature themselves" (140–41). He depicts hunting as pleasurable fun alone with one's gun, offering something like a proto-masturbatory opening to possibilities for being that exceed the enervating options available in the village. To have a determinate space in which one can feel "wildness" is to inhabit place as "a savage." Yet, he argues that such feeling needs to give way to a "higher" perception, in which such impulses are channeled away from "appetite" and "sensual savors" and toward "spiritual life." He notes that "the generative energy, which, when we are loose, dissipates and makes us unclean, when we are continent invigorates and inspires us" (146). He names that process of reorientation "chastity," and this description, along with the notion of managing one's "generative energy," recalls the Grahamite insistence on the need to regulate sexual stimulation, but here, such "energy" is not redirected into the less exciting avenues of conjugal union and livelihood, instead animating a turn away from the "filth" of cleaning and preparing animal food and toward the solitary activity of "imagination" (143). The renunciation of a "sensual"/"savage" investment in meat opens the "channel of purity" in which "Man flows at once to God" (147), suggesting that the semi-masturbatory experience of "wild" pleasure while hunting gives way to the semi-masturbatory experience of "spiritual" *flow*. The one exists in a developmental relationship to the other, such that sustained "acquaintance with Nature" through hunting serves as the necessary precondition for achieving a "higher" understanding that allows one to leave off eating animals.

The kind of selfhood Thoreau suggests one ultimately wants to achieve only passes through "savage" experience as a stage. He asserts, "There is a period in the history of the individual, as of the race, when the hunters are the 'best men,' as the Algonquians called them" (142), adding, "even in civilized communities, the embryo man passes through the hunter stage of development" (143). Moreover, while the killing of animals indicates "the larva state" in "a man," "whole nations" can remain in this condition (144). If some men are "like nations" in their bounded individuation, others are part of "nations" that have failed to develop, whose *wildness* makes them "a part of Nature themselves." Such *savagery* is linked to "the Algonquins," suggesting it serves as a metonymic stand-in for Native peoples on whose homelands New England was built. Moreover, the internalization and surpassing of "savage" activities and relations as part of individual maturation translates the complex geopolitics of Native land tenure into a process of (settler) self-elaboration and development in an alegal, "boundless" space of *wildness*. If traces of Indianness appear in *House of the Seven Gables* as a "worthless" anachronism or as a "tribal" residue, here Native peoples temporally are dislocated as part of individual maturation, divorced from contemporary settler phenomenology. Hunting functioned as a dense symbol of the significant distinctions between Indigenous modes of placemaking and collective decision-making and those at play in U.S. liberal governance and the treaty system.[82] At stake in the definition and disposition of Native "hunting grounds" was the jurisdictional authority of the United States to manage lands *within* its boundaries and to define what would constitute a viable assertion of Native sovereignty and territoriality. Here, that geopolitical struggle appears as a negotiation within (settler) selfhood, as the need to redirect individual pleasure and bodily experience toward more *chaste* ends, and in this way, the institutional imperatives of U.S. legal geography serve as an unacknowledged background for the personal sensation of wildness/wilderness.

My point is less that Thoreau encounters nature through the prism of sovereign or settler selfhood than that the conceptualization of space as "Nature" depends on taking as given extant legalized processes of settlement, which provide the trajectory for oppositional expressions such as Thoreau's. The notion of "Nature" is a point at which two patterns meet: the negation of the dominant political economy in order to imagine alternative modes of being (possibilities for personhood) than those offered in it; and the positioning of Native peoplehood and geopolitics within a state of exception as they are forcibly (and anxiously) incorporated within the jurisdiction of the settler-state. The former draws on the sense of difference in the latter while reconstituting it as the phenomenological experience of "wildness." Indians, then, become the mediating vehicle for imagining an ethically grounded oppositional place of exteriority from which to stage a critique of the state. Such a

sensation of outsideness may give Thoreau ethical leverage on existing "economical and social arrangements," but how is the projection of a horizon
within such ethics predicated on settler colonialism? How does Thoreau-
vian "higher law" function as, in Merleau-Ponty's terms, a "reconstitution"
of a "perceptual tradition" built out of (ongoing) political processes through
which Native lands are made amenable to U.S. sovereignty and available
for nonnative inhabitance? What would a masturbatory experience of the
limits of normative selfhood look like if solitude and the imaginative sens-
ing of place were not shunted to an exceptional elsewhere that supposedly
insulates/differentiates the experience of personhood from implication in
the state-sanctioned dynamics of settlement?

WEAVING SELFHOOD

Addressing these questions requires first offering a clearer sense of what's
at stake in the conversion of Native space into settler potentiality as well as
in the positing of a kind of selfhood free from influence by the "dirty institutions" of the state. In "Economy," in a much commented upon passage,
Thoreau offers an anecdote of Native presence worth quoting at length:

> Not long since, a strolling Indian went to sell baskets at the house of a well-
> known lawyer in my neighborhood. "Do you wish to buy any baskets?" he
> asked. "No, we do not want any," was the reply. "What!" exclaimed the Indian
> as he went out the gate, "do you mean to starve us?" Having seen his indus-
> trious white neighbors so well off,—that the lawyer had only to weave argu-
> ments, and by some magic wealth and standing followed, he had said to
> himself; I will go into business; I will weave baskets; it is a thing which I can
> do. Thinking that when he had made the baskets he would have done his part,
> and then it would be the white man's to buy them . . . I too had woven a kind
> of basket of a delicate texture, but I had not made it worth any one's while to
> buy them. Yet not the less, in my case, did I think it worth my while to weave
> them, and instead of studying how to make it worth men's while to buy my
> baskets, I studied rather how to avoid the necessity of selling them. (12)

As many others have noted, the mention of Thoreau's "basket of a delicate
texture" likely refers to *A Week on the Concord and Merrimack Rivers*, which
he published in 1849 and which sold extremely poorly.[83] In one sense, this

story offers an allegory of the perils of authorship; although despite his injunction to "avoid the necessity of selling," the existence of *Walden* and its presence in the reader's hands suggests his failure to learn that lesson. If Thoreau describes himself as lost in "revery" in the text, his most consistent activity while at Walden was writing. While in residence at the cabin, he drafted two versions of *A Week on the Concord and Merrimack Rivers*, a version of *Walden*, a lecture based on his time at Walden, a lecture on Thomas Carlyle, and the essay "Ktaadn," about his 1846 trip to Maine.[84] Perhaps one could see the emphasis in the passage less as on avoiding "selling" per se than on "the necessity" of doing so. To be an author, from this perspective, is to cultivate a kind of independence in which one can engage in reverie and circulate the resulting textual product without depending on remuneration for one's (masturbatory) efforts. As Thomas Laqueur notes, critics of onanism often correlated it with reading and writing, since "both physiologically and morally, the solitary vice [was seen as] a special case of solitary mental work, and specifically of literary engagement" (305). He adds, "Private reading also bore all the marks of masturbatory danger: privacy and secrecy, of course, but also the engagement of the imagination, self-absorption, and freedom from social constraint" (314). The act of writing can be understood as an extension of an autoerotic giving oneself over to imagination and an investment in a kind of self-speculation, exploring how one can "weave" on one's own without needing buyers/readers. The solitude, mental stimulation, and distance from normative patterns of work and family feared by anti-onanists make possible the exceeding of oneself in reverie.

This lesson is precisely what "the Indian" cannot understand. Where, though, is the space of the basketmaker's autonomous self-elaboration? Where does the Indian go for such "study"? At other points in the text Indians appear as existing earlier and elsewhere (with the exception of the Penobscots camping in Concord, to which I will return), but here he sees a local Native person in the village. As Joshua David Bellin notes in *Demon of the Continent*, the passage "convert[s] a highly charged racial and economic conflict into a sly meditation on the hazards and triumphs of economic independence," indicating that Thoreau cannot admit that "the institutions of the market have had significant effects on the peoples he looks to as exemplars of freedom" (66–67).[85] This moment registers the spatiality of settlement that the text regularly dissimulates/translates as the availability of

"Nature" to nonnatives. From where is this person "strolling"? Thoreau describes the lawyer and other prosperous residents as the man's "neighbors," so he must live fairly close-by. Moreover, his exclamation—"do you mean to starve us?"—indicates a collective situation, presumably one he shares with other local Indians. Who are they, and what has produced the dire circumstances that leave them at the verge of starvation?

We hear nothing of a tribe living in the vicinity, nor were there any state-recognized reservations nearby. However, a number of Native peoples persisted as such in Massachusetts despite the absence of a legally acknowledged land base.[86] In *Firsting and Lasting*, Jean O'Brien observes of nineteenth-century town and county histories throughout southern New England that reading them "reveals a New England thickly populated by 'last' Indians throughout the nineteenth century, and occasionally into the twentieth" (113), suggesting continuing Native existence and modes of collective identification that remain legally invisible: "[M]ost local narrators failed (or refused) to understand the complex regional kinship networks that remained at the core of Indian identity in New England, despite the nearly complete Indian dispossession that English colonists accomplished"; "they refused to understand the persistence of Indian kinship and mobility on the landscape, not to mention their ongoing measured separateness as political entities" (117–18). The process of land loss over the course of the eighteenth century and into the nineteenth often resulted from seizures or sales to pay for debt, despite existing laws that precluded such sale of Native lands, or through the actions of legally appointed guardians who had almost unlimited authority to disburse Native resources as they saw fit.[87] This authority included an ability to squander Native funds. In a petition in 1849, those commonly known as Grafton Indians describe the account of more than two thousand pounds which had been set aside for them as part of the purchase of lands of theirs in the early seventeenth century, "which sum by order of said Court, was confided to Trustees appointed by the legislature to be held for the benefit of the grantors and their descendants for ever. The said tribe having parted with all their lands, and being placed under guardianship of persons appointed by the Government, relied on its protection and on the preservation of their property." They add that "through the negligence and want of fidelity of some of the Trustees, over whom neither the original grantors nor their descendants could have any control, the whole trust fund has been diminished so as almost to be without value and to afford no income."[88] Not only were they dependent on the "income" produced by the trust, their impoverishment was directly due to the malfeasance of government-appointed agents and the lack of any "control" over them, due to the exceptional legal status occupied by Native peoples. Thus, the idea that "the Indian" could inhabit a place apart from the market that would allow the basketmaker and others to "avoid" participation in it brackets the continuing history of settler occupation and expropriation that directly produces his *starving* condition, but even in the absence of any apparent land base for the Graftons or the "we" of whom the basketmaker speaks, they articulate themselves as an enduring collective.

However, the dependence of "the Indian" on selling baskets means that he cannot serve as a model for Thoreau's engagement with wilderness/wildness. Like other New Englanders, Thoreau distinguished between what he considered to be authentic and degraded Indians. Increasingly, true Indian identity was correlated with the notion of pure-bloodedness (as opposed to mixture with other populations, particularly people of African descent) and the retention of what were imagined to be pre-Euro-contact customs (although often based on contemporary images of Plains peoples)—a set of assumptions that "led them to deny the Indianness of Indians."[89] This perception of declension occurs despite the fact that, as indicated in Bird's report, "the uniform legislation of the State has regarded all colored persons residing upon the Indians lands, as Indians, and subject to all the disabilities of Indians" and that "the legislation of the last 180 years has recognized as Indians, all descendants of Indians residing upon Indian lands" (30, 53).[90] For Thoreau, participation in contemporary political economy meant that Indians had lost the primal purity that allowed them to index—and serve as a transit to—the space of "Nature."

This dynamic appears perhaps most directly in "Ktaadn," his 1848 essay about his 1846 trip to Maine (eventually included in the posthumously published *The Maine Woods*). At the center of the piece lies his ascent of Mt. Katahdin, known to Wabanaki peoples as "the central emergence place,"[91] but as part of the preparation for the journey and in the wake of it, Thoreau has occasion to view and interact with Penobscots. He notes while passing Indian Island, the main Penobscot settlement, "I observed some new houses among the weather-stained ones, as if the tribe had still a design upon life"

and that the church does not look properly "Abenaki" ("Good Canadian it
may be, but it is poor Indian"): "These were once a powerful tribe. Politics are all the rage with them now. I even thought that a row of wigwams,
with a dance of pow-wows, and a prisoner tortured at the stake, would be
more respectable than this" (4–5). Later, he adds, "Met face to face, these
Indians in their native woods looked like the sinister and slouching fellows
whom you meet picking up strings and paper in the streets of a city. There
is, in fact, a remarkable and unexpected resemblance between the degraded
savage and the lowest classes in a great city. The one is no more a child of
nature than the other. In the progress of degradation, the distinction of races
is soon lost" (70). Participation in "politics" seems to serve as a principal
symptom of their "degradation," marking their dislocation from "nature"
even while in "their native woods."[92] As Joanne Barker suggests in *Native Acts*,
"Keeping the threats posed by Native governance and territorial rights at bay
demands a reinforcement of racist ideologies and identificatory practices of
Native authenticity. Natives are never quite Native enough to deserve the
distinction and rights granted to them under the law" (6), or, as in Thoreau's
case, an engagement with "the law" marks them as not "quite Native enough"
to be truly Indian. Once Indians appear in some way affected by settlement,
including engaging with the legal and administrative processes through which
their homelands are translated as anomalous enclaves within the state/nation,
they cease to be fully Indian, even as *Indianness* remains available as a topos
for the spatiality of *wildness*. In the pages immediately following the discussion of the "degraded savage[s]," Thoreau describes nonnative movement
"here on the edge of the wilderness" as living "like a primitive man," as wear-
ing "the red face of man": "The very timber and boards, and shingles, of
which our houses are made, grew but yesterday in a wilderness where the
Indian still hunts and the moose runs wild" (70–73). The *politics* by which
land remains Native, or by which Native peoples are dispossessed of it and
left *starving*, only can signify the loss of naturalness, but when not connected
to questions of law or sale, when apparently existing in a jurisdictional and
economic limbo, Native occupancy and land tenure bespeak a "red face of
man," a "primitive" mode of inhabitance/being/personhood from which
one might draw an ethics of "wilderness."

In the anecdote of the basketmaker, Thoreau casts the *degraded* Indian
as the figure for a wrong understanding of writing/working/weaving, positioning himself to take up the truly Indian "study" of nature—of how to live

(onanistically) in a state of exception free from "present economical and social arrangements." The protest of the basketmaker in the name of an otherwise nondescript collective can be considered as a "quasi-event." In *Economies of Abandonment*, Elizabeth Povinelli defines that concept as circumstances in which "nothing rises to the level of an event let alone a crisis" (4), suggesting that such conditions require "legal forms of bad faith"—"not being killed by the state in any way that would be recognizable as state killing" (118).[93] Moreover, when groups develop "alternative social projects" as means of enduring and surviving in these conditions, that labor can create possibilities for critiquing dominant political economy, but having to live in zones of abjection and exhaustion "create[s] such reduced conditions of life that the political desire for them to spawn or foster alternative worlds can seem naïve at best and sadistic at worst" (128). For Thoreau, Indians indicate an "alternative world" of wildness, translating their occupancy in their homelands as the potential for remaking (nonnative) personhood through union with "Nature." However, addressing the political and economic conditions that exceptionalize indigeneity—that produce the quasi-events of impoverishment, debt, diaspora, and dislocation for Native peoples in New England—can only sully the (masturbatory) political desire for an elsewhere beyond normative citizenship. As an act of self-elaboration in solitude, Thoreau's writing/weaving must be other than that of "the lawyer," his "arguments," and the "magic wealth" they produce,[94] and inasmuch as the Indian's basket making can be understood as a response to the lawyer, as occurring within and animated by the circumstances produced through the latter's weaving, it must be "degraded."

However, what lesson might Thoreau learn about the relation between selfhood, space, and law from the basketmaker? What would such an ethics look like? In this vein, William Apess's *Indian Nullification* offers a powerful account and critique of the effects of settler law on Native personhood and dwelling in Massachusetts, emphasizing how nonnative experiences of selfhood and inhabitance need to be contextualized within an ongoing history of expropriation.[95] The text primarily details the assertion by the Mashpees, the largest tribe in Massachusetts holding the most land, of authority over their own governance and land in their late spring/early summer "revolt" in 1833. They refused to let nonnatives continue to log their territory (on Cape Cod in Barnstable County), insisted that the guardianship over them be removed, and demanded that Phineas Fish (the minister paid for by funds from Harvard) be removed and control over the meeting house and the approximately 450 acres he claimed as part of his parsonage be returned to them.[96] As part of chronicling this struggle, the text offers a genealogy of Mashpee subjection to English and then American law,[97] including the passage of the act of 1788 creating a board of five overseers appointed by the governor who were "vested with full power to regulate the police of the plantation; to establish rules for managing the affairs, interests and concerns of the Indians and inhabitants"; and to "improve and lease the lands of the Indians." "No lease, covenant, bond or bargain, or contract in writing" was considered valid "unless approved by the Overseer or guardian" (209).[98] Creating a similar kind of administration as that for other Indian "plantations" in the state, that act also prevented Mashpees from cutting trees, gathering wood or hay, taking any minerals or grain, or planting and improving land unless authorized by the overseers. An act in 1819 gave the guardians additional powers to bind out members of the tribe for up to three years for habitual drunkenness or idleness, allowing guardians to apply the attendant earnings to whatever purpose they thought proper (210).

More than detailing the specific statutory scheme governing the Mashpee tribe, the text explores how this legal regime has affected the Mashpees as a people, as well as other Native peoples. They cannot take up a place outside "politics," since they are constrained to occupy their territory in ways consistent with state law. Apess insists, "[W]hat makes the robbery of my wronged race more grievous is that it is sanctioned by legal enactments" (214). Further, "the Indians are enforced by the laws which deprive them of the use of their own lands to pay a heavy tax, from which they derive no benefit" (188), which instead funds the guardians, the teachers of a school who have not taught them, and the minister who will not preach to them. They do not occupy an exterior space, but offer an intensified example of the kind of intrusion and encumbrance Thoreau seeks to avoid/defer through his movement to the "woods." The potential for Mashpee placemaking remains contingent on "legal enactments," the weavings of lawyers and officials. However, in addition to mapping the administrative grids through which Mashpee landedness must be lived, Apess uses his act of writing to explore the effect of this imposed settler geography on Mashpee selfhood. He observes, "If the reader will take the trouble to examine the laws regarding the Mashpees, he will see those causes of the inevitable and melancholy effect and, I am sure, will come to the conclusion that any people living under them must necessarily be degraded" (200). As opposed to understanding Native peoples as falling away from a precontact ideal of wildness, Apess locates degradation as a function of institutionalized invasion and regulation, which produces a general "melancholy" affecting Native persons' and peoples' sense of themselves and interaction with each other.

This feeling of loss is not for a pure or innocent contact with the wilderness, in which one can "study" how not to be dependent on the market or embroiled in politics, but for the inhabitance of their homelands as a polity not subjected to settler intervention and oversight. Apess asserts, "[W]e see the Indian driven farther and farther by inhuman legislation and wars, and all to enrich a people who call themselves Christians" (213). The text begins with a statement signed by three Mashpee leaders, "The red children of the soil of America address themselves to the descendants of the pale men who came across the big waters to seek among them a refuge from tyranny and persecution," adding as a response to charges that Apess is an outsider who simply came to Mashpee to stir up trouble, "White men are the only persons who have imposed on us" (166). The possibility for settler emancipation from "tyranny," which Thoreau extends to the system of debt in which property holders and wage workers labor, comes through the continuing *imposition* on Native peoples and lands by the "descendants" of the early settlers, who persist in articulating their "enrich[ment]" at the hands of Indians as a benevolent project of uplift.[99] Apess quotes from an article by Benjamin Hallett, a local lawyer and editor who advocated for greater Mashpee self-determination, "It is in the interest of too many to keep the Indians degraded" (201), and Apess suggests, "If we are to judge of the future by experience of the past, we may reasonably suppose that they would profit the tribe by getting possession of their property and making their own advantage of it" (203), adding that in the wake of the Revolution "the whites were no sooner free themselves, than they enslaved the poor Indians" (239).[100] While one could understand Thoreau as arguing against such "possession" in his condemnation of "property" more broadly, the possibility of *freeing* whites from enervating financial dependencies through occupation of the woods necessitates settler access to Native lands, an oppositional "future" or possibility that seems much like Indigenous peoples' "experience of the past." Nonnative *interests* lie in producing the very *degradation* Thoreau bemoans, in order to open a space for the "alternative social project" of masturbatory personhood.

Apess's act of writing, then, does not respond to the discourses of law by constructing a space of nonfungible personhood outside or beyond the political economy of "selling." Instead, the text seeks to *nullify* the legitimacy of the law by tracking its process of emergence, thereby denaturalizing its apparent givenness as a way of ordering and experiencing the landscape. The significance of such a challenge to the state's authority to superintend Native peoples is marked by the rather overdetermined response to the Mashpees' "assertion and resumption of [their] rights" (181): "Many of the advocates of oppression become clamorous, on hearing the truth from a simple Indian's lips," and "some feared that an insurrection might break out among the colored people, in which blood might be shed" (177). This fear achieves its most extreme expression in the governor's suggestion that "to secure the Commonwealth from danger" he might have "to call out perhaps fifty or sixty thousand militia," protecting the nonnative population from perhaps "a hundred fighting men and fifteen or twenty rusty guns" (183).

However, in contesting the authority of the state to hold Indians in "bondage" as wards to government appointed guardians, Apess and the Mashpees do not seek to suspend the legal recognition of Native territories, including the statutes that prevent the sale of reservation land to anyone but fellow tribe members. Petitions from Native peoples in Massachusetts in the 1840s and 1850s indicate a range of efforts to mobilize government action on behalf of protecting "Indian" lands and to address the effects of guardian malfeasance, including the following: the Dudley Indians calling in 1840 for a law that would actually empower guardians and overseers to remove white trespassers; the Fall River Indians in 1846 insisting on the need for a law that would allow for the removal of an incompetent guardian; the request in 1851 of the Chappequiddic Indians for the building of a fence to separate their lands from those of the whites; and the request in 1855 by the Gay Head Indians for a proper survey of the boundary between the reservation and the town of Chilmark.[101] As Earle observes of the perspective of plantation tribes generally in his 1861 report, "they have come to look upon the laws which place them in this position, as their only safeguard from entire ruin," adding, "[I]f those on the larger plantations . . . were placed at once on the same legal footing as other inhabitants of the Commonwealth . . . the

patrimony of many, if not the most of them would soon be gone" (128).[102]
Such anxiety about the potential loss of all institutional acknowledgment for
Indigenous collectivities indexes the broader pattern of systemic destitution
and displacement to which Native people in southern New England had
been subjected for generations—the web of state-sanctioned racialization,
exploitation, exceptionalization, and debt that provides the unacknowledged background for Thoreau's anecdote of the Indian basketmaker (who
appears not even to have the protections of a state-recognized reservation).

In *Indian Nullification*, whites appear as the inheritors of an ongoing project of occupation and expropriation. In Thoreau's observations about the
basketmaker, they occupy parallel positions ("I too had woven a kind of basket") in which he can learn a lesson of independence lost on the unnamed
"Indian." What would it mean for him to see the act of writing/weaving not
as an opportunity to sublate the Indian, taking up the latter's project and bet-
tering it in a space of exception ordered around Indigenous landedness from
which Native peoples have been vacated, but as a chance to understand his
relation to this person (and the "us" who are "starv[ing]") as the condition
for an investigation into the contours and phenomenology of settler selfhood? As opposed to an escape into a fantasy space divorced from the reality
in which one is situated, the scenes of onanistic pleasure in *Walden* indicate
the potential for an increased connection to and awareness of one's location,
of the specificity of place. Thoreau's vision of masturbatory personhood gestures toward a disjunction in daily experience that enables an altered relation to one's surroundings in which the landscape ceases to be familiar.

Walden suggests that withdrawal, reverie, and the deviation from normative bodily habit can produce a palpable sense of disorientation in which
one's location in space becomes the object of embodied contemplation,
attending to the place of one's body in the geography of the everyday and the
historical process through which the sensation of familiarity is produced.
Thoreau notes in the "Conclusion," "I left the woods for as good a reason
as I went there. . . . It is remarkable how easily and insensibly we fall into
a particular route, and make a beaten track for ourselves," adding, "How
worn and dusty, then, must be the highways of the world, how deep the ruts
of tradition and conformity" (215–16). Introducing a similar idea earlier, he
observes in "The Village," "if we go beyond our usual course we still carry in
our minds the bearing of some neighboring cape . . . till we are completely

lost, or turned round. . . . Not till we are lost, in other words, not till we have lost the world, do we begin to find ourselves, and realize where we are and the infinite extent of our relations" (115). Getting "lost," losing one's bearings and becoming "turned round" within an otherwise well-known space, opens the potential for a new sense not only of the place but of one's position within it—"where we are."[103] The taken-for-granted cartography of the everyday becomes invested with new significance having been alienated from its status as the inert milieu of one's routine. In "Where I Lived, and What I Lived For," Thoreau insists that "we inhabitants of New England live this mean life that we do because our vision does not penetrate the surface of things. We think that *is* which *appears* to be. If a man should walk through this town . . . [and] give us an account of the realities he beheld there, we should not recognize the place in his description" (65). As opposed to the sense of withdrawal into a space divorced from contemporary political economy, the text also proposes a reframing of perspective, altering the physical sense of relation to one's surroundings via a (masturbatory) suspension of their givenness. The self becomes the site for an imaginative break with routine that produces a sensuous reorientation (getting "turned round"). The critical project of the text appears here less as locating a space apart in which to discover the fullness of the self than as the making alien of an already occupied place, such that "we should not recognize" it.

Walden's implicit suspicion of the anti-onanist equation of corporeality and nationality allows the experience of disorientation in space also to serve as a disjunction in the narrative of national territoriality. As such, it opens the potential for an engagement with the circumstances of the basketmaker—and, in Apess's terms, the "legal enactments" that produce his "degradation"—rather than envisioning a retreat to an Indianized space of exception (which Thoreau can inhabit better and more fully). However, accessing such potential requires integrating the "strolling Indian" and his experience of starvation into Thoreau's phenomenal engagement with his environment, or rather recalibrating Thoreau's ways of holistically composing an environment, in Merleau-Ponty's terms a "field of possibility" for future action, out of the sensations and material geographies of everyday perception. Reverie suggests a suspension in the normal processing of sense data, a shifted relation to one's surroundings that might allow one to experience oneself and one's relation to place differently, partially through an imaginative disruption of extant modes of constancy that opens one to new (and potentially fairly unsettling) forms of feeling.

This prospective shift, and the ways the text thwarts it through *Indianiza-tion*, appear quite powerfully in the Penobscot example Thoreau offers in "Economy." He notes, "I have seen Penobscot Indians, in this town, living in tents of thin cotton cloth, while the snow was nearly a foot deep around them," and he contrasts the apparent heartiness and cheapness of Indian wigwams, and the kinds of ready lodging available in "the savage state" generally, to the relative scarcity of those who "own a shelter" "in modern civilized society" (19–20). Penobscots appear as a model of thrift, providing a paradigm though which to approach the absence of security and profusion of debt among Thoreau's neighbors. Their presence becomes instructive of how to live in less costly ways by attending to "savage" means of inhabitance in "Nature," implicitly rendered as an eruption into the present of lifeways from some prehistoric past. The text's staging of this relation constitutes something like temporal drag, Thoreau's queer embrace of that which is supposed to have been "forgotten, abandoned, discredited, or otherwise effaced."[104] That sensation of reaching across time, though, displaces the question of territoriality in the present. As discussed at length in the previous chapter, the Penobscots continue to exist as a polity in the moment of Thoreau's writing (and of mine), and given that Concord is more than 250 miles from Penobscot lands in Maine, what are they doing there? Thoreau never asks. However, groups of Penobscots regularly visited eastern and southeastern Massachusetts in the 1840s, selling baskets as well as offering other "public performances and artifacts of *Indianness*" that "grew in importance with the tourist industry."[105] What Thoreau takes as emblematic of authentic Indians' separation from "civilized society," such that they can serve as a transit into the wilderness, more likely illustrates one way Native peoples have adapted to the political economy of settler presence. Not only might Penobscots have longstanding relationships with other Native persons and peoples in the area,[106] but their ways of making possible continued existence as Indigenous people, despite the continued encroachment on their lands (as discussed in chapter 2), entails a more flexible understanding of what constitutes Native place than that allowed by the reservation and guardian system.[107] To engage with their mappings of New England, or those of the basketmaker and the "us" he invokes, would require offering a different

answer to the question "where it was then that *I* lived." That (masturbatory) project of reassessing one's location and experience of emplaced personhood—exceeding the self in reverie—would engender an ethics more
attuned to the ongoing implications of settlement than one that translates
those legacies and effects as the condition for thinking an escape from capitalist political economy, in which one can envision having a "horizon . . . all
to myself."

Moreover, as suggested earlier, Thoreau himself knew quite well about
the continued existence of Penobscot people, given his visits to Old Town
as part of his trips to Maine.[108] Merleau-Ponty suggests, "The *person who*
perceives is not spread out before himself as a consciousness must be; he
has historical density, he takes up a perceptual tradition" (277). Thoreau's
personal "historical density," which includes awareness of the Penobscots
and that "politics are all the rage with them now,"[109] does not eventuate in an
inclusion of that fact into his representation of them, and Native peoples
more broadly, in *Walden*. How does that knowledge go missing? Put another
way, what would it mean to incorporate it into the text's vision of an autonomous relation with the wilderness? His previous contact with Penobscots
gets edited out as not meaningful in his articulation of a model of (sovereign)
selfhood, functioning as insignificant excess in the "perceptual tradition"
through which he engages Indigenous persons and landedness. If "histories
shape 'what' surfaces,"[110] the history of casting Native peoples as aberration (including, in Jean O'Brien's terms, through discourses of "firsting" and
"lasting") leads to the nonsurfacing in Thoreau's account of the relation
between the people he views in Concord and the political struggles occurring in the Penobscot homeland, as well as deferring the implications of
such presence and conflict for understanding nonnative inhabitance as settlement. Beth Freeman suggests in *Time Binds* that "the messiest thing about
being queer" is "the actual meeting of bodies with other bodies and with
objects" (xxi), and that very *messiness*, and the potential for a reoriented
sense of place and engagement with the contours of settler phenomenology,
is excised from *Walden* in ways that produce the sensation of a sovereign "I"
who can return to an estranged sense of the village after sojourning in the
exceptional space of the wilderness.

However, thinking at the limits of the self who can occupy place in this
way reveals how the experience of *independence* rests on the process of

making that land available for settler inhabitation, including the mobilization of Lockean discourses of "waste" discussed in the previous chapter. As
Michael Warner argues in "*Walden's* Erotic Economy," "Always accompanying Thoreau's self-intergrating asceticism . . . is a second resensualizing and
self-dissolving moment" (161), and that dialectic can be understood in terms
of Thoreau's double relation to "filth" and "impurity"—"have no waste;
enjoy your waste" (163)—which marks the text's continued dependence on
the bourgeois modes of personhood that produce the "self" that (pleasur-
ably) can be dissolved (171). Extending this point, I want to suggest that
the legal logics that produce Native land as "waste" awaiting proper occupancy provide the context in which, in *Walden's* terms, Thoreau can "enjoy
the land" as a space of self-dissolution—of merger with "Nature."[111] To ask
about the conditions of possibility for that sensation, the materials out of
which it is woven, involves *turning round* in order to provide "an account of
the realities" that (re)construct the wilderness as such and, thus, the forms
of selfhood experienced there.

Reverie, then, can be conceptualized less as a means of experiencing and
writing a geographical seclusion for which Indians are the imaginative vehicle than as an expression of the embodied disorientation produced by con-
fronting Native presence and/or the ongoing terms of settler occupation as
a feature of the social landscape in the present. Thoreau insists, "We need
to witness our limits transgressed, and some life pasturing freely, where we
never wander" (212), and he also observes, "I fear chiefly lest my expression
may not be *extra-vagant* enough, may not wander far enough beyond the
narrow limits of my daily experience" (216).[112] If not cast in terms of entry
into an elsewhere, the "limits of my daily experience" might refer to the contours of quotidian (settler) personhood and dwelling, especially as oriented
and given trajectory by law and policy. In this sense, solitude can be re-
thought as a tactical disengagement from normative sociality (including the
routines of wage-work and homemaking) that enables an investigation of
how available experiences of subjectivity are woven from extant modes of
placemaking (the exercise of settler sovereignty). In fact, although *Walden*
presents Thoreau's experience with his own "basket of a delicate texture"
(*A Week*) as the occasion for learning how to "avoid the necessity of selling them," the debt that attended the failure of that book due to Thoreau's
responsibility for the unsold majority of the run actually precipitated his

entry into professional surveying, which served as his main source of income for the rest of his life,[113] so that his own acts of weaving/writing engender a greater familiarity with the legal landscape of property, providing a very clear sense of the ways he and his survival are enmeshed with the official cartography of ownership.

Thus, the idea of "wander[ing]" "beyond the narrow limits of . . . daily experience" can mean coming to see the (legal) "realities" of place and personhood occluded in the phenomenology of everyday life—that serve as the background that allows for lived sensations of selfhood to emerge.[114] As Apess suggests in *Indian Nullification*, Native people(s) remain quite palpably aware of the quotidian efficacy of the state's presence in their routine sociality and placemaking, particularly with respect to how "the laws . . . deprive them of the use of their own lands" (188). Thoreau suggests that the basketmaker thought that "when he had made the baskets . . . it would be the white man's [part] to buy them." While Thoreau interprets that idea as a profound misunderstanding of the dynamics of the market, it resonates with the observation in the Earle report that Indians in Massachusetts "have a vague idea that the State has large funds drawn from the sale of lands which would have been theirs, and that this belongs to them as a portion of the interest of the proceeds, or that the State has in some other way become obligated to their ancestors, so that whatever they receive is but a just due, for which the State has received an ample equivalent" (13). Although speaking specifically about those tribes who still receive funds from the state, this comment intimates a sense on the part of Native people(s) not only that their ability to live in their homelands remains deeply affected by state policies but that the state's wealth and existence as such depends on having claimed "land which would have been theirs" and that history of expropriation means that the state bears to them an enduring debt and obligation. As discussed earlier, Thoreau characterizes those to whom farms have been bequeathed as "serfs of the soil" (2), but in seeking to avoid that debt-inducing and enervating condition, in which one is "anchored to a house or farm" (38), he does not consider to what the inheritance of citizenship might "anchor" him or the ways his *emancipation* from "encumbrances" might be predicated on a reiteration of the exceptionalization and voiding of Native sovereignty.

In *Thoreau's Nature*, Jane Bennett argues, "Before disenchanting America, Thoreau inoculates the reader with an undisturbed version of another idealization—Nature" (120). She suggests that the appeal to a "myth" of "Nature" allows for him to draw on his readers' existing sentiments in ways that seek to open them toward "wildness"—"to respect that which resists or exceeds conventional cultural impositions of form" (xxii). However, if "Nature" serves as a crucial "idealization" through which to facilitate critique of U.S. political economy, what ideas, practices, and mappings does that concept reinscribe? What sort of spatiality and selfhood does such an inoculation engender? "Nature" allows for the imagination of modes of being that defy the debt-inducing and enervating forms of labor, homemaking, and patriotic submission that *Walden* suggests characterize routine life in Concord, and the nation more broadly. As against the financial and attendant physical commitments that arise due to investment in property holding and bourgeois family-formation, Thoreau posits something of a queer retreat into the wilderness, by which to enjoy the land and evade the "dirty institutions" of the state. In promoting a bachelor's life in the wilderness, *Walden* upends anti-onanist warnings about the damage to one's health and welfare that comes from "*amorous reveries*." Thoreau makes reverie, and associated forms of apparently unproductive and wasteful activity, into the prism through which to recast normative personhood, emphasizing the *dissipating* consequences of conventional forms of sociality (including marriage) and arguing for the "wholesome" effects of solitude in providing space that liberates the imagination.

 Walden presents retreat into the natural world, and greater intimacy with it, as offering a sustaining alternative to obedience to the supposedly natural laws of self-management and deferral articulated in dominant accounts of proper social order. In the wilderness, a person can discover a kind of selfhood that is nation-like in its autonomy from the demands of law and the market, extending itself in space in ways that suggest the exertion of something akin to sovereignty—although stripped of the latter's sense either of an administrative regime or of competition with the encompassing sovereignty of the nation. However, what exactly constitutes the space of "Nature" as such? While offered as a self-evident designation of what remains outside the affectations, intrusions, and unhealthful commitments of "present economical and social arrangements," its ability to signify the absence of encumbrance (contentless forms of wildness, purity, innocence) suggests that it less indicates an actual locale with particular properties than operates as a form of negation, a placeholder for the possibility of an extrapolitical elsewhere to which one might retreat in order to live out a life of reverie. In its function as a space of exception, "Nature" can be understood as marking the trace of prior Native sovereignty, especially given that the figure of the Indian serves as the privileged means for indicating Thoreau's entry into and occupancy of it. That topos takes up the anomalousness already attributed to Native polities and lands—as nonnational, yet not foreign, islands lying within the acknowledged boundaries of the state/nation—and remakes it as a way of envisioning the potential for a kind of alegal inhabitance in which white men can discover a healthful personhood emancipated from cycles of dependence, sale, and effeminized domesticity. The idea of a fully self-determining (white male) subject who can engage with others as an independent entity, which serves as the background for the text's account of dreaming toward wholeness in the wilderness, can be understood as a reiterated effect of shifts in (white male) legal subjectivity over the prior half-century. The incorporation of Native territories as "public lands," attendant emigration to the West and boom economies there, and the reverberating effects of those processes on life in southern New England (struggling to retain population and suffering from an intensifying land crisis several generations old) lie at the heart of the emergence of the modes of personhood that orient Thoreau's account. The space of the "woods," with its savage/Indian traces, serves as an imaginative site that *extends the shape* of such normative settler selfhood, and it does so in ways that cast the latter as arising from an extrajuridical (queer) experience of wildness.

Thoureau's account of Indianized liberation and wholeness in the wilderness refers to actual Native people either as models of thrift, simplicity, and distance or as a degraded failure in their inability to understand the need for autonomy from the market. From this perspective, reverie marks a disassociation that enables a kind of weaving/writing not dominated by the imperatives of pursuing "wealth and standing" (in contrast to both the basketmaker and the lawyer). However, what are the implications of an ethics that draws on Native people(s) as an example of how to occupy an ajurisdictional space of exception while disowning any need to attend to the varied forms of abjection produced for Indigenous peoples in New England by their abandonment to such a legal limbo? How does the potential for settler freedom in "Nature" depend both conceptually and materially on the on-going and escalating immiseration of peoples like the Mashpees and the Penobscots, and what might a masturbatory ethics attentive to that problem look like? The question is how to understand, in Povinelli's terms, the "alter-native social projects" engendered by Indigenous survival amid institution-alized settler mappings and their exceptionalization of Native sovereignty and territoriality. As Apess suggests in *Indian Nullification*, "[i]t seems to have been usually the object to seat the Indians between two stools, in order that they might fall to the ground, by breaking up their government and forms of society, without giving them any others in their place" (230). At times, Thoreau aligns the imaginative power of reverie with remoteness, binding the possibility of a sensuous experience of the limits of dominant categories and conventions to a sovereign dwelling in a space beyond law, but at other moments in *Walden*, he stages the feeling of solitude and "dreaming awake" as a disorientation in which one's habituated sense of place becomes alien, opening to a remapping of the local geography and one's position within it.

This sensuous experience of becoming "lost" in an area one knows well suggests that the rupture of ordinary routine promised by onanist disengage-ment from "present social and economical arrangements" might not require a withdrawal into a space of wildness. Instead, the process of "witness[ing] our own limits transgressed" might entail a sudden coming-to-awareness of the conditions of settler selfhood, its inscription within a legal landscape in which Native peoples are dislocated and left to "starve." Might the encounter with the basketmaker and the Penobscots prompt less an assessment of them against an authenticating standard, or a temporal displacement of them as residue from a bygone era, than an investigation of Thoreau's own ease of merger with the space of the wilderness from which Indians have been exiled? Becoming conscious of that phenomenology of settlement, and the implicit ethics of exceptionalization and occupation that it enacts, involves a relin-quishing of the notion of a sovereign selfhood existing in a place apart. Instead, the celebration of waste and of unproductive activity, of a break from the quotidian protocols of the state and its logics of property and citizenship, opens onto a recognition of enduring Native presence within contemporary political economy. Such an awareness further highlights the effaced history of imperial superintendence and displacement—the management, translation, and erasure of Indigenous sovereignties—that provides the enframing con-dition of possibility for the sense of settler escape into the wilderness.

4

DREAMING OF
URBAN DISPERSION

Aristocratic Genealogy and
Indian Rurality in *Pierre*

O ver the first half of the nineteenth century, especially in the wake of
the War of 1812 and the completion of the Erie Canal in 1825, New
York City emerged as perhaps the single most important commercial and
trade center in the United States.[1] Along with its increased significance within
regional, national, and international economies came a massive growth in
population that also produced a steady increase in the gap between workers
and the wealthy, engendering a range of socialisms—many of which called
for an alteration in the distribution of land. Reformers understood the cycle
of impoverishment and exploitation in the city as depending on the legal
terms of ownership and sale that structure occupancy outside of it, which
were being challenged by those in the country as well. Starting in 1839,
tenants on manors in the Albany region, the titles for which dated back to
Dutch claims from the seventeenth century, began an organized campaign
of resistance that lasted for more than two decades—the Anti-Rent movement. Those participating in this struggle often engaged in forms of armed
resistance by posing as "Indians." Involving thousands of participants, the
movement reached its peak in the mid- to late 1840s, periodically bursting
into popular view through extensive newspaper coverage and serving as a
major force in state politics for the better part of a decade.[2] In *Pierre*, Herman
Melville also repudiates the manorial system and its genealogical inequities.
Quite early in the novel he presents the "Patroons," as the owners of the
manors were called, as more than willing to use violence to support their
lawful interests and to secure the rents to which those claims entitle them,

mobilizing the state militia as an army against upstart tenants. The narrator observes of patroon claims, "Ranges of mountains, high as Ben Nevis or Snowdon, are their walls, and regular armies, with staffs of officers, crossing rivers with artillery, and marching through primeval woods, and threading vast rocky defiles, have been sent out to distrain upon three thousand farmer-tenants of one landlord, at a blow" (11). The eponymous Pierre Glendinning, the latest prospective inheritor of one such estate ("Saddle Meadows"), appears blissfully unaware of the force necessary to maintain his family's wealth against those who work the land and provide his means of support. Melville himself would have been well aware of these armed struggles given not only his family's residence in the vicinity of Albany throughout the period of greatest tension but the fact that his mother descended from the Van Rensselaers, the wealthiest and longest-standing of the patroons and the ones whose efforts to "distrain" residents in the late 1830s first gave rise to the Anti-Rent movement.[3]

However, while consistently casting the Glendinnings and those of their ilk as embedded in a generationally iterative project of exploitation and expropriation, *Pierre* does not offer a more just paradigm for occupancy. Unlike those in New York City advocating for land reform in the mid-nineteenth century, such as Horace Greeley and George Henry Evans, Melville neither proposes a rethinking of property law nor connects the legal contours of tenant struggle at play upstate to the conditions of laborers in urban space. Once Pierre discovers Isabel, whom he believes to be his illegitimate sister, he and the novel flee to an unnamed metropolis for which New York City provides the de facto referent, largely leaving aside the drama of title in/to the countryside and portraying the city as a site in which to enact ways of being at odds with the legalized aristocratic order in the country. Scholars have explored the violence of inheritance at Saddle Meadows,[4] as well as the novel's engagement with life in the city (reflective of Melville's own periods of residence there),[5] but they have not addressed the significance of the absence of a new vision of landedness in the country and the attendant work performed by the text's removal to the city. Rather than imagining a space in the wilderness freed from the constraints of existing forms of governance from which a new normative framework can emerge, either Lockean toil in the country or occupancy in nature as an exceptional elsewhere as discussed in chapters 2 and 3, *Pierre* abandons non-urban space, portraying "nature" as largely a construction of elite privilege and a zone for its expression. Instead, the text turns to the brutal atomizing anonymity of urban life as the only available alternative to the otherwise intractable entwinements of family, land, and law in the country. *Pierre* eschews a direct struggle with the legal regime of inheritance and landholding in favor of investing in the possibilities for dispersion offered by the city, less proposing a place or mode of placemaking outside existing schemas of property and jurisdiction than gesturing toward an undoing of their dominant tendencies facilitated by the density, heterogeneity, and obscurity of the cityscape.

Pierre explores the ways the genealogical structure of elite property holding in the countryside gives rise to nonnormative forms of desire and identification—incest, homoeroticism, cross-class affection, and bastardy—that themselves cannot be contained within the legal structures governing relatedness and land tenure.[6] The novel proliferates such "secrets," "mysteries," and "ambiguities" and transplants them to the city, where they gain in force. In this way, the text presents the city as a queer space that enables the implosion of the existing normative order, its ruination and collapse in which the text takes a kind of melodramatic and manic glee. Within this frame, the city operates as a relatively alegal kind of place in which the antinormative possibilities fostered by the manor system reach destructive fruition, and the novel refuses to offer a model of proper intimacy and occupancy in its stead, almost entirely bracketing bourgeois homemaking in ways that parallel the absence of an attention to land reform.[7] In doing so, Melville investigates and highlights the ethical appeal of the city's broader enabling of what Elizabeth Povinelli has called "stranger sociality"—the collapse of entrenched, particularly genealogical, connections in favor of anonymity, autonomy, and separation, understood as the predicate for (liberal) freedom.[8]

The city's somewhat entropic queer propensities appear to operate independently of the legal structures at play in the country, casting urban space as an alternative to the shaping force of law and the attendant problem of defining and determining landedness, and this desire to escape modes of state-sanctioned coercion consistently is coded in the text as a gambit to transcend *Indianness*. In addition to the violence of the patroons, the novel registers the displacement of Native peoples, periodically reminding readers of the prior presence of Indians and the role of warfare with them in the eventual assertion of title to Saddle Meadows. Thus, the current land system in the country appears as a product of multiple, and intriguingly cross-referenced, processes of state-backed violence through which a gene-alogically structured hierarchy of landholding illegitimately (re)produces itself. Yet, more than indexing an imperial moment of founding, or even the presence of specific polities and their territorialities (which in upstate New York would mean Haudenosaunee, or Iroquois, peoples),[9] the figure of the Indian in *Pierre* serves as, in Sara Ahmed's terms, a "sticky sign" that comes to encompass all forms of landedness and genealogical continuity in the country, casting the question of non-urban occupancy in its entirety as an anarchronistic, intractable, and ethically impossible muddle.[10] In *Pierre*, as in *House of the Seven Gables*, the genealogical property holding of the wealthy suggests an uncomfortably Indian tendency toward stasis and the illegitimate monopolization of resources, but for Melville, there is no means of redeeming rusticity as an alternative ethics, instead disavowing rural land-edness (associated with Native peoples) in a (settler) fantasy of urban retreat.

The shift to the metropolis serves as the condition of possibility for the dissolution of elite commitments and identifications, born in and borne from the country, but the text's endorsement of the city as a (negative) space of potential for liberation from legalized geographies of property leaves aside the historicity of New York City. Its vitality and immense growth over the prior half-century, as well as its ability to sustain an exponentially increasing population density, depended on the development of an exten-sive commercial and transportation infrastructure stretching north and west across the state and connecting the Atlantic to the Great Lakes region, which required passage through and acquisition of Haudenosaunee lands (espe-cially Oneida and Seneca territory)—a process of dispossession that per-sisted throughout the first half of the nineteenth century. The arguments marshaled by Seneca leaders and intellectuals in the period, such as Maris Bryant Pierce, indicate the force of state-sanctioned expansion needed to enable metropolitan "ambiguities" but also the persistence and scope of the (geo)politics of placemaking from which *Pierre* seeks queer escape in the city. Attending to the struggle in the 1840s for land to the north (over Anti-Rent demands for equitable settlement) and in the western portion of the state (over maintaining the Seneca reservations) highlights the stakes of the text's ethical flight from the question of landedness. Such engagement with struggles over land directs critical attention toward the elements of the novel that suggest how the queer proliferation of lineage-undoing desires in the metropolis depends on backgrounding settlement as an unaddressed but necessary precondition to the drama of urban dispersion.

INHERITING NATURE

Pierre offers a persistent critique of aristocratic landholding in the country, casting it as an extension of European modes of hierarchy. In leveling charges against proprietors upstate, the text clearly draws on elements of the Anti-Rent struggle in the vicinity of Albany, which achieved greatest coherence and visibility in the exact same period as when Melville was living in the area after he had returned from his time in the Pacific.[11] Yet, while in some sense being shaped by the force of that movement, *Pierre* takes a different trajectory, implicitly distinguishing itself not only from arguments made by Anti-Renters but from those of the promoters of land reform who aligned themselves with that movement. As opposed to their Lockean vision of natural right in which legitimate inhabitance depends on agricultural labor on the land, *Pierre* portrays non-urban space as hopelessly bound up in the legalities of elite privilege—as an ethical dead end.

Beginning with an account of the history of the Glendinnings' claims to Saddle Meadows, as well as aligning them with similarly situated patroon families in the region, the text explores the ways genealogy, legal title, and occupancy interarticulate in the experience of an elite embeddedness in the land. The narrator observes, "It has been said that the beautiful country round about Pierre appealed to very proud memories. But not only through the mere chances of things, had that fine country become ennobled by the deeds of his sires, but in Pierre's eyes, all its hills and swales seemed as sanctified through their very long uninterrupted possession by his race" (8). The "possession" does not seem to arise from particular "deeds," whether meaning actions, bills of sale, or official endorsements of ownership, instead emerging out of the very continuity of genealogy itself in ways that *sanctify* the family's control over the land.[12] The "country" becomes an extension of aristocratic "memories," and for this reason, "These far-descended Dutch meadows lie steeped in a Hindooish haze . . . Such estates seem to defy Time's tooth" in ways that "contemporize their fee-simples with eternity" (11). Melville here suggests that for Pierre the land serves as an extension of himself due to his family's generational enmeshment in the landscape. As

Sara Ahmed suggests in *Queer Phenomenology*, "Loving one's home is not about being fixed into a place, but rather it is about becoming part of a space where one has expanded one's body," "creat[ing] new folds, or new contours of what we could call livable or inhabitable space" (11), and the text traces that lived process of orientation.

However, the pacific view of the "fine country" that appears before Pierre's "eyes" clearly belies prior and ongoing forms of struggle. The status of the Glendinning tenants can be traced to particular documents, "haughty rent-deeds" which have an unlimited length that runs "so long as grass grows and water runs, which hints of a surprising eternity for a deed, and seems to make lawyer's ink as unobliterable as the sea" (11). If the claims of the patroons seem to defy history itself ("the mere chances of things"), their renters remain subject to "deeds," but ones whose terms appear equally *eternal*, an unchanging relation of subordination itself *sanctified* by "lawyer's ink." Tenants had contracts that gave them de facto control over their lands for a single life, several lives, or in perpetuity, but those same documents stipulated that, in exchange, they needed to provide rent, offer a day of service each year to the proprietor, and pay to the landlord a percentage (often a quarter) of the price of the sale of the land and improvements from one tenant to another. Failure to fulfill these conditions meant that the land reverted to the direct control of the title holder.[13] Moreover, as noted earlier, "the Patroons" defend their claims through the mobilization of "regular armies, with staffs of officers," that "have been sent out to distrain upon" their tenants (11). The recourse to military force as a way of securing property holding indicates both the repeated rupture of legalized landholding and the official investment in violence as a means of suturing official mappings to the territory against the will of the population that inhabits it. As opposed to Pierre's sense of his and his forebears' presence in this place as due to a kind of immanent genealogical development, the text presents their habitation in the country as, in Gramsci's terms, "hegemony protected by the armour of coercion" (263).

In addressing Glendinning claims, Melville interanimates tenant and Native resistance, but in ways that speak less to an endorsement of Indigenous self-determination than an unexplored dimension of tenant opposition itself. Proprietors' claims to title rest on the prior dislocation of Native peoples. The novel observes that Pierre's paternal great-grandfather took part in "an Indian battle . . . in the earlier days of the colony" over Saddle Meadows and that Pierre's paternal grandfather repelled the "repeated combined assaults of Indians, Tories, and Regulars" during the Revolution (6), earlier "in a night-scuffle in the wilderness before the Revolutionary War" having "annihilated two Indian savages by making reciprocal bludgeons of their heads" (29–30).[14] The combat with tenants, then, in a fashion reiterates the earlier struggles with Indians, a link suggested by the novel's description of the rent-deeds as running "so long as grass grows and water runs"—a phrase taken from the language of negotiation with Native peoples for land cessions.[15] As Jeffory Clymer suggests, the novel portrays "imperialist violence as the necessary precondition for private property" (183).[16]

This linkage parallels newspaper coverage of the Anti-Rent struggle (especially by those committed to the larger goals of land reform), which positioned violence against Indians as presaging the current state-sanctioned regime of property. In *Young America*, George Henry Evans depicts the origin of "Land Monopoly" in the United States as the brutal dislocation of Native peoples:[17]

> A new continent is discovered, and immediately a spirit of competition arises among European powers, who commission their captains to 'discover and CONQUER' or '*take possession of*' lands in America 'not possessed by any Christian prince.' In this thievish and murderous way the land of this State came into the hands of a few persons, who exacted of others conditions for the use of the soil, not only binding themselves, but their heirs, to pay tribute to the Land-Lords, in some cases *for ever*, and in others, *for three lives*, and for various other terms.[18]

Indians mark the first target of a will-to-domination over "lands in America," but that initial set of "thievish and murderous" acts colors the entirety of land tenure in New York. However, after the opening scene of settler occupation, implicitly presumed to have long since been completed in "this State," focus shifts to the plight of the "others" who are *bound* to perpetual toil in order to "pay tribute" to the patroons. This somewhat empty gesture toward Indigenous territoriality, in which white lessees appear to inherit Native peoples' status as the wronged dwellers on the land, can be understood as bearing the impress of the fact that, starting in 1841, Anti-Renters organized resistance to evictions and distress sales by creating cadres that they and their opponents referred to as "Indians," a movement which at its height included perhaps as many as ten thousand men.[19] Insurgents divided themselves into locally based "tribes" that acted autonomously but coordinated with each other in units at various scales (towns, counties, regions), and at each level, there was a governing "chief."[20] Although obliquely invoking indigeneity as a figure of opposition to wrongful exertion of authority over land, those who donned "Indian" garb did not express solidarity with Native peoples.[21]

While alluding to the linkage of tenants with Native peoples, *Pierre* leaves aside their *Indian* modes of resistance. While "the Patroons" called out "regular armies," the novel offers no sense of the organized opposition to which the militia was a response. When later describing Pierre as "prospectively possess[ing] the fee of several hundred farms scattered over part of two adjoining counties," the novel offers this fact as evidence of "the highly graveling doctrine and practice of the world" that "he who is already fully provided with what is necessary for him, that man shall have more, while he who is deplorably destitute of the same, he shall have taken away from him even that which he hath" (261–62). This depiction offers no hint that such "fee" might be the subject of an armed revolt as it was throughout the areas surrounding Albany for the better part of the previous decade. Even more directly, tenants appear as the abject object of landlords' will in the characterization of Pierre's mother's response to their pleas: "Those hill-side pastures, be it said, were thickly sown with a small white amaranthine flower" which the cattle do not want to eat, interfering with dairying, and "for this cause, the disheartened dairy tenants of that part of the Manor, had petitioned their lady-landlord for some abatement in their annual tribute of upland grasses." They cry out, "The small white flower, it is our bane! . . . [F]ree us from the amaranth, good lady, or be pleased to abate our rent!" (342–43).[22] Not only does this scene suggest that farmers continued to pay the "annual tribute" and "rent," but that in the face of such difficulties, their only strategy lies in plaintively petitioning the proprietor to grant them a reprieve.

The absence of tenant mobilization in *Pierre* speaks to the divergence between the normative framings of the movement and the novel: Melville's sense of the countryside as merely an extension of elite power and will. Anti-Renters presented themselves as the proper inheritors both of the legacy of the Revolution and of the labor expended by their fathers in developing the area.[23] On July 4, 1839, tenants of Rensselaerwyck gathered in Berne and adopted a Declaration of Independence that lays out their grievances as well as provides ethical justification for them.[24] They describe themselves as "inhabitants of a land of liberty and legitimate heirs of all its rights and privileges guaranteed by its Constitution and Laws" (60). Their status as citizens makes them "heirs" to certain "guaranteed" protections, casting the landlords as violators of the Constitution, but more than offering a general sense of an American ethos of land tenure violated by patroon claims, the insistence that they will not "any longer tamely surrender that freedom which we have so freely inherited from our gallant ancestors" articulates with the repeated characterization of Van Rensselaer as a "pretended proprietor of our soil" (61). Together these formulations suggest that the current tenant occupants possess a better claim to the land via *inheritance* from their "ancestors" who worked it, the term "soil" highlighting a connection to the ground through agricultural labor rather than the abstract relation of government-endorsed paper.[25] The Declaration supplements this counter-genealogical narrative of sustained tenant inhabitance with references to the war for independence. It asserts, "[W]e consider his [Stephen Van Rensselaer's] proposals in the same light that Dr. Franklin considered the act of the British Parliament imposing stamp duties on certain papers and documents used in the Colonies" (61). Such patriotic associations also appear in newspaper accounts favorable to the Anti-Rent movement, as in the description of the "Indians" as "of the tribe that made a teapot of Boston Harbor" or the observation that "the term *'lawless banditti'* applied to . . . the Anti-Renters is no worse than that of *'rebel'* applied to Gen. Washington and the Anti-Monarchists of '76."[26] From this perspective, the legal system of landholding upstate appears as a relic of patterns of authority and privilege under Great Britain against which the Revolution was fought (as in the argument made by small landholders in Maine, discussed in chapter 2). Thus, Anti-Renters implicitly cast the use of force as a form of self-defense whose moral authority rests on both the protection of lands on which their families have labored and the embodiment of the spirit of '76 in resistance to, in the Declaration's terms, a law "emanating from a foreign monarchy" (61).

Neither of these tacks gains any ground in *Pierre*.[27] Revolution in the novel points toward the absence of transformation, the maintenance of a

continuity in relations of property and their genealogical scaffolding across
the supposed political break engendered by a change in the regime.[28] Pierre's
"was a double revolutionary descent" in which his mother was "the daughter
of a general" (20), in addition to his paternal grandfather having gained
fame for the defense of "a rude but all-important stockade fort" against the
British and their allies (6): "On both sides he sprung from heroes" (20). The
Revolution becomes another moment of glory within the storied history of
patroon nobility, more "deeds of his sires" by which the "fine country" occupied by Saddle Meadows "become[s] ennobled" (8). In this way, the break
with Great Britain less reorders the terms, geographies, and hierarchies of
life in the country than *sanctifies* occupancies and titles like those of the
Glendinnings, reinforcing the government-backed legitimacy of elite landedness. Other allusions to revolutions in the text suggest that they consistently are unable to instigate change that could produce more just relations
of landedness. The novel's early comparison of patroon lineages with those
of the peerage in England specifically points to the actions of Charles II
(after the English Civil War) and George III (in the period of the American
Revolution) in sustaining the latter (9–10), and the novel observes that
upstate New York, in Samuel Otter's terms, "out-Englands England" in the
authenticity of its elite lineage (196). The superior genealogies of the landlords upstate to those created by Charles II testify not only to the reversal
of the revolution in England in the seventeenth century but to the failure
of those revolutionaries' compatriots to generate a new order in the New
World. In addition, a group that includes the woman readers are led to
believe is Isabel's mother "were forced to fly from their native land, because
of the cruel, blood-shedding times there," which Pierre guesses refers to "the
French Revolution."[29] When telling Pierre of his father's youthful exploits in
the city, and apparent courting of this woman, Aunt Dorothea notes rumors
that this woman was "of the noblest birth, and some ways allied to the royal
family" (75–76), suggesting the she was one of the deposed aristocracy. The
novel implicitly contrasts the property-undoing ramifications of revolution
in France with those in the United States, in which elite titles like that of the
Glendinnings remained untouched.[30]

The novel also displaces the Anti-Rent strategy of claiming alternative
genealogies for the land. The story of Charlie Millthorpe, Pierre's tenant
playmate in childhood with whom he is reunited in the city, speaks to the

absence in the text of alternative possibilities for familial continuity that might provide the basis for a counterpolitics that transforms existing legalized geographies of land tenure. The text notes that "Millthorpe was the son of a very respectable farmer," but that status appears somewhat odd given the position held by his ancestors: "Though for several generations the Millthorpes had lived on the Glendinning lands, they loosely and unostentatiously traced their origin to an emigrating English Knight, who had crossed the sea in the time of the elder Charles. But that indigence which had prompted the knight to forsake his courtly country for the howling wilderness, was the only remaining hereditament left to his bedwindled descendants in the fourth and fifth remove" (275–76). Again, flight to the New World appears here as bid for refuge by fallen elites rather than as the pursuit of freedom. Charlie Millthorpe's ancestor crosses the ocean in search of wealth, but this attempt to transform his "indigence" into possibility for his descendants fails. They receive poverty as their sole "hereditament," as opposed to the rent-driven landed wealth of the patroons. The residence of generations of Millthorpes on Glendinning property has produced less a countervailing claim to it based on their actual labor in the soil than a legally sanctioned destitution for which there is no available amelioration. The fact that the Millthorpes' situation can be traced back to the era of Charles I suggests that the regime of landholding to which the they are subjected, and by which they are left destitute, has persisted virtually unchanged despite revolutions in England (including the murder of Charles himself) and against England in the war for U.S. independence. Tenant lineage in the text, therefore, serves less as an alternative framework for placemaking than a sign of the continuity of abjection in the country, made possible by the legalities of elite reproduction.

Moreover, nature in the novel does not function as a potential space for the exercise of self-sovereignty, as in *Walden*,[31] nor does it operate as a site of legitimacy and rejuvenation as in *The House of the Seven Gables*.[32] The narrator insists, "Say what some poets will, Nature is not so much her own eversweet interpreter, as the mere supplier of that cunning alphabet, whereby selecting and combining as he pleases, each man reads his own peculiar lesson according to his own peculiar mind and mood" (342). Instead of providing a set of principles that can guide behavior, and that might offer alternative norms to those currently institutionalized by law, "Nature" supplies an "alphabet" that can be rearranged to serve the interests of whatever one "pleases." It bears no inherent "lesson," but can be mobilized as part of a range of pedagogies, each viewer seizing on elements of the landscape in order to fashion a narrative that suits his "mind and mood." Further, in casting the hierarchical relations of property in the country as utterly intractable, the novel highlights the process by which they are naturalized as a feature of the landscape. The narrator indicates,

> If the grown man of taste possess not only some eye to detect the picturesque in the natural landscape, so also, has he as keen a perception of what may not unfitly be here styled, the *povertiesque* in the social landscape. To such an one, not more picturesquely conspicuous is the dismantled thatch in a painted cottage of Gainsborough, than the time-tangled and want-thinned locks of a beggar, *povertiesquely* diversifying those snug little cabinet-pictures of the world, which, exquisitely varnished and framed, are hung up in the drawing-room minds of humane men of taste[.] . . . They deny that any misery is in the world, except for the purpose of throwing the fine *povertiesque* element into its general picture. (276–77)

Seen from the perspective of men like Pierre, with "drawing-room minds" shaped by the kind of wealth and breeding that grants them "taste," the situation of people like the Millthorpes registers as the *"povertiesque"*—an extension of the picturesque that helps add liveliness and a sense of rustic authenticity when surveying the scene of rural life.[33] As Roger Hecht argues, "Melville turns the picturesque discourse inside out, exposing exactly how it masks both the oppression felt by tenant farmers and the illegitimacy of the land tenure system itself" (38). In addition to illustrating the elite denial-by-aestheticization of tenant "misery," the text here suggests that the apprehension of "the natural" remains shot through with institutionalized relations of property holding.[34]

However, even as the text tracks that ideological conversion of entrenched inequity into aesthetic appreciation of *diversity*, Melville offers no other option through which to articulate the Millthorpes' and other renters' sense of their relation to the land. The novel demonstrates how tenant genealogy gets converted into a means of legitimizing patroon authority, but Melville defers the possibility of telling a different story of non-elite descent in the country. In this way, *Pierre* brackets the implications of alternative narratives (such as those of the Anti-Renters) for characterizing legitimate inhabitance in non-urban space and for imagining the potential for alterations in the existing political economy of landholding.

Thus, while contesting the legitimacy of elite landedness, *Pierre* implicitly dismisses the movement for the redistribution of landed property that intersected with the Anti-Rent coalition.[35] Of those public intellectuals who in some fashion endorsed tenant claims, the most famous proponents of land reform were George Henry Evans and Horace Greeley.[36] Evans's repudiation of the right of the landlords to rent rests on his contention that the "fundamental error, adopted from the monarchical system" that "has remained untouched in our Constitution to this day" is "the Monopoly of the Soil," which undermines "the *Natural Right* of all men to the use of the Soil."[37] He articulates this position from within a Lockean conceptual framework in which productive use of the soil gives one the right to control over it, defending "Indian" actions as protecting "the house that your father built with his own means" and "the fields that your ancestors made out of the wilderness" while asserting the need to "resolve ourselves back into a state of nature" by "securing to every family of the State an Inalienable Freehold." He suggests, "The simple truth is, that no Patroon or any other man ever had or could have, anywhere, a right to take more land than he needed for the use of his family."[38] Similarly, Greeley declares, "Land Reform is the natural and sure basis of all Social and Industrial Melioration" (27). He insists, "By Nature's law, use and improvement can alone vest in any individual a right to call some spot of earth his own, and exclude all others from the enjoyment and benefit thereof," adding, "Man has a natural right to such a portion of the earth not already improved by others as he can cultivate and make fruitful; the act of Government is simply officious and impertinent which assumes to give him this, and it is a gross usurpation and moral nullity to undertake to give him more" (18–19).[39] Echoing the vision of natural law circulated in earlier struggles between small landholders and proprietors (such as those in Maine discussed in chapter 2), Evans and Greeley present a direct engagement with the soil through the labor of "improvement"— the carving of space "out of the wilderness" through one's toil and for one's "family"—as the normative predicate for landholding on which no "act of Government" legitimately can intrude. On this basis, both call for a legal limitation on the amount of land that can be owned by any individual, or that can be inherited if already owned, and for the government to make available to average citizens free land that they can use to provide subsistence for themselves.[40] Within the land reform movement, arguments about the proper relation to "nature" serve as the vehicle for making claims to state action, maintaining an animating confidence in the possibility of reading land, family, and rights together in ways that could provide a moral and practical alternative to the kinds of aristocratic consolidations licensed by existing law.

By contrast, *Pierre* expresses a pronounced distrust with respect to making "nature" the foundation for conceptions of proper inhabitance and political legitimacy. The text casts non-urban landedness less as a model for conceptualizing a (revolutionary) transformation in the political order, or a means of ameliorating existing forms of injustice, than as an intractable ethical dilemma that cannot so much be resolved as displaced. Once Pierre has left for the city, and has begun to write an epic that will "produc[e] some thoughtful thing of absolute Truth" (283), the narrator cautions that, despite Pierre's desire to occupy a position from which he can attain an encompassing perspective (as "the resolute traveler" believes he has found atop "the Alps"), the land offers nothing but layers of accretion: "[B]ecause Pierre began to see through the first superficiality of the world, he fondly weens he has come to the unlayered substance. But, far as any geologist has yet gone down into the world, it is found to consist of nothing but surface stratified on surface. To its axis, the world being nothing more but superinduced superficies" (284–85). Neither the territory nor longstanding emplacement in it can provide anything more than "superficies"; there is no metaphysical or normative ground to be found in a sustained relation to the literal one. From this perspective, the Lockean arguments for land reform appear as yet another "superinduced" layering upon existing political "surface[s]," yet one that takes itself for the discovery of an "unlayered substance." The novel suggests that the sociopolitical terrain of the countryside remains too densely "storied" with patroon property holding either for there to be a full recognition of the shallowness of such claims or a different lesson learned from "nature" upstate. Additionally, those particular *superficialities* are backed by the administrative and disciplinary power of the state, including the mobilization of "regular armies" who work in the service of defending the geography of the manor system. Rejecting the foundationalizing gestures in land reform discourses (including their own investment in reprosexual continuity through figures of familial provision and inheritance), the novel defers the possibility of envisioning or enacting change through any alternative mode of land tenure in the countryside. The seemingly inescapable regime of the *povertiesque* appears to foreclose the potential for imagining a form of occupancy in "nature" that could evade the institutionalized terms of elite landedness.

Moreover, beyond effacing "Indian" opposition to the landlords, thereby casting authority in the country as more unilateral and uncontested than it was, *Pierre* aligns elite property ownership and inheritance with *Indianness* in ways that present landholding itself, rather than patroonery per se, as the problem that needs to be overcome. As discussed earlier, Melville raises the specter of displaced Native peoples, suggests the violence of their dislocation, and alludes to a linkage between them and tenants through the figure of the latter's leases as lasting as "long as grass grows and water runs." The text, however, also presents the patroons and their claims as Indian-like. The novel compares the long hereditary transmission of the "Dutch Manors at the North" to the line of descent flowing from "Pocahontas the Indian Princess," passing down the "blood" of "aboriginal royalty" for "over two hundred years." Further, with respect to elite forms of land tenure upstate, the narrator remarks, "whatever one may think of the existence of such mighty lordships in the heart of a republic, and however we may wonder at their thus surviving, like Indian mounds, the Revolutionary flood, yet survive and exist they do" (11). Later, when Pierre reaffirms his repudiation of "the sumptuousness of his hereditary halls," his grandfather's resting place is characterized as an "Indian-chief grave" (principally due to the burial with him of his "ancestral sword and shield") (261). Although not extensive, such references appear when the narrator or Pierre elaborates a critique of elite property holding, such that the invocation of Indianness seems calculated to confirm and underline the odiousness of manorial society.

More specifically, these associations turn on lineage and a longstanding connection to place. The "lordships" of the landlords somewhat surprisingly have persisted into the present era despite the change in jurisdiction brought by the Revolution. The "flood" of independence failed to alter socio-spatial formations upstate, and in this way, elite control of large swaths of territory, to which other people cannot have access except on patroon terms, continues as an anachronistic feature of the landscape, thus making it analogous to "Indian mounds." The phrase refers to ceremonial centers and burial sites constructed east of the Mississippi and into the Missouri River valley over the course of more than a millennium, ending in roughly the early sixteenth century, by what have come to be called Mississippian peoples. In the late eighteenth and early nineteenth centuries, these kinds of monuments were taken by nonnatives to signify not so much evidence of enduring Indigenous political presence (and thus the limits of rightful nonnative occupancy) as a uniquely American form of ruin that marked the passing of a prior civilization, largely believed to be unrelated to those peoples present on the land at the time of sustained contact with Europeans.[41] As such, they serve in *Pierre* as a means of depicting an enduring connection to a particular location as a deadened and deadening immovability destined to consign one to irrelevance as the inscrutable remnant of a way of life long gone. Similarly, the portrayal of Pierre's grandfather as an "Indian-chief" at the site, and in the mode, of burial also correlates a significant embeddedness in place with entombment and presents that tendency as a familiarly (and familially) *Indian* one. This linkage of mortifying situatedness with social hierarchy in the figure of the "chief" articulates with the earlier allusion to "aboriginal royalty." The text creates a metonymic chain in which the two sides of the notion of sovereignty—an aristocratic structure headed by a monarch-like figure and a clearly delimited territorial domain for the exercise of his authority—are yoked to a sense of archaism and morbidity: "Indian" appears as the self-evident marker of that assemblage. To be *Indian-like* appears to signal a site of ethical impossibility, an unrecuperably undemocratic enmeshment with the land that leaves one as stuck temporally as one is spatially. Moreover, the passage of Indianness genealogically through "blood" further ties it to the lineage of patrician inheritance and an attendant (improper) sense of entitlement to the possession of extensive territory as one's birthright.

Such references are neither particularly frequent nor central to the main narrative, so what seems striking is the apparent obviousness of signaling this set of meanings through the image of the Indian. The figure appears self-evident in conveying this connotative ensemble. As discussed in chapter 2, *House of the Seven Gables* does similar work in its association of the figure of the "tribe" with oppressive forms of familially defined landedness, but there, Lockean conceptions of toil in the wilderness, such as those employed in land reform discourse, provide a means of envisioning a normative kind of inhabitance that exceeds the elite bias of existing law (even if Hawthorne appears skeptical about the possibility of realizing that vision). In *Pierre*, the *Indian* indexes the flaws of territoriality per se; the novel offers no alternative to patroon property holding and indicates the failure of revolution to break up this entrenched geography. Erasing "Indian" resistance by tenants while linking them to Native peoples via the allusion to treaties, the text presents the possession of land (and the countryside itself) as posing an insoluable dilemma. Melville, therefore, abandons the country as the site for ethical imagination in favor of an embrace of the queer possibilities of the city.

Fantasies of Metropolitan Disintegration

In its discussion of Saddle Meadows and the manor system more broadly, the novel illustrates how genealogical, territorial, and legal relations remain inextricably braided together in rural placemaking, marking the presence of an oppressive structure naturalized through/as extended familial relations. Melville positions the space of the city, though, as a counterpoint that undoes that matrix of kinship, land, and law, replacing it with the "mysteries" of personal autonomy and unregulated conduct made possible by the dynamics of urban existence. As discussed in previous chapters, Hawthorne's and Thoreau's texts suggest "nature" as a site from which to critique existing modes of political economy, particularly the escalating forms of speculation at play in the sale of public lands and the debt accrued in acquiring a household for bourgeois homemaking. Rather than finding an exterior (natural) site from which a new (or recuperated) norm might emerge, Melville highlights the possibilities for dissolution represented by the city, welcoming its tendency toward dispersion as an arevolutionary kind of ethical force, one defined by entropic and anarchic forms of negation. For *Pierre*, then, the city functions as something of an exceptional space, but that status is due to its capacity for evading and deferring the realization of normalized geographies of family, property, and legality rather than its ability to found a new normative order.

The novel's vision of the metropolis can be understood simultaneously as a queer project and as a form of settler identification driven by a "pathological relationship to Indigenous sovereignty."[42] In *Queering the Underworld*, Scott Herring notes that the city mystery genre, incredibly and increasingly popular in the mid-nineteenth century, had a clear "formula": "a narrator inspires curiosity in his middle-class audience; tells it a story of startling revelation about urban classifications in cities such as Boston, New York City, Philadelphia, Baltimore, Louisville, and New Orleans; and leaves said middle-class audience with what counts for knowledge about a criminal underworld" (5). The narrator provides a "demystifying" taxonomy for his readers in ways that indicate the proliferation of perversities within the city while also making them the objects of a manageable regime of knowledge production through which they can be contained, and in this way, such texts "contributed to what could be called a hermeneutics of sexual suspicion, a mode of analysis that seeks to expose and to explain away the sexual secrets of modern metropolitan U.S. life" (10).[43] However, in his study, Herring sets out to explore late-nineteenth-century writings that frustrate that impulse toward categorization (and, thus, implicitly toward regulation): "The closer critics examine the following texts, the less the texts reveal and the more they annoy. This is precisely their antihermeneutical point" (21); in doing so, these texts "make rotten a will-to-knowledge" (23).[44] *Pierre* engages in such a project of *annoyance*, of "spoilage and ruination,"[45] less providing insight into the mysteries of the city than emphasizing, in the text's terms, its "ambiguities" in ways that work to undo the (legal) network of family and property that sustains the violences of occupancy upstate.[46]

This investment in the dispersive queer properties of the city appears in the novel as a means of evading the ethical quagmire of landedness, itself cast as a problem of *Indianness*. Jodi Byrd argues that "Indianness becomes a site through which U.S. empire orients and replicates itself by transforming those to be colonized into 'Indians' through continual reiterations of pioneer logics, whether in the Pacific, the Caribbean, or the Middle East" (xiii), adding, "[T]he United States has used executive, legislative, and juridical means to make 'Indian' those peoples and nations who stand in the way of U.S. military and economic desires" (xx). However, in the case of *Pierre*, the attribution of Indianness indicates less the legitimacy of state-initiated or -sanctioned aggression than its illegitimacy, its role in preserving hereditary monopolistic estates that themselves are taken to be oppressive. The very desire to transcend the politics of territoriality, though, indicates unacknowledged forms of settler privilege. In "Writing off Indigenous Sovereignty," Aileen Moreton-Robinson argues that the "possessive investment in patriarchal white sovereignty is enhanced through property ownership"; it "produces affect that is encapsulated in a sense of home and place, mobilising an affirmation of a white national identity" (95). Yet *Pierre* emphasizes not a defined "sense of home and place," but the possibilities for ethical reimagination unleashed by queer deviations and ruptures from the (generational) security of familial landholding. The novel's apprehensions, though, can be understood as signaling, in Moreton-Robinson's terms, forms of "white colonial paranoia, injury[,] and worrying [that] are inextricably tied to an anxiety about dispossession" (102). Melville notes the dispossession of Indigenous peoples that makes Saddle Meadows possible, as well as the ferocity of Pierre's grandfather's assault on Native persons, without offering anything that might constitute remediation for such wrongs nor an acknowledgment of ongoing Indigenous dispossession in New York State throughout this period. That simultaneous "worrying" and foreclosure animates the novel's effort to flee "patriarchal white sovereignty" in its ethical trajectory toward the queer potentials unleashed in/by the city.[47] The mobility imagined in that shift, and in the text's powerful (if perhaps ambivalent) longing for the kinds of anonymous nomadism and "mystery" at play in the space of the city, enacts a queer kind of settler privilege.[48] The novel's desire for freedom from the genealogized geography of state-sanctioned landedness gains meaning through contrast with an *Indianized* rurality. In this way, Melville's ethical orientation toward the city depends on taking the geopolitics of settlement as a "structuring template,"[49] backgrounding the jurisdictional matrix of the settler-state and the expropriation of Indigenous lands that makes possible the urbanity toward which the text moves.

Although Pierre does not move to the city until almost two-thirds of the way through the novel, it appears quite early as an enframing perspective through which to view Saddle Meadows and the manorial system more broadly. After the dedication, the text begins by noting, "There are some strange summer mornings in the country, when he who is but a sojourner from the city shall early walk forth into the fields, and be wonder-smitten with the trance-like aspect of the green and golden world . . . [,] and all Nature, as if suddenly become conscious of her own profound mystery, and feeling no refuge from it but silence, sinks into this wonderful and indescribable repose" (3). The sense of untroubled "Nature" expressed here bespeaks the alienness of the very space being celebrated, that such "wonder" only emerges as a back-formation for one (the "sojourner") who does not actually dwell there.[50] Notably, though, this view privileges not the truth to be found in nature but its "mystery," particularly its uninterpretable "silence." Later the text further aligns this alluring inscrutability with the cityscape. When Isabel protests of life in the city that "this silence is unnatural. . . . The forests are never so still," Pierre replies, "Because brick and mortar have deeper secrets than wood or fell" (231), and the narrator observes of the street on which Pierre lives that "on Sunday, to walk through it, was like walking through an avenue of sphinxes" (269). The deferral or absence of a clear truth makes urban space attractive, as it generates a kind of unknowability ("secrets") at odds with the legalized givenness of property and inheritance in the country—a *mysteriousness* that proliferates more in the avenues Pierre traverses than in the forest. However, Melville less celebrates the metropolis as a kind of locale with its own specificity than positions it as a counterpoint, as a horizon that recedes from the kinds of claims, dynamics, and modes of enforcement at play upstate.

Rather than mapping the particular social networks that emerge in and through the city, *Pierre* revels in urbanity's capacity to disarrange patterns of kinship and the ordered sociality of the countryside, producing democratizing and unpredictable forms of atomization and anonymity. After describing Pierre's view of the landscape, and its "sanctified" status as a "possession" of "his race," the novel juxtaposes this familial and residential continuity with urban life: "In our cities families rise and burst like bubbles in a vat. For indeed the democratic element operates as a subtle acid among us, forever producing new things by corroding the old" (9). "Cities" seem less to serve as an inert setting than actively to make possible the process of "burst[ing]" and dissolving, breaking apart "families" and lines of descent and providing a "democratic" kind of "acid" that does not so much revolutionize or reform the political order as "corrod[e]" it.[51] Such dispersion of the regularities of genealogy and inheritance creates the potential for something "new" to arise, and that kind of creative destruction, and its allure for the text, reappears later in the discussion of Pierre's movement through the city. When Pierre, Isabel, and Delly first enter it, the narrator describes the street lamps as "not so much intended to dispel the general gloom, as to show some dim path leading through it, into some gloom still deeper beyond" (229), and upon leaving Isabel and Delly in order to find lodging for them, Pierre "turned out of the narrow, and dark, and death-like bye-street" only to "find himself suddenly precipitated into the not-yet-repressed noise and contention, and all the garish night-life of a vast thoroughfare, crowded and wedged by day, and even now, at this late hour, brilliant with occasional illuminations, and echoing to very many swift wheels and footfalls" (236). These passages bespeak a kind of enthralled, even titillated, horror at the illegibility of urban space, its extremes and rapid transformations and the overwhelming crush of activity and sensation. Such moments also point toward kinds of fragmentation and ruin engendered by metropolitan density—the "acid" that eats away at "old" social formations. Later, in a scene focused on Pierre's writing routine once he has settled into the Church of the Apostles (about which I will say more shortly), the narrator observes, "One in a city of hundreds of thousands of human beings, Pierre was solitary as at the Pole" (338), and feeling himself to be a "most unwilling states-prisoner of letters" in his room, Pierre at night regularly "began to bend his steps down the dark, narrow side-streets, in quest of the more secluded and mysterious tap-rooms. There he would feel a singular satisfaction, . . . eye[ing] the varied faces of the social castaways, who here had their haunts from the bitterest midnights" (340–41). The terror and squeamishness initially associated with immersion in the disorder, mayhem, and unilluminated "secrets" of urban street life becomes a source of pleasure ("satisfaction"), a desire for a thrilling sort of alienation in which one's isolation (actually made possible by the dwarfing concentration of "hundreds of thousands" in a small radius) allows for becoming a "castaway."[52]

Cumulatively, such descriptions of the disorientation produced by the city index less Pierre's perspective per se than a yearning on the part of the novel itself, a fascination amid initial apparent disgust. Urban space serves not merely as the context for the latter half of the story but as an enabling and generative actor in the process of distending and dissolving the legalized assemblage that sustains manorial property holding.[53] If the Millthorpes are consigned to the generationally iterative misery of the "povertiesque," urban space offers a break from such genealogical entrapment and emplacement, provoking forms of *contention*, *mystery*, and *seclusion* that facilitate an escape from the enduring structure of land, law, and family. In discussing

nineteenth-century city mysteries fiction, David M. Stewart observes that
scholars have underemphasized the "pleasure" such texts offer "based on the
nonproductivity of effects such as anger, weeping, and sexual arousal" (677),
and instead, he emphasizes "the relish with which people read crime literature" (681), adding, "Crime was sensationalized in the popular press, not as
something to be explained and eliminated from city life, but as a source of
mystification and intrigue that overflowed the pages of the exposé . . . and
eroticized urban experience" (684). While city mystery fiction often decries
the horrors and criminality of urban life, "we detect an exhilaration in [its]
engagement with crime that both belies and proceeds from [its] warning[s],"
"creat[ing] a kind of prurient vertigo to which the author himself seems
subject" (688–89). In its continuity with this genre, *Pierre* shares that attraction to the "vertigo" produced by metropolitan intensity and anarchy. Thus,
rather than seeking to reveal queer dimensions of the city, in the sense of
particular extant or incipient sexual subcultures,[54] the novel invests in the
notion of the city as a queer nexus, attributing to the urban a capacity to,
in Herring's terms quoted above, "ruin" the legalized order of lineage and
inheritance in ways that provide an ethical counterpoint to the violence of
Glendinning ownership and inhabitance.[55] The city's queer decompositions
define the trajectory of the novel, offering something like an urban sublime
in which the metropolis emerges as incommensurable (in many ways terri-
fyingly so) with the conventions and logics that shape life beyond it,[56] and
the country appears as a backward zone whose geographies can and must be
negated in the embrace of the democratic corrosions of the city.

The city less introduces a new regime or normative order than creates conditions for the elaboration of disruptive and dispersive propensities generated
within the familial regime of property in the country. The question of lineage and its implications for the generational transference of an estate never lie
far from the itineraries of desire in the novel. Most accounts of the novel characterize the Glendinnings as bourgeois,[57] and from that perspective, incest
appears as a violation or an intensification of the nuclear family.[58] However,
the Glendinnings are not middle class; they are part of a landed elite. In fact,
there are no middle-class families to be found anywhere in the novel.[59] Elite
property holding, conveyed through reproduction and preserved through
carefully orchestrated marital linkages, incites secrets of passion and sensation, and in this way, the text preserves something like Foucault's distinction

between "alliance" and "sexuality," discussed in chapter 1, in the sense that the question of landedness remains at the forefront at Saddle Meadows as opposed to the more mobile and polymorphous proliferation of "mysteries" in the city. However, the kinds of subjective interiority usually attributed to *sexuality* (as opposed to the calculating, wealth-preserving genealogical stratagems of *alliance*) appear in the novel in connection to (and at times to be incited by) the workings of the law of landownership and inheritance.[60]

As one of the principal "ambiguities" in the title, Isabel offers the primary, although not exclusive, queer deformation of lineage through which the novel stages the problem of managing unruly desires generated from within the genealogical order, highlighting the difficulties of defining and securing the boundaries of familial relation.[61] Several years before Isabel's appearance, Aunt Dorothea gives Pierre a portrait of Pierre Sr. painted during his youth that little resembles the official portrait of him hung in the drawing-room (72), and while contemplating it, Pierre's speculations "never voluntarily transgressed that sacred limit, where his mother's peculiar repugnance [toward the youthful portrait] began to shade off into ambiguous considerations," since "all such imaginings" on Pierre's part were "based upon the known acknowledged facts of his father's life" (82). "Ambiguous considerations" suggests relations that exist beyond the terms of the institutional nexus of legally "acknowledged" parentage and marriage, such that they cannot be determined through official designations and modes of evidence but yet still receive their affective charge through that very system. Isabel increases the number of *piercing* and *elusive* "mysteries" that surround the Glendinning family (142), producing "an ever-creeping and condensing haze of ambiguities" (151). The *ambiguity* of her relation to the Glendinnings sets the established *facticity* of familial connections against a speculative "chain of wondering," introducing a fundamental "mystery" into the calculation of relatedness. The apparent givenness of genealogy rests on the *literalizing* power of law to instantiate the real.[62] Isabel's presence, and Pierre's attachment to her, suggests that the seemingly straightforward, natural logic of descent through which Glendinning title is transmitted remains shadowed by supplementary associations, identifications, and desires. The management of genealogy produces its own "secrets," experienced and eroticized as such precisely because they do not follow the normative trajectory of elite reproduction.

The "mystery" borne by Isabel, then, functions as an intensification of kinds of desire incited by the legalized (and gendered) braiding of gene- alogy and landholding in Glendinning family formation. As many have observed, Pierre's connection to Isabel seems to follow from his relationship with his mother, with him referring to Mary Glendinning as "sister" and her calling him "brother," and the text notes his "courteous lover-like adoration" of her (16). Given the recentness of a law allowing married women to own property in the state of New York, only passed in 1848,[63] the creation of a generationally equalizing and somewhat eroticized bond between Mary and Pierre, as well as Mary's refusal to remarry in the wake of her husband's death (5), resonates with the potential of Mary to lose virtually all of the estate to Pierre as the proper inheritor. Reciprocally, his "romantic filial love" for her can be read as responsive to the fact that his father's will was never altered in the wake of his birth (57, 179). A similar dynamic can be seen in Dorothea's feelings toward her brother. Pierre becomes the "warmest and most extravagant" object of her affections due to his being "the likeness, and very soul of her brother," whom she considered "the noblest and hand- somest of brothers" (73), and when looking at the youthful portrait of her brother, she "begin[s] to think" that the subject "is looking at me, and smil- ing at me, and nodding at me" and calling out her name (79), positioning herself as the object of her brother's attractions. In light of her relative mar- ginality within the generational distribution of property,[64] her affections toward her brother and nephew, and the ways they work in and through the portrait, can be understood as incited by inheritance. Moreover, while the novel juxtaposes Isabel with Lucy, Pierre's intended of whom his family approves, what makes Lucy attractive as a mate is precisely her genealogical proximity to Pierre. Mary Glendinning says of the match, "you, Pierre, are going to be married before long . . . not to a Capulet, but to one of our own Montagues" (18), and when Lucy joins Pierre in the city, she tells him that he should describe her to Isabel as a distant relative since there is in fact "some indirect cousinship" between them (311). As Wynn Kelley argues in "*Pierre*'s Domestic Ambiguities," the "stain of incest" in the novel appears as "a necessary element of the family's house and home and has been estab- lished as a family pattern even before the advent of Isabel" (101).[65]

More than incestuous impulses, the dynamics of patroon ownership and inheritance give rise to a variety of nonnormative desires, including a range

of homoeroticisms. Scholars have focused most intently on Pierre's relation with his cousin Glendinning Stanly, whose affection as boys the novel
describes as "a love which only comes short, by one degree, of the sweetest
sentiment entertained between the sexes" (216).[66] They become somewhat
estranged as adults, especially in the wake of Glen's failed courtship of Lucy,
and when Pierre reveals his "marriage" to Isabel and leaves for the city, Glen
refuses him lodging and pretends not to know him while becoming the sole
heir of the Glendinning estate due to Mary's changing of her will. Rather
than seeing their early affection/attraction and its transformation into enmity
as pivoting around a desire for Lucy or reading Lucy as something of a narrative prop for a queer plot, we can approach their relationship, including its
homoerotic dimensions, as a function of their relative positions within the
genealogical order. Not only had Pierre "so victoriously supplanted" Glen
in the pursuit of Lucy (and the enormous wealth of her side of the family
[26]), Glen replaces Pierre in the Glendinning lineage. After Mary signs a
will making Glen her heir, Pierre experiences "something strangely akin to
that indefinable detestation which one feels for any imposter who has dared
to assume one's own name and aspect" (289). Glen has assumed Pierre's
name, and the prior potential for such substitution—the genealogical proximity that makes it possible—seems to shape their emotional inclinations
with respect to each other.

Reciprocally, the erotics surrounding the portrait of Pierre's father and
Pierre's relationship with Charlie Millthorpe suggest the ways same-sex desire in the novel also can arise out of a yearning to escape the genealogical
order of landholding, but a longing that emerges out of its terms and that
achieves expression most readily in the queer dispersions of urban space.
In *Closet Writing/Gay Reading*, James Creech offers an extended reading of
Pierre's "reveries" in front of his father's portrait that draws out the homoerotic dynamics of Pierre's gaze and suggests that Isabel functions as a coded
substitute for an attraction to other men as indicated in his attraction for the
portrait.[67] As Creech notes, Pierre's attraction to the portrait emanates from
"the eroticized spectacle of his father's illicit desire" (152), but what makes
Pierre Sr.'s possible liaison with the French emigrant "illicit" is that she cannot serve as the proper wife of the Glendinning heir. In this way, his "desire"
and the eroticization of it by both Pierre Jr. and Pierre Sr.'s cousin Winwood
(who paints the portrait without the former's knowledge) emanates from

the contravention of the legalized terms of patroon lineage, a sensual fris-
son facilitated by the "democratic" forms of corrosion at play in the city
(where the liaison takes place). Thus, if Pierre's masturbatory relation to
his father's image is certainly homoerotic, it seems less to speak to a kind of
sexual identity than a mode of relation to the manorial protocols of inheritance, a trajectory away from them, which as addressed earlier the text often
designates as "mystery" (askew with respect to the *truth* of lawful relatedness and landholding).

In addition, Charlie Millthorpe's relation with Pierre suggests the possibility for desire across class lines, amplified and given freer range by the
queer potentialities of the city. Readers first hear of Charlie as the reason
why Pierre has come to reside in the Church of the Apostles (275), and
the text indicates that after the death of his father Charlie sold virtually all
their possessions, "converting all into cash departed with his mother and sis-
ters for the city" in which he "really advanced his fortunes in a degree" by
becoming a lawyer (279–80). He indicates his distaste for matrimony, declar-
ing, "By marriage, I might contribute to the population of men, but not the
census of mind" (281). In addition to finding Pierre a place to live, Charlie
shows a strong ongoing interest in Pierre, paying off his debts and mourn-
ing somewhat uncontrollably upon learning of his death in prison (Pierre
poisoned himself in the wake of his arrest for murdering Glen Stanly)—
referring to Pierre as a "heavenly bird": "Ah, Pierre! my old companion,
Pierre;—school-mate—play-mate—friend!—Our sweet boy's walks within
the woods!" (362). Coupled with his inclination not to marry, Charlie's
devotion to Pierre, his "heavenly bird," appears fairly amatory. However,
given their initial acquaintance in the country, that attraction arises from
within the dynamics of the landlord–tenant relationship, an asymmetry that
persists in their later interactions with Charlie offering aid and resources
without expecting (or receiving) anything in return. In this way, Charlie's
attraction to Pierre cannot be separated from the naturalized hierarchies of
manorial land tenure, simultaneously eroticizing that distinction. In doing
so, his affection confounds the apparent impossibility of any relation between
them other than submission or deference, and within the metropolis, liberated from subjection to the terms of elite territoriality, Charlie achieves a
kind of self-sufficiency not available to him upstate, a transformation that
enables greater scope and momentum for his attractions toward Pierre.

The proliferation of perversions in the novel, specifically incest and homo-eroticism, illustrates how the legalized order of lineage engenders a range of "ambiguities" that diverge from the normative pattern of genealogical "truth," further intimating that the city in its separation from the sphere of institutionalized regulation at play in the rural north gives greater latitude to such tendencies. The Church of the Apostles provides an example of such potential.[68] While marveling at the conditions of the urban economy that make possible the Apostles' "precarious" living situation, the text also refers to them as "clannish" and as "organized in a peculiar society" that was "secretly suspected to have some mysterious ulterior object, vaguely connected with the absolute overturning of Church and State" (267–69). The occupation of a single building by a community seeking to reorder extant forms of political economy based on their own avant-garde spiritual principles sounds a great deal like a phalanstery, itself largely considered by those who did not identify as Associationists to be a site for the expression of aberrant desire (one whose Fourierist connotations may also be under-stood as gesturing toward the cause—and limits—of land reform).[69] Reeve Huston notes, "To conservatives throughout New York, 'abolitionism, anti-rentism, fourierism, and agrarianism' were inextricably linked" (188).[70]

If the Apostles themselves appear as a travesty of various reform move-ments, attempting to discern transcendent truth and to found a new norma-tive order rather than embracing the dispersive queer corrosion promised by metropolitan "mysteries," the Church illustrates the city's democratizing processes of mobility and upheaval. The narrator notes of the Church, "In the lower old-fashioned part of the city, in a narrow street—almost a lane—once filled with demure-looking dwellings, but now chiefly with immense and lofty warehouses of foreign importers . . . stood at this period a rather singular and ancient edifice, a relic of a more primitive time" (265). The passage highlights the transformation of the area from primarily residential to almost exclusively commercial in a fairly short period of time, casting the "edifice" as a residue of an earlier time—a "relic." As Nick Yablon argues, the "process of urban restructuring generated ruins and visions of ruin. The redevelopment of mixed-use neighborhoods into financial and retail districts; the relocation of churches to new, middle-class enclaves; and the widening and extension of streets through densely populated slums, all involved the raz-ing of mansions and counting-houses, churches and cemeteries, taverns and tenements, each of which briefly resembled ruins in their half-demolished state" (109). Such *"ruin-effects"* heightened the sense that time somehow sped up in the city, as if entire eras were compressed into only a few years' time leaving little possibility for the sedimentation of the metropolitan land-scape. After being abandoned by its merchant and accountant parishion-ers who themselves had moved uptown, swept there by "the tide of change and progress [that] had rolled clean through its broad-aisle," the Church was "divided into stores, cut into offices, and given for a roost to gregari-ous lawyers," and "so well did the thing succeed, that ultimately the church-yard was invaded for a supplemental edifice, likewise to be promiscuously rented to the legal crowd," who did not like being so far removed from the street thereby leaving the upper stories of the new building available on comparatively cheap terms for renters like the Apostles (266–67).[71] Such rapid turnover and the surge in the number of tenants in ever tighter quar-ters creates the potential for increasing forms of obscurity in which one may be as "solitary as at the Pole" among thousands, who themselves are "social castaways" (338, 341).[72]

That rapidity of transformation, and attendant forms of urban density and anonymity, enables a relative alegality that facilitates the expression and proliferation of "ambiguities" arising and arriving from the country. Having come to the city, found Glen's house shut up, placed Isabel and Delly in a police watch house for safekeeping so as to go find Glen, and been rebuffed by him, Pierre returns to the station to find it in chaos: "The before decent, drowsy place, now fairly reeked with all things unseemly"; "On all sides, were heard drunken male and female voices, in English, French, Spanish, and Portuguese"; "Running among this combined babel of persons and voices, several of the police were vainly striving to still the tumult" (240). While decrying this polyglot profusion of disreputables as "one combined sortie . . . poured out upon earth through the vile vomitory of some unmentionable cellar" (241), the sensational thrill offered by the description of the crush of humanity suggests an attraction on the text's part toward this unseemly assemblage. Perhaps most notable, though, is that the crowd completely overwhelms the ability of the police to control them, suggesting the limi-tations in manifesting governmentally sanctioned modes of placemaking through the enforcement of laws against public offenses. This scene captures the fact that city officials had little ability to order everyday activity on the streets, despite passing numerous regulations, creating a professional police force in 1845, and periodically increasing its size thereafter.[73] Here, the novel also gestures toward the demographic explosion downtown that both produces this rowdy nightlife and the growth of tenements such as the Church of the Apostles. Between 1820 and 1860 the population of the city grew by well over 600 percent, doubling in the decade from 1845 to 1855 alone; most residents could not afford the townhouses being built above 14th Street and so were crowded into increasingly cramped quarters in lower Manhattan.[74]

Rather than commenting on these historical shifts, and the specific political and economic dynamics that created a completely artificial housing shortage, Melville casts such crowding as part of the very being of the city. The intensities, disparities, and anonymities created by such a concentration of people, commerce, and capital appear in *Pierre* as a potential for forms of everyday autonomy not constrained by the terms of family and propriety that predominate upstate, generating a queer social ecology well-suited to the profusion of "mysteries." When Glen and Lucy's brother Fred appear at Pierre's door in order to try to reclaim Lucy after she has chosen to join him and Isabel, asserting that they need to save her from his "depravity" and "pollutedness," Pierre insists that "she is of age by the law:—she is her own mistress by the law," to which she adds that if they seek to remove her "by violence" she has "the ordinary appeal to the law" (327–28). Rather than constructing and enforcing a particular genealogized set of relations, "law" in the city works to insulate what may be considered "depravity" so long as it occurs among consenting adults, less instantiating a normative order than opening a negative space in which the acidic tendencies of the city can articulate with the propulsive "ambiguities" borne from the country. When read alongside Charlie Millthorpe's accession to status and financial independence through becoming a lawyer and the Apostles' inhabitance of their space due to the retreat of lawyers from it, these fleeting references to law in the urban section of the novel suggest less a confrontation with or repudiation of legality than a portrait of how urban authorities' limits, ambivalences, and apathies in regulating occupancy and interaction facilitate increased possibilities for personal predilections, perverse inclinations, and nonfamilial pleasures and associations. If connection to place appears not entirely separable from the law, in contrast to *House of the Seven Gables* and *Walden*, occupancy in the city appears to bear a far more vexed, alienated, and

excessive relation to the state than it does in the country, and the urban section of *Pierre* suggests the operation of principles of placemaking, of democratizing disjunction, neither directly endorsed nor enforced by the state.

Thus, even as *Pierre* at times adopts a tone of scandalized horror with
respect to the supposed excesses of the metropolis, at no point does it suggest rural landholding as a cure for the city's queer propensities—an absence
that notably differentiates it from the land reformers who also take up the
cause of the tenants upstate. As with its effacement of the Lockean arguments made by Anti-Renters and its refusal to envision a more just pattern
of landedness that could replace the manor system, the novel does not
position increased chances for property holding in the country as the cure
to urban ills. By contrast, people like George Henry Evans and Horace
Greeley actively connected the distribution of property outside the city
to the rates of exploitation and poor situation of workers within it. Evans
argues that "[l]and monopoly drives farmers' sons into the overstocked
trades, the traders force them into the cities, where more than half their
earnings are taken from them by the combined forces of Paper Money and
Landlordism, and under this operation their wages are getting lower and
employment more scarce."[75] Similarly, Horace Greeley asserts that "the frequent lack of employment, the scanty reward, and the meager subsistence,
often accorded to Labor" can be traced "directly to the resistless influence
of Land Monopoly" (21). They contend that the inability to make a decent
living in the country due to the relative paucity of available land in the state
as a result of its control by a small collection of owners drives people into
the city where they must struggle with one another and those already there
to get jobs, depressing wages due to the competition. Conversely, the breaking up of "land monopoly" in non-urban areas would promote movement
away from the city in ways that would make wages more competitive and
bring down inflation. Greeley recommends "a change in the Social Condition of the mass of Laborers in their relation to the Soil, as will leave them
really free to accept an offer of employment, in view of all its conditions, or
decline it" (30). Evans observes that a law limiting landholding in the state
to 160 acres would lead to a "gradual emigration from, instead of an influx
to, the cities, till something like that state of decency and comfort would
prevail that would befit a Christian community," and an appeal to Congress
that he authored insists that if public lands were made available for free,

"[c]ity populations would diminish gradually till every inhabitant could be the owner of a comfortable habitation."[76] Whether supporting increased access to territory or not, these linkages of the increased availability of land to labor reform in the cities were commonplaces of political rhetoric in New York state and elsewhere by the late 1840s and early 1850s.[77] The absence of such arguments in *Pierre* highlights the extent to which its trajectory is toward the city as a horizon of ethical aspiration, implicitly understanding the metropolitan landscape as a place from which to escape the violences of "land monopoly" without engaging the complex dialectical relationship between urban and rural economies and placemaking.

The disorientation produced by the compactness and relative ungovernability of urban life—in which the novel takes a sensational thrill, not unlike that of city mystery fiction—provides the condition of possibility for the ruination of the Glendinning family. *Pierre*, though, keeps the struggle over genealogy and property in the foreground even as it illustrates queer processes of urban corrosion. As Priscilla Wald observes, "Pierre as he knows himself does not exist without the law," and "without the law he will find his story untellable" (146).[78] The legalities of land tenure produce a range of feelings and relations that exceed the privileged terms of lineage, and while such queer desires gain space for expression in mystery-laden metropolitan space, they remain oriented toward the terms of landholding in the country, suggesting something of an inability to embrace fully the generative potential of the city's "ambiguities." Pierre chooses to present himself as having married Isabel as part of a "resolution to hold his father's memory untouched, nor to one single being in the world reveal the paternity of Isabel" (177). In doing so, he maintains the integrity of the Glendinning line and the naturalized image of Saddle Meadows as its space of unfolding. Additionally, in response to Glen and Frederic's efforts to reclaim Lucy, Pierre hunts them down with the intent to kill them, shooting Glen before being arrested: "Spatterings of his own kindred blood were upon the pavement; his own hand had extinguished his house in slaughtering the only unoutlawed human being by the name of Glendinning" (360). The act of murdering Glen not only serves as vengeance against him specifically but as an expression of Pierre's desire to *extinguish* "his house," to rupture the genealogical continuity through which the coherence of the estate is maintained in ways that suggest a persistent investment in Saddle Meadows and the Glendinning line.[79] Pierre sees the "murder" of the legally authorized patriarch of Saddle Meadows as the means of resolving or displacing "the ambiguities which hemmed him in" (337).[80] Thus, the novel's plot ends with the collapse of the Glendinning line through the death of the lawful heir and the suicide of the "true" one, suggesting that this agonistic violence unleashed in the city arises as a residue of rural struggles.

However, concluding in this fashion emphasizes the negative momentum of the text's ethics, rupturing the terms of landedness but neither investigating the principles structuring occupancy in the city nor addressing what occurs in the country in the wake of the self-destruction of patroon lineage. The text's conclusion marks the urban decimation of the Glendinning line, undoing the assemblage of genealogy and territory while still remaining immersed and invested in it in its denaturalization. If *Pierre* engages in a project of dissociating the city from the country and celebrating the queer capability of the former to ruin legalized modes of kinship and property holding, it remains focused on dissolution without addressing the construction of the city, the reconstruction of the country in the wake of the manor system, or the relation between those two processes. The text flees from the ethical quagmire of land claims upstate, but in setting the truth-constituting workings of law in the country against the proliferating mysteries of urban life, Melville queers the city in ways that suspend analysis of the networks through which the one is tied to the other. More specifically, in seeking to dispense with the Indianized problem of territoriality, casting it as a rural anachronism ethically superseded in the democratizing kinds of corrosion at work in the metropolis, the novel effaces how the emergence of New York City in the mid-nineteenth century depends on the continuing displacement of Native peoples and, therefore, the ways a queer urban liberation from the question of landedness functions as a form of settler fantasy.

CONQUEST AND THE CITY

To the extent that the novel's move from upstate to the city represents a flight from the multiple and ongoing modes of expropriation and exploitation that make possible the manor system, that transit can be thought of as bearing within it an ethical impulse, a desire to disown the reiterative coercions through which pastoral space is, in Latour's terms, *placed*.[81] From this perspective, *Pierre*'s orientation toward the city's queer proliferation of lineage-and-inheritance-dissolving "mysteries" functions as a repudiation of the history of Indian removal, toward which the text gestures. However, the text also presents the retreat from the rural to the urban as an evasion of the former's *Indianizing* enmeshments in genealogy and landedness. In a sense, Pierre's death in jail in the metropolis, after the death of his mother due to her grief over his "marriage" to Isabel and his murder of Glen, breaks the novel free from Saddle Meadows, as if the Glendinnings' inability to leave behind the desires and attachments generated through patroon property holding itself produces the tragic denouement. Having disposed of all potential heirs, the text is free to indulge in the pleasure of urban "ambiguities," implicitly returning to the perspective of the "sojourner from the city" with which it began (3). To be free from the territorial investments that perpetrate violence against Indians, then, simultaneously entails liberating oneself from the Indian propensity toward rootedness in place, embracing the democratizing, acidic corrosions of city density, mobility, and anonymity. What's at stake, though, in localizing the dispossession of Native peoples into an originary moment (a primal scene of settlement) that can then be segregated temporally and spatially from the space(s) of antinormative queer potential? How does Indian policy persist as part of the ongoing construction of life in the city, and how, then, does the ethics of urban negation—positioning the city as site of the undoing of oppressive systems—function as a mode of settler normalization? What other possibilities for thinking the politics of place emerge when attending to the continuing experiences of settlement in this period by Indigenous peoples on land claimed by New York state?[82]

The novel turns away from Native presence and the politics of settler occupancy, casting them as part of an ambivalent founding moment of association/antagonism that perhaps colors later events without meaningfully participating in them. In *Queer Phenomenology*, Sara Ahmed suggests, "The background [can] be understood as that which must take place in order for something to appear," adding, "a background is what explains the conditions of emergence or an arrival of something as the thing it appears to be in the present" (37–38): "We can think . . . of the background not simply in terms of what is around what we face, as the 'dimly perceived,' but as produced by acts of relegation: some things are relegated to the background in order *to sustain* a certain direction; in other words, in order to keep attention on what is faced. Perception involves acts of relegation which are forgotten in the very preoccupation with what is faced" (31). What are the sets of Indigenous-settler relations "that must take place" in order for the city "to appear"?

Facing the urban as a kind of queer horizon entails relegating Native peoples, and the ongoing effects of Indian policy, to a ruralized elsewhere from which the text seeks escape.[83] The adoption of such a perspective by the novel involves an orientation away from the circumstances faced by Indigenous peoples to the north and west, but that very turning away from the scene of settlement depends on the (re)production of a jurisdictional, commercial, and transportation infrastructure that can sustain the metropolis and migration to it. In this sense, the text renders self-evident as background the policy developments and maneuvers along the route of the Erie Canal, including the displacement of Senecas and Oneidas, that make possible the growing density, anonymity, and mystery of New York City, that transform it into a site for "social castaways" amid "hundreds of thousands of human beings" and engender the sphinx-like proliferation of secrets that eat away at normative modes of lineage.

The key to the rise of New York lay in the positioning of it as a privileged node in expanding commercial networks. Construction of state-funded transportation linkages tied the city to the Great Lakes and beyond, facilitating greater population density in the city through access to a more expansive and cheaper supply of foodstuffs. The Erie Canal was at the center of this development.[84] Begun in 1817 and finished in 1825, its "chief beneficiary was the city of New York, which witnessed a 64 percent population surge during that decade,"[85] and as a result of the canal, "shipping costs from Lake Erie to Manhattan plummeted from a hundred dollars a ton to under nine dollars" while in the same year as the canal's completion "five hundred new mercantile operations opened their doors in the city."[86] Because of the construction of the canal system, Buffalo became "the primary granary depot of the United States in the decades before the Civil War," serving as "America's great transshipment port," and Rochester "became a breadbasket overnight, producing substantial amounts of wheat," making it "the flour capital of the United States."[87] Access to cheap grain, meat, and dairy from upstate and the Great Lakes region made possible the escalating density of New York City, while direct communication with the Old Northwest vastly increased both the opportunities for business ventures based on shipment to and from regions beyond the state and the wealth to be gained from speculative investments in land along the canal route.

The construction of the canal (as well as more local canals that preceded and followed it), the growth of cities in the state that supported and depended on the canal (like Buffalo and Rochester), the land rush along its path, and the emergence of land-based transport via railroad inspired by the success of the Erie Canal all depended on the acquisition of Haudenosaunee lands and the displacement of Six Nations' peoples, particularly the Oneidas and Senecas. In a somewhat perverse recognition of this fact, the first ship to pilot the canal after its completion was called the *Seneca Chief*.[88] The idea for a canal that extended across the state can be traced back to the Western Inland Lock Navigation Company founded by Philip Schuyler in the 1790s.[89] A one-time U.S. senator and surveyor-general of the state of New York, as well as the father-in-law of Alexander Hamilton and Stephen Van Rensselaer III, Schuyler sought access to the Oneida Carrying Place, a sacred area that served as a portage between the Mohawk River and Wood Creek. After helping engineer state purchases of more than five-and-a-half million acres of Oneida lands in the 1780s and the early 1790s, partially for the construction of a road (the Genesee Turnpike) through Oneida territory,[90] Schuyler's company built the Rome Canal. In bridging the gap between these waterways, the canal created a "rudimentary water passage from Albany to Seneca Lake" that "lowered carriage fees of transportation from one hundred dollars to thirty-two dollars per ton, and from Albany to Niagara by half," thereby becoming "the rationale for much grander schemes, namely, the Erie Canal and the branch canal system."[91] Moreover, the idea of placing the western terminus of the canal at Buffalo can be traced to the machinations of the Holland Land Company, which was the holder of preemption rights to much of western New York (including Six Nations, and particularly Seneca, lands) originally acquired from Massachusetts in the wake of the deal in 1786 whereby a conflict between the two states over jurisdiction was resolved by giving the former state jurisdiction and the latter preemption rights that could be sold to private purchasers. Buffalo was founded by the Holland Company, and in campaigning for its status as a node in state transportation networks, which as expected exponentially increased the value of land surrounding Buffalo (including the Senecas' Buffalo Creek reservation), the company was aided by Erastus Granger, the federal Indian agent for the Six Nations from 1804 to 1819.[92] These maneuverings for speculative control over Haudenosaunee lands occurred despite the ratification of the Treaty of Canandaigua in 1794, which promised that "the United States will never . . . disturb the Seneca nation, nor any of the Six Nations, or of their Indian friends" and that their lands "shall remain theirs until they choose to sell the same to the people of the United States who have the right to purchase."[93] In addition, the use of state agreements to acquire Iroquois territory also flouted the various versions of the federal Trade and Intercourse Act passed in the 1790s and early 1800s, which mandated that transfers of Native land should be overseen by the national government.[94]

While by the mid-1830s Oneida lands had been reduced to a small fraction of what they had been just a few decades earlier, the Senecas remained in possession of significant landholdings at the Buffalo Creek, Cattaraugus, Allegany, and Tonawanda reservations, and these territories became the subject of a major public controversy in the late 1830s and 1840s, a struggle that continued through the height of the Anti-Rent Wars and the period in which *Pierre* was written and published.[95] The push for Seneca land driven by rising property values and the growth of the city of Buffalo, themselves a result of the increasing geographic reach and commercial significance of the canal system, led to the effort in 1837 driven by the Ogden Land Company (the successor to the Holland Land Company) to negotiate a treaty to obtain the rest of the Senecas' territory and to facilitate their removal to west of the Mississippi. The result was a treaty of removal and appended contract for the sale of the entirety of four reservations (Buffalo Creek, Tonawanda, Cattaraugus, and Allegany). It originally was submitted in early 1838, but due to Seneca protests and charges of deceit and corruption, the Senate passed a resolution in June that the treaty would be accepted as legitimate and could be proclaimed as such by the president once he was assured that the "free and voluntary assent thereto" had been offered by "the said tribes or bands" when "separately assembled in council."[96] Commissioner Ransom H. Gillet was sent back to Seneca territory twice (from August 1838 into October and in late summer and fall 1839, after the treaty had again been returned by the president) to obtain evidence of Seneca consent. In doing so, he used bribes, held private meetings at his quarters at a nearby tavern, harassed Seneca leaders at their homes at all hours of the day and night, and signed for people who supposedly had consented by proxy. President Van Buren sent a message to the Senate in January 1840 indicating, "No *advance* towards obtaining the *assent* of the *Seneca* tribe *to the amended treaty* was made."[97] Despite this determination, and a three-to-two vote by the Indian Affairs Committee against the treaty, the Senate in March 1840 decided to accept it in a tie vote that was broken by the vice president, and President Van Buren proclaimed it in April 1840.[98]

The implementation of the treaty was delayed for various reasons: the intervention and advocacy of the Quakers (who had missionaries among the Senecas); the determination by Commissioner of Indian Affairs T. Hartley Crawford (backed by the U.S. attorney general) that according to the treaty the Senecas had five years in which to remove; decreasing popular support for the policy of Indian removal in light of the carnage and cost of the Second Seminole War; the resistance to land claims by elites, understood as speculative rather than established through labor, due to the Anti-Rent struggle; and the reduced push by the state government for displacing Haudenosaunee peoples given that Governor William Seward decided not to seek reelection and was, therefore, no longer beholden to Whig party interests in the western part of the state. In a deal struck between the Secretary of War John C. Spencer, the trustees of the Ogden company, and the Quakers in early 1842, in which no Seneca representatives participated but which many Seneca leaders eventually accepted as the best they could get, the Cattaraugus and Allegany reservations were spared, while the Buffalo Creek and Tonawanda ones would be sold. The supplemental Treaty of Buffalo Creek was ratified and proclaimed by August of that year. However, this agreement still did not end the controversy, since those at Tonawanda did not accept the validity of their reservation being included in a deal to which they had not assented. They persisted in a public campaign to have their reservation exempted from the 1842 agreement, including blocking the access of government surveyors to the reservation, sending representatives (led by Ely S. Parker) to Washington to lobby for land retention, and filing a court case (*Fellows v. Blacksmith*) that eventually reached the Supreme Court.[99] Partially prompted by a favorable Supreme Court decision in 1857, federal officials agreed to purchase the lands in Kansas provided for the Tonawanda Senecas in the treaties of 1838 and 1842, and with those funds, the Tonawandas bought back from the Ogden Land Company approximately 7,500 acres of their reservation.[100]

Lasting almost twenty years, the Senecas' fight to retain their lands in the wake of the Treaty of 1838 illustrates the immense implications for Native peoples of state-sponsored transportation networks and attendant forms of land speculation, as well as the limits of *Pierre*'s account of urban space as the site to which one might flee from the legacy of Indian dispossession (itself cast as completed long ago). Seneca narrations of their landedness in their struggle against removal provide a more multivalent way of envisioning ongoing Indigenous locatedness and participation in the present. In his *Address on the Present Condition and Prospects of the Aboriginal Inhabitants of North America, with Particular Reference to the Seneca Nation* (1838), delivered in Buffalo and soon after circulated as a pamphlet, Seneca chief Maris Bryant Pierce provides an account of Seneca sovereignty that emphasizes less a primordial relation to the land stretching back beyond memory than the ways the experience of peoplehood in the present moment arises out of the reservations' position as nodes within geographically expansive networks of information, goods, and technologies.[101] The text begins by noting that Pierce is "by blood" "of the race of people" about whose "condition and circumstances" he will speak, and he juxtaposes this act of Native self-representation with the fact that "hitherto our cause has been advocated almost exclusively, though ably and humanely, by the friends of human right and human weal, belonging by *nature* to a different, and by *circumstances* and *education*, to a superior race of men" (3). That gesture toward white *superiority*, and the benefits of the civilization program, though, quickly becomes the occasion for drawing attention to the struggle over land that has forestalled Native adoption of nonnative practices and technologies. In contrast to the narrative "reiterated so frequently" that "it is the *doom* of the Indian to disappear—to vanish like the morning dew, before the advance of civilization," Pierce points to "the page which records the dealings . . . of the early white settlers and of their successors, down even to the present day" as providing evidence that not only do Native people not "lack the competency" to take up "civilized" ways but that forms of white invasion provide the explanation for why they have not done so more extensively (4–5). He posits the arrival of "some beings from fairy land" or "distant planet" who come among whites and who "dazzle and amaze you . . . till finally they . . . claim the *right* to your possessions, and of hunting you, like wild beasts, from your long and hitherto undisputed domain," asking, "how ready would *you* be to be taught of *them*?" (5–6). Thus, as opposed to indicating a dislocation in time in which Indians must catch up to whites, the text casts the reluctance to adopt nonnative practices as a response to invasion, as an ongoing spatial relation rather than a temporal gap.

Moreover, Pierce inverts the narrative used to license removal (from New York and elsewhere) in which Native peoples are cast as hunters with a proclivity toward *wandering*, an absence of a determinate sense of place, and a desire to remain unaltered by present "circumstances." He highlights nonnative violence by characterizing it as "hunting" Indians "like wild beasts," suggesting that whites are the ones who endorse murderously roving bands. Additionally, the text later describes the Trail of Tears as the Cherokees being "hunted at the point of the bayonet . . . , from their homes and possessions and country, to the 'terra incognita' beyond the Mississippi," after having already "redeem[ed] the Indian character from the foul aspersions that it is not susceptible of civilization and Christianization" (9–10). In depicting the prospective land of the Senecas in the west as "terra incognita," a phrase repeated later (13), the text suggests that this territory remains unknown to Seneca people, a space to which they have no attachments and about which they have virtually no information. While its remoteness from their current location appears in nonnative accounts as enabling something like a trip back in time to a space of innocence free from white intrusion, Pierce indexes and mocks this sentiment that the territory in Kansas constitutes "a western wilderness beyond the white man's reach, where an Eden lies in all its freshness of beauty" (17). In response to this image of "a wilderness of game," he asserts, "I deny that we could possess *such a territory* this side of the shores of the Pacific, with *safety*, *free of molestation*, and in *perpetuity*" (15).[102] As opposed to placing the Senecas beyond time, sealed off from the fall into modern civilization, removal only defers for a brief period the scene of dispossession.[103]

Arguments in favor of such an ostensible move through space, supposedly in order to restore conditions of purity in which Native people(s) can be their desired hunting and wandering selves, posit a temporality of Indianness which, Pierce suggests, bears little relation to Senecas' understandings of themselves: "Having said thus much as to our condition after a removal, under the supposition that we wish to return and continue in the habits of life which prevailed when the country was first taken possession of by the

Europeans, I proceed now to say, that we do not wish to do so," adding that "we desire to renounce those habits of mind and body, and adopt in their stead those habits and feelings . . . which result from the cultivation and enlightening of the moral and intellectual faculties of man" (16). Although apparently affirming the terms of the civilization program, this line of argument notes that Senecas cannot "return" to the past any more than anyone else and insists on their modernness and the effectivity and desirability of the forms of "cultivation" in which they have engaged over the centuries since the onset of European presence. While perhaps overemphasizing uniformity in the embrace of new beliefs, practices, and technologies,[104] the text invokes a Seneca phenomenology in which current "habits of mind and body" have replaced prior "habits and feelings." That process indicates not so much a tragic loss as a condition of possibility for Seneca engagement with the circumstances in which they are enmeshed at the present moment. Although presented as a means of preserving Indian authenticity, the portrayal of the Senecas as properly belonging amid "nature" displaces them to a sphere beyond the reach of nonnative influence, a locale itself equated with the rural.

In this way, the justifications for removal to which Pierce responds offer the converse perspective to *Pierre*—a moving frontier of improvement and urbanization versus the city as a space apart from which to retreat from the violences of the country. If these two perspectives seem to have opposing ethical charges, an investment in expansion rather than a withdrawal from it, they both rely on defining urbanity as antithetical to Indianness, equating the latter with an elsewhere in which the past lives in ways that make that space discontinuous with metropolitan modernity. As against this segregation of Native peoples into a place that can be distinguished temporally, either as "Eden" or a properly surpassed period in history, Pierce underlines not just Seneca currentness, participating as they do in the contemporary life of the region, but the value of Seneca lands due to their privileged location within extant formations of trade, population movement, and information transfer—the very thing that makes the territory attractive for nonnative exploitation and expropriation. The text does make what might be thought of as a more expected argument based on enduring Seneca connections to their lands, observing, "The graves of our fathers and mothers and kin are here, and about them still cling our affections and memories. Here is the theatre on which our tribe has thus far acted its part in the drama of its existence,

and about it are wreathed the associations which ever bind the human affections to the soil, whereon one's nation, and kindred, and self, have arisen and
acted" (13).[105] This moment emphasizes cross-generational linkages to the
land in which popular "affections and memories" tie the Senecas to the specific place they occupy in ways that cannot be reproduced in some western
locale, even if they are provided with an equivalent amount of territory.
However, just after this articulation, the "Address" changes its tack, indicating, "We are here situated in the midst of facilities for physical intellectual
and moral improvement; we are in the midst of the enlightened; we see their
ways and their works, and can thus profit by their example. We can avail ourselves of their implements, and wares and merchandise, and once having
learned the convenience of using them, we shall be led to deem them indis-
pensable" (13). The "soil" in question becomes significant not solely, or perhaps even primarily, for its historical role as the "theatre" for the "drama of
[the tribe's] existence" but for its position in proximity to "enlightened"
modes of knowledge-production, instruction, and commerce.

Living "here" entails being "situated in the midst" of social formations that
facilitate "improvement" of various sorts. Seneca lands function as something of a hub for (or at least lie hub-adjacent to) the interconnections and
transfers made possible by the Erie Canal and its heirs. The location of the
reservations, then, opens onto, in Merleau-Ponty's terms, a collective "field
of possibility," which they are unwilling to change for another space with a
diminished "horizon." In this vein, Pierce responds with incredulity to the
notion that the Senecas would be better off moving to the West: "What!
leave a fertile and somewhat improved soil—a home in the midst of civilization and christianity, where the very breezes are redolent of improvement
and exaltation,—where, by induction as it were, we must be pervaded by
the spirit of enterprise,—where books, and preaching, and conversation,
and business and conduct, whose influence we need, are all around us[?]"
(16–17). From this perspective, *rural* and *urban* as ways of designating the
relative density of the population and built environment mean less than the
ability to gain access to chains of transmission for goods, information, and
persons trained in needed skills. Eschewing a perspective based on concentration, the text indicates that the Senecas occupy an advantageous position within processes of distribution. As Pierce insists, "let us enjoy the
advantages which our location affords us" (18).

The "Address" suggests how the valorization of the urban as such implic-itly entails not only the ruralization of Native peoples but also the Indianiza-tion of the countryside, casting Indigenous landholding as extraneous to life in the city while also defining the latter in opposition to a bucolic space understood as somehow occupying an earlier period than the city itself. Ignoring the persistent takings of Native lands that make possible the various networks that sustain the growth of New York City, *Pierre* conveys a sense of the city as an exceptional space freed from the ethical conundrums and violences with respect to landedness present upstate. In this way, the logics and policies driving Haudenosaunee removal function as an unacknowl-edged background to Melville's identification with the urban. As against this commonsensical displacement of Native peoples to a rural beyond, Pierce's "Address" insists that the Senecas, and by extension other Indige-nous peoples surrounded by nonnative communities, function as full par-ticipants in a shared modernity even if not completely in control of the circumstances they confront in the context of escalating settler presence, demands, and interference.[106] Seneca opposition helps put into relief the implicit ways *Pierre* is oriented, specifically how settler expansion across the state functions as the background against which to register the possibility of movement to the city (itself appearing as, in Merleau-Ponty's terms, "ready made" rather than dependent on and sustained through ongoing disposses-sion in adjacent regions).

Furthermore, attention to Seneca resistance to settler expropriation high-lights the ways that Melville's vision of freedom relies on a conception of subjectivity that cannot be divorced from the legal norms of the settler-state. As discussed earlier, *Pierre* contrasts the proliferation of queernesses in the city to the strict management of familial relation, coupling, and inheritance in the country, embracing, in Povinelli's terms, the forms of "stranger social-ity" made available by the density and relative alegality of metropolitan life. In *League of the Iroquois*, Lewis Henry Morgan describes the Six Nations as "a people without a city" (59), later observing, "Without the influence of cities, which no people construct who live in the hunter-state, and the important consequences which result from the aggregation of society into large communities, the government of the Iroquois would doubtless have retained its oligarchical form through many generations" (140).[107] As noted in chapter 2, "oligarchical" here refers less to rule by an elite than to the system of governance through clans, which Morgan explains in the following way: "[T]he [Iroquois] League was established upon the principles, and was designed to be but an elaboration, of the Family Relationships" (60). Similarly, the novel presents lineage-based claims to land as inherently oppressive, anachronistic, and antidemocratic, and to the extent that Pierre's retreat to the city constitutes a desire on the part of the novel to escape the ethical miasma of landedness, it simultaneously functions as a break with legally regulated genealogy, *bursting* the family as the normative unit around which to orient social life in favor of an image of an aggregation of "social castaways." In this way, the text implicitly treats the autonomous individual as the subject of democratizing urban impulses.

This vision of semi-sovereign selfhood, as indicated in previous chapters, recirculates ideologies and legal forms that emerge from the settler acquisition of Native lands. The struggle over the Treaty of Buffalo Creek, though, illustrates the political and legal stakes, as well as unexamined assumptions, of the foreclosure of genealogy. Or more specifically, Morgan's text illustrates the ways that, from the perspective of Euramerican discourses of sexuality and kinship, Seneca forms of governance appear as a somewhat bloated mode of (pre-urban) family formation.[108] Yet, the insistence by the Senecas at various points during the struggle to retain their reservations in the late 1830s and 1840s that their clan-based modes of consensus need to be acknowledged and respected as a process of political decision-making draws attention to the ways the imposition of a normative model of individuality, such as that privileged in *Pierre*, abets the appropriation of Native lands.

During the controversy over the treaty of 1838, U.S. officials insisted that the assent of a majority of Seneca chiefs was necessary in order for it to be considered valid.[109] However, that framing of legitimacy presupposes a political system in which chiefs function something like elected officials and in which policy is decided by a centralized body based on the votes of a preponderance of legislators. That model has little relation to extant Seneca political formations in the period, which were ordered around the eight clans: belonging to a clan passed through one's mother; they were led by clan mothers who chose Seneca leaders; and the chiefs remained accountable to, and could be removed by, the clans.[110] In a memorial to the president protesting the treaties of 1838 and 1842, Tonawanda leaders note that the treaty process "took away our *independence* by prescribing the manner in which our assent should be given, namely, by the signatures of a majority of our chiefs in open council, when, in fact, by our national laws, it was and still is necessary that *all* of the chiefs should be of one mind; that they must *unanimously* agree to make a treaty."[111] The importance of *unanimity*, though, lies less in agreement by a select set of leaders than broad assent expressed by and through the various networks that coalesce around the chiefs. An earlier memorial in 1839 from leaders from the Buffalo Creek reservation to the governor of Massachusetts, asking him to intercede on the Senecas' behalf, offers the following:

> As in the declaration of war, so in matters relative to our lands the chiefs can do nothing, unless the power has been specially delegated to them for the purpose, at the time. The sales which have heretofore been made, have, without a single instance, been made in the following manner, viz: The question was first discussed by the chiefs, if they thought best to sell, then the question was put to the warriors and women, who, through their speakers, gave their opinion to the council, if they thought best to sell, then the chiefs appointed a speaker to say to the commissioner that the papers might be presented, as they had concluded to sell. The deed was then signed by as many as were chosen for that purpose, sometimes more and sometimes less.[112]

The petition emphasizes the ways chiefs do not act as legislators free to enact whatever policy they wish. Instead, the decision to engage in a treaty emerges out of an extensive process of consultation in which the council of women—as clan mothers and the ones to whom chiefs are responsible— directly takes part.[113] In the absence of an engagement with this clan-based method of collective decision-making, the United States simply is inventing leaders, forms of political subjectivity, and modes of voice that travesty the claim of treaty-based consent.[114]

Moreover, the question of who constitutes a valid leader with whom a treaty may be negotiated opens into a broader geography of continuing Haudenosaunee presence and relation that exceeds the specific territoriality of the Senecas. As noted at several points in Seneca memorials and accounts by the Quakers when arguing for a new treaty prior to 1842, the assent of other members of the Iroquois Confederacy and the performance of a formal Condolence Ceremony through which the new chief would be raised were necessary to licensing someone as a leader.[115] Ongoing connections to other Haudenosaunee peoples, then, suggests the persistence of a network among the Six Nations (in many ways similar to the Wabanaki Confederacy discussed in chapter 2) at odds with state mappings and the desire to cast the Senecas as an isolated entity on an increasingly constricted landbase.

While *Pierre* certainly is not about Seneca removal, does not comment on it in any explicit way, and cannot be understood as contributing to it,[116] the novel's critique of family-based landholding takes as a given that genealogy functions as a stultifying constraint, especially when defined and backed by the power of law. That understanding of the union of law and family as oppressive and regressive draws on and recirculates the ideology of individual political subjectivity at play in majority rule, itself used to dismiss Haudenosaunee modes of governance as backward and illegitimate or to efface them entirely.[117] Acknowledging Seneca struggles over the decade before *Pierre*'s publication, then, highlights how Melville's disavowal of genealogy gains momentum from the legal privileging of individualism as the axiomatic form of political subjectivity. In addition, the text's Indianization of the manor system can be understood as drawing on extant representations of Native kinship systems like the Seneca clans—and their role in Indigenous sociospatiality—as an inappropriate/archaic way of life that cannot function as a proper mode of contemporary governance. In this way, the text's investment in the corrosive propensities of the city as against the legally constituted and enforced familialism of property law in the country not only implicitly anchors the text's vision in the dispossession of Indigenous lands that facilitates the exponential growth of New York City in the mid-nineteenth century but recirculates the atomizing equation of freedom with afamilial individualism that helps engender those displacements.

If *Pierre* remains unconcerned with the ongoing presence of Haudenosaunee peoples after its citation of them as an originary context, it does register the significance of territoriality in representing the negotiation between (apparent) truth and ambiguity as a struggle for control over land. Melville disjoints such images from reference to actual conflict and inhabitance, either the "Indian" opposition of the Anti-Renters or the resistance to Indian removal in the state, but they appear scattered throughout the narrative in ways that suggest a nagging, residual unease with the question of legitimate occupancy. After Pierre first encounters Isabel, not knowing who she is, the narrator characterizes Pierre's vertiginous replaying of that experience in his mind: "He felt that what he had always before considered the solid land of veritable reality, was now being audaciously encroached upon by bannered armies of hooded phantoms" (49). The mystery surrounding Isabel appears here as an invading army, coming to claim the land from those who believe they legitimately possess it. Similarly, after Pierre completes his second interview with Isabel, the narrator observes that once one believes oneself to "have come to the Ultimate of Human Speculative Knowledge," "[s]udden onsets of new truth will assail him, and overturn him as the Tartars did China, for there is no China Wall that man can build in his soul, which shall permanently stay the irruptions of those barbarous hordes which Truth ever nourishes in the loins of her frozen, yet teeming North, so that the Empire of Human Knowledge can never be lasting in any one dynasty, since Truth still gives new Emperors to the earth" (166–67). In this moment, "Truth" assaults the existing regime from the "North" even as it then gives rise to a "new Emperor" who, in turn, will be overrun by "barbarous hordes." These examples suggest that whatever may count as "truth" cannot be stable and "solid," cannot itself function like a sovereign state or a property claim in their putatively rooted and bounded territoriality. Instead, *ambiguity* contributes to a greater (less rigid and legally fixated) form of "truth" by repudiating foundational grounding. These moments insist on mobility, displacement, and the undermining of the existing order as key features of a real *advancement* in human knowledge, one correlated with the mysteries and density of the city.[118]

When read against the grain, the discussion of Enceladus offers something like an allegory for a substantive engagement with the layered struggles over land that the novel eschews in its flight to the city. After Pierre is visited by his cousin Glen Stanly and Lucy's brother Frederic in an effort to reclaim her, he fantasizes about murdering them, and sitting in his room, "Pierre was solitary as at the Pole" (337): "Now he began to feel that in him, the thews of a Titan were forestallingly cut by the scissors of fate" (339). Once he has returned to the apartment at the Apostles from a night among "the social castaways," he slips into a trancelike state in which he imagines Saddle Meadows and the nearby mountain, which he characterizes as "the phantasmagoria of the Mount of the Titans" (341–42), and fronting the mountain, "among the recumbent sphinx-like shapes thrown from the rocky sweep," he spots a rock formation he identifies as Enceladus "the most potent of all the giants" (345)—the Titan with whom he identifies himself. The child of Titan (himself the son of siblings) and Titan's "mother Terra," Enceladus "was both the son and grandson of an incest" (347). In this section, Pierre dreams his way back upstate, suggesting that he remains haunted by Glendinning property claims and the matrix of family, law, and territory they represent from which he has sought escape. As critics have noted, the figure of Enceladus recalls the mysteries and perversities of the Glendinning line and the attendant difficulties of defining the contours and limits of family while simultaneously indexing the problem of how to understand the generational relation to land.[119] In particular, the immersion of Enceladus in/as rock suggests to Pierre an effort to climb the mountain, "to regain his paternal birthright by fierce escalade" (347), as well as the futility of doing so. Pierre can neither surmount nor escape his relation to Saddle Meadows and the lineage from which he comes, can neither fully embrace the mysteries that surround him nor settle into a convenient legal fiction that functions as "truth." Instead, he remains caught within an impossible position that motivates his murderous assault on Glen and Frederic, indicating a tragic inability to forget his "paternal" genealogy and the "birthright" of an estate that mires him in the countryside.

However, this eruption of territoriality at the close of the novel also might be read otherwise, as an impression on *Pierre* of the questions of jurisdiction, sovereignty, and collective placemaking whose deferral largely makes possible the novel's queer displacement of the politics of occupancy. If Pierre identifies with Enceladus as an expression of "sphinx-like" mystery lodged in the landscape, the figure also recalls the struggle over the land toward which the text gestures in its discussion of tenant miseries.[120] As discussed earlier, the novel displaces the Anti-Rent War, avoiding any depiction of organized and armed tenant opposition as well as of the broader movement for land reform for which Anti-Rent served as a prominent and powerful icon, but in his tortured eruption from the apparently placid and charming countryside, Enceladus expresses a sense of barely suppressed conflict and serves as a trace of a history of such struggle.

In Pierre's vision, the mountain when viewed from the Saddle Meadows household appears lovely. However, as one actually approaches it, "long and frequent rents among the mass of leaves revealed horrible glimpses of dark-dripping rocks, and mysterious mouths of wolfish caves" (343): "Stark desolation, ruin, merciless and ceaseless, chills and gloom,—all here lived a hidden life, curtained by that cunning purpleness, which, from the piazza of the manor house, so beautifully invested the mountain once called Delectable, but now styled Titanic" (344). When examined more closely by moving out from the manor into the rest of the estate, the seeming ease and givenness of Glendinning ownership is revealed to be quite fraught, indicating a "hidden life" that has been "curtained" by the naturalization of patroon title. Despite Enceladus's seeming stillness, his immersion in rock, he "still turn[s] his unconquerable front toward that majestic mount" (345), and speaking of all of the rocks, the narrator notes, "no longer petrified in all their ignominious attitudes, the herded Titans now sprung to their feet, flung themselves up the slope, and anew battered at the precipice's unresounding wall" (346). While Pierre's vision concentrates on the "most potent" of the giants, Enceladus takes his place among all "the herded Titans," signaling a collective project of reclamation that continues despite the seeming impossibility of their quest. To the extent that the text here foregrounds the inevitability of failure, the senselessness of their struggle and the rage it produces, Melville aligns Pierre's "Titanic vision" with a "chain" that he must "drag at his o'erfreighted feet" (347), indexing Pierre's fatal failure to surrender the impotence-inducing connection to the country and embrace the dispersive potential of urbanity.[121] Yet, dwelling within the anxieties about the politics of rural occupancy rather than seeking to evade them through a move to the metropolis, one can see in the space of "nature" an unresolved struggle over legitimate placemaking that amplifies in a refracted way the passing reference at the beginning of the novel to the "regular armies" employed by the patroons to quell an otherwise textually unacknowledged (series of) renter uprising(s) (11).

In light of the novel's patterns of Indianization, the Enceladus section further can suggest how Anti-Rent agitation (including the use of "Indian" disguises and "tribal" organization) points back toward the broader problem of legitimizing land claims and the limits of legal discourse in doing so. The Anti-Rent movement and land reform posit an alternative Lockean vision of generationally accreting relations to land, locating this vision within the normative legacy of the American Revolution and presenting access to territory as one of the principles at stake in the struggle for independence. *Pierre*

eschews both Lockean landedness and the idea of revolutionary transformation. The figure of Enceladus, though, suggests less an effort—or failure—
to break from a prior regime than the latter's survival, traces of which are
misrecognized from afar as if they were merely expressions of "nature" (the
immanent continuity of the countryside with itself). The "herded Titans"
suggest a genealogically overdetermined collectivity evidence of whose
prior presence persists in/as the landscape in ways that resemble quite powerfully the situation of the Senecas and other Haudenosaunee peoples in the
period. When viewed from a perspective attentive to the ongoing pursuit
of self-determination by Indigenous peoples, what initially appears as a
conflict among settlers—in which *Indians* function as a mutable symbol of
ethical (im)possibility—morphs into a sign of the slipperiness of claims
to the land in light of the survival of a prior geopolitics of sovereignty. The
momentum of Melville's representation of the Titanic mountain pushes
toward a sense of Pierre's identification with Enceladus as a wrong one, as an
orientation toward estates upstate in the interest of reclaiming "his paternal
birthright" that indicates a failure to abandon genealogy and landedness as
hopelessly compromised. Yet, when read with an eye toward the Six Nations
and the modes of settler dispossession at play in and beyond this period, this
section of the novel suggests the palimpsestic quality of occupancy as well
as the everyday experience of previous political geographies as if they were
an expression of "the vigorous hand of Nature's self" (346). From this perspective, the flight to the metropolis functions less as an escape from this
history than an extension of it.

In this vein, an investment in the queer dispersions made possible by
the cityscape operates less as a break from the oppressive dynamics of rural
inhabitance than an evasion of the signs of continuing geopolitical contestation and an attempt to foreclose a sense of the violence through which the
extant system of governance secures inhabitance in both the country *and the
city*. The move to the urban as a site of ethical promise, in its supposedly
negative relation to the impositions and regulations of the law, then, appears
more as an effort to extricate oneself from exposure to formations of Indianness—including the Indianization of the country as backward, anachronistic, and mired in its own (properly superseded) particularity. Rather than
repudiating the backward-looking glance from the urban to the rural, as
the novel does, the somewhat askew view of the Titan-littered landscape

sketched above suggests a project of seeing the endurance of Indigenous peoples and an attendant engagement with the inscription and normalization of settlement as an accreting, generational dynamic that shapes non-natives' lived sense of place.

As in the possibilities offered by nonnuclear familial and household formation when unbound from a Lockean imaginary (as discussed in chapter 2) and of autoerotic reorientation freed from the process of securing a space apart for the expression of sovereign settler selfhood (addressed in chapter 3), *Pierre*'s critique of the ways legally regulated modes of lineage, property, and inheritance are presented and experienced as an immanent relation to the land itself potentially opens onto an engagement with the ways the experience of place is mediated by habituated patterns of normalization and "nature"-alization. The desire to flee from the space of Indianness in order to evade the scene of settler occupation is another *ambiguity* produced from within settler colonialism—a fantasy of escaping the orbit of histories of violence through the inhabitance of an elsewhere. The trajectory toward the metropolis, though, does not enable a (queer) transcendence of such ongoing legacies of struggle. In addition, the novel's fascination with, if also terror about, the autonomy of strangers in the cityscape implicitly takes a model of individualized personhood (separate from any form of collective belonging other than a de facto one to the state whose jurisdiction extends over the place in question) as normative, and it does so in ways that efface that ideal's embeddedness in extant settler legal norms, which help secure access to Indigenous lands by displacing Native modes of political legitimacy and forms of decision making. While *Pierre* suggests that claims to territory and processes of displacement constitute a crisis in contemporary ethics, the attendant anxieties about inhabitance and political belonging cannot be remediated through nonnatives' removal of themselves to an ostensibly less compromised location within the nation. The notion that such a place exists is itself a prominent feature of settler ethics and phenomenology.

While Melville expresses greater regret over the expropriation of Indigenous lands than Hawthorne or Thoreau, *Pierre*'s engagement with what it portrays as the *past* of Indian dislocation equally insulates nonnative ethics, subjectivity, and placemaking from the consequences of settler invasion, never mind its ongoing contemporaneity. All seal off Indigenous sovereignty into an Indianness that signals an anachronistic intrusion of what *was* into what *is*, an aberrant residue within nonnative modes of inhabitance, person-hood, and association. In doing so, they clear space for the articulation of oppositional projects of self-elaboration—Lockean, natural, metropolitan—that appear to have nothing to do with the tribal traces that sprinkle their texts. Melville's investment in the city as a perversely democratizing space that distends the legal-genealogical order of property looks quite different from Hawthorne's mobilization of the arguments of small property holders for the right to labor in the wilderness and Thoreau's effort to evade debt-inducing ownership through inhabitance in "Nature." Yet, *Pierre* also searches for a place beyond state regulation, itself cast as abetting a destructive and oppressive system of land tenure that benefits elites at the expense of every-one else. In this sense, he casts the city as a space apart, one that distends and corrodes the legal order at play in the country, leaving aside the ways that the growth of New York depends on the continuing expropriation of Haudenosaunee lands throughout this period. Similarly, Hawthorne's re-circulation of the image of "toil" by "actual settlers" effaces Wabanaki geog-raphies (signaled by the "Indian deed"), and Thoreau's retreat into the wild draws on the exceptionalization of Indigenous homelands in New England while evading how settler access to a supposedly unencumbered space of liberty depends on the abjection of Native people (producing the circum-stances of the basketmaker).

My aim, though, has not been to restore absented Native contexts or to locate proper Indigenous referents for the figures of Indianness that appear intermittently in these writings. Rather, considering the eruptions of other-wise irrelevant or marginal signs of indigeneity draws attention to the ques-tion of how settler colonialism operates when Native people(s) are not in the picture, how it functions as an ordinary mode of framing and experi-ence. Instead of seeking to fill in Native histories and presence, *Settler Com-mon Sense* has sought to explore the ways that nonnative conceptions and sensations of personhood, place, and belonging realize settlement as a con-tinuing phenomenon, taking as their template the legal and administrative processes through which Native land is incorporated into the jurisdiction of the settler-state and is made available for occupancy by nonnatives. In *Native Acts*, Joanne Barker argues that, as against scholarly and political efforts to produce a vision of authentic indigeneity, "[t]he challenge, then, is not how to capture the truth or the essence of the Native in the category of the Native; it is not about which discourse 'gets it right.' Rather it is to think through the kinds of historical circumstances that have been created to produce coherence in what 'the Native' means and how it functions in any given historical moment or articulatory act" (19). Flipping this analysis over, the challenge is not to remedy settler colonialism by generating a proper Native subject that nonnatives can recognize and with whom they can identify, but to think through the historical circumstances that cohere settler phenomenology as an anchor for nonnative sense-making and action in the world. Reading *The House of the Seven Gables*, *Walden*, and *Pierre* for traces of that dynamic in mid-nineteenth-century New England and New York functions as a way of locating how everyday forms of orientation that are predicated on settler occupation (and, reciprocally, that project a horizon of possibility shaped around the normalization of settlement) contour these texts' articulations, in ways that are not *about* (the portrayal of) Indians. They envision the potential for an ethics opposed to state policy, differently configured in each case, while implicitly making U.S. jurisdiction over "domestic" space and the displacement of Indigenous peoples a necessary background for their acts of political imagination.

These texts' queer interventions into the political economy of property holding, then, gain momentum from the impress of the legal geographies of settlement on quotidian experience (and the ongoing materialization of the former through the latter). From a particular critical vantage point, the idea of *queering* settler common sense might mean indicating how forms of queerness (however construed) might enable a critique or disjointing of settler colonialism. However, the various queernesses, and queer spaces, envisioned in the texts addressed here do not necessarily facilitate a challenge to settler sovereignty. Instead, their counterhegemonic potential works through a reinstantiation of the self-evidence of nonnative modes of jurisdiction and occupation. In this way, queering settler common sense might entail examining how relations, inclinations, imaginings, formations that might be collated as "queer" do not inherently escape the orbit of the continuing U.S. imperial absorption of Native peoples and territories. Such queer potentialities, in fact, may directly contribute to settlement by envisioning themselves as against, beyond, askew with respect to the state and its mappings.[122]

Conversely, though, analytical strategies employed within queer studies do offer the potential for intervening in this dynamic. All three of the texts I've discussed offer points of unevenness in which the potential for an else-where separate from the demands and impositions of the law itself becomes disjointed, riven by the nagging presence of political conflict over inhabi-tance and the contours of governance (the Indian deed, the basketmaker, the figure of Enceladus). The attention within queer studies to embodied feelings of rupture, disorientation, backwardness—to sensations that suggest a dislocation with respect to normative experiences of space and time—opens onto the possibility of attending to those moments when settler sen-soria reach their limits, confronted by Indigenous presence and persistent legacies of settler violence and expropriation. Taking up intellectual meth-ods from queer studies in reading such textual, and lived, occasions, though, is not equivalent to a reading of them *as queer*, instead drawing on such crit-ical strategies to highlight forms of contingency, contention, and negotiation routinely edited out in the (re)construction of a sense of settler constancy as the basis for nonnatives' assessment of and interaction with their environ-ment. In *The Amalgamation Waltz*, Tavia Nyong'o suggests of efforts to read the mixed-race body as redemptive of histories of U.S. racism, "is it not pos-sible to unyoke racial hybridity from its association with progressive, hetero-sexual time? Into what alternate temporalities might it then fall?" (176–77), and similarly, I have explored how unyoking queer intellectual tools from the location and validation of forms of queerness (as a distinct identity, pol-itics, mode, style, etc.) might enable an engagement with the temporality of *Indianness*—the cutting of indigeneity out of contemporary sensation and its being made anomalous in ways that allow nonnative affective formations to operate as if they were not intimately enmeshed with the reproduction of settler sovereignty.

My emphasis on the ongoing construction of settler geographies, sense impressions, and subjectivities in ordinary experience—the routine remak-ing of settlement through everyday forms of perception and action—raises the question of how such patterns might be disjointed. I have sought to address that potential in my readings, moving away from a sense of pre-given structure and toward ways of conceptualizing the regularities of settler colo-nialism as performative and processual, but my goal has not been to offer a ready means by which nonnatives might recognize and seek to remedy their continuing participation in projects of imperial occupation. Instead, I've highlighted the difficulty of locating unstated, implicit settler orientations, especially when they are not enunciated with respect to things *Indian*. Rather than suggesting the ease with which nonnatives might feel otherwise, I have aimed to sketch the ubiquity of sensory, emotional, political, and ethical investments in settlement and the ways that they do not function as conscious commitments that might be refuted, debunked, and repudiated. Highlighting the pervasiveness and recalcitrance of settler common sense works as a way of insisting on the need to read its enduring presence across the historical and cultural terrain of life in the United States. In *This Is Not a Peace Pipe: Toward a Critical Indigenous Philosophy*, Dale Turner observes that "[w]e cannot hope to fully understand the meaning and content of Aboriginal rights without understanding first how colonialism has been woven into the normative political language that guides contemporary . . . legal and political practices," adding that "[t]he project of unpacking and laying bare the meaning and effects of colonialism will open up the physical and intellectual space for Aboriginal voices to participate in the legal and political practices of the state" (30–31). Investigating how the givenness of settler legal and political practices has been woven into the nonnormative visions offered by Hawthorne, Thoreau, and Melville illustrates how the continuing effects of colonialism provide the horizon for these authors' ethical efforts to reimagine inhabitance, personhood, and association with others. Such analysis does not center on the representation of Native sovereignty, but it does seek to demonstrate methodologically what it might mean to proliferate a commitment to Indigenous self-determination, exceeding figurations of Indianness in favor of the difficult work of attending to how nonnative modes of being-in-the-world realize settler colonialism as their animating condition of possibility.

Notes

INTRODUCTION

1. This introduction serves as a more of sketch than a fully fleshed-out contextualization of my work in existing scholarship. For such references/engagements, see chapter 1.

2. I have chosen not to capitalize "nonnative" for two reasons, one stylistic and the other substantive: such capitalization looks typographically awkward to me; and I choose to distinguish in a more pronounced way between when I am referring to persons who are not Indigenous and those who are.

1. ORDINARY LIFE AND THE ETHICS OF OCCUPATION

1. For differently configured efforts to define settler colonialism, see Bruyneel; Coombes; Ford; Fujikane and Okamura; Goldstein; Jacobs; Johnston and Lawson; Morgensen; Niezen; Razack; Stasiulis and Yuval-Davis; Veracini; Wolfe, *Settler*.

2. For a sampling of extant queer analysis of nineteenth-century writing in the United States, see Castiglia; Castiglia and Looby; Coviello, *Tomorrow's*; Crain; Herring, *Queering*; Luciano; Moon; Nyong'o; Packard; Somerville; Stokes.

3. On the history and persistence of this trope, see P. Deloria, *Indians*; Dippie; Elmer; B. Miller; J. O'Brien, *Firsting*.

4. While I will directly address studies from the past twenty years, important earlier work includes that of Louise Barnett, Brian Dippie, Richard Drinnon, Leslie A. Fiedler, Myra Jehlen, Annette Kolodny, Robert F. Sayre, and Richard Slotkin. I am focusing here on nonnative representations, but for work on Native self-representation in the nineteenth century, see L. Brooks; Carlson; Carpenter; Cheyfitz, "The (Post)Colonial"; Justice, *Our Fire*; Kelsey; Konkle, *Writing*; Michaelsen; Murray; Peyer; Piatote; Rasmussen; Rifkin, *Manifesting*; Rifkin, *When*; Round; C. Walker; Warrior, *The People*; Weaver; Womack; Wyss.

5. In this vein, rather than seeking representations that allow for the consolidation of "the Indian" as a type that could serve as the object of (critical) sympathy, I am interested in tracing how figurations of Indianness participate in a broader set of normalizations that cast the conditions of settlement as given. On the problem of the (romantic) "type" with respect to enslavement, see Baucom.

6. The scholarly discourse of "settler colonialism" decidedly tends to be skewed toward Anglophone examples and histories in ways that leave aside other modes less committed to extermination/replacement but still ordered around the absorption of Indigenous peoples and lands into a state dominated by nonnatives. With respect to Hispanophone modes of imperialism and settler colonialism, see Brysk; Escalante; Mignolo; Diane Nelson; Radding; Saldaña-Portillo; Seed.

7. Both Wolfe and Moreton-Robinson address Australia in their earlier writings and extend their analyses to the United States in later work. Although I primarily focus on the United States, their formulations about both settler-states, and settler colonialism as a phenomenon, have been incredibly important in addressing Native peoples on lands claimed by the United States, and as with their work, I hope that mine might also speak to other settler-state contexts.

8. Thanks to Dana E. Powell for directing me to Latour as a way of thinking about the workings of Native–settler negotiations of sovereignty, and thanks to Matt Mullins, whose dissertation work prompted me to consider Latour's writings in greater detail.

9. For critiques of this scholarly habit with respect to the nineteenth century, see Garrison; Mandell, *Tribe*; Rosen. Thanks to Beth Piatote for helping me clarify this point.

10. For nonphenomenological explorations of how the history of federal Indian policy becomes part of everyday forms of nonnative self-understanding and boundary maintenance, see Biolsi; Fujikane and Okamura; Morgensen. For discussion of this process in Hispanophone settler colonialisms, see Alonso; Diane Nelson. For discussion of the ways state policies and legalities become part of quotidian experience, see also Das; Dayan; Povinelli, *Economies*; Salamon; Scott; Taussig; Wagner.

11. On "assemblage," see DeLanda; Protevi; and Puar. Some have critiqued the concept for rushing too quickly to a sense of malleability that leaves aside the continuity and durability of particular social identities, formations, and inequities. However, it emphasizes a process of putting together that directs attention toward how categories, relations, and subjugations continually are stabilized and maintained while also suggesting that an imperial formation like settlement might have a range of parts (institutions, discourses, practices, etc.) that interact in varied ways.

12. Work on affect, the everyday, and phenomenology largely does not investigate the enframing (geo)political ground on which such sensations occur, in Bryd's terms the "territoriality of conquest" (125). Instead, it tends to emphasize moments of perception and its possibilities for introducing new or unexpected relations rather than its capacity actively to enact forms of continuity. For discussion of this tendency, see Anderson; Dean. For examples, see Bennett, *Enchantment*; Dumm, *Politics*; Massumi; Seigworth and Gregg; K. Stewart. This dynamic also is present in Latour's work, but I have chosen to emphasize less the ways mediation makes

possible the unexpected than the ways it indicates the ongoing, active production of stability and regularity.

13. On Native structures of feeling, see also Brant; Carpenter; Driskill, "Stolen"; Goeman; Gould; Justice, "Go Away"; Piatote; Ramirez; Warrior, "Your Skin."

14. For other efforts to explore how affect, including eroticism, does not necessarily function in liberatory ways, see Berlant, *Cruel*; Holland; Povinelli, *Economies*.

15. For critiques of the politics of settler-states' recognition of Indigenous sovereignties and self-determination, see Barker; Coulthard; Dennison; Engle; Garroutte; Goeman; Lyons; B. Miller; Diane Nelson; Niezen; Povinelli, *Cunning*; Raibmon; Ramirez; Simpson, "Subjects"; Turner.

16. Thanks to Zach Laminack, whose dissertation work prompted me to engage more fully with Merleau-Ponty. On the relation between phenomenology and personhood as a kind of property of the state, see Salamon. For discussion of phenomenology (broadly conceived) in relation to processes of racialization, specifically blackness, see Allewaert; Holland; Ngai; Scott. The relation of nonwhite subjects to the kinds of settler sensoria I address are historically and conceptually fraught, but for reasons I elaborate further later, I would like to hold off on collapsing settler phenomenology into whiteness, instead maintaining a heuristic and semi-binaristic distinction between settlers and Natives so as to highlight forms of experiencing place and personhood that attach to modes of settler governance rather than to a specific racial identity.

17. In *Political Affect*, John Protevi addresses the ways system-level dynamics exceed the interactions/tendencies of individual elements, describing the system-generating effects that maintain forms of regularity as "feedback," and what I am characterizing as momentum functions similarly, although at the level of personal experience.

18. On the proliferation and institutionalization of "geographical literarcy" in the American colonies and early-republic (through the notation and diffusion of surveying techniques, use of national maps as decoration and part of material culture, and integration of geographical texts into the educational system), see Brückner. For discussion of how representations of and engagement with the landscape function as a means of articulating an expansive notion of American personhood, see Jehlen; R. Wilson.

19. On this simultaneous continuity and reframing, see Atack, Bateman, and Parker, "Northern"; Belich; Brückner; Calloway, *Scratch*; Coviello, *Intimacy*; Gates, *History*; Jensen; Jones; Dana Nelson, *National*; Rockwell; E. White; Yirush. On this reformulation of capacities from within one historical formation in the emergence of another, see Sassen.

20. On the failure of progressive arguments to account for the affective dimensions and dynamics of what is being critiqued, as well as its integration into nonconscious everyday patterns, see Berlant, *Cruel*; Bryson; Massumi; Protevi; Sedgwick.

21. On the ways such templates were gendered in the nineteenth century, potentially leading to different relations to place, see Jehlen; Kilcup; Kolodny, *Lay*.

22. Thanks to Audra Simpson for pushing me to clarify the role of vanishing/erasure in theorizing common sense and to Beth Piatote for calling on me to address the role of discourses of temporality in this process.

23. On racialization as a process of making anomalous in the nineteenth century, see Nyong'o.

24. See Rifkin, "Indigenizing." For a very different account of settler affect around histories of Indigenous dispossession, one concerned more centrally with processes of commemoration that explicitly address Native presence, see Elliott.

25. While not pursuing exactly Gerald Vizenor's discussion of "Indian" as a "simulation," my discussion of tropes of Indianness owes a debt to his theorization of the ways figurations of Indianness substitute for (rather than point to) engagements with Native peoples and "the tribal real." See Vizenor.

26. Notably, Morrison often gestures toward the presence of Native peoples and settler colonialism while then understanding them in terms of the presence of "race" which is equated with blackness, such as in referencing the "conquest" of the continent (3), suggesting that "what was distinctive in the New" of the New World was "the presence of the unfree" in bondage (48), citing "the desire for a limitless empty frontier" (51), and characterizing black male characters in Hemingway's writing as "Tontos all" (82).

27. See Perea. For a discussion of the role of mid- to late-nineteenth-century ethnological discourse in helping create the black/white binary as the primary mode of racial understanding in the United States, see Ben-Zvi.

28. I should note that I am not suggesting the complete absence of work on intersections of African American and Native histories in the nineteenth century. Such scholarship, though, largely has turned on either the possession of slaves by Native people, the presence of people of African descent as tribal members (particularly in New England), or white participation in benevolent campaigns against removal and/or slavery. For recent examples, see James Brooks; Chang; Lowery; Mandell, *Tribe*; Miles; Miles and Holland; Portnoy; Saunt; J. Sweet.

29. On the international dimensions of black freedom struggles, see Baucom; Doyle; Gilroy; Hartman; Kazanjian; Silva; Singh; Stephens; Sundquist, *To Wake*; Von Eschen. I should note, though, that Byrd's study seeks to explore relations between Indigenous peoples and nonwhite, nonnative populations in ways that are not inherently triangulated through whites, and the effort to foreground such relations among people of color might be understood as at odds with my effort to specify modes of everyday settlement by focusing primarily on the experiences of and texts by whites. In doing so, however, I do not mean to suggest a generic settler subject that displaces differential racial privilege (something akin to, "well, we're all settlers"), nor do I seek to downplay the role of race among nonnatives in shaping the

experience and stakes of participation in settler colonial dynamics. Rather, I aim to address everyday dynamics of settlement in ways that do not understand nonnative people of color as unimplicated in such processes, even while recognizing the vastly disproportionate benefits of settlement that accrue to whiteness and white people.

30. See also V. Deloria; Moreton-Robinson, "Writing off Treaties"; Rifkin, *Manifesting*; Wolfe, "Settler."

31. See also Andersen; Coombes; Jacobs; Johnston and Lawson; Miller et al.; Moreton-Robinson, *Whitening*; Razack.

32. I should note, though, that Morgensen presents racism toward nonnative people of color as itself an integral part of settler colonialism's operation as a fundamentally white supremacist formation. See also Fujikane and Okamura; Lawrence and Dua.

33. Byrd argues that "imperialism has forced settlers and arrivants to cathect the space of the native as their home" (xxxix). Using the term "arrivants" to name non-natives of color allows Byrd to recognize the endemic and profound force of various racisms in the process by which many people of color, or their ancestors, came to occupy land claimed by the United States; the central role played by U.S. imperialism in engendering those displacements and diasporas; and the enduring subjection of various nonnative populations to forms of unfreedom, exploitation, dispossession, and state-sanctioned (or organized) terror. In emphasizing how such dominations generate a *cathexis* to the "domestic" space of the nation that further enables and expands settler colonialism, she powerfully articulates the ways that part of the violence of other racializations in the United States lies in their making "arrivants" identify with and through settlement as a condition of participation within the nation.

34. I also do not think this difficulty is solved by recognizing that whiteness has international dimensions in terms of the United States' relation to other peoples and countries. See Kazanjian; Lowe; Silva. Such studies illustrate how international relations are shaped around racial ideologies, imperatives, and systems of value, but in doing so, "race" still functions conceptually as more or less a way of indicating forms of invidious distinction among populations rather than as a way of addressing the forced translation between systems of governance in which one arrogates to itself a metapolitical authority to define what constitutes the terrain of "politics" per se.

35. On the emergence of "Indian" as a form of racial identification in New England by whites, and self-identification for Native peoples, see Den Ouden; Mandell, *Tribe*; Shoemaker; D. Silverman, *Red*; J. Sweet.

36. For discussion of the lexical variability of the term "queer," see Chen, 57–88. For various understandings of queerness in relation to normative kinship formations, see Ahmed, *Queer*; Berlant and Warner; Edelman; Eng; Ferguson, *Aberrations*; Freeman, *Wedding*; Gray; Halberstam; Povinelli, *Empire*; Rifkin, *When*; Weston, *Families*.

37. For "heterosexual imaginary," see Ingraham.

38. While "reorientation" speaks to the issues of movement, environment, and perception within phenomenology, it resonates with José Muñoz's notion of disidentification.

39. On the emergence of bourgeois homemaking in the U.S. in the early nineteenth century, see Boydston; Coontz; Dillon; Merish; Rifkin, *When*.

40. For examples, see Castiglia and Looby; Coviello, *Tomorrow's*; Crain; Herring, *Queering*; McGarry; Moon; Packard.

41. For examples, see Abdur-Rahman; Brandzel; Chen; C. Cohen; Driskill et al; Ferguson, *Aberrations*; Freeman, *Wedding*; Hong and Ferguson; Justice, "Notes"; Luibhéid; Miranda, *Bad*; Morgensen; Povinelli, *Empire*; Puar; Rodríguez; Ross; Scott; Shah; A. Smith; Somerville; Stokes; Stoler; Tompkins.

42. Scholars in Native studies have offered a critique of such formulations, which sometimes travel under the name of "queer diaspora." See Driskill, "Doubleweaving"; Driskill et al.; Morgensen; A. Smith.

43. See also Coviello, *Tomorrow's*; Dinshaw et al; Freccero; Goldberg and Menon; McCallum and Tuhkanen; McGarry; Nealon; Scott.

44. For discussion of temporality in relation to other modes of colonization, see Chakrabarty; Fabian; McClintock; Young, *White*.

45. Freeman's invocation of "prosthetic memory" also seems applicable here: "Prosthetic memories are neither the scars of originary trauma nor the proprietary result of long, slow cultural inculcation like that of family heritage or ethnic birthright: they belong to nobody and everybody at once and are detachable from the context that produced them" (*Time*, 159–60).

46. On this history of canonization, see Cheyfitz, "Matthiessen's"; Pease.

47. For strong defenses of multiculturalism as a political project, even while acknowledging the problems of its (uneven) institutionalization, see Lauter; Newfield; Stam and Shohat. For critique of it as a project of containing and/or disavowing ongoing structural racisms, see Ahmed, *On Being*; Chow; Ferguson, *Reorder*; Lee; Melamed; Reddy; Sharpe.

48. See Bryson; Guillory; Lauter; Melamed.

49. In this vein, my dissertation project, focused on nonfiction writings by Native Americans and Mexican Americans in the antebellum period, continually was greeted with the question, "but is it literary?"—an "innocent" question that does a great deal of boundary work.

50. See also Lee; Melamed.

51. In *Muting White Noise*, James Cox explores the obverse of my aim here: how Native authors have produced "red readings" of canonical texts, signifying on them in ways that illustrate Native presence and settler violence.

52. On this dynamic within contemporary settler multiculturalism, see Povinelli, *Cunning*.

2. Romancing the State of Nature

1. The territory now known as the state of Maine was part of Massachusetts from 1692 until it became its own state in 1820, as part of the compromise that brought Missouri into the union as a slave state.

2. Versions of this same conflict were occurring at numerous other places beyond that particular stretch of territory in Maine. See Gates, *History*, 59–74; Huston, 33–35; Moody; A. Taylor, *Liberty*, 4–9, 44–45; E. White, 1, 73–121.

3. Shurtleff, *Concise* 31.

4. His mother's family, the Mannings, were landholders and in service to proprietors in Maine, although in an area south of the Kennebec, and Hawthorne resided on Manning lands in Maine in the 1810s during the conflict. Moreover, he attended Bowdoin College just in the wake of the end of the conflict, and a lifelong friend whom he met there, Horatio Bridge, was the son of one the chief attorneys for the proprietors (who later became a proprietor himself) of the Plymouth Patent on the Kennebec. In 1837 Hawthorne and Bridge visited Montpelier, the crumbling former residence of Henry Knox—the proprietor of the Waldo Patent. See Griffiths; Mellow, 12–35, 86–93; A. Taylor, *Liberty*, 244–46; Wineapple, 22–57.

5. Thanks to Peter Coviello for helping me to clarify my sense of the relation between Hawthorne's text and Lockean ideology as an orientation rather than an endorsement.

6. See Atack, Bateman, and Parker, "The Farm"; Belich; Larson; M. Morrison; Rousseau; Sánchez; Charles Sellers; Van Atta.

7. On Hawthorne's politics and political service, see Cheyfitz, "Irresistibleness"; Davis, 77–104; Levine, 129–33; Mellow; Murphy, 92–95; Reynolds; Wineapple.

8. This ideology, though, came under greater stress as the economy picked up again in the late 1840s and many Democrats began to seek opportunities to promote trade. The expansionism of the late 1840s and early 1850s enabled the extension of domestic markets and greater participation in foreign ones while also allowing annexed territories to be presented as a boon to an increasingly urbanized populace seeking the benefits and moral uplift of Lockean landedness as homesteaders on the frontier. See Atack, Bateman, and Parker, "Northern"; Eyal; Gates, *History*, 177–248; Hietala.

9. See also Bellis, 30–50. For a differently configured interpretation of the place of the state and nationalism in Hawthorne's writing, see Berlant, *Anatomy*.

10. Hawthorne's idea of "romance" in the novel usually is interpreted as a way of addressing the function of art and/or as a commentary on the penetration of technology and the market into everyday life. See Bellis, 30–50; Castiglia, 256–93; Davis, 35–52; M. Gilmore; Michaels; Milder, "Other"; Millington 105–53; Sundquist, *Home*, 86–142; Thomas, 71–90; Trachtenberg. For discussion of "romance" as a means of meditating on masculine modes of emergent middle-class notions of privacy, see Shamir, 147–74.

11. On Hawthorne's romance as about property and title, see Michaels; Thomas, 71–90.

12. Scholars often have described the novel as expressive of middle-class norms. See Arai; Brown, 63–95; H. Jackson; Lang, 30–41; Loman, 65–70, 86–95; Pfister, 144–61. For readings that see the text as having a more ambivalent or critical relation to bourgeois domesticity, see Baym; Castiglia, 256–93; Levine, 119–47; Millington 105–53; Murphy 83–96; Shamir 147–74.

13. Historians have suggested the powerful connections between the social upheaval in and around Salem that produced the Salem witch trials and the loss of property in, and displacement from, Maine due to ongoing conflict with Native peoples. See Baker and Kences; McWilliams, "Indian John"; Norton.

14. See H. Jackson, 273–75; Levine, 136. The idea of the House may be based on the experience of Hawthorne's cousin Suzanna Ingersoll, who had to engage in a legal fight to assert rights to a seven-gabled mansion in Salem. See Mellow, 175, 325–26; Wineapple, 142–43.

15. I will continue to capitalize "House" to indicate the House of the Seven Gables.

16. On the importance of Locke to the novel, see Michaels. Brook Thomas argues, "The Indian deed establishes a seemingly legitimate line of ownership from the Indians to the present-day ruling class, but Hawthorne grants no sanctity to the line of inheritance established by written documents," instead "imagin[ing] a more radical Jacksonian narrative by implying that the Indian deed would not be honored by white settlers of the land." This description of the settlers in Maine "implies that the virgin condition of America allowed a reenactment of the Lockean state of nature in which ownership was established by labor" (72–73).

17. This passage actually comes from an 1844 notebook entry by Hawthorne himself (Bellis, 185).

18. See Arai. Gillian Brown argues that the novel displaces women's domestic labor, but the portrayal of Phoebe less effaces the work of middle-class domesticity than connects her facility with housework to other kinds of honorable "toil" in the country. When Phoebe arrives in the city, Hepzibah, who has opened a shop in the House to try to remedy her lack of funds, finds that Phoebe has far greater ability as a saleswoman than she. Phoebe declares, "Oh, I have done all the shopping for the family, at our village-store. . . . And I have had a table at a fancy fair, and made better sales than anybody," adding, "You shall see that I am as nice a little sales-woman, as I am a housewife" (58). On Phoebe's commercial talents, see Brown, 77–81; M. Gilmore, 177–78; Millington, 115; Streeby, "Haunted."

19. While writing *House*, Hawthorne was living in a rented house in the Berkshires, a non-urban space that suggests something of the "country" to which he refers. See Mellow, 321–84; Wineapple, 218–44. On non-urban space in Massachusetts in this period, see Binford; Clark, *Roots*; Thornton. On the turn to non-urban

spaces as regenerative amid the growing pressures of commercialization, see D'Amore, "Thoreau's"; Newbury; Newman; Stowe.

20. See Griffiths, 434–35; A. Taylor, *Liberty*, 37–47; Williamson, 2:97, 161–62, 190–91, 238, 338, 398–99. Knox is a possible inspiration for Colonel Pyncheon. See Griffiths.

21. On this history, see Eves; Khan; Sturtevant; A. Taylor, *Liberty*; Williamson, 2:532, 606–8, 613–16.

22. On Shurtleff's background, see A. Taylor, *Liberty*, 101–5.

23. Shurtleff credits "Sullivan's late history" as the basis for his ideas about legitimate title (16). On Sullivan, who was from Maine and became governor of Massachusetts in 1808, see A. Taylor, *Liberty*, 216–17; Williamson, 2:401, 416, 606–7, 610.

24. Such a position is a bit odd for a man who had worked as a lawyer for the Plymouth Company and Henry Knox (A. Taylor, *Liberty*, 216), but he adds the caveat that "unless the purchase is made, to promote a settlement of a number, in similar circumstances of *want* and distress" (140), offering a potential out for proprietors.

25. On the importance of Locke in the colonies and the early republic, see Arneil, 168–200; Dworetz; Freyer; Konkle, "Indigenous"; Slauter, "Reading"; Tully, *Approach*, 137–76; Robert Williams; Yirush.

26. On English notions of "waste" land, see Macmillan; Seed; Robert Williams; Yirush.

27. On the intellectual context in and against which Locke writes, see Arneil; Ivison, "Locke"; Macpherson; Tully, *Approach*.

28. In fact, the majority of the pamphlet is framed as a speech by the Goddess of Freedom.

29. On Ely, see Moody; A. Taylor, *Liberty*, 105–14.

30. We are told that Hepzibah is willed a "life-estate" by the prior owner, but actual ownership is willed to Jaffrey (20).

31. See Millington, 157; Thomas, 55.

32. See Bellis 33–34.

33. This incident reflects the fact that the Waldo Patent almost was revoked after the Revolution due to the Loyalist leanings of its current holders. See A. Taylor, *Liberty*, 39.

34. The link to Englishness also implicitly alludes to running public concerns, and Democratic Party charges, about the intimate relation between the commercialization of the frontier and British investments. See M. Morrison. On massive British investment on the U.S. frontier in this period, see Belich.

35. Brook Thomas notes, "Hawthorne's sketch of the history of the House of the Seven Gables suggests that the present system has a faulty foundation," but "he goes on to question the possibility that any human product can intentionally be made to coincide with natural law" (45).

36. On Democratic Party rhetoric, see Eyal; Feller; Hietala; Jensen; M. Morrison; Charles Sellers; Van Atta.

37. This dynamic can be understood, in Gramsci's terms, as a kind of "criticism [that] makes possible a process of differentiation and change in the relative weight of the elements the old ideologies used to possess. What was previously secondary and subordinate, or even incidental, is now taken to be primary—becomes the nucleus of a new ideological or theoretical complex" (195). Further, as Raymond Williams argues in *Marxism and Literature*, dominant formations offer "a version of the past which is intended to connect with and ratify the present. What it offers in practice is a sense of *predisposed continuity*," and for this reason, "It is significant that much of the most accessible and influential work of the counter-hegemony is historical" (116).

38. See Latour, *Reassembling*.

39. The last major alteration had occurred in the early 1840s, when Congress passed legislation decreasing the price of western lands and the acreage in each purchasable unit while vastly increasing preemption rights. While supported as a boon to farmers who wanted to work the land themselves, critics worried lower costs and the absence of public bidding would encourage gaming of the law by speculators. See Atack, Bateman, and Parker, "Northern"; Gates, *History*, 145–76, 219–47; Jensen, 171–86; Lause; M. Morrison; Van Atta. The acquisition in the 1840s by the United States of tens of millions of acres of public land in former Mexican territory and Oregon exponentially magnified this problem, which is part of what drove the controversies leading to the Compromise of 1850. See Hietala, 95–131. Hawthorne was well aware of these issues when writing *House*, signing a Free Soil petition against the terms of the compromise (particularly the Fugitive Slave Law) in spring 1851. See Levine, 132; Reynolds, 183; Wineapple, 242–43. David Reynolds argues with respect to *House*, "It is not difficult not to see in that romance a veiled critique of the Mexican War and the ill-gotten gain of massive new territory, including California" (153–54). For a reading of the text as more ambivalent about U.S. expansionism, see Murphy, 83–96.

40. On the crucial role of public lands in the crisis of 1837, in particular President Jackson's specie circular, see Anthony, "Banking"; Gates, "Role"; Rohrbough, 221–49, 271–94; Rousseau; Sánchez, 28–41; Charles Sellers, 346–47, 353–54.

41. See Eyal. On the effects of economic dislocation in Salem in this period, see Michaels, 164–65.

42. Versions of the phrase "actual settlers" that Hawthorne uses to describe small landholders in Maine were used repeatedly in statutes with respect to the public lands in the 1840s and 1850s. See Jensen, 179.

43. Anthony, "Banking," 725.

44. On the figure of the asylum in the novel, see Knadler.

45. See Thomas, 86.

46. In contrast, Jaffrey's wealth has no direct relation to any sort of work at all. After his death, Hepzibah and Clifford as his next of kin inherit "a couple of hundred thousand . . . and some say twice as much" (225), but other than Jaffrey's time as a judge and in politics, readers learn nothing of how he acquired his fortune. Either it was what remained of the "great wealth" willed to him by his uncle (18–19), which was gained through indeterminate "investments" (165), or Jaffrey had his own somewhat speculative portfolio.

47. See also Anthony, "Banking."

48. For a different version of such a reading, see Sundquist, *Home*, 86–142.

49. Numerous critics have noted the oddity of the ending. See Brown, 76; Castiglia, 269–70; Davis, 134–37; M. Gilmore, 172–73; Lang, 40–41; Millington, 148–53; Murphy, 91–92; Reynolds, 177; Streeby, "Haunted"; Trachtenberg, 478.

50. One, though, could read the genre of the romance as itself part of Hawthorne's "attempt to imagine and experience the labor of authorship as a form of nonmanual labor . . . aligned with and economically dependent on the manual" (Newbury, 697)—a kind of work that is other than urban and is connected to the toil in the country.

51. Ahmed, *Queer*, 15.

52. Latourian hybridity is not to be confused with that articulated by Homi Bhabha, or inhabiting such critical figures as "the borderland," "mestizaje," "encounter/contact," and "the middle ground." See Bhabha. For critiques of such postcolonial notions of mixture, see Spivak; Young, *Colonial*.

53. See A. Taylor, *Liberty* (esp. 89–121, 181–207). On previous association of whites in Maine with Indians, see K. Morrison, 105–6. On the association of backcountry whites with Indians in the American colonies and early republic, as well as the ways settlers might see Native peoples as providing a model for their own development of modes of collectivity with which to oppose centralized administrative policy, see E. White. On the equation of respectability and landed wealth with the territory itself (and with forms of Indianness) in elite discourse in the late eighteenth century and early nineteenth century, see Hallock, 177–216.

Notably, the act of whites disguising themselves as "Indians" in Maine repeatedly was described as "blackening" themselves. See Sturtevant, 274; A. Taylor, *Liberty*, 87, 89, 115, 117. In this vein, the references to the blackness of white characters in *House* usually has been interpreted as an allusion to slavery, but given the role of settler struggle in Maine as an intertext for the novel, it may signal Indianness. On blackness in the novel, see Anthony, "Class"; H. Jackson, 281–87; Levine, 140–42; Michaels, 168–78; Murphy, 83–84, 95–96. On the complex overlaps between discourses of blackness and Indianness in eighteenth- and nineteenth-century New England, see Den Ouden; Mandell, *Tribe*; J. O'Brien, *Dispossession*; Reynolds, 25, 84–85; D. Silverman, *Faith*, 223–73.

54. Huston, 107–30; Kades, 945; Lause, 23–24. I will address this movement in greater detail in chapter 4.

55. Williamson, 2:616. See also A. Taylor, *Liberty,* 224, 228.

56. Most famously this strategy was used in the Boston Tea Party. See P. Deloria, *Playing,* 10–37.

57. See Den Ouden; J. O'Brien, *Dispossession;* D. Silverman, *Faith.*

58. Here I am drawing on Craig Yirush's marvelous account in *Settlers, Liberty, and Empire.* On the relation between natural rights arguments and the appropriation of Native lands in the late colonial period, see also Banner, 10–111; Calloway, *Scratch;* Dowd, *War under Heaven;* Hinderacker; Hurt, 3–27; Jones, *License,* 1–119; Robertson, 3–27; E. White; R. White, 223–365.

59. Latour, *Reassembling,* 196.

60. Timothy Powell incorrectly suggests that the deed actually was bartered for the House's grounds (43).

61. See Powell, 30–48. Other critics also have read the deed as offering a critique or qualification of white expansionism. See Levine, 136; Murphy, 84–85. On Hawthorne's earlier critique of colonial English relations with Native peoples in the founding of Salem, see Colacurcio; Reynolds, 154.

62. In "The Governance of the Prior," Elizabeth Povinelli observes, "The priority of the prior person (or people) as a natural right of all persons and the people as such emerged as an impediment to the previous logics of kingly seizure and to the emergent logic of colonial governance" (17). However, when confronted with extant polities in spaces over which the English sought to exert authority, the "natural right" of priorness runs into a problem, the existence of Indigenous peoples whose presence "challeng[es] what kinds of entities and relations can be the basis of a sovereign claim" (15).

63. I should note that not all nonnatives have the same access to claims-making through labor and that labor in the antebellum period often serves as a means of arguing for the rights of whites as against African Americans, whose racial linkage to slavery often is perceived as disqualifying them from serving as self-possessed, Lockean political subjects. See Coviello, *Intimacy;* Roediger; Stanley. However, African Americans also made claims to national belonging and citizenship through invocations of labor, seeking to enact a Lockean narrative that similarly displaces Native sovereignties. See Rifkin, "Home"; Ruffin, 25–55. On this dynamic in the Caribbean, see S. Jackson.

64. For discussion of the ways liberal systems of value can depend for their normative appeal on the effacement of Indigenous geopolitics, see Ivison, *Postcolonial;* Povinelli, *Cunning;* Tully, *Strange;* Turner.

65. In *John Locke and America,* Barbara Arneil observes, "the question 'How was private property created by the first men?' is for Locke the same question as 'Who has just title to appropriate the lands of America now?'" (134)

66. As Tully observes, "The juxtaposition gives the impression that land which is not put under labour intensive cultivation for the market is wasted or is not used beneficially," and "[t]hus, by definition, a political society only comes into being on the basis of, and to govern, a regime of private property created by expanding needs and intensive agricultural production for the market" (*Approach*, 163–64). See also Arneil, 146–51; Macpherson, 203–14.

67. In *Why We Left*, Joanna Brooks offers a wonderful discussion of the ways forms of enclosure and land dislocation in Great Britain produced transatlantic migration. See also Cheyfitz, *Poetics*.

68. In "Locke, Liberalism and Empire," Duncan Ivison notes that "in order to define the nature and scope of rights, claims have to be made about the nature of persons, and particularly about those qualities or powers to which the rights refer, or are intended to protect" (97). Locke correlates generic personhood with a particular way of inhabiting space, and in the next section, I will explore further the implications of this linkage for addressing the novel's notions of selfhood, sexuality, and inheritance.

69. Merleau-Ponty, 277, 509.

70. For an overview of Penobscot history, see Kolodny, "Summary"; MacDougall. Hawthorne might have known something about the contemporary Penobscots given that Henry David Thoreau had interacted with them as early as 1838 and certainly in his trip to Maine in 1846, and Thoreau and Hawthorne knew each other well from Hawthorne's time living on Emerson's property (The Old Manse) in the early 1840s and remained in touch, at least intermittently, afterward. See Cain, 36–37, 51; Harding, *Days*, 137–41, 192, 236, 308–9; Sayre, 104, 155–93; Wineapple, 157–76. Additionally, Penobscots actually came to the Concord, Salem, and Worcester areas with some regularity during the 1830s and 1840s. See Doughton, 210; Harding, *Days*, 107; Mandell, *Tribe*, 140; Thoreau, *Walden*, 19.

71. On the running conflicts over that period, which have been described as the Anglo-Abenaki Wars, see Baker and Reid; Belmessous; Bourque, 147–208; L. Brooks, 1–51; Calloway, *Western*; Ghere, "Diplomacy"; Ghere, "Mistranslations"; Haefeli and Sweeney; K. Morrison; Walker, Conkling, Buesing; Williamson, 2:9–345.

72. See Baker and Reid. On the negotiation of seventeenth-century deeds just west of Penobscot territory, see Baker, "A Scratch."

73. In *The Unmasked Nabob of Hancock County*, Ely repeatedly refers to General Knox's proprietary claims as based on a "spurious patent."

74. Williamson, 1:240.

75. Williamson, 2:190–91. On Madockawando, see MacDougall, 64–75.

76. See Baker, "A Scratch"; Belmessous; Bourque, 141–42; Ray. For similar kinds of agreements in Massachusetts and southern New Hampshire in roughly the same period, see Leavenworth.

77. Bourque, 121; Ghere, "Diplomacy," 122; MacDougall, 62.

78. See Belmessous; Ghere, "Mistranslations"; Ghere and Morrison; Williamson, 2:67, 92, 113, 145–46, 258–59.

79. Calloway, *Dawnland*, 116–17. The full reply is reprinted in Calloway, *Dawnland*, 115–18.

80. Pawling, 36–37; Walker, Conkling, and Buesing, 58. This agreement reiterates the terms of one with the colonial government in 1769. See Kolodny, "Summary" 13. On Penobscot participation in the Revolution more broadly, see MacDougall, 93–106.

81. Pawling, 44–54. This tactic was used by the U.S. government with respect to numerous peoples, including Revolutionary allies, throughout the 1780s and into the mid-1790s. See Banner; Barnes; Hurt; Jones; Prucha, *American*; A. Taylor, *Divided*. William Williamson notes that as of 1783, approximately two-thirds of Maine was still not appropriated by nonnatives (Williamson, 2:506).

82. Answer of the Indian Chiefs to the Commissioner delivered by Oronoe 4th Sept. 1784, legislative packet for March 11, 1797, chapter 86, Resolve for carrying out agreement with Penobscot Indians, and directions to the Quarter Master General (Massachusetts State Archives).

83. L. Brooks, xxi.

84. On the role of claims about the British lack of geographical knowledge of the colonies as a significant part of revolutionary stagings of the legitimacy of American self-rule, see Brückner, 51–97.

85. See Havard, 139; Pawling, 40, 68; Prins, 109; Speck, *Penobscot*, 203–29; Williamson, 2:67.

86. On the Wabanaki confederacy, see Borque, 235–44; L. Brooks, 1–50; Calloway, *Dawnland*, 3–23; Calloway, *Western*, 166–67, 193–96; Havard, 34–35, 122; MacDougall, 75–83; K. Morrison; Prins; Speck, "Eastern"; W. Walker; Walker, Conkling, and Buesing; Williamson, 2:217. There has been scholarly disagreement over how to understand the social geography of the areas that became northern Massachusetts and Maine prior to sustained European contact in the early seventeenth century. For varying perspectives, see Baker, "Finding"; Bourque, 103–9; Prins; Snow; Speck, *Penobscot*, 12–24. For discussion of Indigenous peoples to the west surrounding the Connecticut River and the Lake Champlain corridor up to the St. Lawrence River, see Brooks, 1–50; Calloway, *Western*; Haefeli and Sweeney. The terms "Wabanaki" and "Abenaki" sometimes are used as synonyms but commonly designate different groups, the former east of the Kennebec River and the latter west of the Connecticut River. However, they share related languages and a complex history of shifting political alliances and kinship relations with each other. For a powerful statement of the existence of a somewhat cohesive Wabanaki sense of territoriality and identity, extending to at least the late nineteenth century, see Brooks, 246–54. Micah Pawling suggests that the notion of a Wabanaki "cultural homeland" can displace some of the problems in trying to define/impose tribal distinctions, especially in earlier periods (24).

87. See Bourque, 124, 127; MacDougall, 49, 66; K. Morrison, 34–36; Prins, 104–7; Snow, 301–3.

88. See Bourque, 111–45; Kolodny, "Summary," 7; MacDougall, 54–67; K. Morrison.

89. Quoted in Bourque, 144.

90. See Bourque, 173–75, 193, 235–41; Havard, 37, 252–53; Speck, "Eastern"; W. Walker; Walker, Conkling, and Buesing. The treaties of the eighteenth century that include the Penobscots also routinely include neighboring peoples as well. See Calloway, *Dawnland,* 107–18; Williamson, 2:145–46, 258–59.

91. See Speck, "Eastern," 498; Walker, Conkling, and Buesing, 72.

92. MacDougall, 11; Speck, "Eastern," 498, 503–5; W. Walker, 114, 116–18, 123; Walker, Conkling, and Buesing, 71–73.

93. Pawling, 73–81; Williamson, 2:571. Micah Pawling notes that this treaty only established a southern boundary for the Penobscots, rather than a specific area to be surveyed and that, as a result, the Penobscots continued to possess most of the river's watershed—a territory "more than half of the state's present-day size" (78, 87).

94. Report of the commissioners, legislative packet for Feb. 26, 1796, chapter 97, Resolve appointing commissioners to treat with the Penobscot Indians (Massachusetts State Archives).

95. Translation of the Answer of the Indians Aug. 5, 1796, legislative packet for March 11, 1797, chapter 86, Resolve for carrying out agreement with Penobscot Indians, and directions to the Quarter Master General (Massachusetts State Archives).

96. Message from the governor, legislative packet for June 23, 1797, chapter 45, Resolve on the message from the governor, respecting certain complaints of the Penobscot Indians and appointing an agent and directing the quartermaster general to make provision, and grant for that purpose (Massachusetts State Archives).

97. Pawling, 133–34; Williamson, 2:669.

98. Petition of Penobscot Indians, legislative packet for February 13, 1818, chapter 120, Resolve on the Petition of Penobscot Indians (Massachusetts State Archives).

99. See Ferland; Pawling, 146–48.

100. Walker, Conkling, and Buesing, 75.

101. On the numerous petitions sent by Penobscots to state officials in the late eighteenth and nineteenth centuries, see Pawling, 84–151.

102. On the role of the federal government in administering expansion in the West in the mid-nineteenth century, see Hietala; Prucha, *American Indian Treaties*; Rockwell; Trennert. On the persistent narrative of the United States as lacking much in the way of a state apparatus before the late nineteenth century, see Jensen; Novak; Rockwell; Sylla.

103. On the dismissal of Native peoples in southern New England as not appropriately "Indian" in the eighteenth and nineteenth centuries, see Den Ouden; Mandell, *Tribe*; J. O'Brien, *Firsting*; D. Silverman, *Faith*.

104. Prucha, *Documents*, 15. This violation of the terms of the various Trade and Intercourse Acts by the states became a major legal issue starting in the 1970s when peoples in New England sought and received federal recognition as tribes and won suits for the acknowledgment of their rights to large swaths of land. In Maine such judgments opened up the possibility of Penobscot and Passamaquoddy claims to approximately two-thirds of the state prior to the Maine Indian Claims Settlement Act in 1980 (Prucha, *Documents*, 297–99). Notably the Penobscots were seen as more authentically Indian than many other groups in New England. As James Sullivan notes in his "History of the Penobscott Indians" (1804), they "are the only native savages, which have lived unmixed with the white people and negroes, preserving the savage aboriginal manners of life, within the commonwealth of Massachusetts" (210). On the process of federal recognition and land settlement in Maine, see Brodeur; MacDougall, 1–35; Rolde, 10–54. On the significance of referring to agreements with the Penobscots in the late eighteenth and nineteenth centuries as "deeds" rather than "treaties," see Pawling, 60, 146. Notably, Henry Knox, who was the Secretary of War under President Washington and was a vocal proponent of treaties with Native peoples instead of warfare, had direct financial interests in Penobscot and Passamoquoddy lands, likely contributing to Massachusetts's decision to treat Indian affairs as a state matter. See Rolde, 22–24; A. Taylor, *Liberty*.

105. The vast expansion of available "public land" in the late 1840s through purchases of Native territories and the Mexican-American War set off fears of renewed speculation, such as those that produced earlier financial panics and depressions, but Hawthorne does not address the problem of land tenure in those spaces which are of most concern. As Gretchen Murphy wryly observes of the text's ending, "They light out not to the territories but to the suburbs" (91–92).

106. On possessive individualism, see E. Cohen; Collier, Maurer, and Suárez-Navez; Coontz; Dillon; Macpherson; Merish; Shamir.

107. Castiglia, 281.

108. For example, the text associates Holgrave and Phoebe's courtship with Eden (152, 216). This sense of endorsing heteroromance is amplified by the fact that Hawthorne referred to his wife Sophia as "Phoebe" and that he often characterized their first home together, which he called "the Old Manse," as "Eden." See Loman, 17; Wineapple, 157–77. However, in describing Clifford's feelings about the House's garden, the narrator notes, "It was the Eden of a thunder-smitten Adam, who had fled for refuge thither out of the same dreary and perilous wilderness, into which the original Adam was expelled" (107). That sensation of a return to a foundational state of wholeness in nature, one that turns back the clock to a purer time, exceeds the terms of hetero-desire.

109. See Castiglia, 263–64; Levine, 135–36; Thomas, 54.

110. See Blumin; Boydston; Coontz; Cott, *Bonds*; D'Emilio and Freedman.

111. Some critics have suggested that the text contests the idea of a biological transference of capacities and tendencies. Robert Levine notes that the House and Pyncheon wealth largely are not conveyed from parents to children, instead following less linear routes and thereby indicating "mixed-up" "bloodlines" that sever Pyncheon "degeneration" from actual "inbreeding" (140), and Christopher Castiglia argues that the text presents the notion of "family character"—the impression of "interior predisposition[s]" conveyed naturally through reproduction—as itself a back formation from the legal matrix of family-formation, property holding, and land tenure (269, 278–79). On the text's characterization of certain characters as un-Pyncheon-like, see Arai.

112. Some critics have suggested that the shift from elite lineage to bourgeois homemaking in the novel signals an embrace of whiteness as a kind of property. See Anthony, "Class"; H. Jackson. However, the text's depiction of "blood" primarily as a vector of degeneration seems to work against the claim of an investment in the coherence and value of whiteness. For a slightly differently configured critique of such readings, see Levine, 119–47. Moreover, *House* does not offer an account of the affective richness of bourgeois homemaking, a feature which Ezra Tawil has argued is central in the construction of familially defined racial difference in the early to mid-nineteenth century (92–128).

113. See Coontz; D'Emilio and Freedman; Godbeer; Shammas.

114. In *Interior States*, Christopher Castiglia suggests that the text models forms of "*queer interiority*": "Hawthorne's characters are queered by excessive and inscrutable emotions, devotion to the past, anti-social reclusiveness, economic and biological non-productivity, and lack of control over bodily functions" (278).

115. Gretchen Murphy presents the union of Holgrave and Phoebe, and Holgrave's turn to "laws" at the end, as a symbolic rejoinder to what Hawthorne considered to be the excesses of U.S. expansionism, their marriage suggesting a relative, regulative compromise in envisioning U.S. domestic space (83–96).

116. See Chambers-Schiller.

117. See Chambers-Schiller; Cott, *Public*; Isenberg; Stanley.

118. See Basch; Cott, *Public*, 24–55; Isenberg, 155–90; Shammas, 53–82.

119. On the relation between Clifford and contemporaneous discourses of insanity and institutionalization, see Knadler.

120. See Anthony, "Class," 254. On the prominence of fears of masturbation (particularly by men) in the mid-nineteenth-century United States, see Bertolini; Burbick, 77–95; Castiglia, 168–215; Fowler; Graham; Haynes; Nissenbaum, 25–38; Sokolow, 77–99. I will address this issue further in chapter 3.

121. Additionally, the railroad's association with movement west, and attendant forms of speculation, makes it a problematic figure in the text, and when Clifford

and Hepzibah disembark, they see the remains of a church and a farmhouse—
figures of traditional village life in New England—which prompts them to return
to Salem, suggesting a (perhaps ambivalent) connection to country life that con-
travenes Clifford's manic *nomadism*. See Bellis, 44–47; Levine, 146–47; Millington,
149–51; Murphy, 89–91.

122. Further, as suggested in the text's emphasis on Phoebe and Holgrave's
"country"-inspired participation in the market, the alternative *House* offers to aristocratic title and government power is not an anticapitalist embrace of proletarianism
or socialism. Critics tend to offer a fairly monolithic sense of the "capitalism" the text
is read either as refusing or confirming (in the form of an endorsement of middle-
class domesticity). See Anthony, "Class"; Brown, 63–95; Lang, 30–41; Michaels;
Millington, 105–53; Pfister, 146; Streeby, "Haunted"; Thomas, 71–90. The text's
perspective can be contrasted with the more broadly socialist ideas about wealth
and land reform in the period, such as those championed by the National Reform
Association. See Jensen, 171–205; Lause; Newman; Zahler.

123. On Fourierism in the United States, see Delano; Guarneri; Loman; Spurlock. The community of Brook Farm, in which Hawthorne lived for a time in the
early 1840s, eventually became a Fourierist phalanx, but not while he was there. On
his time at Brook Farm, see Mellow, 178–87; Newbury; Wineapple, 144–54. For the
influence of Fourierism on Hawthorne's work, see Loman; Pfister, 156–59.

124. As Loman notes, "the garden also recalls the Fourierist attempt to reconcile
city and nature"—"the regenerative garden is analogous to those demanded by
Fourierist theorists" (58). On mesmerism in the novel, see Anthony, "Class," 260–
61; Brown, 86–90; Davis, 131–32; Lang, 35–37; Loman, 98–99; Michaels, 173–78;
Millington, 137–40; Sundquist, *Home*, 86–142.

125. The linking of Holgrave to Fourierism and other countercultural movements, though, seems less obscure in light of their connection to land reform movements, particularly as led by the National Reform Association, in the late 1840s.
See Lause, 35–46; Wilentz, 335–43; Zahler, 52–56. I will address this topic further
in chapter 4.

126. On Fourierism and other similar movements as forms of "middle-class radicalism," see Spurlock.

127. Bieder, 35, 43.

128. Trautmann, 36–57. On Morgan's career and significance more broadly, see
Bieder, 194–246; Kuper; Trautmann.

129. On the linking of Native peoples to forms of aristocracy, through both the
figure of the "noble savage" and the notion of primitive despotism, see Onuf, 30–39.

130. If Morgan's categories in *League* to some extent come out of Blackstone,
Blackstone's formulations often invoke or allude to Locke's. See Arneil, 176–82. On
Blackstone's extensive popularity in the United States, see Basch, 43–44; Welke,
27–28.

131. See Levine, 136.

132. Luciano does not explore this dimension of settler–Indigenous relations, such as in her argument that the history and modes of grief performed by William Apess's "Eulogy on King Philip" operate in the service of gaining Indians inclusion within U.S. citizenship (53–56).

133. Luciano, 21.

3. Loving Oneself Like a Nation

1. Sayre 60. This idea also was circulated by some of the initial reviews of *Walden* (Bellin, *Demon* 59) and gets repeated at times in Thoreau criticism. See Richardson, 219; Robinson, 96; Sayre, ix, 203.

2. See L. Brooks, 163–218; Doughton; Mandell, *Tribe*; J. O'Brien, *Firsting*; O'Connell; Plane and Button; D. Silverman, *Faith*; D. Silverman, "Impact."

3. On the becoming Indian of nonnatives, see Byrd; P. Deloria, *Playing*; Green; Huhndorf; Simpson, "Captivating."

4. On the representation of Indians in Thoreau's writing, see Bellin, *Demon*, 58–70; Bellin, "Taking"; Bellis, 121–41; Frost; P. Gilmore; Gura, "Thoreau's"; Maddox, 131–68; Mielke, 93–114; Dana Nelson, "Thoreau"; Paryz, 123–50; Richardson, 219–23; Robinson (esp. 29–47); Sayre; B. Taylor. On the place of westward expansion in Thoreau's writing, see Schneider, "Climate." As a counterpoint, see Buell, "Manifest."

5. This line in *Walden* may be a play on Ralph Waldo Emerson's earlier remark that "man shall treat with man as a sovereign state with a sovereign state" (Newman, 113).

6. On contemporary accounts that characterized Thoreau as selfish and eccentric, see Abelove; Myerson, *Emerson and Thoreau*, 371–414. On the ways contemporary scholarship has characterized Thoreau as self-obsessed and immature, see B. Taylor, 1–13.

7. On the erotics of Thoreau's writing, see Abelove; Coviello, *Tomorrow's* chap. 1; Harding, "Thoreau's"; Kaplan, 177–205; Walls, 124–26, 142–44; Warner.

8. Raymond Williams, 110–11.

9. My argument here resonates with Scott Morgensen's discussion of the ways "queer primitivism" enacts a settler colonial relation to place even as it seems to provide a more radical alternative to the homonormative embrace of the nuclear family, nationalism, private property, and consumerism (161–94).

10. While I will address readings of *Walden* from within political theory and ecocriticism as relevant, I should note that interpreting Thoreau's account of nature as dependent on settler jurisdiction raises questions about the enframing assumptions of both approaches. The former tends to presume the coherence of the U.S. nation-state and usually to position it as a horizon of political legitimacy/aspiration. For examples, see Kaplan, 177–205; Mariotti; Rosenblum; B. Taylor. The latter

often treats the "natural" world as a referential given rather than a back-formation from the politics of jurisdiction (the conditions through which spaces come to appear as beyond/outside politics). For examples, see Buell, *Environmental*; Cafaro, 139–73; Knott; McKusick; Myers; Richardson; Robinson; Rossi. On the problem of the concept of "nature" due to its tendency to reify certain locales, its usual association with purity, its articulation as the absence of mediation, its racialized equation with nonwhite persons, and its implicit alignment with class-inflected notions of leisure, see Allewaert; Cronon, "The Trouble"; Latour, *Politics*; Mazel; Morton; Newman; Phillips; Ruffin.

11. On *Walden* as seeking to offer alternative ways of being amid the problems of worsening conditions of work and livelihood, see Fanuzzi; Gleason; Grusin; Neufeldt; Newman; Newbury; B. Walker.

12. See Coontz, 73–160; Coviello, *Intimacy*, 25–57; Dillon, 11–48, 116–96; Keyssar, 3–43; Merish, 29–87; Dana Nelson, *National*, 26–60; Rohrbough; Charles Sellers; Welke, 21–62; E. White; Zagarri.

13. On this dynamic, see Fanuzzi.

14. See Atack, Bateman, and Parker, "Northern"; Gross, "Culture"; Yanella.

15. See Atack, Bateman, and Parker, "Farm"; Feller; Gates, *History*, 145–76, 219–47; Lause; M. Morrison; Van Atta; Zahler, 81–146.

16. On the use of the figure of enslavement to describe the wrongful subjection of whites, see Kazanjian; Roediger; Sánchez-Eppler; Slauter, *State*; Stanley.

17. See Burbick, 61.

18. Thoreau's analysis of "cost" neither opens into a broader critique of capitalist exploitation, distinguishing his work from extant socialisms (including those championed by other Transcendentalists such as Orestes Brownson), nor does it repudiate bodily excess per se. See Grusin; Gura, *American*; Newman.

19. See Boydston; G. Brown; Cott, *Bonds*; Dillon; Merish; Shamir.

20. On the relation between Thoreau's writing and advice manuals on domesticity and homebuilding, see D'Amore, "Thoreau's"; Gleason; Tichi. For discussion of how Thoreau's account of privacy and household-construction resonates with bourgeois norms of masculinity, see Shamir, 175–228. On women readers' identification with *Walden* despite its sexism, see Wider.

21. On Thoreau's representation of the Fields, and Irish immigrants more broadly, see Gleason; Rosenblum; Yanella.

22. On the nineteenth-century discursive nexus of women, commodity consumption for the home, and the production of bourgeois affect and subjectivity, see Merish. On the discursive nexus of eating, overconsumption, sensuality, and improper domesticity in the period, see Tompkins, 53–88.

23. In "Chastity and Sensuality," an unpublished essay, Thoreau offers perhaps his most explicit discussion of the *beastliness* of marital lust, asserting, "If it is the result of a pure love, there can be nothing sensual in marriage" (274), adding, "Love

and lust are far asunder" (275–76). Notably, neither Thoreau nor any of his siblings ever married, and he also had a series of maiden aunts (Harding, *Days,* 112).

24. The review is reprinted in Myerson, 381–86.

25. The tract went through ten editions in fifteen years (Sokolow, 78). On Graham and his legacy, see Burbick, 77–95; Nissenbaum; Sokolow; Tompkins, 53–88. Although Graham backed away from discussing masturbation in the wake of *A Lecture to Young Men,* the text remained immensely popular and helped inspire the numerous other such books and pamphlets in the following decades. On the emergence of antimasturbation discourses in the wake of the publication of *Onania* (1712), see Laqueur.

26. When addressing onanism's medical dimensions, authors often highlighted the dangers of losing such a vital fluid, the cost to the body of producing semen (seen as a precious distillation of blood), and the consequently destructive effects of increasingly frequent ejaculations, facilitated by the practice of masturbation in solitude.

27. Graham would have been particularly sensitive to the dangers of indebtedness given his childhood poverty, due to his father's death and problems with the will. See Nissenbaum, 8–13.

28. On the drift of figures of moral rectitude and positive self-making (such as "enterprise," "profit," and "industry") toward more limited associations with market activities and gain over the course of the first half of the nineteenth century, see Neufeldt, 23–52.

29. Here, Fowler does recur to arguments about the loss of sperm in particular, but the general cast of his argument follows the broader logic of Graham's physiology. See also Sokolow, 85.

30. As Nissenbaum suggests, "Inverting the process by which traditional political theorists had used 'organic' language to describe the social order, Graham applied the rhetoric of late-eighteenth-century republican social philosophy to the individual human organism" (19). See also Burbick, 78–86.

31. Graham's work draws on late eighteenth- and early-nineteenth-century French physiology, as translated and republished in Philadelphia in the late 1820s and early 1830s. However, he does not take up the French notion of the state as the principal agent for ensuring and managing health. See E. Cohen, 68–205.

32. See Nissenbaum, 119–20.

33. John Ware suggests in *Hints to Young Men*: "Domestic life, and the domestic relations, are the essential element of human happiness and human progress, so far as our moral and spiritual character are concerned" (29–30). On Owenite understandings of marriage and property, see Spurlock, 23–72. On how Graham's warnings about sexual overstimulation in marriage ironically help bolster the free-love movement, see Nissenbaum, 158–73; Sokolow, 127–42.

34. The logic goes, as Laqueur suggests, something like this: "[W]hen something incorporeal, something not quite real, created excitement, it was more dangerous

than if the body were responding to something more real, something present there and then" (207). For Graham, this problem extends beyond masturbation per se to the problem of "a disproportionate exercise of the brain" in childhood education (62, 155).

35. Financial and land speculation in the period, especially in the wake of the Panic of 1837, often was characterized as a kind of "dream." See Anthony, "Banking"; Sánchez, *Reforming*.

36. As an example, see Woodward, 46–49, 63–65. On the masturbatory resonance of "reverie" in the period and its connection to the "liminal" state of bachelorhood, a new social status emergent in the early nineteenth century, see Bertolini; Castiglia, 211–15.

37. See Burbick, 64; Nissenbaum, xi, 138; Packer, 255; Shelden, 245. However, as Stephen Nissenbaum notes, Graham's theory of vegetarianism—that meat overstimulates the body and thus breaks down one's physical constitution—differed significantly from more classical arguments in its favor (about indulging the gross/animal urges at the expense of higher/rational impulses), which appear far closer to Thoreau's own (39–40).

38. Thoreau likely would have been exposed to antimasturbation writing not only due to its incredible popularity but specifically through Bronson Alcott (a fellow Transcendentalist resident of Concord), given that Bronson's cousin was William Alcott. William, who was quite close with Bronson, was a famous health advocate, a Grahamite, and himself wrote about the dangers of masturbation. See Burbick, 104–12; Nissenbaum, 146–47; Shelden, 242–43; Sokolow, 88, 154–55; Tompkins, 73–77. A testimonial from Alcott was included in later editions of Graham's *Lectures to Young Men* as well as reprinted in other masturbation tracts as an advertisement for Graham's text. See Graham, 3–4; Woodward, 70–71. On the relation between *Walden* and young men's guides of the period, including some of the writers who also wrote about masturbation, see Burbick, 57–74; Neufeldt; Newbury; B. Walker.

39. In his eulogy for Thoreau, Emerson described him as "the bachelor of thought and Nature" (Myerson, 420). In *America's Bachelor Uncle*, Bob Pepperman Taylor takes up this description as a way of thinking about Thoreau's depiction of "nature" and its relation to U.S. political life.

40. Masturbation repeatedly was cited as a leading cause of insanity. See Fowler, 32; Sokolow, 89.

41. As Christopher Castiglia notes of the emergent connection between financial profligacy and sexual deviance in the period, "Writers throughout the 1850s deployed fantasy, daydreams, and reveries as a crucial archive of critique and imaginative reconstruction—of democratic possibility," in which "'normal' intimacies [are] revealed as speculative investments with highly dubious payoffs" (211).

42. See Harris; Rifkin, *When*, 45–98; Tawil, 92–128.

43. On "seriality" as a crucial feature of settler experience in the backcountry in the colonial period, see E. White.

44. At times in his journals, Thoreau talks about relating to nature as a "lover." See Walls, 143, 150. On the role of pleasure in Thoreau's conception of selfhood, see Cafaro, 38–44; Warner.

45. As the OED notes, *milking* serves as slang for masturbation from at least the early seventeenth century onward. However, Thoreau continually returns to notions of "chastity" and "continence" as a way of describing this process of imaginative excess, drawing on masturbatory figurations but dissociating them from actual orgasm. His ambivalence toward pleasure might be understood as helping shape his rejection of Fourierism, with that theory's emphasis on the fulfillment of the "passions." See the discussion of Fourierism in chapter 2. Although American Associationists downplayed this aspect of Fourierist philosophy, Thoreau may have been familiar with it given his interactions with Henry James Sr., a well-known Fourierist who translated *Love in the Phalanstery* (1848), which was the principal vehicle for bringing information on Fourier's theories of sexuality and marriage to U.S. readers. See Spurlock, 69–71. On Thoreau's connection to James as well as Horace Greeley Jr., the newspaper editor and prominent Fourierist supporter, see Harding, *Days,* 145–56, 186–87, 211–14; Richardson, 131–34; Sattelmeyer, "*Walden,*" 12–13. Thoreau had expressed hostility to the socialistic designs of Brook Farm even before it formally became a Fourierist community, saying he would rather "keep bachelor's hall in hell" than join. See Harding, *Days,* 124–26; Richardson, 101–3. On the erotics of deferral and future potential in *Walden,* see Coviello, *Tomorrow's,* 29–47.

46. The term "onanism" derives from the name of the biblical figure Onan, who is punished for spilling his seed, or is claimed to have been so in *Onania* and afterward. See Laqueur, 15, 112–35. Many rejected this reading of the Bible, including those who adopted a Grahamite understanding of masturbation as one particularly intense version of nervous overstimulation. See Graham, 88. In repeatedly speaking of his relation to his seed(s) and the ground, then, Thoreau plays on this association. Additionally, beans were not a cash crop for farmers in Concord, despite being iconically associated with New England, so Thoreau's invocation of them would have highlighted the fact that his acts of planting were not practical nor designed to make possible a commercial self-sufficiency. See Gross, "Great." On the pleasures and economies of excess in *Walden,* see Grusin; Warner.

47. On *Walden* as a response to the failed project of the American Revolution, see Bellis, 135–36; Cavell.

48. On the relation between health and "Nature" in Thoreau's work, see also Burbick, 57–74; Christopher Sellers. On the relation between visions of solitude and the meaning of liberty in the revolutionary era, see Slauter, *State,* 215–40.

49. In the essays "Resistance to Civil Government," "Walking," and "Life without Principle," Thoreau offers more strident assertions of his distance from the state,

all of which either were published before *Walden* or based on lectures delivered while he was in the process of writing it. See Hyde, 123–46, 147–78, 195–214.

50. As Milette Shamir notes, "The image of the nation as a house not divided but cluttered, spun out of control and feminized, is the contrasting image to the integrity of Thoreau's model cabin" (205). See also Rosenblum, 17–18.

51. My reading here resonates with Myra Jehlen's notion of "incarnation" as well as Rob Wilson's articulation of the "American sublime."

52. On the relation between conceptions of self-possession and state sovereignty in the wake of the Treaty of Westphalia, see E. Cohen, 61–81; Elmer, 1–20. Morris B. Kaplan argues that "Thoreau appears to envision a new American founding, a community of sovereign individuals" (187). Thoreau's vision of sovereign selfhood, though, resonates with but is not reducible to the "sovereignty of the individual" as articulated by Stephen Pearl Andrews, which entailed a more explicit free-love argument than that made by Thoreau. See James, Greeley, and Andrews. On Andrews, see Spurlock, 107–29. Thoreau's depiction of individual sovereignty also can be understood in terms of conceptions of "self-culture" at play in Transcendentalism and Unitarianism more broadly. See Gura, *American*; Neufeldt; Newman; Packer.

53. For different accounts of this dynamic, see Abrams; Bennett, *Thoreau's*; Fanuzzi; Mariotti.

54. See R. Wilson. As against the understanding of *Walden* as pastoral, some scholars have read it as taking part in the tradition of the georgic, which illustrates, in Michael G. Ziser's terms, a "concern with man's active, pragmatic, and specific relationship to the natural world around him" (176). On the georgic as an effaced mode in colonial American and antebellum writing, see also T. Sweet. On the limits of Thoreau's semipastoral representation of Walden with respect to its actual historical situation, see Gross, "Culture"; Maynard, 15–94; Sattelmeyer, "Depopulation."

55. I am drawing on McKusick and Buell as examples of a broader phenomenon in both Thoreau scholarship and ecocriticism more broadly. Lance Newman suggests that "wilderness is not a place outside town, but a monument we have built to desires that capitalism cannot fulfill" (196), and in *American Literary Environmentalism*, David Mazel compares the assertion of nature's unquestionable, empirical facticity to the supposedly self-evident materiality of sexed embodiment as critiqued by Judith Butler (xiv–xviii). For a discussion of Thoreau's engagement with non-human life and investigation of physical phenomena less dependent on the kinds of totalizations that attend the notion of "the natural world," see Walls. On the problems for environmental politics of taking Thoreau as a model, see Chaloupka; Kroeber; Phillips. Rob Nixon offers a broader critique of the "transcendental" tendencies in environmental thinking and practice (234–62). On women's modes of engagement with "nature" in the nineteenth century that could provide a model of "emotional intelligence" more attuned to questions of environmental justice, see Kilcup. For examples of Afro-Americanist ecocriticism, which explicitly addresses

the complexities of raced relations with place and "nature," see Allewaert; Outka; Ruffin.

56. On this dialectic between the "wild" and "wilderness," see Bennett, *Thoreau's*; Dumm, "Thoreau's"; Knott, 49–82; McKusick, 141–69; Schneider; Walls. On the "tonic of wildness" as distinguished from the proliferation in the period of "tonics" sold to remedy various maladies, see Bellin, "Taking," 12–16; Burbick, 67.

57. Here I differ from Jane Bennett's reading of Thoreau's account of "nature" as a "heteroverse" (that "does not form a unified or self-sufficient whole" [*Thoreau's*, xx]), Shannon Mariotti's presentation of it as a focus on "nonidentical" particulars (in Adorno's sense of the term), and Laura Dassow Walls's interpretation of it as a (Humboldtian) process of immanent self-transformation.

58. On institutionally realizing the "literal," and derealizing that which is cast as "figurative," see Bracken; Cheyfitz, *Poetics*; Rifkin, *Erotics*.

59. For Agamben, life in the state of exception entails the possibility of infinite harm as the object of state-sanctioned violence beyond any legal redress, a situation for which the Nazi concentration camp serves as the paradigm. For varied ways of mobilizing Agamben's analysis for thinking about U.S. federal Indian policy, see Byrd, 185–220; Rifkin, "Indigenizing"; Shaw.

60. See also Morton. I should note that I am not suggesting the inefficacy or falsity of ecology as a science. On the ways humanities scholars often remain unaware of the actual dynamics of the scientific practice and discipline of ecology, see Philipps. On the ways public claims made in the name of "Science" differ from methodologies and knowledge-claims within scientific disciplines, see Latour, *Politics*. For readings of Thoreau's relation to the entities and processes he observes as experimental, see Cafaro; Cameron; Walls.

61. While Thoreau imagines "Nature" as beyond the state, later preservationist policies enact this sense of exception as a function of the state, in ways that continue to displace Native peoples. See Mazel; Spence.

62. As the official reports on Indian affairs in the state in 1848 and 1861 observe, there were Native peoples who received state assistance but did not have lands recognized as legally distinct—either in terms of possessing common lands or having individual titles under special rules (such as that they could not be sold to anyone other than tribal members). These groups were included as distinct entities having their own entries in both reports.

63. See Bird, 9, 15, 16, 19, 25, 71.

64. On the use of negation as a tactic of self-definition and self-determination by Native peoples, see Simpson, "On Ethnographic."

65. While pointing to the actual absence of post-Revolution federal treaties with peoples in New England, this assertion also appears as something of a response to the use of the example of the Cherokees by the Mashpees and their advocates in the mid-1830s in order to prompt those concerned about Indian removal in the South

to turn their attention to the oppressive conditions faced by Indians in Massachu-setts. See Apess, *Indian,* 177, 192, 196, 200–201, 205, 208, 226, 238–39. In addition, the choice of "nullification" in the title of Apess's text points to the "Nullification Crisis" a few years earlier, in which South Carolina claimed the right to refuse federal law (specifically with respect to tariffs). The legislation enabling President Jackson to use force to exert federal supremacy was facilitated by the resolution of the constitutional crisis created by *Worcester v. Georgia* (1832), a case that turned on Georgia's absence of legislative authority over the Cherokee Nation. See Ellis, 102–22; Garrison, 190–96; Kucich; Norgren, 123–28.

66. For differently configured accounts of the ways "nature" serves as "exception" in settler–Indigenous relations in the American colonies and the early United States, see Elmer, 145–46, 209–17; Mazel. On the relation between Thoreau's conception of "Nature" and emergent ideas of middle-class leisure, tourism, and suburban retreat, see Binford; D'Amore; Newbury; Newman; Shamir, 75–208; Stowe.

67. Such a connection can be traced back to at least the seventeenth century, in which Indian presence marked a space as the "howling wilderness" as in Mary Rowlandson's narrative. See M. Cohen; Cronon, "The Trouble"; Mazel, 35–58. For discussion of the making of Native peoples into a figure for "nature" in ways that efface issues of Indigenous sovereignty, see Goldberg-Hiller and Silva; Harkin and Lewis; Schweninger. For discussion of eighteenth-century discourses of engage-ment with the landscape as less involving "playing Indian" than featuring uneven engagements with Native peoples, see Hallock.

68. In his journal and other writings, Thoreau consistently links the figure of the Indian with "Nature." For examples, see P. Gilmore, 35–36; Richardson, 106; Robinson, 39; Sayre, 33. Thoreau's representation of Native people(s) in *Walden* cannot be understood as resulting from a lack of research, given the extensive read-ing of sources indicated by his "Indian notebooks." See Johnson, "Into"; Sayre, 101–22. Also, if as I argue *Walden* can be understood as drawing on and reinforcing the exceptionalization of Native peoples, such a dynamic does not mean that Thoreau actively endorsed removal. In fact, advocacy by his mother played an important role in moving Emerson to write his letter decrying the displacement of the Cherokees, suggesting that Thoreau's family was staunchly antiremoval (Harding, *Days,* 74; Sayre, 147).

69. See L. Brooks, 163–97; Mandell, *Tribe.* On nineteenth-century writing about logging, see Kilcup, 75–132. Ecocriticism often repeats the gesture of linking Indians with nature, implicitly confirming this genealogy. For examples, see Buell, *Environmental,* 76–77, 108, 135–36; McKusick, 166–68; Myers, 75–85. For eco-critical examinations of place explicitly concerned with Native sovereignty, see Adamson; Cronon, *Changes;* Hallock; Kilcup; Schweninger. In addition to promot-ing the relocation of Native peoples, the deforestation of Native lands due to logging can be thought of as, in Rob Nixon's terms, "displacement without moving," making

inhabitance unsustainable in a given location or making impossible the practice of extant lifeways that characterize a people's or population's modes of inhabitance.

70. See also Sayre 74. On Samoset, see Salisbury, 114–16.

71. Similarly, in "Former Inhabitants; and Winter Visitors," he states: "I came to town still, like a friendly Indian, when the contents of the broad open fields were all piled up . . . , and half an hour sufficed to obliterate the tracks of the last traveller" (178). In "Taking the Indian Cure," Joshua David Bellin argues that Thoreau plays Indian in ways reminiscent of other nonnatives in the period who presented themselves as purveyors of Indian medicine.

72. See also Robinson, 77–99; Christopher Sellers; Warner.

73. For a discussion of the ways accounts of enslavement often merged black bodies into the environment in ways that could provide alternative models for envisioning ecological personhood, see Allewaert. For discussion of "nature" as a space of trauma for African Americans due to histories of enslavement and lynching, see Outka.

74. The following sketch draws on a range of sources. While I will offer citations for particular examples, in general see Atack, Bateman, and Parker, "Northern"; Belich; Clark, *Social*; Coontz; Coviello, *Intimacy*; Freyer; Gates, *History*; Gross, "Culture"; Horwitz; Jensen; Keyssar; McCoy; Rockwell; Rohrbough; Charles Sellers; Shammas; Van Atta; Welke.

75. Atack, Bateman, and Parker, "Northern," 323; Belich, 65, 229.

76. I should note that this ideology of autonomous freeholders individually buying and settling land for use does not easily match the fact of transplantation of communities west as well as rampant forms of speculation (of various sorts and scales), which I discussed in chapter 2.

77. Atack, Bateman, and Parker, "Northern," 292.

78. For a discussion that directly links the acquisition of Native lands, the removal of Native peoples, and the vast expansion of the "public lands" and the machinery and business of managing their sale, see Rohrbough. On the immensity and significance of the civilian bureaucratic apparatus of Indian affairs in the nineteenth century, see Rockwell. For discussion of the unevenness in the ways that land to the West was envisioned by nonnatives with respect to a notion of integrated national space/identity, see LeMenager.

79. Jensen, 181–89. One historian has referred to the Armed Occupation Act of 1842 as "the direct forebear of the Homestead Act twenty years later" (quoted in Rockwell, 135).

80. Such conflicts include the battles in the Ohio Valley and against the Cherokee Chickamaugas in the 1790s, with Tecumseh and his allies and in the Creek Red Stick War in the 1810s, in the Seminole wars over the 1820s and 1830s, in the Black Hawk War, against Comanches in Texas in the 1840s and 1850s, and uprisings in New Mexico and California in the late 1840s and early 1850s. Spending on the

military accounted for over 90 percent of federal expenditures each year from 1808 to 1848 (Rockwell, 24). On the role of military land bounties in the decision of *Johnson v. McIntosh* (1823), a pivotal Indian law case still used as precedent which finds that Native peoples only have a right of "occupancy" due to the European rights of "discovery," see Robertson.

81. The kind of intertwined political and property-holding selfhood addressed here, though, does not appear ex nihilo in the early nineteenth century, instead emerging out of earlier modes of subjectivity in the backcountry (of Maine, western Pennsylvania, Kentucky, western New York, and the Ohio country) and the sort of Lockean arguments supporting colonial political claims (including over Indian lands in the backcountry) circulating before the Revolution. See Calloway, *Scratch*; Hinderaker; Jones; E. White; Yirush. I am suggesting an intensification, amplification, expansion, and greater institutionalization of such tendencies in the early nineteenth century.

82. See Rifkin, *Manifesting*.

83. Since Thoreau had agreed to pay for copies that did not sell, he actually was in debt to the publisher until 1853, most of the time he was composing *Walden*. See Harding, *Days*, 246–54; Newbury, 706; Packer, 193, 242; Richardson, 194–96; Sayre, 66.

84. Richardson, 154. William Cain suggests that during this period Thoreau was "less of a sojourner in nature than he was a maker of books" (34). On *Walden* as about the act of writing and its possibilities for self-remaking and social reorientation, see Cavell.

85. On the specific kinds of patterns in southern New England Native basket making in the nineteenth century, and their significance for thinking about both forms of collective Native identity not registered by the state and the participation of men in this form of cultural production, see McMullen, "Native." On Native basket making in New England more broadly, see Lester; McMullen and Handsman; Neuman.

86. See Bird; Doughton; Earle; Guardians of Indian Plantations and Related Records, 1788–1865 (Massachusetts State Archives); McMullen, "What's." The "us" to whom the basketmaker refers might be the descendants of those who lived at Nashoba, a praying town near Concord, many of whom left in the wake of King Philip's War to live at Natick. However, some remained, others may have returned in the wake of the dissolution of Natick in the late eighteenth and early nineteenth centuries, and Natick itself was less than fifteen miles from Concord. See Mandell, *Behind* 17, 28–32. On the history of Natick in the eighteenth century, see J. O'Brien, *Dispossession*. Thoreau himself had been reading about the history of Natick in the wake of his trip to Cape Cod in 1849 (Johnson, 79–80).

87. See Banner, 49–84; Kwashima, 53–62, 182–85; Mandell, *Behind*; Mandell, *Tribe*; J. O'Brien, *Dispossession*; D. Silverman, *Faith*, 157–222. If guardians in

Massachusetts largely could not authorize sale of lands without legislative approval, they could approve leases to nonnatives through which lands functionally were lost, and often lessees later claimed the lands as their own, illegal takings that retroactively could be approved by the legislature or that Native peoples often could not contest for lack of funds or guardian approval of expenditures for such cases.

88. Petition of John Hector and others, legislative packet for April 4, 1849, chapter 49, Resolve on the petition of John Hector and others, descendants of the Hassanamessett Tribe of Indians (Massachusetts State Archives).

89. J. O'Brien, *Firsting*, xv. See also Den Ouden; Mandell, 143–94; D. Silverman, *Faith*, 223–73; D. Silverman, *Red*.

90. See also Chappaquiddick and Christiantown Indian accounts and correspondence, 1811–1865 (box 3, folder 15), Guardians of Indian Plantations and Related Records, 1788–1865 (Massachusetts State Archives); Petition of Hawaswee and others, legislative packet for March 9, 1855, chapter 15, Resolve on the petition of Howaswee and others, overseers of the Gay Head Indians (Massachusetts State Archives).

91. L. Brooks, *Common*, 17.

92. See Bellin, "Taking," 21–35; Frost, 30–31; P. Gilmore, 44–47; Maddox, 148–58; Paryz, 123–50; B. Taylor, 42. For ecocritical celebrations of *The Maine Woods*, particularly "Ktaadn," see Buell, *Environmental*, 12–13; Knott, 49–81; McKusick, 141–69; Robinson, 130–39. The discussions of *The Maine Woods*, particularly of Thoreau's representation of Joe Polis, do not account for the complexity of Penobscot internal politics at the time. See the discussion in chapter 2.

93. Povinelli's argument resonates with Rob Nixon's discussion of "attritional violence" (2), particularly the effects of environmental degradation on marginalized populations.

94. See Newbury, 702–7.

95. As Renée L. Bergland notes, Thoreau very well may have engaged with various Mashpees during his 1849 stay in a hotel owned by Solomon Attaquin, the brother of one of the first selectmen chosen in the wake of the 1833 "revolt" (115). This stay was part of his weeklong trip to Cape Cod from which emerged his (posthumously published) *Cape Cod*. See Richardson, 201–4. He also had read from Reverend Gideon Hawley's writings reflecting on his time as a preacher at Mashpee (Johnson, 81).

96. The guardianship was removed in March 1834, making Mashpee into a formal district with somewhat greater official control over their own lands and disallowing collection of wood except by members of the tribe. The guardian was replaced by a formal process of election for a clerk, selectmen, and constables as well as a commissioner appointed by the governor, who held many similar oversight and approval powers to that of the guardian; and in 1853, the commissioner was replaced with a treasurer, who had greatly diminished powers. The fund from which

Phineas Fish was paid was split in 1836 to allow some to go to a preacher chosen by the Mashpees; control over the meeting house became shared in 1839; and in 1845 Fish gave up the parsonage (from which he had continued to collect wood and to sell it to others despite the 1834 law). See Bird, 24–38; Campisi, 80–109; Earle, 46–67; Konkle, *Writing*, 119–31; Mandell, *Tribe*, 96–102; Nielson. On the failed struggle of the Mashpees for state and federal recognition as a "tribe" through a court battle in the 1970s, see Brodeur; Campisi; Clifford, 277–348. The Mashpees did achieve federal recognition in 2007 through the tribal acknowledgment process originally set up by the Bureau of Indian Affairs in 1978.

97. At the time, the name used was "Marshpee."

98. The text extensively quotes from various articles, pamphlets, and legislative records with connecting commentary by Apess. For a reading of the implications of this intertextuality, see Gaul.

99. The text repeatedly compares the Mashpees' desire for liberation from the guardian system to the American Revolution. See Apess, *Indian*, 167, 195, 201, 204, 239. Part of this appeal also lies in describing their oppression as unconstitutional, a move that has been interpreted by some as asserting individual rights as U.S. citizens rather than arguing for recognition and sovereignty as an Indigenous polity. For such readings, see Bergland, 112–16; Carlson, 91–121; Doolen, 145–83; Gaul. On how Apess seeks to make use of U.S. legal designations and patriotic discourse while refunctioning them in the interest of sovereignty, see Kucich. For a wonderful reading of Apess as making an argument for dual Native citizenship (in one's tribal nation as well as the United States) that anticipates just such a legal formulation as it emerged in the early twentieth century, see J. O'Brien, *Firsting*, 180–91.

100. At various points, the text describes Indians as enslaved or in "bondage." See Apess, *Indian*, 167, 187, 201, 203, 205, 217, 239, 240. On Apess's references to slavery in his work, specifically their relation to chattel slavery and potential alliances between Native people and African Americans, see Doolen, 145–83.

101. Petition from guardian of the Dudley Indians, legislative packet for March 14, 1840, chapter 34, Act to protect the Indian lands from trespassers and intruders (Massachusetts State Archives); Letter from James Arnold, legislative packet for April 14, 1846, chapter 216, Act concerning Guardians and Treasurers of Indian Tribes and others (Massachusetts State Archives); Letter from Leavitt Thaxter, legislative packet for May 20, 1851, chapter 68, Resolve in favor of the Chappequiddic Indians (Massachusetts State Archives); and Petition of Hawaswee and others, legislative packet for March 9, 1855, chapter 15, Resolve on the petition of Howaswee and others, overseers of the Gay Head Indians (Massachusetts State Archives).

102. The supposed emancipation offered by citizenship is imposed on Native people(s) in Massachusetts in 1869, removing the legal protections for Native land as well. See Campisi, 112–16; Mandell, *Tribe*, 195–217; J. O'Brien, *Firsting*, 191–99; Plane and Button; Rosen, 155–79; D. Silverman, *Faith*, 266–73.

103. On this potential for disorientation and reorientation in Thoreau's writings, see Abrams; Bennett, *Thoreau's*; Cavell; Mariotti; B. Taylor.

104. Freeman, *Time*, xvi.

105. Mandell, *Tribe*, 140. See also Harding, *Days*, 107. On some Penobscots' regular trips to Worcester in the 1830s to attend the Catholic church there, see Doughton, 210.

106. Of the praying towns created in the seventeenth century for converted Native people(s), Wamesit was among the closest to Concord, and the Pennacooks who lived there had longstanding relations with northern and western peoples that may have persisted as part of Wabanaki geographies. See Leavenworth; Mandell, *Behind*, 16, 27–29. On Abenaki networks in the centuries preceding this period, which include the Pennacooks, see L. Brooks; Calloway, *Western*; Haefeli and Sweeney.

107. On enduring relations in the late eighteenth and nineteenth centuries among Native peoples across New England, as well as into New York and the Great Lakes region, see Joanna Brooks; L. Brooks; Haefeli and Sweeney; Lopenzina; Mandell, *Tribe*; D. Silverman, *Red*; A. Taylor, *Divided*.

108. Thanks to Lisa Brooks for suggesting I address this point and its significance for reading *Walden*. In fact, many of the references to Indians in *Walden* are inserted after Thoreau's trip to Maine in 1853, which served as the basis for "Chesuncook," included in the posthumously published *Maine Woods*. See Richardson, 293–96.

109. Thoreau, *Maine Woods*, 4–5.

110. Ahmed, *Queer*, 44.

111. In *Writing Nature*, Sharon Cameron contrasts Thoreau's *Journal* with *Walden*, arguing that the former challenges a sense of discrete, controlling selfhood through the encounter with the multiplicity and untotalizable dynamics of nature, in ways that suggest that it is unterritorializable. What I am suggesting, though, is that the issue is the substantialization of "nature" as a kind of thing/space/entity/process to which one could have a relation, arguing that constructing a space or experience called "nature" in this way emerges out of a history of settlement, and a feeling of sovereign selfhood, that makes possible the phenomenological sensation of an unmediated relation to extrapolitical place. Similarly, in *Ariel's Ecology*, Monique Allewaert suggests that the "plantation zone" occasioned a merger of the slave body with the natural world that can offer alternative ways of envisioning ecological personhood, and while not equating black and white experiences of embodiment and relation to nonhuman entities and topographies (including the land), I do want to raise the question of how such mergers and the potentials they offer may themselves be predicated on kinds of (settler) sovereignty-installing and (Native) sovereignty-clearing gestures that are resonant with, though not identical to, those at play in *Walden*.

112. On the significance of notions of "extravagance" and remaining within "due bounds" within mid-nineteenth-century health discourse, see Burbick, 50.

113. See Chura, 73–74, 87. As Chura notes, Thoreau's chief client for much of his surveying career was the town of Concord.

114. On the political significance of an erotics of self-undoing, see Hart.

4. Dreaming of Urban Dispersion

1. On the rise of New York City in this period, see Blackmar; Burrows and Wallace, 429–774; Foley; Kelley, *Melville's*; Larson, 47–63; Spann; Wilentz.

2. On the Anti-Rent Wars, see Bruegel; Christman; Huston; McCurdy; Summerhill. For a fictional account from the perspective of the landlords, see Cooper, *Redskins*. This text is the final installment in James Fenimore Cooper's Littlepage trilogy, chronicling the life of a single family and their lands in New York from the colonial period through the mid-nineteenth century written during the mid-1840s at the height of the Anti-Rent conflict. On Cooper's own manorial inheritance, see Lopenzina; A. Taylor, *William*. Melville likely was aware of Cooper's writings in this period, given that Cooper was a close friend of his uncle, Peter Gansevoort (H. Parker, 93; Robertson-Lorant, 5).

3. See Delbanco, 17–20, 63–91; Otter, 199; H. Parker, 3, 125–65, 339–475; Robertson-Lorant, 3–5, 305–7. On the close relationship between Melville's sister Augusta and Cornelia Patterson Van Rensselaer (Stephen Van Rensselaer's daughter), which also entailed Melville visiting the Van Rensselaer Manor House, see H. Parker, 156, 162, 301, 347–48, 409, 467, 473, 526. Most explicitly, the Glendinnings are modeled on the Van Cortlandts, a patroon family with three generations of Pierres. See Clymer, 176; N. Nixon, 723.

4. See Clymer; Fredricks, 98–111; Hecht; Levine, 147–62; N. Nixon; Oshima; Otter, 172–207; Slouka; Spanos.

5. See Augst; Castiglia, 270–77; Kelley, *Melville's*, 145–61; N. Nixon.

6. My sense of the novel's queer project resonates with Samuel Otter's reading of the text's relation to sentimental writing, pushing it past its generic limits in ways that do not suggest the distance associated with "irony." See Otter, 208–54. I argue that *Pierre* does so with respect to conventions of lineage and property in ways that suggest their own disorganizing internal tendencies and how they are amplified by life in the city.

7. Although, for a wonderful reading of the role of a desire for male domesticity in Melville's writing, see S. Wilson.

8. See Povinelli, *Empire*.

9. The Haudenosaunee, otherwise known as the Iroquois League or Six Nations, consists of the following peoples: Mohawks, Oneidas, Onondagas, Cayugas, Senecas, and Tuscaroras. By the early 1790s the council fire had been moved from Onondaga to Seneca territory (Buffalo Creek), largely due to the movement of

Onondagas (the traditional keepers of the council fire) to Buffalo Creek in the wake of the destruction of their villages during the American Revolution (it returned to Onondaga in 1847 after the loss of the Buffalo Creek reservation). See Hauptman, *Conspiracy*, 78, 108, 214.

10. Ahmed, *Cultural Politics*, 91–93.

11. Melville lived in the area from 1844 to 1847. On this period in Melville's life, see Delbanco, 62–91; Robertson-Laurent 123–65. On this period in the Anti-Rent struggle, see Christman; Huston, 107–74; McCurdy, 128–286; Summerhill, 71–84.

12. See Hecht, 41.

13. There were approximately 260,000 leasehold tenants, about a twelfth of the state's population (Huston, 3). On the difficulties of legally defining the meaning of "landlords" and "tenants," see McCurdy.

14. Melville's grandfathers had played important roles in the Revolution: his father's father took part (as a "Mohawk") in the Boston Tea Party, and his mother's father defended Fort Schuyler from Mohawk attacks (much like Pierre's). See H. Parker, 3–6; Robertson-Lorant, 2–5, 305.

15. Scholarship on *Pierre* traces this phrase to a statement by President Andrew Jackson as part of an effort in 1829 to negotiate for the removal of the Creeks to what would become Indian Territory. See Clymer, 177; Hecht, 43; Otter, 200. That connection itself might arise from Brian Dippie's use of a quotation from Jackson to this effect as an epigraph to one of his chapters (45). However, the phrase was used at least as early as the 1780s in negotiations with the Oneidas. See Tiro, 79. For a later usage by Red Jacket in the 1810s, see Stone 300–301.

16. Samuel Otter observes, "The emphasis on 'race' in the opening pages of *Pierre* . . . reminds us that Saddle Meadows has been 'sanctified' through blood, particularly the blood of Indian battles" (195). On the complexities of racial lineage in the novel, see Levine, *Dislocating*, 147–62; Oshima.

17. Evans was one of the chief proponents of land reform in the period, helping found the National Reform Association. See Lause, 9–20; Wilentz, 326–62; Zahler, 13–40. On Evans's writings in the Anti-Rent struggle during its height in the mid-1840s, see McCurdy, 173–80, 206–15, 221–27.

18. "Anti-Rent War—Shocking Effects of Patroonery," *Young America*, August 16, 1845, 2. See also "The New Constitution: No. III, Plan for Restoring the Land of New York to the People," *Young America*, June 28, 1845, 2, 14. For a reversal of this discourse that suggests its familiarity, in which the dispossession of Indians is tied to the supposed dispossession of landlords via the demands of Anti-Renters, see Cooper, *Redskins*. For an analysis in the period critiquing patroon claims (specifically that of the Van Rensselaers) to have gotten land by purchase from Indians, see Pepper, 6–8.

19. Huston, 116; McCurdy, 71–74. The "Indians" first appeared as such in 1840 in the wake of the "Helderberg War," an armed conflict that arose from Stephen Van

Rensselaer IV's efforts to collect back rent to pay the debts left in the wake of the death of his father (Stephen Van Rensselaer III) in 1839. See Christman, 36–41. For a mock epic rendition of the Helderberg War, see Schoolcraft, *Helderbergia*. On the earlier appearance of a smaller "Indian" tenant movement, see Bruegel, 1417–18.

20. See Christman; Huston.

21. As Reeve Huston observes, "The braves claimed to be the aboriginal inhabitants of estate lands, who had long since given way to white settlement by moving to new lands beyond the Rocky Mountains," and in a proclamation from Delaware county, the insurgents asserted that "as the land did not belong to the landlords they having no title," it "must of course belong to the Indians," further indicating, "It is presumed, however, that if the 'Indians' succeed in establishing *their* title, they will immediately retire to their home beyond the Rocky Mountains—or somewhere else" (121).

22. A similar sense of quiescence emerges around Mrs. Glendinning's decision to exile Delly Ulver due to her affair with a married man, an edict that appears not only to be uncontested by Delly and her parents but incontestable (94–103).

23. See "The Pro and Con of Anti-Rent," *New-York Daily Tribune*, September 6, 1845, 2.

24. Christman, 15–22; McCurdy, 1, 15–16; Summerhill, 61–62. The document is reprinted in Foner, 59–63. Page numbers will be cited parenthetically.

25. Somewhat ironically, that very continuity can be understood as due to the terms of the leases themselves, which militated against the kind of generational fractioning and mobility increasingly prominent in southern New England over the course of the eighteenth and early nineteenth centuries discussed in chapters 2 and 3.

26. "Anti-Rent Movements," *Working Man's Advocate*, September 14, 1842, 1; "The Struggles of Feudalism," *Young America*, April 26, 1845, 2.

27. The absence of Anti-Rent modes of agency and normative framings in the text might be understood as Melville's response to the almost total collapse of the movement in the late 1840s due to the following: ferocious state response to "Indian" mobilizations (resulting in hundreds of arrests); the criminalization of "masks or other disguises" in January 1845; the legislative successes of the Anti-Rent Party in 1844, 1845, and 1846 (resulting in a splintering of goals and pressure to disown "Indian" violence); the ratification of the constitution of 1846, which outlawed leases of longer than twelve years and eliminated the quarter-sales (although only relevant to contracts made "hereafter"); and the movement to institute lawsuits against the titles of landlords (given legislative backing in 1848) which further fragmented an already fracturing coalition. See Christman; Huston; McCurdy; Summerhill. Some scholars incorrectly suggest that legal developments in the late 1840s and early 1850s invalidated the patroon leases. See Bruegel, 1398, 1424; N. Nixon, 724–25.

28. Here I diverge from Dominic Mastronianni's account of the novel as offering something like a theory of permanent revolution. See also Jehlen, 185–226.

29. As Robert Levine notes, this reference could as easily be to the Haitian Revolution as the one in Paris (156).

30. Invoking the French Revolution in the early 1850s also alludes to the thwarted series of popular revolts in France and other European nations in 1848, which by 1852 had been defeated with the restoration of monarchical, or broadly dictatorial, regimes. On the relation of "the European 1848" to Melville's work, particularly *Moby-Dick* and *Pierre*, see Rogin, 102–86. On the response of American politicians to these revolutions and counterrevolutions, particularly Young America Democrats, see Eyal, 93–115.

31. As Nicola Nixon observes, "The rural in *Pierre* is no Walden-like retreat from urban strife . . . nor is it a mythologized frontier" (731). On the novel's representation of "nature" as an ideologically loaded figuration, see also Delbanco, 196–97; Hecht; Higgins and Parker, 32–34; Oshima; Otter, 172–207; Rogin, 155–86; Slouka; Snediker; Sundquist, *Home,* 150–53.

32. Here my argument differs from those who characterize the logic of *Pierre* as Lockean. See Clymer, 182; Dimock, 148.

33. On the relation between the novel and extant forms of landscape painting, see Otter, 172–207.

34. In this way, the novel can be seen as responding to just such mobilizations of "nature" in the discourses of elite landholding in the late eighteenth and early nineteenth centuries. See Hallock, 177–216.

35. On the linkage of Anti-Rent with broader land reform movements in popular media accounts at the time, see Zahler, 49–52. On the fault lines in Anti-Rent politics around commitment to land reform, see Christman, 253–78; McCurdy, 234–59; Summerhill, 83–85. On the central role of Thomas Devyr in mediating the relation between the land reform movement (largely working out of New York City) and the Anti-Rent struggle, see Christman.

36. George Henry Evans's attention was directed to the conflict over manorial land tenure through Devyr. See Christman, 69–72. After having left New York to work on his farm in New Jersey in 1835 in the wake of setbacks to the labor movement, Evans returned to publishing in 1841 and became the most visible and vocal advocate of land reform as one of the cofounders of the National Reform Association and in his newspaper editorship in the mid-1840s (specifically, *The Working Man's Advocate*, which became *Young America*). On Evans and the changing context of radicalism in New York in the 1830s and 1840s, see Lause, 1–46; Wilentz, 172–255, 326–62. Horace Greeley, who became editor of the *New York Daily Tribune* in 1841, also served as a prominent commentator on both the Anti-Rent struggle and land reform, coming to the latter through his interest in Fourierism in the early 1840s and Evans's efforts to attract such socialists to the free soil movement. See Greeley, 272–99; Lause, 40–41; Wilentz, 337–99; Zahler, 41–56. The fact that Evans

was a nominal Democrat and Greeley a stalwart Whig sometimes led them to different conclusions in their coverage of Anti-Rent matters, especially controversies around "Indian" violence. See McCurdy, 167–68, 205–33.

37. "The New Constitution: No III. Plan for Restoring the Land of New York to the People," *Young America*, June 28, 1845, 2; "Mr. Watson's Oration," *Young America*, July 26, 1845, 2.

38. "The Sun on Feudalism," *Young America*, April 12, 1845, 2–3; "The New Constitution: No III. Plan for Restoring the Land of New York to the People," *Young America*, June 28, 1845, 2; "The Harbinger—Satanstoe—Anti-Rentism and 'Indian Outrages' Justified—Right to Land," *Young America*, August 9, 1845, 2.

39. See also "The Pro and Con of Anti-Rent," *New-York Daily Tribune*, September 6, 1845, 2.

40. See "Vote Yourself a Farm," 120–24; Greeley, 311–17.

41. See Schoolcraft, *Notes*, 40–45; Snyder; Stone, 14–15; Wallace, 131–43; Yablon, 47–49.

42. Moreton-Robinson, "Writing off Indigenous," 95.

43. On the equation of nonnormative sexual identity with urban spaces, see Gray; Halberstam; Herring, *Another*; Weston, *Long*, 30–56.

44. For a similar set of critical investments, organized around anonymity in Walt Whitman's work, see Coviello, *Intimacy*, 127–56. On "bad reading" as a means of negotiating the embodied experiences and knowledges of engaging with a public of urban strangers, see Millner.

45. Herring, *Queering*, 21.

46. As Thomas Augst observes, in contrast to the truth-ensuring dynamics of city mystery fiction, "Melville insists that we see urban identity as both unstable and elusive" (62). On city mystery fiction, see also Erickson; Kelley, *Melville's*, 94–161; Looby; Millner; D. Stewart. For a different reading of Melville's relation to the genre, see Kelley, *Melville's*, 94–96. For broader discussion of sensation fiction in the nineteenth century, see Cvetkovich; Denning; Streeby, *American*.

47. Thanks to Nancy Bentley for helping me formulate this point.

48. As Hiram Perez suggests in "You Can Have My Brown Body and Eat It, Too!" modern "gay" identity powerfully correlates with "mobility," especially in envisioning the possibility of separating oneself from "the heteronormative confines of the traditionally defined 'home' and 'family,'" but as he notes, "Conceptually and materially, that freedom and self-determination are premised on the property of whiteness" (177–78).

49. Latour, *Reassembling*, 196.

50. On the perspective adopted by this moment, see Snediker.

51. See also Mastronianni, 408–11; N. Nixon, 735.

52. For a reading of this dynamic in the novel more focused on alienation and estrangment, see Augst. In *Fever Reading*, Michael Millner addresses the attraction

to popular writings on scandal in the period, arguing that they stage "the drama of evidence" in ways that engage the "complex emotional language circulating around system trust" such that one can learn to "tak[e] action within the complexities of the system" (115–17), and *Pierre*'s proliferation of urban "mystery" can be seen as drawing on the same pleasures of unknowing, although explicitly distinguished from what is cast as the legalized/genealogized will-to-knowledge and ownership in the country.

53. In this way, the novel draws on the binarizing powers of sensation in which "a dramatic encounter between clearly differentiated entities" allows for the management of anxiety "because [the binary] render[s] intelligible that which is anxiety-producing precisely because it is not susceptible to such ordering" (Cvetkovich, 33–34).

54. For readings that suggest the text seeks to do so, especially with respect to the Church of the Apostles, see Castiglia, 276–77; Kelley, "*Pierre*'s."

55. This reading draws on Jordan Stein's discussion of queer analysis in his engagement with *Blithedale Romance*. He articulates his critical aim as "to collect into the history of sexuality versions of queerness that never accede to discourse," and he defines "queerness" as "a variety of social, sexual, or stylistic aberrances distinguished by some particularity irreducible enough that they would be difficult to collect into generic categories," focusing on "the novel's attempt to represent something whose properties and principles were incoherent" (212–13). However, rather than seeking to mark a heretofore, or historically as yet, uncategorizable kind of "aberrance," Melville's emphasis on the city's capacity to proliferate "mysteries," anonymities, and disjunctions privileges the making "incoherent" of genealogy and property as itself a value.

56. For a very different account of the democratizing work of the sublime in *Pierre*, see Fredricks. On the "sublime" as an ideologically loaded mode in U.S. writing, see Outka; R. Wilson.

57. For examples, see Brown, 135–69; Creech; Dimock, 140–75; Hecht; Kelley, "*Pierre*'s"; G. Silverman; Weinstein, 159–84.

58. On the meaning of incest plots in late eighteenth- and early-nineteenth-century narratives, see Dalke; Dillon, 118–39; Samuels; Stern, 26–29. For a reading of nineteenth-century incest plots as suggesting the limits of linking sentiment to the family, see Hendler, 113–46; Weinstein, 173.

59. The only exception might be Reverend Falsgrave, about whom we learn that he was the "child of a poor northern farmer who had wedded a pretty seamstress" (98), but Mrs. Falsgrave already has died prior to the beginning of the novel.

60. Such an analysis of the role of the law in inciting desire might be understood as an account of the effects of "the law of the father," but my reading is less psychoanalytic than an engagement with the novel's portrayal of the queer "affective economies" engendered by the laws of property and inheritance. See Ahmed,

Cultural. For interpretations of the text that read it as either an exploration of Pierre's psyche or indicative of Melville's, see Flory; Higgins and Parker; Kelley, *Melville's,* 145–61; Milder, "Ugly"; Robertson-Laurent, 304–17; Sundquist, *Home,* 143–86.

61. A number of scholars have suggested that Pierre's incestuous connection with Isabel functions as an assault on "the family"—to dissolve it, create forms of equality not found in bourgeois homemaking, produce greater mutability of roles, or suggest the impossibility of escaping the orbit of familial relatedness. For examples, see Brown, 158–59; Castiglia, 271–72; Dill, 713–16; G. Silverman, 353–56; Weinstein, 159–84.

62. See Fredricks, 97; Weinstein, 182. On this general dynamic, see Cheyfitz, *Poetics.*

63. See Basch; Weinauer, 145–47. On the married women's property acts more broadly, see Cott, *Public,* 24–77; Isenberg.

64. On the continuing tendency to leave real estate to sons, see Basch, 101–7.

65. Jeffory Clymer argues, "Mary thus rejects marriage for herself and imagines her son's marriage as an incestuous affair that keeps property within the family, and her entire character is built around the project of rendering Glendinning family property immune from any form of expropriation" (180). See also Jehlen, 203–4.

66. See Clymer, 190; Creech, 126–30; Higgins and Parker, 120–22; N. Nixon, 729–30; Rogin, 175; Weinstein, 166.

67. Creech, 134–52. For different readings of the erotics of subjection to his father's legacy, see Arsi; Jehlen, 185–226.

68. In *Interior States,* Christopher Castiglia argues that the Church of the Apostles "recall[s] other values than those represented by the lawyers and businessmen" inhabiting the floors below them, "becom[ing] one of the first literary examples of functional queer subculture in the new American cityscape": "The tragic irony of *Pierre* is that at the romance's conclusion its protagonist sits in the midst of a powerful model of counter-sociality, struggling desperately to invent just such an alternative from the frayed materials of his past, never noticing that what he seeks is all around him as his present" (276–77).

69. See the discussion of phalanxes, phalansteries, Fourierism, and their perverse associations in chapter 2. On the text's critique of various ways of imagining social reform through its depiction of the Apostles, see Weinstein, 177.

70. On the relation between Fourierism and land reform, see the discussion in chapter 2. Additionally, the novel lambastes the Apostles' "deluded" use of flesh brushes and their "insane, heterodoxical notions about the economy of [the] body," including eating the "crumbs of Graham crackers" (298–300). In this way, the text suggests that they are extremist adherents of various health reform movements, collated and conflated with one another through allusion to Sylvester Graham. See the discussion of Graham in chapter 3. Also, the Church resembles the Grahamite

boardinghouse in New York during this period, which was frequented by Horace Greeley. See Burrows and Wallace, 533; Nissenbaum, 140–57.

71. On this shift in the vicinity of Wall Street, and lower Manhattan generally, in the early to mid-nineteenth century, see Blackmar, 183–213; Burrows and Wallace, 586–602; Foley; Spann, 3–5, 94–116; Yablon, 128–30. Melville would have been familiar with this alteration in the composition of downtown real estate and the steady movement of middle-class and wealthier families uptown, given that his family moved north in this wave several times when he lived in the city as a child before his father's bankruptcy, and during the period in which Melville wrote *Pierre* his brother Allan's office actually was located on Wall Street (in a building that replaced a church and cemetery in ways quite reminiscent of the Church of the Apostles). See H. Parker, 22–49; Robertson-Lorant, 21–43; Yablon, 138.

72. See Kelley, *Melville's*, 199–200.

73. See Blackmar, 149–82; Spann, 39–43, 313–40.

74. Yablon, 117; Spann, 118. On the Manhattan real-estate market in the nineteenth century, see Blackmar.

75. "More of It," *Young America*, August 16, 1845, 2. See also "To Silas Wright, Governor of the State of New York," *Young America*, September 6, 1845, 2.

76. "The New Constitution: No. III. Plan for Restoring the Land of New York to the People," *Young America*, June 28, 1845, 14; "Vote Yourself," 121.

77. See Zahler, 57–146.

78. See also Weinauer.

79. See Higgins and Parker, 112–43; Jehlen, 185–226; Otter, 238; Toner, 247; Wald, 126–56.

80. His attitude toward Glen's inheritance of the estate mirrors his yearning to find something beneath the secrets and lies of the world, which he pursues through his writing. Pierre desires to find some kind of ultimate truth—"an answer" that can "get a Voice out of Silence" (208). See Spanos; Sundquist, 143–86. On the addition of Pierre's career as a writer as something of an afterthought once the rest of the novel had been completed, see Higgins and Parker.

81. Latour, *Reassembling*, 195.

82. While I will be addressing Indigenous presence in New York state in the mid-nineteenth century and its relation to New York City, the city itself was built on top of Indigenous lands acquired through sale and coercion in the seventeenth and eighteenth centuries. See Burrows and Wallace, 3–76; Grumet.

83. On the representation of Native peoples as non-urban, even anti-urban, see Goeman; Ramirez; Rifkin, *Erotics*, 215–66; Thrush.

84. On the history and effects of the Erie Canal, see Burrows and Wallace, 429–52; Hauptman, *Conspiracy*, 1–5, 82–162; Larson, 49–51, 100–102; Sheriff; Yablon, 19–61.

85. Yablon, 64.

86. Burrows and Wallace, 431, 450.

87. Hauptman, *Conspiracy*, 3, 101, 164.

88. Dennis 194; Hauptman, *Conspiracy*, 1.

89. On this company and its impact on the Oneidas, see Hautpman, *Conspiracy*, 58–85.

90. On Oneida land losses in the 1780s and 1790s, see Graymont; Hauptman, *Conspiracy*, 58–81; Lehman; D. Silverman, *Red*, 125–48; A. Taylor, *Divided*; Tiro, 65–95. Melville's maternal grandfather, Peter Gansevoort, actually was one of the commissioners appointed in 1788 by the state of New York to treat with Haudenosaunee peoples for further land cessions (Graymont, 456).

91. Hauptman, *Conspiracy*, 82–85.

92. Ibid., 102–4.

93. Reprinted in Report of the Committee on Indian Affairs, 17–20. On the Treaty of Canandaigua, see Campisi and Starna; Jemison and Schein.

94. See Graymont. For excerpts from these laws, see Prucha, *Documents*, 14–15, 17–21. On the significance of this failure to follow federal law and the importance of this lapse for late-twentieth-century land claims by Native peoples in New York and New England, particularly by the Oneidas, see Hauptman and McLester; Horsman; Shattuck; Tiro, 96–168.

95. On the Treaty of Buffalo Creek (1838) and its aftermath, including the struggle of the Tonawanda Senecas to reacquire their reservation, see Conable; Genetin-Pilawa, 29–50; Gonzales, 182–220; Hauptman, *Conspiracy*, 175–212; Hauptman, *Tonawanda*; Report of the Committee on Indian Affairs; Society of Friends, *Case*; Society of Friends, *Further*; Valone. Ostensibly, the treaty had to do with exchanging Menominee lands purchased for the Senecas, and other Six Nations peoples, in the early 1830s for territory in Kansas, but representatives from the Ogden Land Company sought to use this transfer as a pretext for extinguishing all Seneca claims to lands in New York. Although the validity of Six Nations' rights to (former) Menominee lands was a subject of some controversy and legal wrangling over the 1820s and early 1830s, some Haudenosaunees, particularly among the Oneidas, did choose to remove to the Green Bay area. See Conable, 99–106; Horsman; Tiro, 143–52.

96. Quoted in Conable, 157. The resolution itself was passed with more than a two-thirds majority, which is the constitutional threshold for approving a treaty. Despite the fact that it says nothing as to how precisely to measure "assent," the Senate's resolution was interpreted by the commissioner, the Ogden Land Company, and other non-Senecas involved in the controversy, as indicating the need to gain signatures from a majority of the chiefs. On various calculations of numbers of chiefs, and therefore of legitimate majorities of them, see Society of Friends, *Case*, 33–34, 137–38.

97. Society of Friends, *Case*, 18.

98. The Quakers pointed out that this tie vote did not rise to the two-thirds minimum constitutionally necessary for a treaty (Society of Friends, *Further*, 27–28).

99. The case was enabled by an act passed by the New York state legislature in 1845 giving Indians the right to sue for recovery of their land on the same basis as citizens of the state (Conable, 295). See *Fellows v. Blacksmith*. In their struggle, Tonawanda Senecas solicited and received aid from local whites and nationally established figures like Henry Rowe Schoolcraft, Ambrose Sevier, and Lewis Cass. This aid included a petition campaign largely led by Lewis Henry Morgan. See Conable, 286–99; Genetin-Pilawa, 39–44. On the significance of Lewis Henry Morgan's work, see the discussion of him in chapter 2. Both Morgan and Schoolcraft published important works on the Iroquois in this period. See Morgan, *League*; Schoolcraft, *Notes*.

100. However, more Seneca land was lost on the Allegany reservation in the late 1840s and early 1850s due to the construction of the Erie Railroad, completed in April 1851. See Hauptman, *Iroquois*, 117–18.

101. Born in 1811, Pierce was a chief on the Buffalo Creek reservation and participated in the struggle against the Treaty of 1838 during his breaks while attending Dartmouth College, in which he had enrolled in 1836. On Pierce, and Seneca writing in the period more broadly, see Carlson, 39–65; Ganter, "Red Jacket"; Konkle, *Writing*, 224–87; Littlefield; Vernon.

102. In *Appeal to the Christian Community*, Nathaniel T. Strong, another Seneca chief, offers just such a perspective, endorsing the sale of their New York lands (6–7).

103. Pierce also notes that in the proposed western territory, "[t]he proximity of our then situation to that of other and more warlike tribes, will expose us to constant harassing by them; and not only this, but the character of those worse than Indians, those *white borderers* who infest, yes *infest*, the western border of the white population, will annoy us more fatally than even the Indians themselves" (16).

104. On tensions among Senecas over forms of Euroamerican influence, especially as they were perceived to play a role in the push for removal, see Carlson, 39–65; Conable; Dennis; Ganter, *Collected*; Gonzales, 182–220; Hauptman, *Tonawanda*; Rothenberg; Stone; Strong.

105. This rhetoric reflects that which appears in Seneca petitions to the government against removal. See Society of Friends, *Case*, 178–79; Report of the Committee of Indian Affairs, 26.

106. See Lyons.

107. On Morgan's relationship with the Tonawanda Senecas, largely through the Parker family, see Armstrong, 1–13; Michaelsen, 84–106; A. Parker, *Life*, 79–91; Trautman, 36–57.

108. See Rifkin, *When*, 51–77.

109. The Senate's resolution in June 1838 that sent the revised treaty back to the Senecas does not mention anything about a "majority," instead indicating the need to present the treaty "to each of said tribes or bands separately assembled in council" returning it to the president when "they have given their free and voluntary assent thereto." The resolution is reproduced in Report of the Committee on Indian Affairs, 48–49. The insistence on having a "majority" of Seneca "chiefs" sign likely comes in the instructions to the treaty commissioner from Commissioner of Indian Affairs Crawford (Society of Friends, *Case,* 15).

110. On Seneca clan structures, see Abler, "Seneca Moieties"; Bonvillian; Doxtator; Mann; Morgan, 78–103; Namias, "Introduction"; A. Parker, *History,* 28–31, 61–89; Rothenberg. On the challenge to matrilineal clans posed by the patriarchal dynamics of Handsome Lake's revelations and religion, as well as the Quakers, see Dennis.

111. Report of the Committee of Indian Affairs, 11. See also Morgan, 111; Schoolcraft, *Notes,* 124. In the wake of the proclamation of the Treaty of Buffalo Creek in 1840, the Quakers continued to maintain that a majority of chiefs was necessary to legitimize the treaty, insisting that threshold had not been reached. See Society of Friends, *Further,* 23, 37–38. This vision allowed the Quakers to see the supplemental treaty of 1842 (which they had negotiated with the U.S. government and the Ogden company without any Seneca participation) as valid once a majority of Seneca chiefs had assented, despite the fact that no Tonawanda leaders had agreed. See Conable, 249–82; Hauptman, *Tonawanda,* 45–60.

112. Society of Friends, *Case,* 186.

113. The Quakers note as part of advocating for the repeal of the treaty of 1838, "By the established laws and usages of the nation, the clans select from their most intelligent members, such as by their qualifications for usefulness in council, are considered proper to fill the office of chief" (Society of Friends, *Case,* 15).

114. In a memorial to the president in December 1839, Seneca leaders decry the practice of presenting certain persons as chiefs who have not achieved that status through Seneca processes (Society of Friends, *Case,* 182).

115. Society of Friends, *Case,* 16, 182, 244–45. On the history and legacy of the Condolence Ceremony, see Fenton.

116. Melville actually was in Buffalo briefly in mid-1840, during an intense period of the controversy (H. Parker, 171–76), and he may have become aware of it during that time.

117. The Senecas of the Allegany and Cattaraugus reservations did adopt majority rule and a republican form of government in 1848. See F. Cohen, 8–9; Doxtator; Genetin-Pilawa, 44–49; S. O'Brien, 97–109.

118. The images of invasion and armed conflict over territory, however, do not themselves fit the novel's representation of urban space. Given that the novel takes place in the vicinity of Wall Street, which was named after the wall initially built to

keep Native people out of the original Dutch settlement, the image does speak to the history of Native presence in New York City. See Grumet.

119. See Brown, 159; Jehlen, 214–15; Kelley, "*Pierre's*," 109; Otter, 246–47; Rogin, 181; Slouka, 147–57.

120. See Hecht, 45.

121. Describing the rock figure, the narrator observes, "Marsy gave arms to the eternally defenseless, but nature, more truthful, performed an amputation, and left the impotent Titan without one serviceable ball-and-socket above the thigh" (346). See Robertson-Lorant, 316; Slouka, 150–55; Sundquist, *Home,* 169–71.

122. On the endurance of this tendency in nonnative queer self-articulation, see Morgensen.

Bibliography

Abelove, Henry. "From Thoreau to Queer Politics." *Yale Journal of Criticism* 6, no. 2 (1993): 17–27.

Abdur-Rahman, Aliyyah I. *Against the Closet: Black Political Longing and the Erotics of Race.* Durham: Duke University Press, 2012.

Abler, Thomas S. "Seneca Moieties and Hereditary Chieftainships: The Early-Nineteenth-Century Political Organization of an Iroquois Nation." *Ethnohistory* 51, no. 3 (2004): 459–88.

Abrams, Robert E. "Image, Object, and Perception in Thoreau's Landscapes: The Development of Anti-Geography." *Nineteenth-Century Literature* 46, no. 2 (1991): 245–62.

Adamson, Joni. *American Indian Literature, Environmental Justice, and Ecocriticsm: The Middle Place.* Tucson: University of Arizona Press, 2001.

Agamben, Giorgio. *Homo Sacer: Sovereign Power and Bare Life.* 1995. Translated by Daniel Heller-Roazen. Stanford: Stanford University Press, 1998.

Ahmed, Sara. *The Cultural Politics of Emotion.* New York: Routledge, 2004.

———. *On Being Included: Racism and Diversity in Institutional Life.* Durham: Duke University Press, 2012.

———. *Queer Phenomenology: Orientations, Objects, Others.* Durham: Duke University Press, 2006.

Allewaert, Monique. *Ariel's Ecology: Plantations, Personhood, and Colonialism in the American Tropics.* Minneapolis: University of Minnesota Press, 2013.

Alonso, Ana María. *Thread of Blood: Colonialism, Revolution, and Gender on Mexico's Northern Frontier.* 2nd ed. Tucson: University of Arizona Press, 1997.

Andersen, Chris. "From Difference to Density." *Cultural Studies Review* 15, no. 2 (2009): 80–100.

Anderson, Ben. "Modulating the Excess of Affect: Morale in a State of 'Total War.'" In *The Affect Theory Reader*, edited by Melissa Gregg and Gregory J. Seigworth, 161–85. Durham: Duke University Press, 2010.

Anthony, David. "Banking on Emotion: Financial Panic and the Logic of Male Submission in the Jacksonian Gothic." *American Literature* 76, no. 4 (2004): 719–47.

———. "Class, Culture, and the Trouble with White Skin in Hawthorne's *The House of the Seven Gables.*" *Yale Journal of Criticism* 12, no. 2 (1999): 249–68.

Apess, William. "Eulogy on King Philip, as Pronounced at the Odeon, in Federal Street, Boston." 1836. In *A Son of the Forest and Other Writings*, 103–38. Edited by Barry O'Connell. Amherst: University of Massachusetts Press, 1997.

———. *Indian Nullification of the Unconstitutional Laws of Massachusetts Relative to the Marshpee Tribe; or, The Pretended Riot Explained.* 1835. In *On Our Own Ground: The Complete Writings of William Apess, a Pequot*, 163–274. Edited by Barry O'Connell. Amherst: University of Massachusetts Press, 1992.

Arai, Keiko. "'Phoebe Is No Pyncheon': Class, Gender, and Nation in *The House of the Seven Gables.*" *Nathaniel Hawthorne Review* 34, nos. 1–2 (2008): 40–62.

Armstrong, William H. *Warrior in Two Camps: Ely S. Parker, Union General and Seneca Chief.* Syracuse: Syracuse University Press, 1978.

Arneil, Barbara. *John Locke and America: The Defence of English Colonialism.* Oxford: Clarendon Press, 1996.

Arsi, Branka. "Melville's Celibatory Machines: *Bartleby, Pierre*, and 'The Paradise of Bachelors.'" *diacritics* 35, no. 4 (2005): 81–100.

Atack, Jeremy, Fred Bateman, and William N. Parker. "The Farm, the Farmer, and the Market." In *The Cambridge Economic History of the United States*, edited by Stanley L. Engerman and Robert E. Gallman, 245–84. New York: Cambridge University Press, 2000.

———. "Northern Agriculture and the Western Movement." In *The Cambridge Economic History of the United States*, edited by Stanley L. Engerman and Robert E. Gallman, 285–328. New York: Cambridge University Press, 2000.

Augst, Thomas. "Melville, at Sea in the City." In *The Cambridge Companion to the Literature of New York*, edited by Cyrus R. K. Patell and Bryan Waterman, 58–75. New York: Cambridge University Press, 2010.

Baker, Emerson W. "Finding the Almouchiquois: Native American Families, Territories, and Land Sales in Southern Maine." *Ethnohistory* 51, no. 1 (2004): 73–100.

———. "'A Scratch with a Bear's Paw': Anglo-Indian Land Deeds in Early Maine." *Ethnohistory* 36, no. 3 (1989): 235–56.

Baker, Emerson W., and James Kences. "Maine, Indian Land Speculation, and the Essex County Witchcraft Outbreak of 1692." *Maine History* 40, no. 3 (2001): 159–89.

Baker, Emerson W., and John G. Reid. "Amerindian Power in the Early Modern Northeast: A Reappraisal." *William and Mary Quarterly*, 3rd ser., 61, no. 1 (2004): 77–106.

Banner, Stuart. *How the Indians Lost Their Land: Law and Power on the Frontier.* Cambridge: Harvard University Press, 2005.

Barker, Joanne. *Native Acts: Law, Recognition, and Cultural Authenticity.* Durham: Duke University Press, 2011.

Barnes, Celia. *Native American Power in the United States, 1783–1795.* Madison, N.J.: Farleigh Dickinson University Press, 2003.

Barnett, Louise. *The Ignoble Savage: American Literary Racism, 1790–1890.* Westport, Conn.: Greenwood Press, 1975.

Basch, Norma. *In the Eyes of the Law: Women, Marriage, and Property in Nineteenth-Century New York.* Ithaca: Cornell University Press, 1982.

Baucom, Ian. *Specters of the Atlantic: Finance Capital, Slavery, and the Philosophy of History.* Durham: Duke University Press, 2005.

Baym, Nina. "The Heroine of *The House of the Seven Gables;* or, Who Killed Jaffrey Pyncheon?" *New England Quarterly* 77, no. 4 (2004): 607–18.

Belich, James. *Replenishing the Earth: The Settler Revolution and the Rise of the Anglo-World, 1783–1939.* New York: Oxford University Press, 2009.

Bellin, Joshua David. *The Demon of the Continent: Indians and the Shaping of American Literature.* Philadelphia: University of Pennsylvania Press, 2001.

———. "Taking the Indian Cure: Thoreau, Indian Medicine, and the Performance of American Culture." *New England Quarterly* 79, no. 1 (2006): 3–36.

Bellis, Peter J. *Writing Revolution: Aesthetics and Politics in Hawthorne, Whitman, and Thoreau.* Athens: University of Georgia Press, 2003.

Belmessous, Saliha. "Wabanaki versus French and English Claims in Northeastern North America, c. 1715." In *Native Claims: Indigenous Law against Empire, 1500–1920,* 107–28. New York: Oxford University Press, 2011.

Bennett, Jane. *The Enchantment of Modern Life: Attachments, Crossings, and Ethics.* Princeton: Princeton University Press, 2001.

———. *Thoreau's Nature: Ethics, Politics, and the Wild.* Thousand Oaks, Calif.: Sage, 1994.

Ben-Zvi, Yael. "Where Did Red Go? Lewis Henry Morgan's Evolutionary Inheritance and U.S. Racial Imagination." *CR: The New Centennial Review* 7, no. 2 (2007): 201–29.

Bergland, Renée L. *The National Uncanny: Indian Ghosts and American Subjects.* Hanover, N.H.: University Press of New England, 2000.

Berlant, Lauren. *The Anatomy of National Fantasy: Hawthorne, Utopia, and Everyday Life.* Chicago: University of Chicago Press, 1991.

———. *Cruel Optimism.* Durham: Duke University Press, 2011.

Berlant, Lauren, and Michael Warner. "Sex in Public." *Critical Inquiry* 24, no. 2 (1998): 548–66.

Bertolini, Vincent J. "Fireside Chastity: The Erotics of Sentimental Bachelorhood in the 1850s." *American Literature* 68, no. 4 (1996): 707–37.

Bhabha, Homi. *The Location of Culture.* New York: Routledge, 1994.

Bieder, Robert E. *Science Encounters the Indian, 1820–1880: The Early Years of American Ethnology.* Norman: University of Oklahoma Press, 1986.

Binford, Henry C. *The First Suburbs: Residential Communities on the Boston Periph-ery, 1815–1860*. Chicago: University of Chicago Press, 1985.

Biolsi, Thomas. *Deadliest Enemies: Law and Race Relations on and off Rosebud Reser-vation*. Minneapolis: University of Minnesota Press, 2001.

Bird, F. W., Whiting Griswold, and Cyrus Weekes. *Report of the Commissioners Relating to the Conditions of the Indians in Massachusetts*. Boston: Massachusetts General Court, 1849.

Blackmar, Elizabeth. *Manhattan for Rent, 1785–1850*. Ithaca: Cornell University Press, 1989.

Blumin, Stuart M. *The Emergence of the Middle Class: Social Experience in the Ameri-can City, 1760–1900*. New York: Cambridge University Press, 1989.

Bonvillain, Nancy. "Iroquoian Women." In *Studies on Iroquoian Culture*, edited by Nancy Bonvillain, 47–58. Rindge, N.H.: Franklin Pierce College, 1980.

Bourque, Bruce J. *Twelve Thousand Years: American Indians in Maine*. Lincoln: Uni-versity of Nebraska Press, 2001.

Boydston, Jeanne. *Home and Work: Housework, Wages, and the Ideology of Labor in the Early Republic*. New York: Oxford University Press, 1990.

Bracken, Christopher. *Magical Criticism: The Recourse of Savage Philosophy*. Chi-cago: University of Chicago Press, 2007.

Brandzel, Amy. "Queering Citizenship? Same-Sex Marriage and the State." *GLQ* 11, no. 2 (2005): 171–204.

Brant, Beth. *Writing as Witness: Essay and Talk*. Toronto: Women's Press, 1994.

Brodeur, Paul. *Restitution: The Land Claims of the Mashpee, Passamaquoddy, and Penobscot Indians of New England*. Boston: Northeastern University Press, 1985.

Brooks, James F., ed. *Confounding the Color Line: The Indian–Black Experience in North America*. Lincoln: University of Nebraska Press, 2002.

Brooks, Joanna, ed. *The Collected Writings of Samson Occom, Mohegan*. New York: Oxford University Press, 2006.

———. *Why We Left: Untold Stories and Songs of America's First Immigrants*. Minne-apolis: University of Minnesota Press, 2013.

Brooks, Lisa. *The Common Pot: The Recovery of Native Space in the Northeast*. Min-neapolis: University of Minnesota Press, 2008.

Brown, Gillian. *Domestic Individualism: Imagining Self in Nineteenth-Century Amer-ica*. Berkeley: University of California Press, 1990.

Brückner, Martin. *The Geographic Revolution in Early America: Maps, Literacy, and National Identity*. Chapel Hill: University of North Carolina Press, 2006.

Bruegel, Martin. "Unrest: Manorial Society and the Market in the Hudson Valley, 1780–1850." *Journal of American History* 82, no. 4 (1996): 1393–424.

Bruyneel, Kevin. *The Third Space of Sovereignty: The Postcolonial Politics of U.S.–Indigenous Relations*. Minneapolis: University of Minnesota Press, 1997.

Brysk, Alison. *From Tribal Village to Global Village: Indian Rights and International Relations in Latin America*. Stanford: Stanford University Press, 2000.

Bryson, Bethany. *Making Multiculturalism: Boundaries and Meaning in U.S. English Departments*. Stanford: Stanford University Press, 2005.

Buell, Lawrence. *The Environmental Imagination: Thoreau, Nature Writing, and the Formation of American Culture*. Cambridge: Harvard University Press, 1995.

———. "Manifest Destiny and the Question of the Moral Absolute." In *The Oxford Handbook of Transcendentalism*, edited by Joel Myerson, Sandra Herbert Petrulionis, and Laura Dassow Walls, 183–97. New York: Oxford University Press, 2010.

Burbick, Joan. *Healing the Republic: The Language of Health and the Culture of Nationalism in Nineteenth-Century America*. New York: Cambridge University Press, 1994.

Burnham, Michelle. *Captivity and Sentiment: Cultural Exchange in American Literature, 1682–1861*. Hanover: Dartmouth College Press, 1997.

Burrows, Edwin G., and Mike Wallace. *Gotham: A History of New York City to 1898*. New York: Oxford University Press, 1999.

Byrd, Jodi. *The Transit of Empire: Indigenous Critiques of Colonialism*. Minneapolis: University of Minnesota Press, 2011.

Cafaro, Philip. *Thoreau's Living Ethics:* Walden *and the Pursuit of Virtue*. Athens: University of Georgia Press, 2004.

Cain, William E. "Henry David Thoreau, 1817–1862: A Brief Biography." In *A Historical Guide to Henry David Thoreau*, edited by William E. Cain, 11–60. New York: Oxford University Press, 2000.

Calloway, Colin G., ed. *Dawnland Encounters: Indians and Europeans in Northern New England*. Hanover, N.H.: University Press of New England, 1991.

———. *The Scratch of a Pen: 1763 and the Transformation of North America*. New York: Oxford University Press, 2006.

———. *The Western Abenakis of Vermont, 1600–1800*. Norman: University of Oklahoma Press, 1990.

Cameron, Sharon. *Writing Nature: Henry Thoreau's Journal*. New York: Oxford University Press, 1985.

Campisi, Jack. *The Mashpee Indians: Tribe on Trial*. Syracuse: Syracuse University Press, 1991.

Campisi, Jack, and William A. Starna. "On the Road to Canandaigua: The Treaty of 1794." *American Indian Quarterly* 19, no. 4 (1995): 467–90.

Carlson, David J. *Sovereign Selves: American Indian Autobiography and the Law*. Urbana: University of Illinois Press, 2006.

Carpenter, Cari M. *Seeing Red: Anger, Sentimentality, and American Indians*. Columbus: Ohio State University Press, 2008.

Castiglia, Christopher. *Interior States: Institutional Consciousness and the Inner Life of Democracy in the Antebellum United States*. Durham: Duke University Press, 2008.

Castigilia, Christopher, and Christopher Looby. "Introduction: Come Again? New Approaches to Sexuality in Nineteenth-Century U.S. Literature." *ESQ: A Journal of the American Renaissance* 55, no. 3–4 (2009): 195–209.

Cavell, Stanley. *The Senses of Walden.* 1972. Chicago: University of Chicago Press, 1992.

Chakrabarty, Dipesh. *Provincializing Europe: Postcolonial Thought and Historical Difference.* Princeton: Princeton University Press, 2000.

Chaloupka, William. "Thoreau's Apolitical Legacy for American Environmentalism." In *A Political Companion to Henry David Thoreau,* edited by Jack Turner, 205–28. Lexington: University Press of Kentucky, 2009.

Chambers-Schiller, Lee Virginia. *Liberty, a Better Husband: Single Women in America: The Generations of 1780–1840.* New Haven: Yale University Press, 1984.

Chang, David A. *The Color of the Land: Race, Nation, and the Politics of Landownership in Oklahoma, 1832–1929.* Chapel Hill: University of North Carolina Press, 2010.

Chen, Mel Y. *Animacies: Biopolitics, Racial Mattering, and Queer Affects.* Durham: Duke University Press, 2012.

Cheyfitz, Eric. "The Irresistibleness of Great Literature: Reconstructing Hawthorne's Politics." *American Literary History* 6, no. 3 (1994): 539–58.

———. "Matthiessen's *American Renaissance:* Circumscribing the Revolution." *American Quarterly* 41, no. 2 (1989): 341–61.

———. *The Poetics of Imperialism: Translation and Colonization from* The Tempest *to* Tarzan. Philadelphia: University of Pennsylvania Press, 1997.

———. "The (Post)Colonial Construction of Indian Country: U.S. American Indian Literatures and Federal Indian Law." In *The Columbia Guide to American Indian Literatures of the United States since 1945,* edited by Eric Cheyfitz, 1–124. New York: Columbia University Press, 2006.

Chow, Rey. *The Protestant Ethnic and the Spirit of Capitalism.* New York: Columbia University Press, 2002.

Christman, Henry. *Tin Horns and Calico: A Decisive Episode in the Emergence of Democracy.* New York: Henry Holt and Company, 1945.

Chura, Patrick. *Thoreau the Land Surveyor.* Gainesville: University Press of Florida, 2010.

Clark, Christopher. *The Roots of Rural Capitalism: Western Massachusetts, 1780–1860.* Ithaca: Cornell University Press, 1990.

———. *Social Change in America: From the Revolution through the Civil War.* Chicago: Ivan R. Dee, 2006.

Clifford, James. *The Predicament of Culture: Twentieth-Century Ethnography, Literature, and Art.* Cambridge: Harvard University Press, 1988.

Clymer, Jeffory A. "Property and Selfhood in Herman Melville's *Pierre." Nineteenth-Century Literature* 61, no. 2 (2005): 171–99.

Cohen, Cathy J. "Punks, Bulldaggers, and Welfare Queens: The Radical Potential of Queer Politics?" *GLQ* 3, no. 4 (1997): 437–65.

Cohen, Ed. *A Body Worth Defending: Immunity, Biopolitics, and the Apotheosis of the Modern Body*. Durham: Duke University Press, 2009.

Cohen, Felix S. *On the Drafting of Tribal Constitutions*. Edited by and introduced by David E. Wilkins. Norman: University of Oklahoma Press, 2006.

Cohen, Matt. *The Networked Wilderness: Communicating in Early New England*. Minneapolis: University of Minnesota Press, 2009.

Colacurcio, Michael J. "'Red Man's Grave': Art and Destiny in Hawthorne's 'Mainstreet'." *Nathaniel Hawthorne Review* 31, no. 2 (2005): 1–18.

Collier, Jane F., Bill Maurer, and Liliana Suárez-Navaz. "Sanctioned Identities: Legal Constructions of Modern Personhood." *Identities* 2, nos. 1–2 (1997): 1–27.

Conable, Mary H. "A Steady Enemy: The Ogden Land Company and the Seneca Indians." PhD diss. University of Rochester, 1994.

Coombes, Annie E., ed. *Rethinking Settler Colonialism: History and Memory in Australia, Canada, Aotearoa New Zealand and South Africa*. New York: Manchester University Press, 2006.

Coontz, Stephanie. *The Social Origins of Private Life: A History of American Families, 1600–1900*. New York: Verso, 1988.

Cooper, James Fenimore. *The Redskins*. Vol. 6 of *Works of J. Fenimore Cooper*. New York: Peter Fenelon Collier, 1893.

Cott, Nancy F. *The Bonds of Womanhood: "Woman's Sphere" in New England, 1780–1835*. New Haven: Yale University Press, 1977.

———. *Public Vows: A History of Marriage and the Nation*. Cambridge: Harvard University Press, 2000.

Coulthard, Glen S. "Subjects of Empire: Indigenous Peoples and the 'Politics of Recognition' in Canada." *Contemporary Political Theory* 6 (2007): 437–60.

Coviello, Peter. *Intimacy in America: Dreams of Affiliation in Antebellum Literature*. Minneapolis: University of Minnesota Press, 2005.

———. *Tomorrow's Parties: Sex and the Untimely in Nineteenth-Century American Literature*. New York: New York University Press, 2013.

Cox, James H. *Muting White Noise: Native American and European American Novel Traditions*. Norman: University of Oklahoma Press, 2006.

Crain, Caleb. *American Sympathy: Men, Friendship, and Literature in the New Nation*. New Haven: Yale University Press, 2001.

Creech, James. *Closet Writing/Gay Reading: The Case of Melville's* Pierre. Chicago: University of Chicago Press, 1993.

Cronon, William. *Changes in the Land: Indians, Colonists, and the Ecology of New England*. New York: Hill and Wang, 1983.

———. "The Trouble with Wilderness; or, Getting Back to the Wrong Nature." In *Uncommon Ground: Rethinking the Human Place in Nature*, edited by William Cronon, 69–90. New York: Norton, 1996.

Cvetkovich, Ann. *Mixed Feelings: Feminism, Mass Culture, and Victorian Sensational-ism.* New Brunswick: Rutgers University Press, 1992.

Dalke, Anne. "Original Vice: The Political Implications of Incest in the Early American Novel." *Early American Literature* 23 (1988): 189–201.

D'Amore, Maura. "Thoreau's Unreal Estate: Playing House at Walden Pond." *The New England Quarterly* 82, no. 1 (2009): 56–79.

Das, Veena. *Life and Words: Violence and the Descent into the Ordinary.* Berkeley: University of California Press, 2007.

Davis, Clark. *Hawthorne's Shyness: Ethics, Politics, and the Question of Engagement.* Baltimore: Johns Hopkins University Press, 2005.

Dayan, Colin. *The Law Is a White Dog: How Legal Rituals Make and Unmake Persons.* Princeton: Princeton University Press, 2011.

Dean, Tim. "Bareback Time." In *Queer Times, Queer Becomings,* edited by E. L. McCallum and Mikko Tuhkanen, 75–100. Albany: State University of New York Press, 2011.

DeLanda, Manuel. *A New Philosophy of Society: Assemblage Theory and Social Complexity.* New York: Continuum, 2006.

Delano, Sterling F. *Brook Farm: The Dark Side of Utopia.* Cambridge: Harvard University Press, 2004.

Delbanco, Andrew. *Melville: His World and Work.* New York: Vintage Books, 2005.

Deloria, Philip J. *Indians in Unexpected Places.* Lawrence: University Press of Kansas, 2004.

———. *Playing Indian.* New Haven: Yale University Press, 1998.

Deloria, Vine, Jr. *Custer Died for Your Sins: An Indian Manifesto.* 1969. Norman: University of Oklahoma Press, 1988.

D'Emilio, John, and Estelle B. Freedman. *Intimate Matters: A History of Sexuality in America.* 2nd ed. Chicago: University of Chicago Press, 1997.

Denning, Michael. *Mechanic Accents: Dime Novels and Working Class Culture.* New York: Verso Books, 1987.

Dennis, Matthew. *Seneca Possessed: Indians, Witchcraft, and Power in the Early American Republic.* Philadelphia: University of Pennsylvania Press, 2010.

Dennison, Jean. *Colonial Entanglements: Constituting a Twenty-First Century Osage Nation.* Chapel Hill: University of North Carolina Press, 2012.

Den Ouden, Amy E. *Beyond Conquest: Native Peoples and the Struggle for History in New England.* Lincoln: University of Nebraska Press, 2005.

Dill, Elizabeth. "That Damned Mob of Scribbling Siblings: The American Romance as Anti-novel in *The Power of Sympathy* and *Pierre.*" *American Literature* 80, no. 4 (2008): 707–38.

Dillon, Elizabeth Maddock. *The Gender of Freedom: Fictions of Liberalism and the Literary Public Sphere.* Stanford: Stanford University Press, 2004.

Dimock, Wai-chee. *Empire for Liberty: Melville and the Poetics of Individualism.* Princeton: Princeton University Press, 1989.

Dinshaw, Carolyn, Lee Edelman, et al. "Theorizing Queer Temporalities: A Round-table Discussion." *GLQ* 13, no. 2–3 (2007): 177–95.

Dippie, Brian W. *The Vanishing America: White Attitudes and U.S. Indian Policy.* Lawrence: University Press of Kansas, 1982.

Doolen, Andy. *Fugitive Empire: Locating Early American Imperialism.* Minneapolis: University of Minnesota Press, 2005.

Doughton, Thomas L. "Unseen Neighbors: Native Americans of Central Massa-chusetts, A People Who Had 'Vanished.'" In *After King Philip's War: Presence and Persistence in Indian New England,* edited by Colin G. Calloway, 207–30. Hanover, N.H.: University Press of New England, 1997.

Dowd, Gregory Evans. *War under Heaven: Pontiac, the Indian Nations, and the British Empire.* Baltimore: Johns Hopkins University Press, 2002.

Doxtator, Deborah. "What Happened to the Iroquois Clans? A Study of Clans in Three Nineteenth Century Rotinonhysonni Communities." PhD diss. University of Western Ontario, 1996.

Doyle, Laura. *Freedom's Empire: Race and the Rise of the Novel in Atlantic Modernity, 1640–1940.* Durham: Duke University Press, 2008.

Drinnon, Richard. *Facing West: The Metaphysics of Indian-Hating and Empire-Building* (1980). Norman: University of Oklahoma Press, 1997.

Driskill, Qwo-Li. "Doubleweaving Two-Spirit Critiques: Building Alliances between Native and Queer Studies." *GLQ* 16, no. 1–2 (2010): 69–92.

———."Stolen from Our Bodies: First Nations Two-Spirits/Queers and the Jour-ney to a Sovereign Erotic." *SAIL* 16, no. 2 (2004): 50–64.

Driskill, Qwo-Li, Chris Finley, Brian Joseph Gilley, and Scott Lauria Morgensen, eds. *Queer Indigenous Studies: Critical Interventions in Theory, Politics, and Litera-ture.* Tucson: University of Arizona Press, 2011.

Dumm, Thomas L. *A Politics of the Ordinary.* New York: New York University Press, 1999.

———. "Thoreau's Solitude." In *A Political Companion to Henry David Thoreau,* edited by Jack Turner, 326–39. Lexington: University Press of Kentucky, 2009.

Dworetz, Steven M. *The Unvarnished Doctrine: Locke, Liberalism, and the American Revolution.* Durham: Duke University Press, 1990.

Earle, John Milton. *Report to the Governor and Council, Concerning the Indians of the Commonwealth, under the Act of April 6, 1859.* Boston: William White, 1861.

Edelman, Lee. *No Future: Queer Theory and the Death Drive.* Durham: Duke Univer-sity Press, 2004.

Elliott, Michael A. *Custerology: The Enduring Legacy of the Indian Wars and George Armstrong Custer.* Chicago: University of Chicago Press, 2007.

Ellis, Richard E. *The Union at Risk: Jacksonian Democracy, States' Rights, and the Nul-lification Crisis.* New York: Oxford University Press, 1987.

Elmer, Jonathan. *On Lingering and Being Last: Race and Sovereignty in the New World.* New York: Fordham University Press, 2008.

Ely, Samuel. *The Deformity of a Hideous Monster, Discovered in the Province of Maine, by a Man in the Woods, Looking after Liberty.* Boston, 1796.

———. *The Unmasked Nabob of Hancock County: or, The Scales Dropt from the Eyes of the People.* Portsmouth, N.H.: Charles Pierce, 1796.

Eng, David. *The Feeling of Kinship: Queer Liberalism and the Racialization of Intimacy.* Durham: Duke University Press, 2010.

Engle, Karen. *The Elusive Promise of Indigenous Development: Rights, Culture, Strategy.* Durham: Duke University Press, 2010.

Erickson, Paul. "New Books, New Men: City-Mysteries Fiction, Authorship, and the Literary Market." *Early American Studies* 1, no. 1 (2003): 273–312.

Escalante, Emilio del Valle. *Maya Nationalisms and Postcolonial Challenges in Guatemala: Coloniality, Modernity, and Identity Politics.* Santa Fe: School for Advanced Research Press, 2009.

Eves, Jamie H. "'The Acquisition of Wealth, or of a Comfortable Subsistence': The Census of 1800 and the Yankee Migration to Maine, 1760–1825." *Maine History* 35, nos. 1–2 (1995): 6–25.

Eyal, Yonatan. *The Young America Movement and the Transformation of the Democratic Party, 1828–1861.* New York: Cambridge University Press, 2007.

Fabian, Johannes. *Time and the Other: How Anthropology Makes Its Object.* New York: Columbia University Press, 1983.

Fanuzzi, Robert. "Thoreau's Urban Imagination." *American Literature* 68, no. 2 (1996): 321–46.

Feller, Daniel. *The Public Land in Jacksonian Politics.* Madison: University of Wisconsin Press, 1984.

Fellows v. Blacksmith, 60 U.S. 366 (1857).

Fenton, William N. *The Great Law of the Longhouse: A Political History of the Iroquois Confederacy.* Norman: University of Oklahoma Press, 1998.

Ferguson, Roderick. *Aberrations in Black: Toward a Queer of Color Critique.* Minneapolis: University of Minnesota Press, 2004.

———. *The Reorder of Things: The University and Its Pedagogies of Minority Difference.* Minneapolis: University of Minnesota Press, 2012.

Ferland, Jacques. "Tribal Dissent or White Aggression? Interpreting Penobscot Indian Dispossession between 1808 and 1835." *Maine History* 43, no. 2 (2007): 125–70.

Fiedler, Leslie A. *The Return of the Vanishing American.* New York: Stein and Day, 1968.

Flory, Wendy Stollard. "Melville and Isabel: The Author and the Woman Within in the 'Inside Narrative' of *Pierre.*" In *Melville and Women,* edited by Elizabeth Schultz and Haskell Springer, 121–40. Kent, Ohio: Kent State University Press, 2006.

Foley, Barbara. "From Wall Street to Astor Place: Historicizing Melville's 'Bartleby.'" *American Literature* 72, no. 1 (2000): 87–116.

Foner, Philip S., ed. *We the Other People: Alternative Declarations of Independence by Labor Groups, Farmers, Women's Rights Advocates, Socialists, and Blacks, 1829– 1975.* Urbana: University of Illinois Press, 1976.

Ford, Lisa. *Settler Sovereignty: Jurisdiction and Indigenous People in America and Australia, 1788–1836.* Cambridge: Harvard University Press, 2011.

Foucault, Michel. *The History of Sexuality.* Vol. 1. 1976. Translated by Robert Hurley. 1978. New York: Vintage Books, 1990.

Fowler, Orson S. *Amativeness: or Evils and Remedies of Excessive and Perverted Sexuality, Including Warning and Advice to the Married and Single.* New York: Fowler and Wells, 1844.

Freccero, Carla. *Queer/ Early/ Modern.* Durham: Duke University Press, 2006.

Fredricks, Nancy. *Melville's Art of Democracy.* Athens: University of Georgia Press, 1995.

Freeman, Elizabeth. *The Wedding Complex: Forms of Belonging in Modern American Culture.* Durham: Duke University Press, 2002.

———. *Time Binds: Queer Temporalities, Queer Histories.* Durham: Duke University Press, 2010.

Freyer, Tony A. "Business Law and American Economic History." In *The Cambridge Economic History of the United States,* edited by Stanley L. Engerman and Robert E. Gallman, 435–82. New York: Cambridge University Press, 2000.

Frost, Linda. "'The Red Face of Man,' the Penobscot Indian, and a Conflict of Interest in Thoreau's *Maine Woods.*" *ESQ: A Journal of the American Renaissance* 39, no. 1 (1993): 21–47.

Fujikane, Candace, and Jonathan Y. Okamura, eds. *Asian Settler Colonialism: From Local Governance to the Habits of Everyday Life in Hawai`i.* Honolulu: University of Hawai`i Press, 2008.

Ganter, Granville, ed. *The Collected Speeches of Sagoyewathca, or Red Jacket.* Syracuse: Syracuse University Press, 2006.

———. "Red Jacket and the Decolonization of Republican Virtue." *American Indian Quarterly* 31, no. 4 (2007): 559–81.

Garrison, Tim Alan. *The Legal Ideology of Removal: The Southern Judiciary and the Sovereignty of Native American Nations.* Athens: University of Georgia Press, 2002.

Garroutte, Eva Marie. *Real Indians: Identity and the Survival of Native America.* Berkeley: University of California Press, 2003.

Gates, Paul. *History of Public Land Law Development.* Washington D.C.: Government Printing Office, 1968.

———. "The Role of the Land Speculator in Western Development." 1942. In *The Jeffersonian Dream: Studies in the History of American Land Policy and Development,*

6–22. Edited by Allan G. and Margaret Beattie Bogue. Albuquerque: University of New Mexico Press, 1996.

Gaul, Theresa Strouth. "Dialogue and Public Discourse in William Apess's *Indian Nullification*." *American Transcendental Quarterly* 15, no. 4 (2001): 275–92.

Genetin-Pilawa, C. Joseph. *Crooked Paths to Allotment: The Fight over Federal Indian Policy after the Civil War*. Chapel Hill: University of North Carolina Press, 2012.

Ghere, David L. "Diplomacy and War on the Maine Frontier, 1678–1759." In *Maine: The Pine Tree State from Prehistory to the Present*, edited by Richard W. Judd, Edwin A. Churchill, and Joel W. Eastman, 120–42. Orono: University of Maine Press, 1995.

———. "Mistranslations and Misinformation: Diplomacy on the Maine Frontier, 1725–1755." *American Indian Culture and Research Journal* 8, no. 4 (1984): 3–26.

Ghere, David L., and Alvin H. Morrison. "Searching for Justice on the Maine Frontier: Legal Concepts, Treaties, and the 1749 Wiscasset Incident." *American Indian Quarterly* 25, no. 3 (2001): 378–99.

Gilmore, Michael T. "The Artist and the Marketplace in *The House of the Seven Gables*." *ELH* 48, no. 1 (1981): 172–89.

Gilmore, Paul. "The Indian in the Museum: Henry David Thoreau, Okah Tubbee, and Authentic Manhood." *Arizona Quarterly* 54, no. 2 (1998): 25–63.

Gilroy, Paul. *The Black Atlantic: Modernity and Double Consciousness*. Cambridge: Harvard University Press, 1993.

Gleason, William. "Re-Creating *Walden*: Thoreau's Economy of Work and Play." *American Literature* 65, no. 4 (1993): 673–701.

Godbeer, Richard. *Sexual Revolution in Early America*. Baltimore: Johns Hopkins University Press, 2002.

Goeman, Mishuana. *Mark My Words: Native Women Mapping Our Nations*. Minneapolis: University of Minnesota Press, 2013.

Goldberg, Jonathan, and Madhavi Menon. "Queering History." *PMLA* 120, no. 5 (2005): 1608–17.

Goldberg-Hiller, Jonathan, and Noenoe Silva. "Sharks and Pigs: Animating Hawaiian Sovereignty against the Anthropological Machine." *SAQ* 110, no. 2 (2011): 429–46.

Goldstein, Alyosha. "Where the Nation Takes Place: Proprietary Regimes, Antistatism, and U.S. Settler Colonialism." *SAQ* 107, no. 4 (2008): 833–62.

Gonzales, Christian Michael. "Cultural Colonizers: Persistence and Empire in the Indian Antiremoval Movement, 1815–1859." PhD diss. University of California, San Diego, 2010.

Gould, Janice. "Disobedience (in Language) in Texts by Lesbian Native Americans." *ARIEL: A Review of International English Literature* 25, no. 1 (1994): 32–44.

Graham, Sylvester. *A Lecture to Young Men on Chastity. Intended Also for the Serious Consideration of Parents and Guardians.* 4th ed. Boston: George W. Light, 1838.

Gramsci, Antonio. *Selections from the Prison Notebooks.* Edited and translated by Quintin Hoare and Geoffrey Nowell Smith. New York: International Publishers, 1971.

Gray, Mary L. *Out in the Country: Youth, Media, and Queer Visibility in Rural America.* New York: New York University Press, 2009.

Graymont, Barbara. "New York State Indian Policy after the Revolution." *New York History* 57, no. 4 (1976): 438–74.

Greeley, Horace. *Hints toward Reforms, in Lectures, Addresses, and Other Writings.* New York: Harper and Brothers, 1850.

Green, Rayna. "The Pocahontas Perplex: The Image of Indian Women in American Culture." *Massachusetts Review* 16, no. 4 (1975): 698–714.

Griffiths, Thomas Morgan. "'Montpelier' and 'Seven Gables': Knox's Estate and Hawthorne's Novel." *New England Quarterly* 16, no. 3 (1943): 432–43.

Gross, Robert A. "Culture and Cultivation: Agriculture and Society in Thoreau's Concord." *Journal of American History* 69, no. 1 (1982): 42–61.

———. "The Great Bean Field Hoax: Thoreau and the Agricultural Reformers." *Virginia Quarterly Review* 61, no. 3 (1985): 483–97.

Grumet, Robert S. *First Manhattans: A History of the Indians of Greater New York.* Norman: University of Oklahoma Press, 2011.

Grusin, Richard. "Thoreau, Extravagance, and the Economy of Nature." *American Literary History* 5, no. 1 (1993): 30–50.

Guarneri, Carl J. *The Utopian Alternative: Fourierism in Nineteenth-Century America.* Ithaca: Cornell University Press, 1991.

Guillory, John. *Cultural Capital: The Problem of Literary Canon Formation.* Chicago: University of Chicago Press, 1993.

Gura, Philp F. *American Transcendentalism: A History.* New York: Hill and Wang, 2007.

———. "Thoreau's Maine Woods Indians: More Representative Men." *American Literature* 49, no. 3 (1977): 366–84.

Haefeli, Evan, and Kevin Sweeney. *Captors and Captives: The 1704 French and Indian Raid on Deerfield.* Amherst: University of Massachusetts Press, 2003.

Halberstam, J. Jack. *In a Queer Time and Place: Transgender Bodies, Subcultural Lives.* New York: New York University Press, 2005.

Hallock, Thomas. *From the Fallen Tree: Frontier Narratives, Environmental Politics, and the Roots of a National Pastoral, 1749–1826.* Chapel Hill: University of North Carolina Press, 2003.

Harding, Walter. *The Days of Henry Thoreau: A Biography.* 1962. New York: Dover Publications, Inc., 1982.

———. "Thoreau's Sexuality." *Journal of Homosexuality* 21, no. 3 (1991): 23–45.

Harkin, Michael E., and David Rich Lewis, eds. *Native Americans and the Environment: Perspectives on the Ecological Indian*. Lincoln: University of Nebraska Press, 2007.

Harris, Cheryl I. "Whiteness as Property." *Harvard Law Review* 106, no. 8 (1993): 1707–91.

Hart, Lynda. *Between the Body and the Flesh: Performing Sadomasochism*. New York: Columbia University Press, 1998.

Hartman, Saidiya. *Lose Your Mother: A Journey along the Atlantic Slave Route*. New York: Farrar, Straus and Giroux, 2008.

Hauptman, Laurence M. *Conspiracy of Interests: Iroquois Dispossession and the Rise of New York State*. Syracuse: Syracuse University Press, 1999.

———. *The Iroquois in the Civil War: From Battlefield to Reservation*. Syracuse: Syracuse University Press, 1993.

———. *The Tonawanda Senecas' Heroic Battle against Removal*. Albany: State University of New York Press, 2011.

Hauptman, Laurence M., and L. Gordon McLester III. Introduction to *The Oneida Indian Journey: From New York to Wisconsin, 1784–1860*, edited by Laurence M. Hauptman and L. Gordon McLester III, 9–18. Madison: University of Wisconsin Press, 1999.

Havard, Gilles. *The Great Peace of Montreal of 1701: French-Native Diplomacy in the Seventeenth Century*. Translated by Phyllis Aronoff and Howard Scott. Montreal: McGill-Queen's University Press, 2001.

Hawthorne, Nathaniel. *The House of the Seven Gables*. 1851. Edited by Robert S. Levine. New York: Norton, 2006.

Haynes, April. "The Trials of Frederick Hollick: Obscenity, Sex Education, and Medical Democracy in the Antebellum United States." *Journal of the History of Sexuality* 12, no. 4 (2003): 543–74.

Hecht, Roger. "Rents in the Landscape: The Anti-Rent War in Melville's *Pierre*." *ATQ* 19, no. 1 (2005): 37–50.

Hendler, Glenn. *Public Sentiments: Structures of Feeling in Nineteenth-Century American Literature*. Chapel Hill: University of North Carolina Press, 2001.

Herring, Scott. *Another Country: Queer Anti-Urbanism*. New York: New York University Press, 2010.

———. *Queering the Underworld: Slumming, Literature, and the Undoing of Lesbian and Gay History*. Chicago: University of Chicago Press, 2007.

Hietala, Thomas R. *Manifest Design: Anxious Aggrandizement in Late Jacksonian America*. Ithaca: Cornell University Press, 1985.

Higgins, Brian, and Herschel Parker. *Reading Melville's* Pierre; or, The Ambiguities. Baton Rouge: Louisiana State University Press, 2006.

Hinderaker, Eric. *Elusive Empires: Constructing Colonialism in the Ohio Valley, 1673–1800*. Cambridge: Cambridge University Press, 1997.

Holland, Sharon. *The Erotic Life of Racism*. Durham: Duke University Press, 2012.

Hong, Grace Kyungwon, and Roderick A. Ferguson, eds. *Strange Affinities: The Gender and Sexual Politics of Comparative Racialization*. Durham: Duke University Press, 2011.

Horsman, Reginald. "The Origins of Oneida Removal to Wisconsin, 1815–1822." In *The Oneida Indian Journey: From New York to Wisconsin, 1784–1860*, edited by Laurence M. Hauptman and L. Gordon McLester III, 53–69. Madison: University of Wisconsin Press, 1999.

Horwitz, Morton J. *The Transformation of American Law, 1780–1860*. Cambridge: Harvard University Press, 1979.

Huhndorf, Shari M. *Going Native: Indians in the American Cultural Imagination*. Ithaca: Cornell University Press, 2001.

Hurt, R. Douglas. *The Indian Frontier, 1763–1846*. Albuquerque: University of New Mexico Press, 2002.

Huston, Reeve. *Land and Freedom: Rural Society, Popular Protest, and Party Politics in Antebellum New York*. New York: Oxford University Press, 2000.

Hyde, Lewis, ed. *The Essays of Henry David Thoreau*. New York: Farrar, Strauss and Giroux, 2002.

Ingraham, Chrys. "The Heterosexual Imaginary: Feminist Sociology and Theories of Gender." *Sociological Theory* 12, no. 2 (1994): 203–19.

Isenberg, Nancy. *Sex and Citizenship in Antebellum America*. Chapel Hill: University of North Carolina Press, 1998.

Ivison, Duncan. *Postcolonial Liberalism*. New York: Cambridge University Press, 2002.

———. "Locke, Liberalism and Empire." *The Philosophy of John Locke: New Perspectives*, edited by Peter R. Anstey, 86–105. New York: Routledge, 2003.

Jackson, Holly. "The Transformation of American Family Property in *The House of the Seven Gables*." *ESQ: A Journal of the American Renaissance* 56, no. 3 (2010): 269–92.

Jackson, Shona. *Creole Indigeneity: Between Myth and Nation in the Caribbean*. Minneapolis: University of Minnesota Press, 2012.

Jacobs, Margaret D. *White Mother to a Dark Race: Settler Colonialism, Maternalism, and the Removal of Indigenous Children in the American West and Australia, 1880–1940*. Lincoln: University of Nebraska Press, 2011.

Jakobsen, Janet R. "Queer Is? Queer Does? Normativity and the Problem of Resistance." *GLQ* 4, no. 4 (1998): 511–36.

James, Henry, Horace Greeley, and Stephen Pearl Andrews. *Love, Marriage, and Divorce and the Sovereignty of the Individual*. 1853. New York: Source Book Press, 1973.

Jehlen, Myra. *American Incarnation: The Individual, the Nation, and the Continent*. Cambridge: Harvard University Press, 1986.

Jemison, G. Peter, and Anna M. Schein, eds. *Treaty of Canandaigua 1794: 200 Years of Treaty Relations between the Iroquois Confederacy and the United States.* Santa Fe: Clear Light Publishers, 2000.

Jensen, Laura. *Patriots, Settlers, and the Origins of American Social Policy.* New York: Cambridge University Press, 2003.

Johnson, Linck C. "Into History: Thoreau's Earliest 'Indian Book' and His First Trip to Cape Cod." *ESQ: A Journal of the American Renaissance* 28, no. 2 (1982): 75–88.

Johnston, Anna, and Alan Lawson. "Settler Colonies." In *A Companion to Postcolonial Studies,* edited by Henry Schwarz and Sangeeta Ray, 361–76. Malden, Mass.: Blackwell, 2000.

Jones, Dorothy V. *License for Empire: Colonialism by Treaty in Early America.* Chicago: University of Chicago Press, 1982.

Justice, Daniel Heath. "'Go Away, Water!': Kinship Criticism and the Decolonization Imperative." In *Reasoning Together,* edited by The Native Critics Collective (Craig S. Womack, Daniel Heath Justice, and Christopher B. Teuton, eds.), 147–68. Norman: University of Oklahoma Press, 2008.

———. "Notes toward a Theory of Anomaly." *GLQ* 16, nos. 1–2 (2010): 207–42.

———. *Our Fire Survives the Storm: A Cherokee Literary History.* Minneapolis: University of Minnesota Press, 2006.

Kades, Eric. "The End of the Hudson Valley's Peculiar Institution: The Anti-Rent Movement's Politics, Social Relations, and Economics." *Law and Social Inquiry* 27 (2002): 941–65.

Kaplan, Morris B. *Sexual Justice: Democratic Citizenship and the Politics of Desire.* New York: Routledge, 1997.

Kazanjian, David. *The Colonizing Trick: National Culture and Imperial Citizenship in Early America.* Minneapolis: University of Minnesota Press, 2003.

Kelley, Wyn. *Melville's City: Literary and Urban Form in Nineteenth-Century New York.* New York: Cambridge University Press, 1996.

———. "*Pierre*'s Domestic Ambiguities." In *The Cambridge Companion to Herman Melville,* edited by Robert S. Levine, 91–113. New York: Cambridge University Press, 1998.

Kelsey, Penelope Myrtle. *Tribal Theory in Native American Literature: Dakota and Haudenosaunee Writing and Indigenous Worldviews.* Lincoln: University of Nebraska Press, 2008.

Keyssar, Alexander. *The Right to Vote: The Contested History of Democracy in the United States.* Rev. ed. New York: Basic Books, 2009.

Khan, B. Zorina. "'Justice of the Marketplace': Legal Disputes and Economic Activity on America's Northeastern Frontier, 1700–1860." *Journal of Interdisciplinary History* 39, no. 1 (2008): 1–35.

Kilcup, Karen L. *Fallen Forests: Emotion, Embodiment, and Ethics in American Women's Environmental Writing, 1781–1924.* Athens: University of Georgia Press, 2013.

Knadler, Stephen. "Hawthorne's Genealogy of Madness: *The House of Seven Gables* and Disciplinary Individualism." *American Quarterly* 47, no. 2 (1995): 280–308.

Knott, John R. *Imagining Wild America: Wilderness and Wildness in the Writings of John James Audubon, Henry David Thoreau, John Muir, Edward Abbey, Wendell Berry, and Mary Oliver.* Ann Arbor: University of Michigan Press, 2002.

Kolodny, Annette. *The Lay of the Land: Metaphor as Experience and History in American Life and Letters.* Chapel Hill: University of North Carolina Press, 1984.

———. "A Summary History of the Penobscot Nation." In Joseph Nicolar, *The Life and Traditions of the Red Man*, 1–34. Edited by Annette Kolodny. Durham: Duke University Press, 2007.

Konkle, Maureen. "Indigenous Ownership and the Emergence of U.S. Liberal Imperialism." *American Indian Quarterly* 32, no. 3 (2008): 297–323.

———. *Writing Indian Nations: Native Intellectuals and the Politics of Historiography, 1827–1863.* Chapel Hill: University of North Carolina Press, 2004.

Kroeber, Karl. "Ecology and American Literature: Thoreau and Un-Thoreau." *American Literary History* 9, no. 2 (1997): 309–28.

Kucich, John J. "William Apess's Nullifications: Sovereignty, Identity and the Mashpee Revolt." In *Sovereignty, Separatism, and Survivance: Ideological Encounters in the Literature of Native North America*, edited by Benjamin D. Carson, 1–16. Newcastle upon Tyne: Cambridge Scholars, 2009.

Kuper, Adam. *The Reinvention of Primitive Society: Transformations of a Myth.* 1988. London: Routledge, 1997.

Kwashima, Yasuhide. *Puritan Justice and the Indian: White Man's Law in Massachusetts, 1630–1763.* Middleton: Wesleyan University Press, 1986.

Lang, Amy Schrager. *The Syntax of Class: Writing Inequality in Nineteenth-Century America.* Ann Arbor: University of Michigan Press, 2003.

Laqueur, Thomas W. *Solitary Sex: A Cultural History of Masturbation.* New York: Zone Books, 2003.

Larson, John Lauritz. *The Market Revolution in America: Liberty, Ambition, and the Eclipse of the Common Good.* New York: Cambridge University Press, 2010.

Latour, Bruno. *Politics of Nature: How to Bring the Sciences into Democracy.* Translated by Catherine Porter. Cambridge: Harvard University Press, 2004.

———. *Reassembling the Social: An Introduction to Actor-Network Theory.* New York: Oxford University Press, 2005.

———. *We Have Never Been Modern.* 1991. Translated by Catherine Porter. Cambridge: Harvard University Press, 1993.

Lause, Mark A. *Young America: Land, Labor, and the Republican Community.* Urbana: University of Illinois Press, 2005.

Lauter, Paul. *Canons and Contexts.* New York: Oxford University Press, 1991.

Lawrence, Bonita, and Enakshi Dua. "Decolonizing Antiracism." *Social Justice* 32, no. 4 (2004): 120–43.

Leavenworth, Peter S. "'The Best Title That Indians Can Claim': Native Agency
and Consent in the Transferal of Penacook-Pawtucket Land in the Seventeenth
Century." *New England Quarterly* 72, no. 2 (1999): 275–300.

Lee, James Kyung-Jin. *Urban Triage: Race and the Fictions of Multiculturalism.* Minneapolis: University of Minnesota Press, 2004.

Lehman, J. David. "The End of the Iroquois Mystique: The Oneida Land Cession
Treaties of the 1780s." *William and Mary Quarterly*, 3rd ser., 47, no. 4 (1990):
523–47.

LeMenager, Stephanie. *Manifesting and Other Destinies: Territorial Fictions of the
Nineteenth-Century United States.* Lincoln: University of Nebraska Press, 2004.

Lester, Joan. "Art for Sale: Cultural and Economic Survival." In *Enduring Traditions:
The Native Peoples of New England*, edited by Laurie Weinstein, 151–67. Westport, Conn.: Bergin and Garvey, 1994.

Levine, Robert S. *Dislocating Race and Nation: Episodes in Nineteenth-Century American Literary Nationalism.* Chapel Hill: University of North Carolina Press, 2008.

Littlefield, Daniel F., Jr. "'They Ought to Enjoy the Home of Their Fathers': The
Treaty of 1838, Seneca Intellectuals, and Literary Genesis." In *Early Native Ameri-
can Writing: New Critical Essays*, edited by Helen Jaskoski, 83–103. New York:
Cambridge University Press, 1996.

Locke, John. *Two Treatises of Government* and *A Letter Concerning Toleration.* Edited
by Ian Shapiro. New Haven: Yale University Press, 2003.

Loman, Andrew. *"Somewhat on the Community-System": Fourierism in the Works of
Nathaniel Hawthorne.* New York: Routledge, 2005.

Looby, Christopher. "George Thompson's 'Romance of the Real': Transgression
and Taboo in American Sensation Fiction." *American Literature* 65, no. 4 (1993):
651–72.

Lopenzina, Drew. "'The Whole Wilderness Shall Blossom as the Rose': Samson
Occom, Joseph Johnson, and the Question of Native Settlement on Cooper's
Frontier." *American Quarterly* 58, no. 4 (2006): 1119–45.

Lowe, Lisa. *Immigrant Acts: On Asian American Cultural Politics.* Durham: Duke
University Press, 1996.

Lowery, Malinda Maynor. *Lumbee Indians in the Jim Crow South: Race, Identity, and
the Making of a Nation.* Chapel Hill: University of North Carolina Press, 2010.

Luciano, Dana. *Arranging Grief: Sacred Time and the Body in Nineteenth-Century
America.* New York: New York University Press, 2007.

Luibhéid, Eithne. *Entry Denied: Controlling Sexuality at the Border.* Minneapolis:
University of Minnesota Press, 2002.

Lyons, Scott Richard. *X-Marks: Native Signatures of Assent.* Minneapolis: University
of Minnesota Press, 2010.

MacDougall, Pauleena. *The Penobscot Dance of Resistance: Tradition in the History of
a People.* Lebanon: University of New Hampshire Press, 2004.

MacMillan, Ken. *Sovereignty and Possession in the English New World: The Legal Foundations of Empire, 1576–1640*. New York: Cambridge University Press, 2009.

Macpherson, C. B. *The Political Theory of Possessive Individualism: Hobbes to Locke*. New York: Oxford University Press, 1962.

Maddox, Lucy. *Removals: Nineteenth-Century American Literature and the Politics of Indian Affairs*. New York: Oxford University Press, 1991.

Mandell, Daniel R. *Behind the Frontier: Indians in Eighteenth-Century Eastern Massachusetts*. Lincoln: University of Nebraska Press, 1996.

———. *Tribe, Race, History: Native Americans in Southern New England, 1780–1880*. Baltimore: Johns Hopkins University Press, 2008.

Mann, Barbara Alice. *Iroquoian Women: The Gantowisas*. New York: Peter Lang, 2000.

Mariotti, Shannon L. *Thoreau's Democratic Withdrawal: Alienation, Participation, and Modernity*. Madison: University of Wisconsin Press, 2010.

Massumi, Brian. *Parables for the Virtual: Movement, Affect, Sensation*. Durham: Duke University Press, 2002.

Mastronianni, Dominic. "Revolutionary Time and the Future of Democracy in Melville's *Pierre*." *ESQ: A Journal of the American Renaissance* 56, no. 4 (2010): 391–423.

Matthiessen, F. O. *American Renaissance: Art and Expression in the Age of Emerson and Whitman*. 1941. New York: Oxford University Press, 1968.

Maynard, W. Barksdale. *Walden Pond: A History*. New York: Oxford University Press, 2004.

Mazel, David. *American Literary Environmentalism*. Athens: University of Georgia Press, 2000.

McCallum, E. L., and Mikko Tuhkanen, eds. *Queer Times, Queer Becomings*. Albany: State University of New York Press, 2011.

McClintock, Anne. *Imperial Leather: Race, Gender and Sexuality in the Colonial Contest*. New York: Routledge, 1995.

McCoy, Drew R. *The Elusive Republic: Political Economy in Jeffersonian America*. Chapel Hill: University of North Carolina Press, 1980.

McCurdy, Charles W. *The Anti-Rent Era in New York Law and Politics, 1839–1865*. Chapel Hill: University of North Carolina Press, 2001.

McGarry, Molly. *Ghosts of Futures Past: Spiritualism and the Cultural Politics of Nineteenth-Century America*. Berkeley: University of California Press, 2008.

McKusick, James C. *Green Writing: Romanticism and Ecology*. New York: St. Martin's Press, 2000.

McMullen, Ann. "Native Basketry, Basketry Styles, and Changing Group Identity in Southern New England." In *Algonkians of New England: Past and Present*, edited by Peter Benes and Jane Montague Benes, 76–88. Boston: Boston University Press, 1993.

————. "What's Wrong with This Picture? Context, Conversion, Survival, and the Development of Regional Native Cultures and Pan-Indianism in Southeastern New England." In *Enduring Traditions: The Native Peoples of New England*, edited by Laurie Weinstein, 123–50. Westport, Conn.: Bergin and Garvey, 1994.

McMullen, Ann, and Russell G. Handsman, eds. *A Key into the Language of Wood-splint Baskets*. Washington, Conn.: American Indian Archaeological Institute, 1987.

McWilliams, John. "Indian John and the Northern Tawnies." *New England Quarterly* 69, no. 4 (1996): 580–604.

Mehta, Uday Singh. *Liberalism and Empire: A Study in Nineteenth-Century British Liberal Thought*. Chicago: University of Chicago Press, 1999.

Melamed, Jodi. *Represent and Destroy: Rationalizing Violence in the New Racial Capitalism*. Minneapolis: University of Minnesota Press, 2011.

Mellow, James R. *Nathaniel Hawthorne in His Times*. Boston: Houghton Mifflin, 1980.

Melville, Herman. *Pierre; or the Ambiguities*. 1852. New York: Penguin Books, 1996.

Merish, Lori. *Sentimental Materialism: Gender, Commodity Culture, and Nineteenth-Century American Literature*. Durham: Duke University Press, 2002.

Merleau-Ponty, Maurice. *Phenomenology of Perception*. 1945. Translated by Colin Smith. 1958. New York: Routledge, 2002.

Michaels, Walter Benn. "Romance and Real Estate." In *The American Renaissance Reconsidered*, edited by Walter Benn Michaels and Donald Pease, 156–82. Baltimore: Johns Hopkins University Press, 1985.

Michaelsen, Scott. *The Limits of Multiculturalism: Interrogating the Origins of American Anthropology*. Minneapolis: University of Minnesota Press, 1999.

Mielke, Laura L. *Moving Encounters: Sympathy and the Indian Question in Antebellum Literature*. Amherst: University of Massachusetts Press, 2008.

Mignolo, Walter D. *Local Histories/Global Designs: Coloniality, Subaltern Knowledges, and Border Thinking*. Princeton: Princeton University Press, 2000.

Milder, Robert. "The Other Hawthorne." *New England Quarterly* 81, no. 4 (2008): 559–95.

————. "'The Ugly Socrates': Melville, Hawthorne, and the Varieties of Homoerotic Experience." In *Hawthorne and Melville: Writing a Relationship*, edited by Jana L. Argersinger and Leland S. Pearson, 71–111. Athens: University of Georgia Press, 2008.

Miles, Tiya. *Ties That Bind: The Story of an Afro-Cherokee Family in Slavery and Freedom*. Berkeley: University of California Press, 2006.

Miles, Tiya, and Sharon Holland, eds. *Crossing Waters, Crossing Worlds: The African Diaspora in Indian Country*. Durham: Duke University Press, 2006.

Miller, Bruce Granville. *Invisible Indigenes: The Politics of Nonrecognition*. Lincoln: University of Nebraska Press, 2003.

Miller, Robert J., Jacinta Ruru, Larissa Behrendt, and Tracey Lindberg. *Discovering Indigenous Lands: The Doctrine of Discovery in the English Colonies*. New York: Oxford University Press, 2010.

Millington, Richard H. *Practicing Romance: Narrative from and Cultural Engagement in Hawthorne's Fiction*. Princeton: Princeton University Press, 1992.

Million, Dian. "Felt Theory: An Indigenous Feminist Approach to Affect and History." *Wicazo Sa Review* 24, no. 2 (2009): 53–76.

Millner, Michael. *Fever Reading: Affect and Reading Badly in the Early American Public Sphere*. Durham: University of New Hampshire Press, 2012.

Miranda, Deborah. *Bad Indians: A Tribal Memoir*. Berkeley, Calif.: Heyday, 2013.

———. "Dildos, Hummingbirds, and Driving Her Crazy." *Frontiers* 23, no. 2 (2002): 135–49.

Moody, Robert E. "Samuel Ely: Forerunner of Shays." *New England Quarterly* 5, no. 1 (1932): 105–34.

Moon, Michael. *Disseminating Whitman: Revision and Corporeality in* Leaves of Grass. Durham: Duke University Press, 1991.

Moreton-Robinson, Aileen. "Whiteness, Epistemology, and Indigenous Representation." In *Whitening Race: Essays in Social and Cultural Criticism*, edited by Aileen Moreton-Robinson, 75–88. Canberra: Aboriginal Studies Press, 2004.

———, ed. *Whitening Race: Essays in Social and Cultural Criticism*. Canberra: Aboriginal Studies Press, 2004.

———. "Writing Off Indigenous Sovereignty: The Discourse of Security and Patriarchal White Sovereignty." In *Sovereign Subjects: Indigenous Sovereignty Matters*, edited by Aileen Moreton-Robinson, 86–104. Crows Nest, N.S.W.: Allen and Unwin, 2007.

———. "Writing Off Treaties: White Possession in the United States Critical Whiteness Studies Literature." In *Transnational Whiteness Matters*, edited by Aileen Moreton-Robinson, Maryrose Casey, and Fiona Nicoll, 81–96. New York: Rowman and Littlefield, 2008.

Morgan, Lewis Henry. *League of the Iroquois*. 1851. Edited by William N. Fenton. New York: Corinth Books, 1962.

Morgensen, Scott Lauria. *Spaces between Us: Queer Settler Colonialism and Indigenous Decolonization*. Minneapolis: University of Minnesota Press, 2011.

Morrison, Kenneth M. *The Embattled Northeast: The Elusive Ideal of Alliance in Abenaki-Euramerican Relations*. Berkeley: University of California Press, 1984.

Morrison, Michael A. "Distribution or Dissolution: Western Land Policy, Economic Development, and the Language of Corruption, 1837–1841." *American Nineteenth-Century History* 1, no. 1 (2000): 1–33.

Morrison, Toni. *Playing in the Dark: Whiteness and the Literary Imagination*. 1992. New York: Vintage Books, 1993.

Morton, Timothy. *Without Nature: Rethinking Environmental Aesthetics*. Cambridge: Harvard University Press, 2007.

Muñoz, José Esteban. *Disidentifications: Queers of Color and the Performance of Politics*. Minneapolis: University of Minnesota Press, 1999.

Murphy, Gretchen. *Hemispheric Imaginings: The Monroe Doctrine and the Narratives of U.S. Empire*. Durham: Duke University Press, 2005.

Murray, David. *Forked Tongues: Speech, Writing, and Representation in North American Indian Texts*. Bloomington: Indiana University Press, 1991.

Myers, Jeffrey. *Converging Stories: Race, Ecology, and Environmental Justice in American Literature*. Athens: University of Georgia Press, 2005.

Myerson, Joel, ed. *Emerson and Thoreau: The Contemporary Reviews*. New York: Cambridge University Press, 1992.

Namias, June. Introduction to *A Narrative of the Life of Mrs. Mary Jemison*, 3–45. Norman: University of Oklahoma Press, 1992.

Nealon, Christopher. *Foundlings: Lesbian and Gay Historical Emotion before Stonewall*. Durham: Duke University Press, 2001.

Nelson, Dana. *National Manhood: Capitalist Citizenship and the Imagined Fraternity of White Men*. Durham: Duke University Press, 1998.

———. "Thoreau, Manhood, and Race: Quiet Desperation versus Representative Isolation." In *A Historical Guide to Henry David Thoreau*, edited by William E. Cain, 61–94. New York: Oxford University Press, 2000.

Nelson, Diane M. *A Finger in the Wound: Body Politics in Quincentennial Guatemala*. Berkeley: University of California Press, 1999.

Neufeldt, Leonard N. *The Economist: Henry Thoreau and Enterprise*. New York: Oxford University Press, 1989.

Neuman, Lisa K. "Basketry as Economic Enterprise and Cultural Revitalization: The Case of the Wabanaki Tribes of Maine." *Wicazo Sa Review* 25, no. 2 (2010): 89–106.

Newbury, Michael. "Healthful Employment: Hawthorne, Thoreau, and Middle-Class Fitness." *American Quarterly* 47, no. 4 (1995): 681–714.

Newfield, Christopher. *Unmaking the Public University: The Forty-Year Assault on the Middle Class*. Cambridge: Harvard University Press, 2008.

Newman, Lance. *Our Common Dwelling: Henry Thoreau: Transcendentalism, and the Class Politics of Nature*. New York: Palgrave Macmillan, 2005.

Ngai, Sianne. *Ugly Feelings*. Cambridge: Harvard University Press, 2007.

Nicoll, Fiona. "Reconciliation in and out of Perspective: White Knowing, Seeing, Curating, and Being at Home in and against Indigenous Sovereignty." In *Whitening Race: Essays in Social and Cultural Criticism*, edited by Aileen Moreton-Robinson, 17–31. Canberra: Aboriginal Studies Press, 2004.

Nielson, Donald M. "The Mashpee Indian Revolt of 1833." *New England Quarterly* 58, no. 3 (1985): 400–420.

Niezen, Ronald. *The Origins of Indigenism: Human Rights and the Politics of Identity.* Berkeley: University of California Press, 2003.

Nissenbaum, Stephen. *Sex, Diet, and Debility in Jacksonian America: Sylvestor Graham and Health Reform.* Westport, Conn.: Greenwood Press, 1980.

Nixon, Nicola. "Compromising Politics and Herman Melville's *Pierre.*" *American Literature* 69, no. 4 (1997): 719–41.

Nixon, Rob. *Slow Violence and the Environmentalism of the Poor.* Cambridge: Harvard University Press, 2011.

Norgren, Jill. *The Cherokee Cases: The Confrontation of Law and Politics.* New York: McGraw Hill, 1996.

Norton, Mary Beth. "George Burroughs and the Girls from Casco: The Maine Roots of Salem Witchcraft." *Maine History* 40, no. 4 (2001–2): 259–77.

Novak, William J. "The Myth of the 'Weak' American State." *American Historical Review* 113, no. 3 (2008): 752–72.

Nyong'o, Tavia. *The Amalgamation Waltz: Race, Performance, and the Ruses of Memory.* Minneapolis: University of Minnesota Press, 2009.

O'Brien, Jean. *Dispossession by Degrees: Indian Land and Identity in Natick, Massachusetts, 1650–1790.* New York: Cambridge University Press, 1997.

———. *Firsting and Lasting: Writing Indians out of Existence in New England.* Minneapolis: University of Minnesota Press, 2010.

O'Brien, Sharon. *American Indian Tribal Governments.* Norman: University of Oklahoma Press, 1989.

O'Connell, Barry. Introduction to *On Our Own Ground: The Complete Writings of William Apess, a Pequot,* edited by Barry O'Connell, xiii–lxxvii. Amherst: University of Massachusetts Press, 1992.

Onuf, Peter S. *Jefferson's Empire: The Language of American Nationhood.* Charlottesville: University Press of Virginia, 2000.

Oshima, Yukiko. "Isabel as a Native American Ghost in Saddle Meadows: The Background of Pierre's 'Race.'" *Leviathan: A Journal of Melville Studies* 5, no. 2 (2003): 5–17.

Otter, Samuel. *Melville's Anatomies.* Berkeley: University of California Press, 1999.

Outka, Paul. *Race and Nature: From Transcendentalism to the Harlem Renaissance.* New York: Palgrave Macmillan, 2008.

Packard, Chris. *Queer Cowboys and Other Erotic Male Friendships in Nineteenth-Century American Literature.* New York: Palgrave Macmillan, 2005.

Packer, Barbara L. *The Transcendentalists.* Athens: University of Georgia Press, 2007.

Parker, Arthur C. *The History of the Seneca Indians.* 1926. Long Island, N.Y.: Ira J. Friedman, Inc., 1967.

———. *The Life of General Ely S. Parker: Last Grand Sachem of the Iroquois and General Grant's Military Secretary.* Buffalo: Buffalo Historical Society, 1919.

Parker, Hershel. *Herman Melville, A Biography.* Vol. 1, *1819–1857.* Baltimore: Johns Hopkins University Press, 1996.

Paryz, Marek. *The Postcolonial and Imperial Experience in American Transcendentalism.* New York: Palgrave Macmillan, 2012.

Pawling, Michah Abell. "Petitions and the Reconfiguration of Homeland: Persistence and Tradition among Wabanaki Peoples in the Nineteenth Century." PhD diss., University of Maine, 2010.

Pease, Donald. *Visionary Compacts: American Renaissance Writings in Cultural Context.* Madison: University of Wisconsin Press, 1987.

Pepper, C., Jr. *Manor of Rensselaerwyck.* Albany, N.Y.: J. Munsell, 1846.

Perea, Juan F. "The Black/White Binary Paradigm of Race." In *Critical Race Theory: The Cutting Edge,* edited by Richard Delgado and Jean Stefancic, 344–53. 2nd ed. Philadelphia: Temple University Press, 2000.

Perez, Hiram. "You Can Have My Brown Body and Eat It, Too!" *Social Text* 24, nos. 84–85 (2005): 171–92.

Peyer, Bernd C. *The Tutor'd Mind: Indian Missionary Writers in Antebellum America.* Amherst: University of Massachusetts Press, 1997.

Pfister, Joel. *The Production of Personal Life: Class, Gender, and the Psychological in Hawthorne's Fiction.* Stanford: Stanford University Press, 1991.

Phillips, Dana. *The Truth of Ecology: Nature, Culture, and Literature in America.* New York: Oxford University Press, 2003.

Piatote, Beth. *Domestic Subjects: Gender, Citizenship, and Law in Native American Literature.* New Haven: Yale University Press, 2013.

Pierce, Maris Bryant. *Address on the Present Condition and Prospects of the Aboriginal Inhabitants of North America, with Particular Reference to the Seneca Nation.* 1838. Philadelphia: J. Richards, Printer, 1839.

Plane, Ann Marie, and Gregory Button. "The Massachusetts Indian Enfranchisement Act: Ethnic Contest in Historical Context, 1849–1869." In *After King Philip's War: Presence and Persistence in Indian New England,* edited by Colin G. Calloway, 178–206. Hanover, N.H.: University Press of New England, 1997.

Portnoy, Alisse. *Their Right to Speak: Women's Activism in the Indian and Slave Debates.* Cambridge: Harvard University Press, 2005.

Povinelli, Elizabeth A. *The Cunning of Recognition: Indigenous Alterities and the Making of Australian Multiculturalism.* Durham: Duke University Press, 2002.

———. *Economies of Abandonment: Social Belonging and Endurance in Late Liberalism.* Durham: Duke University Press, 2011.

———. *The Empire of Love: Toward a Theory of Intimacy, Genealogy, and Carnality.* Durham: Duke University Press, 2006.

———. "The Governance of the Prior." *interventions* 13, no. 1 (2011): 13–30.

Powell, Timothy. *Ruthless Democracy: A Multicultural Interpretation of the American Renaissance.* Princeton: Princeton University Press, 2000.

Prins, Harald E. L. "Turmoil on the Wabanaki Frontier, 1524–1678." In *Maine: The Pine Tree State from Prehistory to the Present*, edited by Richard W. Judd, Edwin A. Churchill, and Joel W. Eastman, 97–119. Orono: University of Maine Press, 1995.

Protevi, John. *Political Affect: Connecting the Social and the Somatic*. Minneapolis: University of Minnesota Press, 2009.

Prucha, Francis Paul. *American Indian Treaties: The History of a Political Anomaly*. Berkeley: University of California Press, 1994.

———. *Documents of United States Indian Policy*. 3rd ed. Lincoln: University of Nebraska Press, 2000.

Puar, Jasbir K. *Terrorist Assemblages: Homonationalism in Queer Times*. Durham: Duke University Press, 2007.

Radding, Cynthia. *Wandering Peoples: Colonialism, Ethnic Spaces, and Ecological Frontiers in Northwestern Mexico, 1700–1850*. Durham: Duke University Press, 1997.

Raibmon, Paige Sylvia. *Authentic Indians: Episodes of Encounter from the Late-Nineteenth-Century Northwest Coast*. Durham: Duke University Press, 2005.

Ramirez, Renya K. *Native Hubs: Culture, Community, and Belonging in Silicon Valley and Beyond*. Durham: Duke University Press, 2007.

Rasmussen, Birgit Brander. *Queequeg's Coffin: Indigenous Literacies and Early American Literature*. Durham: Duke University Press, 2012.

Ray, Roger B. "Maine Indians' Concept of Land Tenure." *Maine Historical Society Quarterly* 13 (1974): 28–51.

Razack, Sherene H., ed. *Race, Space, and the Law: Unmapping a White Settler Society*. Toronto: Between the Lines, 2002.

Reddy, Chandan. *Freedom with Violence: Race, Sexuality, and the U.S. State*. Durham: Duke University Press, 2011.

Report of the Committee on Indian Affairs, to whom were referred sundry petitions and memorials from Citizens of New York, and others, praying that the Tonawanda band of the Seneca tribe of Indians may be exempted from the operation of the treaty of the 20th May 1842. 29th Cong., 2nd sess. S. doc. 156.

Reynolds, Larry J. *Devils and Rebels: The Making of Hawthorne's Damned Politics*. Ann Arbor: University of Michigan Press, 2008.

Richardson, Robert D., Jr. *Henry Thoreau: A Life of the Mind*. Berkeley: University of California Press, 1986.

Rifkin, Mark. *The Erotics of Sovereignty: Queer Native Writing in the Era of Self-Determination*. Minneapolis: University of Minnesota Press, 2012.

———. "'A home made sacred by protecting laws': Black Activist Homemaking and Geographies of Citizenship in *Incidents in the Life of a Slave Girl*." *differences: A Journal of Feminist Cultural Studies* 18, no. 2 (2007): 72–102.

———. "Indigenizing Agamben: Rethinking Sovereignty in Light of the 'Peculiar' Status of Native Peoples." *Cultural Critique* 72 (Fall 2009): 88–124.

———. *Manifesting America: The Imperial Construction of U.S. National Space.* New York: Oxford University Press, 2009.

———. *When Did Indians Become Straight? Kinship, the History of Sexuality, and Native Sovereignty.* New York: Oxford University Press, 2011.

Robertson, Lindsay G. *Conquest by Law: How the Discovery of America Dispossessed Indigenous Peoples of Their Lands.* New York: Oxford University Press, 2005.

Robertson-Lorant, Laurie. *Melville: A Biography.* New York: Clarkson Potter, 1996.

Robinson, David M. *Natural Life: Thoreau's Worldly Transcendentalism.* Ithaca: Cornell University Press, 2004.

Rockwell, Stephen J. *Indian Affairs and the Administrative State in the Nineteenth Century.* New York: Cambridge University Press, 2010.

Rodríguez, Juana María. *Queer Latinidad: Identity Practices, Discursive Spaces.* New York: New York University Press, 2003.

Roediger, David R. *The Wages of Whiteness: Race and the Making of the American Working Class.* Rev. ed. New York: Verso, 2007.

Rogin, Michael Paul. *Subversive Genealogy: The Politics and Art of Herman Melville.* New York: Alfred A. Knopf, 1983.

Rohrbough, Malcolm J. *The Land Office Business: The Settlement and Administration of American Public Lands, 1789–1837.* New York: Oxford University Press, 1968.

Rohy, Valerie. *Anachronism and Its Others: Sexuality, Race, Temporality.* Albany: State University of New York Press, 2009.

Rolde, Neil. *Unsettled Past, Unsettled Future: The Story of Maine Indians.* Gardiner, Maine: Tilbury House Publishers, 2004.

Rosen, Deborah A. *American Indians and State Law: Sovereignty, Race, and Citizenship, 1790–1880.* Lincoln: University of Nebraska Press, 2007.

Rosenblum, Nancy L. "Thoreau's Democratic Individualism." In *A Political Companion to Henry David Thoreau,* edited by Jack Turner, 15–38. Lexington: University Press of Kentucky, 2009.

Ross, Marlon B. "Beyond the Closet as Raceless Paradigm." In *Black Queer Studies: A Critical Anthology,* edited by E. Patrick Johnson and Mae G. Henderson, 161–89. Durham: Duke University Press, 2005.

Rossi, William. "Thoreau's Transcendental Ecocentrism." In *Thoreau's Sense of Place: Essays in American Environmental Writing,* edited by Richard J. Schneider, 28–43. Iowa City: University of Iowa Press, 2000.

Rothenberg, Diane. "The Mothers of the Nation: Seneca Resistance to Quaker Intervention." In *Women and Colonization: Anthropological Perspectives,* edited by Mona Etienne and Eleanor Leacock, 63–87. New York: Praeger, 1980.

Round, Philip H. *Removable Type: Histories of the Book in Indian Country, 1663–1880.* Chapel Hill: University of North Carolina Press. 2010.

Rousseau, Peter L. "Jacksonian Monetary Policy, Specie Flows, and the Panic of 1837." *Journal of Economic History* 62, no. 2 (2002): 457–88.

Ruffin, Kimberly N. *Black on Earth: African American Ecoliterary Traditions*. Athens: University of Georgia Press, 2010.

Salamon, Gayle. *Assuming a Body: Transgender and Rhetorics of Materiality*. New York: Columbia University Press, 2010.

Saldaña-Portillo, María Josefina. "'How Many Mexicans [is] a horse worth?': The League of United Latin American Citizens, Desegregation Cases, and Chicano Historiography." *SAQ* 107, no. 4 (2008): 809–32.

Salisbury, Neal. *Manitou and Providence: Indians, Europeans, and the Making of New England, 1500–1643*. New York: Oxford University Press, 1982.

Samuels, Shirley. *Romances of the Republic: Women, the Family, and Violence in the Literature of the Early American Nation*. New York: Oxford University Press, 1996.

Sánchez, María Carla. *Reforming the World: Social Activism and the Problem of Fiction in Nineteenth-Century America*. Iowa City: University of Iowa Press, 2008.

Sánchez-Eppler, Karen. *Touching Liberty: Abolition, Feminism, and the Politics of the Body*. Berkeley: University of California Press, 1997.

Sassen, Saskia. *Territory, Authority, Rights: From Medieval to Global Assemblages*. Updated ed. Princeton: Princeton University Press, 2008.

Sattelmeyer, Robert. "Depopulation, Deforestation, and the Actual Walden Pond." In *Thoreau's Sense of Place: Essays in American Environmental Writing*, edited by Richard J. Schneider, 235–43. Iowa City: University of Iowa Press, 2000.

———. "*Walden*: Climbing the Canon." In *More Day to Dawn: Thoreau's* Walden *for the Twenty-First Century*, edited by Sandra Petrulionis and Laura Dassow Walls, 11–27. Amherst: University of Massachusetts Press, 2007.

Saunt, Claudio. *Black, White, and Indian: Race and the Unmaking of an American Family*. New York: Oxford University Press, 2006.

Sayre, Robert F. *Thoreau and the American Indians*. Princeton: Princeton University Press, 1977.

Scheckel, Susan. *The Insistence of the Indian: Race and Nationalism in Nineteenth-Century American Culture*. Princeton: Princeton University Press, 1998.

Schneider, Richard J. "'Climate Does Thus React on Man': Wildness and Geographic Determinism in Thoreau's 'Walking.'" In *Thoreau's Sense of Place: Essays in American Environmental Writing*, edited by Richard J. Schneider, 44–60. Iowa City: University of Iowa Press, 2000.

Schoolcraft, Henry R. *Helderbergia: or the Apotheosis of the Heroes of the Antirent War*. J. Munsell: Albany, 1855.

———. *Notes on the Iroquois*. 1847. East Lansing: Michigan State University Press, 2002.

Schweninger, Lee. *Listening to the Land: Native American Literary Responses to the Landscape*. Athens: University of Georgia Press, 2008.

Scott, Darieck. *Extravagant Abjection: Blackness, Power, and Sexuality in the African American Literary Imagination*. New York: New York University Press, 2010.

Sedgwick, Eve Kosofsky. *Touching Feeling: Affect, Pedagogy, Performativity*. Durham: Duke University Press, 2003.

Seed, Patricia. *American Pentimento: The Invention of Indians and the Pursuit of Riches*. Minneapolis: University of Minnesota Press, 2001.

Seigworth, Gregory J., and Melissa Gregg. "An Inventory of Shimmers." In *The Affect Theory Reader*, edited by Melissa Gregg and Gregory J. Seigworth, 1–25. Durham: Duke University Press, 2010.

Sellers, Charles. *The Market Revolution: Jacksonian America, 1815–1846*. New York: Oxford University Press, 1991.

Sellers, Christopher. "Thoreau's Body: Towards an Embodied Environmental History." *Environmental History* 4, no. 4 (1999): 486–514.

Shah, Nayan. *Stranger Intimacy: Contesting Race, Sexuality, and the Law in the North American West*. Berkeley: University of California Press, 2011.

Shamir, Milette. *Inexpressible Privacy: The Interior Life of Antebellum American Literature*. Philadelphia: University of Pennsylvania Press, 2006.

Shammas, Carole. *A History of Household Government in America*. Charlottesville: University of Virginia Press, 2002.

Sharpe, Jenny. "Postcolonial Studies in the House of U.S. Multiculturalism." In *A Companion to Postcolonial Studies*, edited by Henry Schwarz and Sangeeta Ray, 112–25. Malden, Mass.: Blackwell, 2000.

Shattuck, George C. *The Oneida Land Claims: A Legal History*. Syracuse: Syracuse University Press, 1991.

Shaw, Karen. "Creating/Negotiating Interstices: Indigenous Sovereignties." In *Sovereign Lives: Power in Global Politics*, edited by Jenny Edkins, Véronique Pin-Fat, and Michael J. Shapiro, 165–87. New York: Routledge, 2004.

Shelden, Mary Lamb. "Health and the Body." In *The Oxford Handbook of Transcendentalism*, edited by Joel Myerson, Sandra Herbert Petrulionis, and Laura Dassow Walls, 241–48. New York: Oxford University Press, 2010.

Sheriff, Carol. *The Artificial River: The Erie Canal and the Paradox of Progress, 1817–1862*. New York: Hill and Wang, 1996.

Shoemaker, Nancy. *A Strange Likeness: Becoming Red and White in Eighteenth-Century North America*. New York: Oxford University Press, 2004.

Shurtleff, James. *A Concise Review of the Spirit Which Seemed to Govern in the Time of the Late American War, Compared with the Spirit Which Now Prevails; with the Speech of the Goddess of Freedom, Who Is Represented as Making Her Appearance upon the Alarming Occasion*. Augusta, Maine: Peter Edes, 1798.

Silva, Denise Ferreira da. *Toward a Global Idea of Race*. Minneapolis: University of Minnesota Press, 2007.

Silverman, David J. *Faith and Boundaries: Colonists, Christianity, and Community among the Wampanoag Indians of Martha's Vineyard, 1600–1871*. New York: Cambridge University Press, 2005.

————. "The Impact of Indentured Servitude on the Society and Culture of Southern New England Indians, 1680–1810." *New England Quarterly* 74, no. 4 (2001): 622–66.

————. *Red Brethren: The Brothertown and Stockbridge Indians and the Problem of Race in Early America*. Ithaca: Cornell University Press, 2010.

Silverman, Gillian. "Textual Sentimentalism: Incest and Authorship in Melville's *Pierre*." *American Literature* 74, no. 2 (2002): 345–72.

Simpson, Audra. "Captivating Eunice: Membership, Colonialism, and Gendered Citizenships of Grief." *Wicazo Sa Review* 24, no. 2 (2009): 105–29.

————. "On Ethnographic Refusal: Indigeneity, 'Voice' and Colonial Citizenship." *Junctures* 9 (2007): 67–80.

————. "Subjects of Sovereignty: Indigeneity, the Revenue Rule, and Juridics of Failed Consent." *Law and Contemporary Problem* 71, no. 3 (2008): 191–216.

Singh, Nikhil Pal. *Black Is a Country: Race and the Unfinished Struggle for Democracy*. Cambridge: Harvard University Press, 2004.

Slauter, Eric. "Reading and Radicalization: Print, Politics, and the American Revolution." *Early American Studies* 8, no. 1 (2010): 5–40.

————. *The State as a Work of Art: The Cultural Origins of the Constitution*. Chicago: University of Chicago Press, 2009.

Slotkin, Richard. *Regeneration through Violence: The Mythology of the American Frontier, 1600–1860*. 1973. Norman: University of Oklahoma Press, 2000.

Slouka, Mark Z. "Demonic History: Geography and Genealogy in Melville's *Pierre*." *ESQ: A Journal of the American Renaissance* 35, no. 2 (1989): 147–60.

Smith, Andrea. "Queer Theory and Native Studies: The Heteronormativity of Settler Colonialism." *GLQ* 16, nos. 1–2 (2010): 41–68.

Smith, Bruce R. "Premodern Sexualities." *PMLA* 115, no. 3 (2000): 318–29.

Snediker, Michael D. "*Pierre* and the Non-Transparencies of Figuration." *ELH* 77, no. 1 (2010): 217–35.

Snow, Dean R. "The Ethnohistoric Baseline of the Eastern Abenaki." *Ethnohistory* 23, no. 3 (1976): 291–306.

Snyder, Christina. *Slavery in Indian Country: The Changing Face of Captivity in Early America*. Cambridge: Harvard University Press, 2010.

Society of Friends. *The Case of the Seneca Indians in the State of New York: Illustrated by Facts*. Philadelphia: Merrihew and Thompson, 1840.

————. *A Further Illustration of the Case of the Seneca Indians in the State of New York, in a Review of a Pamphlet Entitled "An Appeal to the Christian Community, &c.," by Nathaniel T. Strong*. Philadelphia: Merrihew and Thompson, 1841.

Sokolow, Jayme A. *Eros and Modernization: Sylvester Graham, Health Reform, and the Origins of Victorian Sexuality in America*. Rutherford: Farleigh Dickinson University Press, 1983.

Somerville, Siobhan. *Queering the Color Line: Race and the Invention of Homosexuality in American Culture*. Durham: Duke University Press, 2000.

Spann, Edward K. *The New Metropolis: New York City, 1840–1857*. New York: Columbia University Press, 1981.

Spanos, William V. "Pierre's Extraordinary Emergency: Melville and 'The Voice of Silence.'" 2 parts. *boundary 2* 28, nos. 2–3 (2001): 105–55.

Speck, Frank G. "The Eastern Algonquian Wabanaki Confederacy." *American Anthropologist* 17, no. 3 (1915): 492–508.

———. *Penobscot Man*. 1940. Orono: University of Maine Press, 1998.

Spence, Mark David. *Dispossessing the Wilderness: Indian Removal and the Making of the National Parks*. New York: Oxford University Press, 1999.

Spivak, Gayatri Chakravorty. *A Critique of Postcolonial Reason: Toward a History of the Vanishing Present*. Cambridge: Harvard University Press, 1999.

Spurlock, John C. *Free Love: Marriage and Middle-Class Radicalism in America, 1825–1860*. New York: New York University Press, 1988.

Stam, Robert, and Ella Shohat. *Race in Translation: Culture Wars around the Postcolonial Atlantic*. Durham: Duke University Press, 2012.

Stanley, Amy Dru. *From Bondage to Contract: Wage Labor, Marriage, and the Market in the Age of Slave Emancipation*. Cambridge: Cambridge University Press, 1998.

Stasiulis, Daiva, and Nira Yuval-Davis. "Introduction: Beyond Dichotomies—Gender, Race, Ethnicity and Class in Settler Societies." In *Unsettling Settler Societies: Articulations of Gender, Race, Ethnicity and Class*, edited by Daiva Stasiulis and Nira Yuval-Davis, 1–38. London: SAGE, 1995.

Stein, Jordan Alexander. "*The Blithedale Romance*'s Queer Style." *ESQ: A Journal of the American Renaissance* 55, nos. 3–4 (2009): 211–36.

Stephens, Michelle Ann. *Black Empire: The Masculine Global Imaginary of Caribbean Intellectuals in the United States, 1914–1962*. Durham: Duke University Press, 2005.

Stern, Julia. *The Plight of Feeling: Sympathy and Dissent in the Early American Novel*. Chicago: University of Chicago Press, 1997.

Stewart, David M. "Cultural Work, City Crime, Reading, Pleasure." *American Literary History* 94, no. 1 (1997): 676–701.

Stewart, Kathleen. *Ordinary Affects*. Durham: Duke University Press, 2007.

Stokes, Mason. *The Color of Sex: Whiteness, Heterosexuality, and the Fictions of White Supremacy*. Durham: Duke University Press, 2001.

Stoler, Ann Laura. *Race and the Education of Desire: Foucault's History of Sexuality and the Colonial Order of Things*. Durham: Duke University Press, 1995.

Stone, William L. *The Life and Times of Red-Jacket, or Sa-Go-Ye-Wat-Ha: Being the History of the Six Nations*. New York: Wiley and Putnam, 1841.

Stowe, William W. "Transcendental Vacations: Thoreau and Emerson in the Wilderness." *New England Quarterly* 83, no. 3 (2010): 482–507.

Streeby, Shelley. *American Sensations: Class, Empire, and the Production of Popular Culture*. Berkeley: University of California Press, 2002.

———. "Haunted Houses: George Lippard, Nathaniel Hawthorne, and Middle-Class America." *Criticism* 38, no. 3 (1996): 443–72.

Strong, Nathaniel T. *Appeal to the Christian Community on the Conditions and Prospects of the New-York Indians, In Answer to a Book, Entitled* The Case of the New-York Indians, *and Other Publications of the Society of Friends*. Buffalo: Press of Thomas and Co., 1841.

Sturtevant, Lawrence M. "The Riot at Damariscotta Bridge." *New England Quarterly* 60, no. 2 (1987): 264–78.

Sullivan, James. *The History of the District of Maine*. Boston: I. Thomas and E. T. Andrews, 1795.

———. "The History of the Penobscott Indians." In *Collections of the Massachusetts Historical Society*, 9:207–32. Boston: Hall and Hiller, 1804.

Summerhill, Thomas. *Harvest of Dissent: Agrarianism in Nineteenth-Century New York*. Urbana: University of Illinois Press, 2005.

Sundquist, Eric J. *Home as Found: Authority and Genealogy in Nineteenth-Century American Literature*. Baltimore: Johns Hopkins University Press, 1979.

———. *To Wake the Nations: Race in the Making of American Literature*. Cambridge: Harvard University Press, 1998.

Sweet, John Hope. *Bodies Politic: Negotiating Race in the American North, 1730–1830*. Philadelphia: University of Pennsylvania Press, 2006.

Sweet, Timothy. *American Georgics; Economy and Environment in Early American Literature*. Philadelphia: University of Pennsylvania Press, 2002.

Sylla, Richard. "Experimental Federalism: The Economics of American Government, 1789–1914." In *The Cambridge Economic History of the United States*, edited by Stanley L. Engerman and Robert E. Gallman, 483–542. New York: Cambridge University Press, 2000.

Taussig, Michael. *The Magic of the State*. New York: Routledge, 1997.

Tawil, Ezra F. *The Making of Racial Sentiment: Slavery and the Birth of the Frontier Romance*. New York: Cambridge University Press, 2008.

Taylor, Alan. *The Divided Ground: Indians, Settlers, and the Northern Borderland of the American Revolution*. New York: Vintage Books, 2007.

———. *Liberty Men and Great Proprietors: The Revolutionary Settlement on the Maine Frontier, 1760–1820*. Chapel Hill: University of North Carolina Press, 1990.

———. *William Cooper's Town: Power and Persuasion on the Frontier of the Early American Republic*. New York: Vintage Books, 1996.

Taylor, Bob Pepperman. *America's Bachelor Uncle: Thoreau and the American Polity*. Lawrence: University Press of Kansas, 1996.

Thomas, Brook. *Cross-Examinations of Law and Literature: Cooper, Hawthorne, Stowe, and Melville*. New York: Cambridge University Press, 1987.

Thoreau, Henry David. "Chastity and Sensuality." In *Henry D. Thoreau: Early Essays and Miscellanies*, 268–78. Edited by Joseph J. Moldenhauer and Edwin Moser, with Alexander C. Kern. Princeton: Princeton University Press, 1975.

———. *The Maine Woods: A Fully Annotated Edition*. Edited by Jeffrey S. Kramer. New Haven: Yale University Press, 2009.

———. *Walden*. 1854. In *Walden and Resistance to Civil Government*, 1–223. Edited by William Rossi. 2nd ed. New York: Norton, 1992.

Thornton, Tamara Platkins. *Cultivating Gentlemen: The Meaning of Country Life among the Boston Elite, 1785–1860*. New Haven: Yale University Press, 1989.

Thrush, Coll. *Native Seattle: Histories from the Crossing-Over Place*. Seattle: University of Washington Press, 2007.

Tichi, Cecelia. "Domesticity on Walden Pond." In *A Historical Guide to Henry David Thoreau*, edited by William E. Cain, 95–122. New York: Oxford University Press, 2000.

Tiro, Karim M. *The People of the Standing Stone: The Oneida Nation from the Revolution through the Era of Removal*. Amherst: University of Massachusetts Press, 2011.

Tompkins, Kyla Wazana. *Racial Indigestion: Eating Bodies in the Nineteenth Century*. New York: New York University Press, 2012.

Toner, Jennifer DiLalla. "The Accustomed Signs of the Family: Rereading Genealogy in Melville's *Pierre*." *American Literature* 70, no. 2 (1998): 237–63.

Trachtenberg, Alan. "Seeing and Believing: Hawthorne's Reflections on the Daguerrotype in *The House of the Seven Gables*." *American Literary History* 9, no. 3 (1997): 460–81.

Trautmann, Thomas R. *Lewis Henry Morgan and the Invention of Kinship*. Berkeley: University of California Press, 1987.

Trennert, Robert A., Jr. *Alternative to Extinction: Federal Indian Policy and the Beginnings of the Reservation System, 1846–1851*. Philadelphia: Temple University Press, 1975.

Tully, James. *An Approach to Political Philosophy: Locke in Contexts*. New York: Cambridge University Press, 1993.

———. *Strange Multiplicity: Constitutionalism in an Age of Diversity*. New York: Cambridge University Press, 1995.

Turner, Dale. *This Is Not a Peace Pipe: Towards a Critical Indigenous Philosophy*. Toronto: University of Toronto Press, 2006.

Valone, Stephen J. "William Seward, Whig Politics, and the Compromised Indian Removal Policy in New York State, 1838–1843." *New York History* 82, no. 2 (2001): 107–34.

Van Atta, John R. "'A Lawless Rabble': Henry Clay and the Cultural Politics of Squatters' Rights, 1832–1841." *Journal of the Early Republic* 28, no. 3 (2008): 337–78.

Veracini, Lorenzo. *Settler Colonialism: A Theoretical Overview*. New York: Palgrave Macmillan, 2010.

Vernon, H. A. "Maris Bryant Pierce: The Making of a Seneca Leader." In *Indian Lives: Essays on Nineteenth- and Twentieth-Century Native American Leaders*, edited by L. G. Moses and Raymond Wilson, 19–43. Albuquerque: University of New Mexico Press, 1985.

Vizenor, Gerald. *Manifest Manners: Postindian Warriors of Survivance*. Hanover: Wesleyan University Press, 1994.

Von Eschen, Penny M. *Race against Empire: Black Americans and Anticolonialism, 1937–1957*. Ithaca: Cornell University Press, 1997.

"Vote Yourself a Farm." 1846. In *The Era of Reform, 1830–1860*, edited by Henry Steele Commager, 123–24. Princeton, N.J.: D. Van Nostrad Company, 1960.

Wagner, Bryan. *Disturbing the Peace: Black Culture and the Police Power after Slavery*. Cambridge: Harvard University Press, 2009.

Wald, Priscilla. *Constituting Americans: Cultural Anxiety and Narrative Form*. Durham: Duke University Press, 1995.

Walker, Brian. "Thoreau's Alternative Economics: Work, Liberty, and Democratic Cultivation." In *A Political Companion to Henry David Thoreau*, edited by Jack Turner, 39–67. Lexington: University Press of Kentucky, 2009.

Walker, Cheryl. *Indian Nation: Native American Literature and Nineteenth-Century Nationalisms*. Durham: Duke University Press, 1997.

Walker, Willard. "The Wabanaki Confederacy." *Maine History* 36 (1997): 110–39.

Walker, Willard, Robert Conkling, and Gregory Buesing. "A Chronological Account of the Wabanaki Confederacy." In *Political Organization of Native North Americans*, edited by Ernest L. Schusky, 41–84. Washington, D.C.: University Press of America, 1980.

Wallace, Anthony F. C. *Jefferson and the Indians: The Tragic Fate of the First Americans*. Cambridge: Harvard University Press, 1999.

Walls, Laura Dassow. *Seeing New Worlds: Henry David Thoreau and Nineteenth-Century Natural Science*. Madison: University of Wisconsin Press, 1995.

Ware, John. *Hints to Young Men on the True Relation of the Sexes*. Boston: Tappan, Whittemore, and Mason, 1850.

Warner, Michael. "*Walden's* Erotic Economy." In *Comparative American Identities: Race, Sex, and Nationality in the Modern Text*, edited by Hortense J. Spillers, 157–74. New York: Routledge, 1991.

Warrior, Robert. *The People and the Word: Reading Native Nonfiction*. Minneapolis: University of Minnesota Press, 2005.

———. "Your Skin Is the Map: The Theoretical Challenge of Joy Harjo's Erotic Poetics." In *Reasoning Together*, edited by The Native Critics Collective (Craig S. Womack, Daniel Heath Justice, and Christopher B. Teuton, eds.), 340–52. Norman: University of Oklahoma Press, 2008.

Weaver, Jace. *That the People Might Live: Native American Literatures and Native American Community*. New York: Oxford University Press, 1997.

Weinauer, Ellen. "Women, Ownership, and Gothic Manhood in *Pierre*." In *Melville and Women*, edited by Elizabeth Schultz and Haskell Springer, 141–60. Kent: Kent State University Press, 2006.

Weinstein, Cindy. *Family, Kinship, and Sympathy in Nineteenth-Century American Literature*. New York: Cambridge University Press, 2004.

Welke, Barbara Young. *Law and the Borders of Belonging in the Long Nineteenth-Century United States*. New York: Cambridge University Press, 2010.

Weston, Kath. *Families We Choose: Lesbians, Gays, Kinship*. New York: Columbia University Press, 1991.

———. *Long Slow Burn: Sexuality and Social Science*. New York: Routledge, 1998.

White, Ed. *The Backcountry and the City: Colonization and Conflict in Early America*. Minneapolis: University of Minnesota Press, 2005.

White, Richard. *The Middle Ground: Indians, Empires, and Republics in the Great Lakes Region, 1650–1815*. Cambridge: Cambridge University Press, 1991.

Wider, Sarah Ann. "'And What Became of Your Philosophy Then?': Women Reading *Walden*." In *More Day to Dawn: Thoreau's* Walden *for the Twenty-First Century*, edited by Sandra Petrulionis and Laura Dassow Walls, 152–70. Amherst: University of Massachusetts Press, 2007.

Wilentz, Sean. *Chants Democratic: New York City and the Rise of the American Working Class, 1788–1850*. New York: Oxford University Press, 1984.

Williams, Raymond. *Marxism and Literature*. New York: Oxford University Press, 1977.

Williams, Robert A., Jr. *The American Indian in Western Legal Thought: The Discourses of Conquest*. New York: Oxford University Press, 1992.

Williamson, William D. *The History of the State of Maine; From Its First Discovery, A.D. 1602, to the Separation, A.D. 1820, Inclusive*. 2 vols. Maine: Hollowell, 1832.

Wilson, Rob. *American Sublime: The Genealogy of a Poetic Genre*. Madison: University of Wisconsin Press, 1991.

Wilson, Sarah. "Melville and the Architecture of Antebellum Masculinity." *American Literature* 76, no. 1 (2004): 59–87.

Wineapple, Brenda. *Hawthorne: A Life*. New York: Random House, 2003.

Wolfe, Patrick. *Settler Colonialism and the Transformation of Anthropology: The Politics and Poetics of an Ethnographic Event*. New York: Cassell, 1999.

———. "Settler Colonialism and the Elimination of the Native." *Journal of Genocide Research* 8, no. 4 (2000): 387–409.

Womack, Craig. *Red on Red: Native American Literary Separatism*. Minneapolis: University of Minnesota Press, 1999.

Woodward, Samuel Bayard. *Hints for the Young, in Relation to the Health of Body and Mind*. 4th ed. Boston: George W. Light, 1840.

Wyss, Hilary E. *English Letters and Indian Literacies: Reading, Writing, and New England Missionary Schools, 1750–1830*. Philadelphia: University of Pennsylvania Press, 2012.

Yablon, Nick. *Untimely Ruins: An Archaeology of American Urban Modernity, 1819–1919*. Chicago: University of Chicago Press, 2009.

Yanella, Philip R. "Socio-Economic Disarray and Literary Response: Concord and *Walden.*" *Mosaic* 14, no. 1 (1981): 1–24.

Yirush, Craig. *Settlers, Liberty, and Empire: The Roots of Early American Political Theory, 1675–1775*. New York: Cambridge University Press, 2011.

Young, Robert J. C. *Colonial Desire: Hybridity in Theory, Culture, and Race*. New York: Routledge, 1995.

———. *White Mythologies: Writing History and the West*. New York: Routledge, 1990.

Zagarri, Rosemarie. "The Rights of Man and Woman in Post-Revolutionary America." *William and Mary Quarterly*, 3rd ser., 55, no. 2 (1998): 203–30.

Zahler, Helene Sara. *Eastern Workingmen and National Land Policy, 1829–1862*. New York: Columbia University Press, 1941.

Ziser, Michael G. "*Walden* and the Georgic Mode." In *More Day to Dawn: Thoreau's Walden for the Twenty-First Century*, edited by Sandra Petrulionis and Laura Dassow Walls, 171–88. Amherst: University of Massachusetts Press, 2007.

Index

55–56; nationalism and, 55; nature
and, 48, 157; nuclear family model
and, 78; personhood and, 57; politi-
cal discourses and, 41; property
holding and, xviii, 53, 57; queerness
and, 28; reproductivity and, 77;
romance and, 53, 78, 201n10; skepti-
cism of, 157; speculation/property
law and, 87; on Thoreau, 91, 92
Hecht, Roger, 152
Hector, John, 223n88
Helderberg War, 227–28n19
Hemingway, Ernest, 198n26
Herring, Scott, 158, 162
Higgins, Ned, 80
"Higher Laws" (Thoreau), 99, 120
History of the District of Maine, The
(Sullivan), 48, 61, 66
*History of the Indian Wars in New
England* (Hubbard), 70–71
Holland, Sharon, 6, 9
Holland Land Company, 175, 176
homemaking, xviii, 83, 98, 135, 137;
bourgeois, 26, 77, 78, 87, 92, 100,
106, 115, 119, 143, 157, 200n39,
211n112, 232n61; conjugal, 42, 82,
99–100; couple-centered, 79;
imaginary/political economy of, 25;
modular forms of, 85; nuclear family,
28; proper, 90; rejection of, 95
Homestead Act, 221n79
homesteading, xix, 54, 97
homo/hetero, institutionalization of,
26
homoeroticism, xviii, 143, 165, 166, 167
House of the Seven Gables, The
(Hawthorne), xvii, xix, 3, 47, 50, 56,
57, 66, 67, 70, 86, 87, 90, 92, 93,
108, 144, 156–57, 169, 192; characterizations of, 78; elite claims/

inheritance and, 88–89; estate-
building in, 48; imperial legacy and,
42; Indian deed and, 75; Indianness
and, 121; labor/property and, 39–
40; labor/wilderness and, 63; nature
and, 58, 151; queernesses of, 41;
writing of, 40, 202n19
household: couple-centered, 78;
formation, 79, 214n20; self-
reproducing, 85; semi-Lockean, 83;
sustaining, 99
Hubbard, Governor: Penobscots and,
73–74
Huston, Reeve, 167, 228n21

identification, 25, 124, 126, 143
identity, 6, 86, 111, 197n16, 199n35;
bourgeois, 98; gay, 230n48;
imposed, 113; Indigenous, 20, 116,
124, 222n85; individual, 93;
national, 12, 23, 24, 159, 221n78;
nonnative modes of, 5; personal, 15,
105; racial, 20, 24; settler, 157–58;
social, 196n11; urban, 230n46;
whiteness and, 106
ideologies, 34, 201n5; racial, 199n34;
settler, 43; sovereignty-making, 14
imagination, xviii, 16, 123, 190; actual
possession and, 106; nonnative, 108
imperialism, 22, 196n6, 196n11,
199n33
improvement, 73, 86, 109, 181
In a Queer Time and Place (Halberstam),
25
incest, xviii, 143, 164, 167, 187,
231n58
independence, 97, 107, 109, 134–
35, 151, 183; economic, 123;
fight for, 15, 61–62; wilderness
and, 60

aristocratic mode of, xxi; defining,
157; elite, 153, 155; ethical miasma
of, 183; forms of, 144; Indigenous,
16, 18, 19, 94, 131, 134; inhabitance
and, 28; legitimate, 57; Lockean,
189, 201n8; management of, 30;
rural, xxii, 144, 154; transmission of,
96; vision of, 142
landholding, 47, 83, 93, 97, 155, 165,
166, 171; bourgeois, 110; extrapolitical basis for, 61; familial, 80,
159, 185; genealogy and, 164;
hierarchy of, 144; Indigenous, 61,
181; legalized, 146; political
economy of, 100; as republican self-
sovereignty, 95; rural, 170
landlords, 155, 170, 227n13
landscape, 156, 160, 189; deforming of,
110; legal, 136, 139; natural, 152;
social, 31, 152
Laqueur, Thomas, 101, 215n34
Latour, Bruno, 46, 53, 64, 75, 112, 172,
196n8, 196n12; on post-Renaissance
constitution, 58; on social/
explanatory tool, 9; structuring
template and, 62
law, 1, 53, 60, 64, 89, 127, 151, 163;
Anglo-American, 75; bodily, 108;
constitutional, 102; criminal, 73–74;
discourses of, 130; enforcement of,
168; English, 62; exception and,
111; introducing, 2; moral, 55–56;
municipal, 49; national, 108, 184;
natural, 44, 49, 56, 57, 58, 67, 137,
203n35; power of, 185; Roman, 84;
rule by, 55; settler, 13, 88; state, 57,
60; union of, 185
*League of the Ho-de-no-sau-nee, or
Iroquois* (Morgan), 83–84, 182,
212n130

Lecture to Young Men on Chastity, A
(Graham), 93, 100, 104, 215n25
Leverett, Thomas, 68
Levine, Robert, 78, 211n111, 229n29
Locke, John, 202n16, 203n27,
212n130; importance of, 203n25;
land distribution and, 65; Native
peoples and, 89; on ownership, 48;
personhood and, 207n68; political
society and, 49, 65; private property
and, 206n65; social structures/social
convention and, 65; sociospatiality
and, 66
logic, 38, 53, 101, 229n32; settler, 42;
social, 29
Loman, Andrew: on Fourierism, 82,
212n124
Loron, treaty and, 69
Luciano, Dana, 29–30, 77, 86, 90,
213n132

Maddox, Lucy: Indian–white
relationships and, 5
Madockawando, 68, 71
Maine Indian Claims Settlement Act
(1980), 210n104
Maine Woods, The (Thoreau), 125,
223n92, 225n108
Making Multiculturalism (Bryson), 33
Making of Racial Sentiment, The
(Tawil), 21
Maliseets, 70
mappings, 14, 69; Indigenous, 71, 113;
settler, 90
Mariotti, Shannon, 219n57
marriage, 83; Owenite critique of, 103;
socialist critique of, 103; unsexy,
103
Marxism and Literature (Williams),
204n37

MARK RIFKIN is professor of English and women's and gender studies at the University of North Carolina at Greensboro. He is the author of *Manifesting America: The Imperial Construction of U.S. National Space, When Did Indians Become Straight? Kinship, the History of Sexuality, and Native Sovereignty*, and *The Erotics of Sovereignty: Queer Native Writing in the Era of Self-Determination* (Minnesota, 2012).